THE ETHICS OF ORGANIZATIONAL TRANSFORMATION

THE ETHICS OF ORGANIZATIONAL TRANSFORMATION

Mergers, Takeovers, and Corporate Restructuring

EDITED BY
W. Michael Hoffman,
Robert Frederick, and
Edward S. Petry, Jr.

FOREWORD BY
Gregory H. Adamian

From the Seventh National Conference on Business Ethics
Sponsored by the Center for Business Ethics at Bentley College

Q

QUORUM BOOKS
NEW YORK • WESTPORT, CONNECTICUT • LONDON

HD
2746.5
.N38
1989
/4 8874
may 1990

Library of Congress Cataloging-in-Publication Data

National Conference on Business Ethics (7th : 1987 : Bentley College)
  The ethics of organizational transformation : mergers, takeovers, and corporate restructuring / edited by W. Michael Hoffman, Robert Frederick, and Edward S. Petry, Jr. : foreword by Gregory H. Adamian.
      p.   cm.
  "From the Seventh National Conference on Business Ethics, sponsored by the Center for Business Ethics."
  Held Oct. 16–17, 1987 at Bentley College.
  Bibliography: p.
  Includes index.
  ISBN 0–89930–391–9 (lib. bdg. : alk. paper)
  1. Consolidation and merger of corporations—Moral and ethical aspects—Congresses. 2. Corporate reorganizations—Moral and ethical aspects—Congresses. I. Hoffman, W. Michael.
  II. Frederick, Robert. III. Petry, Edward S. IV. Bentley College. Center for Business Ethics. V. Title.
  HD2746.5.N38   1987
  174'.4—dc19   88–18507

British Library Cataloguing in Publication Data is available.

Library of Congress Catalog Card Number: 88–18507
ISBN: 0–89930–391–9

First published in 1989 by Quorum Books

Greenwood Press, Inc.
88 Post Road West, Westport, Connecticut   06881

Printed in the United States of America

The paper used in this book complies with the Permanent Paper Standard issued by the National Information Standards Organization (Z39.48–1984).

10 9 8 7 6 5 4 3 2 1

Contents

Tables and Figures

Foreword

GREGORY H. ADAMIAN

At the very least, the recent spate of corporate mergers and acquisitions has enriched both our language and our store of cultural folk heroes. We now routinely speak of such colorful but previously obscure concepts as "greenmail," "golden parachutes," "white knights," and "shark repellent." We are also treated to dashing figures like T. Boone Pickens, Ronald Pearlman, and Carl Icahn as they brazenly raid the corporate boardroom, striking fear in the hearts of complacent managers everywhere.

But there is a more somber side to this phenomenon we have broadly named "organization transformation." The distressing sight of Wall Street traders led from their offices in handcuffs is only its most obvious manifestation.

Four years ago at the National Conference on Business Ethics, I said that the "burden of ethical responsibility must be borne by all, for no person, no society is immune from the contagion in which widespread ethical irresponsibility can destroy us." And, unhappily, it does appear that unethical behavior is becoming more common in our country. It seems to have afflicted all our important institutions: in Washington, a group of White House officials operated a kind of secret government; two prominent religious leaders were found to have misused the enormous contributions of their followers; in 1987 major league pitchers were caught scuffing balls with sandpaper, while hitters were widely thought to be using bats doctored with cork, and more recently, U.S. servicemen have been convicted of espionage.

Of course, most relevant to those reading this is the blight of insider trading that has accompanied what Ivan Boesky termed "merger mania." But even before we begin to consider the ethical implications of transgressions like those Boesky committed, we must reflect on the larger economic effect that such takeovers entail.

Defenders of a brisk "external market for corporate control," as it is sometimes called, assert that such activity is simply an indication of a healthy economy. Mergers and acquisitions signify competition, and competition can only benefit the economic life of the nation. Takeovers improve managerial performance, advocates believe, and generally enhance corporate accountability. Assets are shifted to more productive enterprises while less profitable pursuits are dropped.

Opponents argue that the benefits of takeovers are limited and that their effects are more often debilitating. Corporations, they declare, are not simply another commodity to be traded on an inadequately regulated market. The main beneficiaries of a large merger are most likely to be the lawyers and investment bankers who negotiate the deal. And finally, detractors claim that management becomes not more efficient, but less so, as it neglects long-term planning in favor of short-term gain, ever wary of an approaching raider.

This profound disagreement, as well as evidence of a general ethical deterioration, gives new urgency to this topic. It is hard to imagine a time when serious consideration of the relationship between the practical world of commerce and the sometimes rarefied world of ethical thought was more necessary. We must reemphasize our commitment as leaders of business, labor, academe, and government to the powerful union between business and ethics. And Bentley College remains dedicated to educating business students who well know the inseparable nature of that union.

One consequence of the work of the National Conference on Business Ethics should be to alter the extremely cynical regard in which the endeavors of big business are held. Public confidence in the business world, long eroding, has been further decayed by these recent scandals.

So the task before us is a considerable one. It is only through participation in forums such as this that we can begin to chart a path through the morass of moral uncertainty, professional disagreement, and waning public trust that has accompanied the boom in mergers and acquisitions. But if we approach our work with intellectual energy and moral rigor, then we can begin to form the new, positive consensus that our nation needs.

Acknowledgments

The Seventh National Conference on Business Ethics and other activities of the Center for Business Ethics were made possible in part by grants from the following: Arvin Industries; Robert W. Brown, M.D.; Champion International Corporation; The Council for Philosophical Studies (sponsored by the National Endowment for the Humanities); The General Mills Foundation; General Motors Corporation; The Goodyear Tire and Rubber Company; Midland-Ross, Inc.; The Motorola Foundation; Norton Company; Primerica Corporation; Raytheon Company; The Raytheon Charitable Foundation; Rexnord, Inc.; Richardson-Merrill, Inc.; The Rockefeller Foundation; Semline, Inc.; Stop and Shop Manufacturing Companies; F. W. Woolworth Company; and Exxon Education Foundation. On behalf of the Center, we wish to thank all these contributors and all of the participants of the Seventh National Conference for sharing with us their support and ideas.

Introduction

What are the ethical issues surrounding mergers, takeovers, and corporate restructuring? Do mergers and takeovers serve the public interest? Should they be allowed even if they do not? What about the rights of individuals whose lives can be so dramatically affected by corporate restructuring? Should their rights take precedence over the interests of corporations or the public good?

These questions are being asked more and more frequently by individuals concerned about the long-term economic and social effect of mergers and takeovers, and for good reason. There have been thousands of mergers and takeovers in the late 1980s, and they continue unabated. According to the March 21, 1988, issue of *Business Week*, in the first two months of 1988 more than $50 billion worth of mergers were initiated. Furthermore, as *Business Week* goes on to say, mergers and takeovers have become institutionalized—an accepted way of doing business. As a consequence the American business system is undergoing a fundamental structural change that will have far-reaching repercussions, even for those who may feel most insulated from such distant and sometimes almost incomprehensible events.

For these reasons the ethics of mergers, takeovers, and corporate restructuring was selected to be the topic for the Seventh National Conference on Business Ethics, sponsored by the Center for Business Ethics at Bentley College, and held on October 15 and 16, 1987, on the campus of Bentley College. Representatives of business, labor, government, the media, and colleges and universities from around the country and abroad participated. This volume includes the texts of many of the presentations at the conference.

Featured speakers from corporations included Goodyear Tire and Rubber Company Chairman and CEO Robert E. Mercer; Allied Signal, Inc., Chairman and CEO Edward Hennessy; Control Data Corporation Chairman Emeritus William

C. Norris; and Champion International Corporation Chairman and CEO Andrew Sigler. Although their backgrounds are diverse and their experience with take-overs and corporate restructuring is varied, each of these corporate leaders presented a similar basic message: takeover activity is having a deleterious effect on the American economy. Robert Mercer, for instance, has called the activities of the raiders "economic terrorism," and Andrew Sigler has said that "the whole climate has changed. There is intense pressure for current earnings, so the message is, don't get caught with major (long-term) investments. And leverage the hell out of yourself. Do all of the things we used to consider bad management."

While some of the scholars who spoke during the conference defended corporate takeovers, there were no "raiders" present to offer their own defense, despite the fact that a number of them had been invited to attend. A summary of their basic justification for takeovers, however, is given in the following quote from one of the foremost defenders of takeovers, Michael Jensen:

The takeover market ... provides a unique, powerful, and impersonal mechanism to accomplish the major restructuring and redeployment of assets continually required by changes in technology and consumer preferences. . . . Scientific evidence indicates that activities in the market for corporate control almost uniformly increase efficiency and shareholders' wealth. Yet there is an almost continual flow of unfavorable publicity and calls for regulation and restriction of unfriendly takeovers. Many of these appeals arise from managers who want protection from competition for their jobs and others who desire more controls on corporations. The result, in the long run, may be a further weakening of the corporation as an organizational form and a reduction in human welfare.[1]

Jensen mentions two justifications for takeovers in this passage. The first is economic, and the second is ethical. The economic justification is that mergers and takeovers increase economic efficiency and thus increase the overall amount of goods and services provided by the economy. One of the main reasons they increase efficiency, according to Jensen and others, is that they remove entrenched, uncompetitive, and self-serving managers who have made themselves a soft corporate bed and intend to lie in it. Takeovers are also supposed to streamline inefficient corporate bureaucracies, redeploy underused assets, and improve international competitiveness. In short, mergers and takeovers should be allowed because they serve the main end of the economy: the effective and abundant creation of wealth. As David Scheffman, the director of the Bureau of Economics of the Federal Trade Commission, said in his address, "there is solid evidence that mergers and takeovers have resulted in a more efficient economy."

Jensen's ethical justification is an appeal to the social benefits of mergers and takeovers. The basic idea is that since mergers and takeovers are, in the long term, good for the economy, they are also good for society as a whole. To take just one example, a healthy and efficient economy enhances and sustains non-economic social goods such as the freedom of individuals to pursue their own ends in their own way. For surely without some degree of wealth, freedom is a marginally useful possession.

Thus the arguments for mergers and takeovers take a macro viewpoint—mergers and takeovers are said to be good for the whole economy, and for all of society. These arguments are opposed from both a macro and micro position. The opposing macro position denies that mergers and takeovers are good for the economy. In order to follow this response, we need to look a little more closely at the argument that takeovers improve efficiency.

The defenders of takeovers judge the relative efficiency of a company according to one central standard—stock price. They argue that the stock market accurately assesses the profitability of a company, and that the market's assessment is reflected in the company's stock price. If the stock price is lower than some group of takeover specialists believe it ought to be, or could be, then the most likely reason is that the company has not been managed efficiently. More efficient management could raise the stock price and thus give the shareholders the return they deserve on their investment. Takeover specialists do not do an in-depth study of the target company's management to determine whether it is efficient. All that work is supposed to be done by the stock market. And so, what the takeover specialists do when they take over a company is, in effect, anything they think necessary to raise the stock price to its proper level.

This line of reasoning has been attacked at every point by those who deny that takeovers are good for the economy. They argue, for instance, that stock price does not necessarily reflect the true value of a company. Considering the October 19, 1987, market crash, they may have a good point. Furthermore, they argue that takeover specialists frequently sacrifice a company's long-term profitability by concentrating on raising stock prices in the short term. The raiders skew stock prices by selling off profitable divisions of the company, slashing research and development budgets, and reducing the work force to the lowest possible level. They then take their profits and run, leaving behind a company that may show profits for a brief period of time, but has no real long-term prospects. Thus the takeover specialists skim off profits by manipulating the financial markets while creating no real wealth in terms of added products and services. They are not efficient managers of companies; rather they are efficient destroyers of companies. And even when companies are not broken up, takeovers are often failures in the long term, leaving both sides of the takeover worse off than before. Again according to the March 21 issue of *Business Week*, studies have shown that seven out of ten mergers of the 1960s and 1970s were unsuccessful.

The micro argument against takeovers does not focus on the overall economic effects, but instead on the consequences takeovers have on communities and on the lives of individuals. The main tactic of takeover specialists after they acquire a company is to restructure the company radically in order to improve profits. This frequently involves wholesale layoffs, plant closings, and plant relocation. A number of studies have shown that these maneuvers have devastating effects on communities and on individuals. The argument of those opposed to takeovers is that these effects are not justified by the alleged economic benefits that accrue to the overall economy. The individuals and communities in question are thus unjustifiably harmed by takeovers. Consequently, takeovers should either not be allowed, or they should be allowed only under conditions that do not permit unjustifiable harm to individuals.

These are, in outline, the opposing views on mergers and takeovers. Since many of them are discussed in detail in this volume, we have not attempted to do full justice to their power or subtlety. However, in the space we have remaining we would like to suggest a context, a common ground, from which the opposing views may be assessed and evaluated. The context is the system of values on which capitalism is based, and without which it could not operate.

As Lisa Newton says in chapter 3, "the purpose of business is to convert resources into goods and services, within limits set down by the society." We suggest that the limits set down by society include not only the laws and regulations governing business activity, but also commonly shared values that underlie and support the system of free enterprise. Capitalism does not exist in a value-free vacuum. The main value of capitalism, as the philosopher Richard DeGeorge has pointed out, is individual freedom. A fundamental principle of capitalism is that individuals are in the best position to determine their own good, and should be free to pursue that good to the extent consistent with the right of others to do the same. The classical defense of capitalism, first given by Adam Smith, is that by freely pursuing our own goods, we advance the common good as well. But in order for this to happen we must have the freedom to enter into transactions that satisfy our individual needs and desires. Without the basic value of freedom, our business system simply would not work.

In addition to freedom, capitalism as it has developed in this country is also based on the values of fairness, honesty, and respect for persons. In a free economic transaction both parties to the transaction can have a reasonable expectation of achieving their goals only if the transaction is a fair one. In a fair transaction neither side takes advantage of the other, either by withholding or misrepresenting relevant information, or by using coercion or intimidation to exploit the other's position. Thus a fair economic transaction must also be an honest one, and one in which each party has a basic respect for the other.

What we are suggesting, then, is that economic transactions should be assessed and evaluated within the context of these basic values. Any economic transaction that does not conform to these values should not be tolerated, since any transaction that subverts these values also tends to be destructive of the very system that makes it possible. The reason, for example, that we believe that insider trading should not be allowed is not merely that it is a shabby exhibition of unbridled greed, but that it tends to subvert the value of fairness on which the free enterprise system is founded. Insider trading is the very antithesis of a fair economic transaction. It can only succeed if one party has an unfair advantage over others and exploits that advantage to his or her own benefit. No system founded on the ideas of freedom, fairness, honesty, and respect for persons can permit such a practice if it hopes to survive.

We do not assume, of course, that placing mergers, takeovers, and corporate restructuring in the context we have suggested will provide any easy answers, or that it will settle any of the debates about them contained in this volume. All the hard questions remain. But what it does do is remind us of where the debate must begin, and of the standards against which the eventual answers must be measured. Thus, for instance, it is not simply economic efficiency that is the controlling factor in judging takeovers, since a policy that promotes efficiency alone could just as well be neither free, fair, nor honest. What we must strive for is efficiency within the bounds of the other values we hold. If we must sacrifice some economic efficiency to preserve those other values, then so be it, for only in that way can we preserve the system as a whole.

NOTE

1. Michael C. Jensen, "Takeovers: Folklore and Science," *Harvard Business Review* (November/December 1984), 120.

I

ETHICAL ISSUES IN ORGANIZATIONAL TRANSFORMATIONS: AN OVERVIEW

Corporate Takeovers: The Moral Backdrop

THOMAS DONALDSON

Looking over the remarks of the senior vice-president and chief economist of one of the nation's largest banks the other day I learned that, precisely speaking, takeovers raise no "moral" issues. Frankly, it came as a surprise to me, but the news was somewhat good, since it prompted me to think that my own remarks could be refreshingly brief. So I read on. "A corporate takeover," he continued, "is simply a decision-making process by the buyers . . . [and] I don't see that there are any particular ethical standards that can be applied with respect to that simple transaction . . . where the sellers have, in effect, decided it's best to sell and the buyers, at the same price, have elected to buy."[1] At this point I was worried, for my suspicions were aroused that my chosen field of business ethics was in danger of disappearing. It occurred to me that I might seek other opinions, say, those of the stockholders of a company that had just freely decided to pay wads of money in greenmail to a raider who, at the same price, had freely elected to accept it. I thought it would be interesting to see whether their theory of ethics agreed with the economist's.

The problem, which comes as no surprise to most of you, is that morality occupies no cupboard separate from the remainder of human action, and because it represents that aspect of human behavior which is concerned with the concept of human good, it is, rather, the inevitable shadow of events created by the light of love, war, commerce, or any other fundamental human endeavor.

A further oddity of the bank economist's remarks is that it neglects the reality of the current takeover discussion: for in criticizing and defending takeovers, both sides make vigorous appeals to morality. The greenmail, poison pills, and golden parachutes have often—I think justly—been condemned as an immoral resolution of conflict of interest. And the callousness with which some raiders have treated the human consequences of their actions has driven some critics to invoke moral, indeed sometimes even religious, language. Representative Silvio Conte, a Republican from Massachusetts, must have been inspired by the Sermon on the Mount when he commented on the floor of the House recently:

> Joyous are the large corporations, for they shall benefit from the deduction value of the 46 percent corporate tax rate in their mergers and acquisition.
> Joyous are the corporate raiders, for they shall reap the profits of liquidation.
> Joyous are the corporate lawyers, for wealthy salaries shall be theirs.
> And blessed are the working people of thy country for it is they who subsidize these takeovers.[2]

As a defender of capitalism I am nonetheless puzzled by how exaggerated claims on behalf of the market, having been put to rest in other arenas, seem to achieve new life in current discussions of takeovers. T. Boone Pickens asserted recently that the only duty of management is to maximize the price of the company's stock in the marketplace, and he makes no secret of his belief that the pursuit of such a duty also, conveniently enough, maximizes national well-being.[3] This, of course, is reminiscent of Milton Friedman's dictum that the social responsibility of business is to do nothing more than maximize profits, a notion that today is rejected by approximately four out of five business executives. Among other things, such a view tends to forget that our existing "free" market, as Warren Law has put it, is "really one of man-made regulations in which interest on debt is deductible for taxes while dividends are not, in which pension funds need not pay taxes, and in which six months is the definition of long-term.' "[4]

But Pickens errs even from a purely theoretical perspective. It is time to return to Ethics and Economics 101. Even in a theoretically free market, the only social welfare goal that optimistic theorists can claim is achieved is a state defined as "Pareto Optimality," that is, an equilibrium state in which no one can be made better off without making someone worse off. Now, of course, Pareto Optimality is no small moral consideration, and it jibes with the solid reasoning, much of which originates in Adam Smith, that explains capitalism's remarkable ability to generate wealth and to enhance, in Smith's language, "the wealth of nations." But we ought not forget that Pareto Optimal states can be truly awful; a state in which everyone happens to be malnourished save one extremely wealthy man, could be a Pareto Optimal state. Furthermore, even from the perspective of Pareto Optimality, there are many Pareto Optimal configurations, and some will satisfy moral criteria better than others. The market does not claim, nor does it need to claim, to accommodate basic needs automatically—that is, automatically to ensure that the hungry are fed, the crippled sheltered, or the willing-to-work employed—nor automatically to distribute in accord with the canons of distributive justice. The market, then, does not automatically ensure morally correct outcomes. It is interesting that as a society we are reaching this conclusion nearly two hundred years after a professor of moral philosophy in England reached it. I have in mind, of course, Adam Smith, who never lost sight of the fact that the market works well only against a solid backdrop of moral expectations from its participants. Whenever I read his ideas on the necessary interconnectedness of morality and the market, I am reminded of the remark once made by a citizen of Eastern Europe. "Under capitalism," the citizen remarked, "man exploits man. Under communism," he added, "it is the other way round." I've always appreciated the humor in the remark, for it suggests, I think accurately, that no system is immune from the moral shortcomings of its members, and that no system, not even capitalism—that best of all systems, notable for its remarkable capacity to harness the inevitable, if regrettable, self-interest of people and direct it to the common good—is capable of turning morality into a nothing, of making it unnecessary.

What goes for all business transactions in a market economy goes for transactions in the realm of corporate takeovers as well. But if takeovers, acquisitions, and mergers are, at least from an important perspective, *moral* phenomena, then what follows?

We should begin by distinguishing the moral from the legal aspects of the takeover controversy. Consider the case of one company, Basic Inc.[5] In a situation where Basic's stock was rising in price on higher-than-normal volume, and rumors about takeovers were rife, management explained the situation to confused shareholders as follows: "With respect to the stock market activity in the Company shares, we remain unaware of any present or pending developments which would account for the high volume of trading and price fluctuations in recent months."[6] The truth is that Basic had been engaged in merger talks for many months, and events were approaching a crescendo in which, as it turns out, the company was acquired at a substantial premium over market price. Now you may be surprised to learn that there is ongoing dispute over whether such statements should be deemed illegal. In a similar case the Third Circuit Court determined "that a company could legally claim nothing was happening so long as no merger *agreement* on price and terms had been reached."[7] Some judges seem to think that, at least as a legal matter, it is acceptable for managers under such circumstances to issue false statements to shareholders. While I happen to disagree even with this legal perspective, it must be acknowledged that the legal-moral distinction has valid application elsewhere. Lying to one's spouse about most things is immoral but ought not be illegal. The point for the discussion of takeovers is that we cannot reduce the questions of ethics in takeovers to ones of law, a tendency that the majority of writers on the topic have been prone to adopt. Indeed, it is essential conceptually to keep the issues separate. What Basic's managers said to their shareholders was a lie. It may or may not have been illegal, but as a falsehood without even extenuating circumstances it was clearly immoral and ought not to have been done.

I intend to deal solely with the moral dimension of takeovers, mergers, and acquisitions. We need not settle the thorny legal problem of whether the business judgment rule properly covers management attempts to use various forms of shark repellent in order to know that many such attempts, as Tom Dunfee has noted elsewhere in this volume, reflect conflicts of interest and hence are violations of managerial ethics.

I also think it helpful to parse moral from empirical considerations, or, in other words, to invoke the standard philosophical distinction between what *is* the case, or what *will* be the case on the one hand, and what *ought* to be the case on the other. This is not to deny that empirical studies are crucial for developing a comprehensive moral perspective. (I remain Kantian without, I hope, being crazy.) For example, if we knew, as an empirical matter, how accurate stock prices are with respect to measuring a firm's performance, then we should know better how to evaluate claims that takeovers enhance value and efficiency. In offering the moral-empirical distinction, let us acknowledge that just as empirical considerations are relevant for moral inquiry, so too must moral insight inform the structure of the empirical research agenda. Let me offer an example. We have noted that the market does not automatically handle issues of distributive justice or need satisfaction. It follows that empirical issues that relate to such issues require research. Consider the empirical question most often researched in the area of takeovers: "Do shareholders of *acquired* companies tend to be better off following takeovers?" While important, however, this question leads to a second, and somewhat less researched topic, namely, "Do shareholders of *acquiring* companies tend to be better off?" Now research on this question is less developed than that on the former, but is advancing nonetheless. But this should lead to a still further, and even less well-researched question: "Is *aggregate* shareholder welfare improved?" That is, when we total the welfare of acquired and acquiring shareholders, do we get a positive or negative value? Only one article I have read reflects this sort of research; it appeared in the *California Review of Management*. (The study's data, for what it is worth, suggest that aggregate shareholder value remains about the same before and after takeovers.[8]) Well, now we are getting somewhere, you say! But, moral analysis leads to three further and more difficult empirical questions that no researcher I know of has taken on. First, apart from whether aggregate shareholder welfare is increased or not, are there minority classes of shareholders whose welfare is harmed, and, if so, to what extent? Such information is crucial for answering the moral question of whether all shareholders are treated to a "fair" deal. Second, is aggregate long-term *social* welfare improved as a result of persistent takeover activity? And, finally, if aggregate social welfare is improved, are there minority classes whose welfare is harmed, and if so, to what extent? As a philosopher I am told that the fault of my profession is a tendency to deliver a priori judgments about empirical fact, but the present range of a priori speculation by nonphilosophers about these last three questions in the face of no hard empirical data, would put even Georg Hegel to shame. I have read comments from takeover critics asserting that our country is being picked clean for the sake of creating a few more billionaires. These claims are usually unaccompanied by even a shred of empirical evidence, save anecdotes and reference to the layoffs and firings occurring at a particular recently acquired company. And in the same vein I read the self-confident predictions of takeover masters and takeover defenders that takeovers must be made in the long-run economic interest of the society. Why must takeovers enhance economic welfare? Why must they harm it? As any epistemologist can tell you, the answers to such questions do not carry their truth status on their face. I am similarly struck by the righteous indignation that so many people, especially academics, manifest in asserting the ''nonproductive'' nature of purely financial transactions. It recalls John Stuart Mill's notion of ''unproductive labor'' and Thorstein Veblen's outcry against games of chicane and financial intrigue. But simply because takeover artists and investment bankers do not make kitchen cabinets with their hands does not mean that their labor is unproductive. It may or it may not be, and the answer is a function of their labor's empirical effect on society. Fortunately, however, the criticism often comes from academics who are pounding away on their word processors and whose overall productive contribution to society could never be doubted.

The most common moral point of entry taken to the takeover controversy by those who agree with the preceding is through the so-called ''stakeholder'' model of corporate social responsibility that views the manager as an agent representing the interests of not only shareholders, but a variety of constituencies, including employees, suppliers, and consumers. This is a truly normative, not empirical model, and at least in the context of the proper empirical assumptions, it does offer important insights. According to the model, stockholders are not the only ones with a stake in management's actions. Pickens has been quoted as saying that he is ''amused by people who say that if an arbitrager bought a stock an hour ago, he should not have the right to decide what happens to 40,000 employees.'' The stakeholder model explains clearly why many employees fail to understand the cause for Pickens' amusement.[9] The model also implies that the managerial constituency extends beyond even shareholders and employees, an implication that gains credence whenever we glimpse the panoramic effects of corporate acquisitions. When Chevron closed Gulf's Pittsburgh headquarters, in addition to dismissing or transferring 5,800 people, it ravaged the local community. Gulf had given charitable support to fifty local institutions and was supplied by countless local companies.[10]

But while reflecting important insights, the stakeholder model has serious problems, the two most obvious of which are its inability to provide standards for assigning relative weights to the interests of the various constituencies and its lack—at least within itself—of a normative, justificatory foundation. In application to an issue such as corporate takeovers, then, I believe it should be augmented, and probably even replaced, by another normative apparatus. To those acquainted with my writing, it will come as no surprise that the apparatus I want to recommend for this purpose includes a "social contract" analysis.

I wish here to show the consequences of the application of the social contract model to the specific issue of corporate takeovers. For those unfamiliar with the model, however, a word of explanation is in order. The point of social contract thinking, as I noted in *Corporations and Morality*, is not to dig up the historical causes of the Sumerian or Egyptian kingdoms. It is to clarify the proper moral presuppositions of business power. The argument is that the moral foundations of productive organizations, including corporations, can be understood through the methodology of social contract reasoning. The point is to engage persons in a thought experiment that will use their powers of reason and moral intuition in a manner calculated to achieve moral insight. We are, according to the method, to presume that rational persons living in a state of "nature" (defined in the business contract as the state of individual production) attempt to sketch the terms of a fair agreement between themselves and the productive organizations that they will allow status as a legal *persona ficta*, and will allow access to both natural resources and the existing labor force.

All productive organizations, then, are viewed as engaging in an implied contract with society, one not unlike that employed by John Locke, Jean-Jacques Rousseau, and Thomas Hobbes in understanding the moral and political foundations of the state. The moral raison d'être for the productive organization turns out to be its productive contribution to society, one tempered by a set of reciprocal obligations existing on both sides of the organization/society divide. In pursuing its aims the productive organization is further bound to respect existing human rights, and to accord its actions with canons of justice, both in terms of distribution and general fairness.

The moral justification of the productive organization does not directly include reference to the responsibilities of shareholders because the concept of the productive organization is broader than of the corporation. Society would no doubt find it necessary to maintain productive organizations even if they failed to adopt the form of the jointly held, investor owned corporation; and, however immoral a socialistic society might be for denying the right to property of its citizens, it, like capitalistic society, will possess productive organizations that have many of the same obligations to society as their capitalist counterparts. Rather, to understand why in capitalistic society the social contract demands that managers owe moral duties to shareholders, we must move beyond the general conception of the social contract, and examine a post-contractual source for business responsibility. This post-contractual source is free agreement in the context of human rights, and it generates what we shall call "derivative" obligations. Such "derivative" obligations include rules, personal agreements, contracts, and laws. To illustrate: the right to private property and freedom, expressed in one's power of control over money and goods, constitutes an enabling foundation which, in the context of an agreement or contract, generates most of management's duties to shareholders. I own a sum of money. I have a moral right to own it, and a moral right—within specific limits—to husband and control it. I then enter into an agreement with a corporation wherein it pledges to manage that money, always attempting to serve my interests by maximizing my return on investment. Here it is the rights to property and freedom, exercised in this instance by the corporation and me, along with the ethical sanctity of promises and contracts, that constitute the moral foundation of the company manager's obligation to pursue my interests, and the company's obligation, in turn, to reward the manager as agreed. This does not, by the way, give the manager the right to lie, murder, steal, or break any other valid moral rights in his efforts; but neither does it give him the right to engage in a cozy management buyout in which he uses some of the power granted him in the course of his fiduciary duties to harm my interests and help his own. In a different vein, our shared right of democratic participation, expressed in the laws that our democratically elected representatives shape and apply, constitutes the enabling foundation that underlies the moral validity of our society's laws, including, for example, the regulations of the Securities and Exchange Commission.

This post-contractual class of management duties, that is, the "derivative" duties, are obviously more flexible than those generated by the basic form of the social contract. Where the contract lays down a minimal floor of responsibility—one which is virtually constant over time—derivative duties are almost infinitely plastic. Because they depend upon the substance of agreements, including even political agreements, their range covers all logically possible covenants compatible with the class of obligations. Managers usually are bound to advance the financial interests of shareholders, but they might, as in the instance of nonprofit corporations such as the Red Cross, be bound to serve ends tied to social welfare. It is even morally possible that they would be obligated to encourage bird watching, to collect out-of-bounds basketballs, or to promote the cause of rock opera. Their plasticity is nearly infinite.

The stakeholder model comes close to the understanding expressed in these two classes of duties, but fails to distinguish properly between them. By assuming that managers must weigh and balance the interests of a variety of stakeholders, that is, of employees, of stockholders, of suppliers, consumers, and people in the surrounding community, the stakeholder model correctly apprehends the possibility of conflict between, say, a manager's duty to shareholders and that to consumers. But the model embodies no means of distinguishing between the radically different sources of duty in this question, and thus complicates finding a solution. In most instances, the manager's duty to consumers is formally identical to the duty of any producer to consumer: whether a guild tradesman, an executive of IBM, or the inspector at a communal Soviet tractor works, the manager must provide safe, efficient products—for that is how society understands and frames one's legitimacy as a producer. But a manager's duty to shareholders is dependent on derivative duties, in other words, it is dependent on the laws and regulations governing the system in which the entity operates, securities laws, the nature of the corporate charter, and, further, the nature of any other agreements, fiduciary or otherwise, with the investor.

Furthermore, and closely connected to this, the stakeholder model provides no means for understanding the various responsibilities involved: no means of answering the question as to *why* we should presume that managers actually have such responsibilities to multiple stakeholders. It is not enough to say that people have an interest or a stake in the manager's actions, for this is merely an empirical claim. It must further be shown that the manager is *morally obliged* to seek to satisfy that set of interests. This explains why the stakeholder model is often discussed and assumed, but almost never the subject of a rigorous proof. It also explains why it is especially vulnerable to the Friedmanite cynic who comes along, denies its conclusion, and asserts instead that the social responsibility of business is nothing other than, and nothing more than, the maximizing of return on investment for shareholders. Or to use Pickens' slightly different formulation, to increase the value of the stock in the marketplace.

In a difficult case, as in the takeover controversy, the social contract–derived duties and the post-contractual, or derivative, duties often conflict. For example, the derivative duty to serve shareholders can be in conflict with the social contract–derived duty to enhance employee welfare. For this reason, in the instance of takeovers, we are especially concerned to isolate the derivative duties at issue. Now while the derivative duty most often mentioned in the takeover controversy is simply management's fiduciary duty to increase shareholder wealth, it may well be that other derivative duties require consideration. This is a point that requires further research. Employing R. H. Coase's concept of a firm as a substitute for expensive modes of transacting, an article in the Spring 1987 issue of *Financial Management* argues that a firm's claimants go beyond stockholders and bondholders to include obligations deriving from implied agreements with other groups such as customers and employees. Here the basis is not just that some persons have an interest or stake, but rather that they entered into an implied agreement, and hence may make claims based on a derivative obligation. They distinguish between explicit contractual claims that firms issue, such as wage contracts and product warranties, and implicit claims, such as "the promise of continuing service to customers and job security to employees."[11] The distinguishing feature of implicit claims is that they are "too nebulous and state contingent to reduce to writing at a reasonable cost."[12] For example, Apple Computer introduced the Macintosh in January 1984, promising that a file server would be available in the near future. "Because the disk was not yet fully developed, the costs to Apple of explicitly stating what future characteristics the disk would have were very high. Consequently, Macintosh customers were sold an implicit claim."[13] The authors continue,

Implicit claims are purchased by other corporate stakeholders as well. . . . When a firm hires a new employee, he or she frequently receives promises about the work environment, the evaluation process and the opportunity for advancement, as well as an explicit employment contract. Similarly, managers typically have no formal employment contract, but often perceive an implicit contract that guarantees lifetime jobs in exchange for competence, honesty, loyalty, and hard work.[14]

These implicit claims typically do not have legal status and, what is more, cannot be unbundled and sold separately.[15]

Important for our purposes is the fact that, if correct, certain implicit agreements carry a moral weight influencing both a decision of whether to acquire or to sell a firm, and also the responsibilities of managing that firm in the future. If there are implicit agreements between the corporation and its employees, or between a corporation and its customers, then while it may not be true that a raider is obliged to honor each and every one in the strictest manner possible, such agreements would constitute factors, that is, moral factors, in the decision-making process connected to acquisition and future management. And if, for example, it can be shown—as some have attempted—that an implicit contract exists between employees and shareholders under which dismissal is expected only in the event of personal incompetence or deterioration in a company's profitability, then dismissal resulting simply as a result of a junk-bond takeover must be regarded as unfair.[16] Or, to take another example, if, after a takeover, the credit rating of older bond issues deteriorates to the disadvantage of bond-holders in a context where an implicit agreement can be shown to exist, then the impact upon bondholders must be regarded as unfair.

It must be granted, however, that the most obvious derivative obligations are explicit ones; and while they include the broad range of contractual and legal arrangements that the firm has entered, including commitments to pension funds, unions, and suppliers, the most significant covenants from the perspective of takeovers are clearly those made by managers to shareholders. The not infrequent violations of such agreements by modern managers, through greenmail, golden parachutes, and a broad assortment of shareholder-abusing, shark-repellant strategies, thus stand as probably the most perspicuous moral violations—this time undertaken by managers against the welfare of shareholders—in the takeover panorama.

Next, let us turn to the social contract–derived obligations that are relevant to the takeover controversy. These may for present purposes be reduced to a few important items. Considered as productive organizations, corporations exist primarily to enhance the welfare of two overlapping classes of persons, those who participate in the productive process, and those who consume its products or services. Adam Smith's allegory of the pin factory lies at the heart of the productive organization's greatest potential contribution, and, in turn, its greatest responsibility: the productive organization must produce *efficiently*. It must use its resources to produce high-quality products at the best possible prices, a consideration that shows why all the cries about mismanaged corporations, about insulated and entrenched corporate leaders, and about the possibility of takeovers enhancing efficiency, are not merely *economic* arguments. They are also *moral* arguments. The moral foundation of the modern productive organization lies with its ability to deliver the goods to society and to deliver them efficiently. Hence, when T. Boone Pickens alludes to this aspect of the matter, he may not know it, but he is making a thoroughly *moral* argument. Of course, there are disputes about the extent to which takeovers enhance efficiency—indeed, whether they do at all. But the moral bottom line is that such things must play a role in the moral calculus.

But the social contract also recognizes the interests of organizational contributors, including those extending all the way from the clerk to the chairman of the board, and demands further that corporate activities remain within the boundaries of justice. If I buy a corporation and fire all the black workers, even if I happened to do it in 1930 when this was legal, I no doubt have violated the nondiscrimination principle of concepts of social justice. This illuminates an aspect of the takeover controversy that is often neglected. I do not know which theory of distributive justice you regard as accurate, whether, say, John Rawls', or Michael Sandel's, or Robert Nozick's. But assume for the moment that you adopt a Rawlsian perspective. By insisting that productive organizations adhere to the bounds of justice, it would follow that the social practices that facilitate the existing wave of takeovers would need to satisfy Rawls' difference principle. Hence the practices allowing takeovers could only encourage inequalities in the distribution of wealth insofar as the worse off who are affected thereby become better off.

This may not be a moot point in the instance of takeovers. While again, only empirical inquiry can answer empirical questions, some of the indicators about the effects of takeovers on the "least well-off" is not encouraging. A recent study on who gets advance notice in plant closings or permanent layoffs (in 1983 and 1984), indicates that about 66 percent of all workers in such events received less than two weeks notice, and 32 percent received no notice whatsoever.[17] Of course, these figures represent all plant closings, not just those brought on by takeovers, but it is usually assumed that cost-conscious corporate acquirers tend to reduce labor costs more vigorously than existing management. And takeover activity, as it happens, occurs against a social backdrop in which the least well-off segments of society do not seem be flourishing. In the last few years we have made hundreds of paper millionaires, and a few billionaires, but almost half of the new jobs created from 1979 to 1985 pay less than a poverty-level income—$180 a week.[18] And for the poorest 20 percent of American families, annual incomes (in real dollars) are one-third less than they were fifteen years ago.[19]

To conclude, this chapter suggests, to paraphrase Oscar Wilde, that in takeovers the truth is never pure and rarely simple. It has argued for the need, in the takeover controversy, to separate moral from legal issues and moral from empirical issues. It has affirmed the need to apply a particular normative theory or model capable of functioning as an analytic backdrop for normative research into takeovers. And, in this vein, it has also been argued that the best backdrop is one that uses a combination of social contract–derived, and post-contractual, or derivative, duties, or, in other words, one that uses a combination of the requirements of the social contract between business and society and the free arrangements made by persons in a democratic state. My hope is that by doing so we can move beyond simplicities to insight, both about takeovers and about the other economic phenomena from which they cannot be disconnected. By employing such strategies, I hope we can reject the prejudice of people who think the final litmus test for human justice in takeovers is whether workers simply continue to perform the same jobs they performed in the past. Similarly, I hope we can reject the view of those whose economic faith is greater than the market's ability to satisfy it—and who seem inevitably to define *homo economicus* by looking in the mirror.

NOTES

1. Roy E. Moor, "The Ethics of Corporate Takeovers: A Public Roundtable Discussion," symposium at the Center for Ethics and Corporate Policy, Waltham, Mass., 1986, p. 1.

2. Walter Adams and James W. Brock, "Hidden Costs of Failed Mergers," *New York Times*, June 21, 1987, Business section, p. 1.

3. Warren A. Law, "A Corporation is More than its Stock," *Harvard Business Review* 64, no. 3 (May-June 1986): 80–83.

4. Ibid., 83.

5. Floyd Norris, *Barron's*, August 10, 1987, pp. 13–14, 37–38.

6. Ibid., 13.

7. Ibid., 13–14, 37–38.

8. Murray Weidenbaum and Stephen Vogt, "Takeovers and Stockholders: Winners and Losers," *California Management Review* 29, no. 4 (Summer 1987): 157–84.

9. Law, "A Corporation is More than its Stock," 82.

10. Ibid., 83.

11. Bradford Cornell and Alan C. Shapiro, "Corporate Stakeholders and Corporate Finance," *Financial Management* 16, no. 1 (Spring 1987): 5–14.

12. Ibid., 5–6.

13. Ibid., 6.

14. Ibid., 5.

15. Cornell and Shapiro extend their analysis to show how such implicit claims can be recognized in a new form of balance sheet.

16. This implicit agreement is argued by Warren Law to have been operative for virtually all corporations. See Law, *A Corporation is More than its Stock*, 82.

17. "Battle Over Plant Closings," *New York Times*, August 28, 1987, p. 25.

18. "Where Greed, Unofficially Blessed by Reagan, Has Led," *New York Times*, June 21, 1987, p. 25.

19. Ibid.

Professional Business Ethics and Mergers and Acquisitions

THOMAS W. DUNFEE

Discussions of ethics are typically focused on nonmarket dimensions of human activity and incorporate assumptions about human nature at odds with the rational actor hypothesis underlying much social science theory. Interestingly, though, the language used in those other disciplines implies value-laden judgments of rightness and wrongness. Entrenched management protects itself with golden parachutes, while corporate raiders seek greenmail payments. Managers divert shareholder wealth to serve their own interests, or shirk on the job. Inside traders misappropriate information. Hired gun investment bankers coerce reluctant clients into further use of their services.

Further, the phenomenon of mergers and acquisitions (the more common term) has been subjected to extensive theorizing within the academic disciplines of economics, organizational design, strategic management, law, and public policy analysis. As a result, there may not be need, or room, for further insights from ethical theory. To the extent that a particular practice of organizational transformation might be found wanting by ethical theorists, but supported by analysis in economics, law, and the relevant management disciplines, many social scientists would assume that the other disciplines should dominate.

Questioning the relevance of theories of professional ethics is not an unfair singling out of a "different" discipline. The question of relevancy must be rigorously explored in the context of any theory that is looked to for special insights into a phenomenon.

THE RELEVANCY OF ETHICS TO ORGANIZATIONAL TRANSFORMATION

In order to establish that ethics is a relevant discipline in attempting to understand and evaluate these dimensions of organizational transformation, at least one of the following must be satisfied: (1) general ethical theory must provide independent insight into the phenomenon of organizational transformation; (2) general ethical theory must enlighten social science or legal theory as applied to organizational transformation; (3) concepts of professional business ethics must explain or influence relevant behavior in a novel way. Each of these possibilities will be briefly considered in turn.

Independent Insight from Ethical Theory

If ethical theory does not provide an insight independent of economics or other social sciences, it is merely redundant. The business ethics/social responsibility literature has failed so far to establish novel major concepts or principles relating to organizational transformation.[1] The literature is less helpful on this issue than it is, for example, on employee rights where it provides independent bases for the recognition and definition of particular rights.[2] The applied ethics literature on mergers and acquisitions is sparse and is just beginning to develop. R. Edward Freeman and others are starting to provide some interesting insights. The case may still be made, but at this point, the first condition has not been satisfied.

Supplemental Insight from Ethical Theory

The second test is whether ethical theory can be shown to enlighten the analysis of economics and/or other social science disciplines in a relevant way. There are several ways in which ethical theory might perform this function. One would be to provide a means of evaluating the assumptions made by social science theorists. For example, the rational actor assumptions of economics and finance may be questioned in certain circumstances. We know that certain markets don't clear. There are many examples from sports, entertainment, emergency equipment, and employment. One explanation could be that most individuals act consistently with personal perceptions of fairness and, therefore, may not always act as rational actor assumptions would project.[3] If so, these personal fairness principles may parallel formal ethical theory. At the least, formal ethical theory might increase understanding of certain behaviors and thereby result in more robust social science models.

Ethical Theory and Business Behavior

Ethical theory can also provide a means for evaluating the appropriateness of certain behavioral assumptions underlying social science theories. For example, the agency cost literature in economics and finance operates on the assumption that managers, ipso facto, are egoistic opportunists. Such managers will shirk (work fewer hours for as much pay as they can get), and divert (indulge their own preferences with corporate jets and country club memberships).[4] These often-stated assumptions may cause students to interpret them as norms, how managers are *supposed* to behave. Such a perverse result should be of concern to all business school pedagogues.

The assumption is essentially a factual one. If, indeed, as assumed throughout the social responsibility/business ethics literature, many managers don't act as opportunistic egoists, then much of the explanatory power of the agency cost models may be lost.

Interestingly, the agency cost literature casts a negative light on certain forms of corporate philanthropy. Under its assumptions, managers who are not effectively controlled by shareholders may breach their fiduciary responsibilities and divert corporate resources toward "personalized" corporate philanthropy. Clearly, corporate philanthropy solely designed to benefit the pet charities of senior managers, or even worse, to benefit senior managers personally through publicity or appointments to prestigious boards, is genuinely suspect. Distinctions need to be made concerning the type of charity and the process through which it is implemented. The danger of the agency cost thesis is that corporate philanthropy may come to be seen as ipso facto evidence of "diverting" management. Ethical theory with its emphasis upon just procedures and the intent of actors may help in clarifying what constitutes proper philanthropy.

Thus, in summary, ethical theory must either provide novel analytical tools, or explain or affect behavior. In the next sections, I will posit that professional concepts of business ethics can influence behavior. I will then argue that ethical behavior is desirable not merely because it is a good in and of itself, but because it serves as a foundation for economic efficiency. Finally, I will suggest that the development and reinforcement of concepts of professional business ethics is one very effective way of moving behavior in desirable directions.[5]

PROFESSIONAL ETHICS AND MARKETPLACE BEHAVIOR

The claim is often heard that there has been a recent decline in the level of ethics in business practice. Those asserting that a decline has occurred often point to the insider trading scandals and the controversy surrounding hostile takeovers as proof. Unfortunately, there are no good empirical data to support or challenge this provocative claim.[6] Faced with a lack of definitive data, the question then becomes whether a market dynamic responsible for declining ethics can be identified. One explanation often casually offered is based upon competitive pressures.

Consider the case of five firms competing in a particular market. One firm decides to introduce deceptive advertising. The deception is difficult for consumers to detect, and the dissembling campaign is successful in capturing a greater market share for the miscreant firm. The competitors realize what has happened, and, one by one, they find it necessary to implement similar types of deceptive advertising in order to halt the decline in their market share. The initial firm responds to those actions by cutting back on the quality of its product, again in a way that is hard for the public to perceive.[7] As this cycle of action and reaction continues, the expected result is an inevitable downward spiral in the level of ethics.

But if this negative scenario were descriptive of most business environments in general, one would expect to see little or no evidence of voluntary ethical behavior in the marketplace. The only counterforce to the downward pressure of the Gresham-law-type force would be the threat of legal sanctions or an egoistic fear of the consequences of lost reputation.

Yet, from Johnson & Johnson's pulling of Tylenol, to Ronald McDonald houses, to many thousands of other actions by business firms and individuals, there clearly appears to be a level of ethical behavior that is well above what the "competitive pressures" model would suggest. Why? One explanation may be that there are generally observed, though nebulous, core concepts of professional business ethics that act as a positive extralegal, extramarket force. These principles, by themselves, may act as counterpoints to any tendencies of managers to act opportunistically or antisocially. They might, for example, make managers more resistant to actual conflicts of interest, in turn lessening the agency cost problems that would freely exist in a world of egoists.

A related research question, also currently unresolved, is the extent to which development of professional norms of ethical behavior influences behavior, particularly when accompanied by extensive educational programs. Research on this issue should also focus on whether particular types of business practitioners are more likely to be influenced positively by professional norms of business ethics, and whether certain types of educational programs pertaining to the norms are more effective.

ETHICS AND ECONOMIC EFFICIENCY

This chapter assumes that there is a positive relationship, to a certain point, between the level of ethical behavior and general economic efficiency. Higher levels of ethical behavior should reduce the costs of long-term contracting, limit the direct losses resulting from opportunistic behavior, and improve productivity through greater responsibility and commitment.[8] The legal system cannot compel "high" levels of ethical behavior. The system, based almost entirely on negative sanctions, is too costly, slow, and incapable of effectively reaching most of the types of behaviors encompassed by professional norms of ethics. Ultimately, the legal system can be relied upon only to set a floor prescribing what are the most reprehensible types of behavior.[9]

This chapter further assumes that there is a positive relationship between the composite ethics of a firm's work force and its profitability.[10] A firm that has comparatively lower losses to its own employees will, by that fact alone, have a cost advantage against competitors. This assumption has interesting implications for foreign competition. If, for example, Japanese firms were found to have on average substantially lower losses to their own employees than do the U.S.

firms with whom they compete, the former would have important advantages resulting from nonmarket factors.

GENERAL PRINCIPLES OF BUSINESS ETHICS

Are there generic principles of business ethics capable of serving as norms for business in general, including individual practitioners, firms, and associations? If there are, the principles should satisfy the following tests. They should be: (1) consistent with general ethical theory, (2) pragmatic and understandable, and (3) compatible with the basic function of business in our society. The list of principles suggested below is neither novel nor surprising. Each is capable of justification under various formulations of ethical theory. The parameters of particular principles should vary depending on the method used to justify them. Thus, a principle of good faith may contain broader prescriptive parameters when justified by a Kantian analysis than when justified by a consequentialistic methodology.

The principles have been drafted to be clear and meaningful. They use common language and refer to familiar concepts. All are found in some version or other in certain corporate codes. Businesspeople have responded knowledgeably and positively to presentations concerning the principles.

Obviously the suggested principles, regardless of how justified and formulated, cannot be perpetually treated by practitioners as bright-line rules that provide simple, decisive answers. It is easy to formulate situations in which two or more of the principles will come into conflict. Ethics requires judgment, and no short-form calculus can remove that inherent characteristic.

With the caveats listed above, the following eight principles are presented as a plausible set of general ethical standards.

1. *Honor Confidentiality*

Information is confidential when it is made available to another with the express or implied understanding that it is to be used only for certain purposes. A principle of confidentiality may also pertain to information identified as proprietary or confidential, obtained by means other than direct disclosure by the owner.

2. *Avoid the Appearance of a Conflict of Interest*

A conflict of interest arises when someone has a personal interest that contrasts with a duty owed to another or when mutually exclusive duties are owed to two or more (some call this competing interests). Binding duties may arise out of contractual obligations, noncontractual promises, role relationships (such as agent or trustee), or by law. Potential conflicts of interest can be deflected from becoming actual conflicts by, among other things, full disclosure, having an independent party certify fairness, or abstention.

3. *Willingly Comply with the Law*

This principle involves compliance with the substance of legal provisions. It goes beyond merely employing a cost-benefit analysis of the impact of likely legal sanctions to determine whether to comply with a given rule. Confronting an immoral law might, in certain instances, justify noncompliance. But valid civil disobedience should occur extremely infrequently in business transactions.

4. *Exercise Due Care*

This principle incorporates a concept of professional competency. One who has special training or experience should perform to the level generally expected of those with equivalent qualifications. The principle may be viewed as an ethical standard in that others rely upon and are affected by the quality of work performed by the businesspeople to whom it applies.

5. *Act in Good Faith*

Good faith incorporates a number of attributes, including honoring promises, being fair, employing just procedures, and responding to the reasonable expectations held by others. The essence of the concept is to act so as to sustain a long-term relationship.

6. *Be Faithful to Special Responsibilities*

Special responsibilities that transcend due care and good faith may derive from a particular position or role. Trustees, agents, directors, and senior executives all encounter special duties imposing higher standards of care and complete trustworthiness.

7. *Show Respect for the Liberty and Rights of Others*

Businesspeople, particularly those in supervisory roles, often have the power to affect the ability of others to exercise basic rights. The affected parties have a right to be treated with respect, and to be able, to the extent feasible, to exercise their basic rights as citizens and human beings.

8. *Respect Human Well-Being*

A fundamental principle is to do no harm to others. Although "harm" is a relative concept that is complex and difficult to define, this principle can be seen as generally trumping any of the other seven when conflicts arise.

APPLICATION OF THE PRINCIPLES TO PROBLEMS IN ORGANIZATIONAL TRANSFORMATION

In the next sections, the way in which the principles apply to common issues in organizational transformation will be briefly explored. Space constraints make it impossible to do much more than identify the basic principles applicable to each problem.

Leveraged Management Buyouts

Leveraged management buyouts (LMBOs) involve current managers taking a firm private by purchasing outstanding stock from the shareholders. Leverage is involved in that the managers use the resources of the firm to obtain financing for the stock purchases. Typically, the managers personally put up only a very small percentage of the purchase price.

The basic principles that apply to this situation are conflict of interest, due care, fidelity, and good faith. Management starts with a basic, substantial conflict of interest, in that they have a duty to represent the interests of the corporate shareholders fully, yet are the other party interested in the transaction. The common way in which such potential conflicts are resolved is by having the proposal approved by outside independent authority, and/or independent members of the board who have no direct interest in the transaction. The validity of this process may be questioned because of the enormous potential returns available to the managers, which may exert enormous temptations to conceal plans, coerce reluctant directors, and subtly misrepresent critical aspects of the deal offered to shareholders. Investment banking firms lack true independence in assessing fairness when they directly participate by having an equity interest in the buyout. If an investment banking firm ends up with any interest in the firm, its assessments cannot be independent. Further, the nature of corporate boards of directors are such that, again, it may be very difficult to identify enough nonparticipating directors with the combination of capability and lack of personal interest sufficient to evaluate the fairness of a deal, particularly one that could return millions of dollars to their management colleagues.

All managers of the firm, including those not personally participating in the buyout, have duties of due care, good faith, and fidelity. The process of the leveraged buyout involves substantial and important disclosures to the shareholders. Because of the tax laws and certain accounting factors, a given LMBO may be a win-win situation, with the firm genuinely worth more in the hands of the privatizing managers than it could ever be while publicly held. Nevertheless, shareholders' representatives need accurate and adequate disclosures in order to judge whether an appropriate price is being paid. If, instead, managers have come up with strategies to increase the value of the firm greatly but do not intend to act on them until they own the firm, there is a clear violation of the principle of fidelity.

Typically, ethical issues in organizational transformation are fact dependent, and the evaluation of a particular situation will depend upon the intent and plans of the managers, the type of disclosure that has occurred, and the appropriateness of the price offered for the shares.

Insider Trading

Insider trading calls into play a majority of the principles: fidelity, confidentiality, conflict of interest, willing compliance with the law, due care, and good faith. If a trader uses the information in violation of his/her firm's rules or inconsistently with a client's expectations, there has been a breach of fidelity, good faith, and confidentiality. Many of the recent cases have involved stealing or misappropriating the information.

There are many ways in which a conflict of interest can be involved in insider trading. A manager with knowledge of a major stock repurchase plan may buy in front of his own firm, personally benefiting, while raising the price of purchase to the firm. Or an employee of an investment banking firm may advise a client about a planned acquisition, and then personally purchase stock of the client and sell the information to other traders who together drive up the price of the stock in advance of the client's open market purchases.

Managers responsible for the control of information that becomes easily available to potential insider traders may breach the principle of due care. Although a breach of willing compliance with the law seems obvious here, there are some justifications that may be proffered by wrong-doers. For example, they might argue that the insider trading law is a bad law, which thereby absolves those engaging in the practice; or traders may assert that the scope of the law is not clear, allowing them to construe ambiguities in their own favor. Neither explanation is satisfying in the typical insider trading case. The fact that one disagrees with the policy underlying a law is not sufficient grounds for noncompliance. Insider traders do not act as a form of civil disobedience; they act to enrich themselves. The mere fact that there are some ambiguous areas in a law does not provide carte blanche to violate its fundamental provisions. Almost all the highly publicized insider trading cases have involved core violations of the law.

Golden Parachutes

Golden parachutes are very substantial severance payments arranged in advance for select senior managers to take effect when termination occurs as a result of a designated occurrence, for example, a hostile takeover. The implementation of golden parachutes may involve a conflict of interest when managers directly or indirectly influence the establishment of their own perquisites.

An issue of due care pertains to any manager having responsibility for implementing golden parachutes. Plans that have only a tenuous relationship to the services rendered, or to the retention of good managers, are suspect. Although golden parachutes, appropriately designed, may result in obtaining and retaining superior, truly independent managers, they may also be subject to substantial abuse.

Tin parachutes, diminutive severance plans for lower level managers, raise similar issues on an appropriately smaller scale. Due care, conflict of interest, and fidelity issues are involved whenever the plans have the potential for acting as a takeover defense. If they are designed to be activated only when a hostile takeover occurs, there is good reason to suspect that the three principles are violated. If not, as is apparently typically the case, they are probably consistent with the principles.

Strategies Employed to Deter Hostile Takeovers

Along with insider trading, the phenomenon of hostile takeovers has garnered substantial amounts of recent publicity. Much of the focus of this chapter will be on evaluating the strategies employed by threatened managers to fend off potential hostile bids. Strategies increasingly employed by defensive management have been captured in pithy phrases: poison pill, pac man, crown jewels, white knight. They all raise questions of conflict of interest, due care, and fidelity. Management has a basic obligation to shareholders to maximize return, supplemented by various obligations to important stakeholders.

A hostile takeover bid may drive up the price of the stock and may produce substantial benefits to shareholders. Or, an actual hostile takeover may result in a greatly increased debt burden for the acquired firm, leading toward reduced expenditures on research and development and lowered financial resiliency. These changes reduce shareholder wealth in the long term. But, underlying the uncertainty of outcome to the interests of shareholders is the immutable fact that hostile takeovers are often followed by reductions in the ranks of the captured managers. Thus, regardless of the likely impact upon shareholders, target management has a personal interest in the outcome, creating a potential conflict of interest.

From the viewpoint of professional business ethics, the dependent question thus becomes: Is management employing the defense strategies solely in the shareholders' interests, or are they seeking to preserve their own positions? Full disclosure of the bases for the action, coupled with assessments of fairness by autonomous professionals, and genuinely independent internal approvals may help prevent the potential conflict of interest from becoming an actual one.

The employment of certain defense strategies may also raise questions of due care and fidelity. Some strategies use a "make ugly" notion that getting rid of "excessive" cash or particularly attractive subsidiaries will reduce the chances of acquisition. Hasty acquisitions at high prices of other firms by a potential target may lack due care and may not be in the long-term interests of shareholders. Fire sales of subsidiaries to produce funds for resisting acquirers raise similar questions.

The payment of greenmail is particularly troublesome under the principles of conflict of interest and fidelity. "Greenmail" is the term used to describe a buyback of the shares held by a threatening acquirer (raider) at higher-than-market prices.[11] In some instances, the acquirer has purchased stock in the open market, then made or threatened a tender offer at a substantial premium over the market price. Target management resists the tender offer, uses corporate resources to initiate legal challenges, and then buys back the stock from the potential acquirer at a substantial premium, using corporate resources to make the purchase. Once the purchase is made, the target firm is left with substantial debt burdens and the price of the stock declines, leaving shareholders worse off.

In this scenario we are left with an actual decline in shareholder wealth balanced against management's assertions that shareholders would have been worse off if the payment hadn't occurred. The fact that management has a very significant conflict of interest means that extremely high standards should be imposed to guarantee that management has not given in to self-interest.

The veil-of-ignorance concept may help in formulating appropriate public policy on this issue. If one cannot know in advance whether one will be a shareholder, a manager, a creditor, or an acquirer, what would one then prefer as a matter of public policy? It seems reasonable to assume that when operating behind a veil of ignorance, the public would not prefer an absolute ban on takeovers, or such heavy restrictions as to ban them de facto.

Acquisition Strategies of Corporate Raiders

Much of the debate about hostile takeovers has focused on the motives of the raiders. The raiders portray themselves as champions of the small investor—as concerned only with making sure that self-serving entrenched management lives up to its obligation to maximize shareholder wealth. The management of potential target companies characterizes the raiders quite differently—as financial manipulators concerned only with personal gain and the short term, more interested in inducing greenmail payments or dismembering productive companies than in enhancing wealth for the ordinary shareholder.

The role of the raiders raises the most complex series of issues in this area. The basic principles involved are respect for the rights of others, respect for human well-being, and good faith. Some raiders proclaim a post-acquisition strategic plan to sell off assets, reduce the work force, and lower wage levels. Sometimes this will involve shutting down marginally profitable facilities. When these decisions are justified solely in financial terms, without consideration of the interests of the affected employees and of other dependent stakeholders, they may be criticized as violating the principle of respect for human well-being. These other interests need to be valued in comparable terms with the financial factors in decisions having such a dramatic effect on employees and stakeholders.

Good faith becomes an issue when a raider misrepresents his true intentions. A raider who threatens a takeover after buying shares in the open market, but who is really playing a game of "chicken" with the target management hoping for a buyout, violates the principle of good faith. It is, however, very difficult to identify whether a raider has actually been deceptive. Merely accepting a buyout, particularly under circumstances in which the takeover was unlikely to succeed, is not definitive evidence of a wrongful intent. Intention is always hard to discern, and in the battlefield conditions of many attempted hostile takeovers, may be impossible.

It might be possible to construct an argument that raiders breach an ethical duty when they knowingly induce weak target management to give in and make greenmail payments that are not in the long-term interest of the target shareholders. This argument is quite strained, particularly in the context of large corporations represented by prestigious law and investment banking firms and operating through a complex system of corporate governance. Generally, a potential acquirer should be entitled to assume that target management will act consistently with its legal and ethical duties.

CONCLUSION

This chapter has presented a structure of eight general principles of professional business ethics. The principles have then been applied in a very general sense to several of the major issues involved in organizational transformation. The application of the principles is designed to show that, indeed, concepts of professional ethics for business practitioners may enlighten analysis of complex marketplace phenomena. Much can be gained through efforts to identify and describe meaningful core principles of business ethics that may serve as norms for behavior.

NOTES

1. See for example, Douglas Houston and John Howe, "The Ethics of Going Private," *Journal of Business Ethics* 6 (October 1987): 519 (relies primarily upon efficiency analysis); R. Edward Freeman, Daniel Gilbert, Jr., and Carol Jacobson, "The Ethics of Greenmail," *Journal of Business Ethics* 6 (April 1987): 164 (probably most extensive analysis, relying upon concepts of blackmail and agency, develops persuasive case that public policy in the corporate governance area should not be based on black-white assessments of questioned practices); and, James Horrigan, "The Ethics of the New Finance," *Journal of Business Ethics* 6 (February 1987): 97 (criticizes normative ideas of major theories in modern finance as "pervasive nihilism," suggests as one counterpoint greater ethical concern, but doesn't define it).

2. See, for example, P. Werhane, *Persons, Rights, & Corporations* (Englewood Cliffs, N.J.: Prentice-Hall, 1985); Robert Sass, "The Workers' Right to Know, Participate, and Refuse Hazardous Work: A Manifesto Right," *Journal of Business Ethics* 5 (April 1986): 129; and references cited in both.

3. For an empirical analysis of how concepts of fairness may be a factor in market anomalies, see Daniel Kahneman, Jack Knetsch, and Richard Thaler, *American Economic Review* 76 (September 1986): 728.

4. See Eugene Fama, "Agency Problems and the Theory of the Firm," *Journal of Political Economy* 88 (1980): 288; Michael Jensen and William Meckling, "Theory of the Firm: Managerial Behavior, Agency Costs, and Ownership Structure," *Journal of Financial Economics* 3 (1976): 305.

5. The relationship between education in ethics and behavior is a critically important issue today. The issue is one that is difficult to test effectively due to the inherent problems associated with evaluating behavior. Crude measures, such as liability suits or indictments for business crimes, fall far short of capturing the extralegal dimension that is the heart of professional ethics. Although there is some weak evidence that education in professional ethics does change scores on moral development tests—Goldman and Arbuthnot, "Teach-

ing Medical Ethics: The Cognitive-Developmental Approach," *Journal of Medical Ethics* 5 (1979): 171; William Penn and Boyd Collier, "Current Research in Moral Development as a Decision Support System," *Journal of Business Ethics* 4 (1985): 131; and Linda Klebe Trevino, "Ethical Decision Making in Organizations: A Person-Situation Interactionist Model," *Academy of Management Review* 11 (1986): 601—no empirical link to behavior has been established. Similarly, there is no empirical evidence that such studies fail to change behavior. For the time being, the interim resolution of the issue must depend upon intuitive plausibility. To this writer, at least, it appears far more plausible to assume that education in professional ethics can affect behavior.

6. The only way to answer this recurring question accurately is to have trend data based around the same questionnaire. See Steven Brenner and Earl Molander, "Is the Ethics of Business Changing?" *Harvard Business Review* 55, no. 1 (1977): 57.

7. To the extent that the public can identify the unethical act and respond by turning to more ethical competitors, the market will provide some correction to unethical actions.

8. Losses would include direct employee theft, shirking in the form of unauthorized sick leave, diversion of corporate opportunities, and so on. These are estimated to amount to tens of billions of dollars each year.

9. For a somewhat more elaborate version of this argument, see Thomas Dunfee, "The Case for Professional Norms of Business Ethics," *American Business Law Journal* 25 (1987): 385.

10. This argument is developed extensively in Thomas Dunfee and Diana Robertson, "Work-Related Ethical Attitudes: Impact on Business Profitability," *Business and Professional Ethics Journal* 3, no. 2 (Winter 1984): 25; Thomas Dunfee, "Employee Ethical Attitudes and Business Firm Productivity," *Wharton Annual* 8 (1983): 75.

11. Although the term "raider" is somewhat pejorative, it is used because it most succinctly describes the position and role of the potential acquirer. Alternative terminology is quite awkward.

Takeovers, Makeovers, and Destruction: The Ethics of Corporate Transformation

LISA H. NEWTON

The bulk of my writing over the last few years has concerned corporate excellence, or virtue: the orientations toward people, product, and market that make the best corporations centers of moral endeavor for employees, community, and the nation at large. The recovery of American competitiveness, I have argued, depends on encouragement of the qualities of excellence exemplified by such corporations—faithfulness to employees, who repay faith with careful work; a passion for quality of product; and, above all, a willingness to work for the long term, unconcerned with this or that quarter's "bottom line."

In the current takeover atmosphere, I feel a little like the Physicians Against Nuclear War who came to Fairfield University a year ago to explain their convictions and describe their work. Some of us questioned the involvement of physicians in essentially political activity; after all, isn't there full employment in guarding people's health? Yes, but there's a connection, they argued, and tried to make it plausible to us: It's bad for your health to smoke, to get fat, to incur stress, and it's just as bad for your health to be blown to smithereens by a nuclear bomb—which is very likely to happen to you if things continue the way they're going—so we work for a nuclear freeze. That is very plausible indeed, almost laughable in its plausibility; similarly plausible, laughable, and somehow ill-fitting is my contention that if corporations are to work for excellence in all respects, they must make sure they are not destroyed by one of these junk-bond, bust-up raiders, for when you are dismantled, you cease to exist, and then excellence is very difficult to achieve. The hostile takeover is at the least the terrorist bomb of American industry, not fatal to the whole world but exploding individual corporations apparently at random, turning America's corporate scene into an extended Beirut where long-term investments and commitments are unwise and, in general, not undertaken.

So we shall have little excellence, little competitiveness, much ado about finance and its yuppies, much scorn for the old-line managers of companies that actually manufacture products, until the takeover mania is past. So I will have to write about the takeovers. In my attempts to get an ethical handle on this activity, I have been increasingly drawn to the ancient truisms about political and economic life: that just as the wages of sin is death, so the wages of making money without creating wealth is government regulation; that those who forget history are condemned to repeat it; and that ultimately, its ability to produce virtuous individuals may be the best test of a society's efficiency.

THE NATURE OF THE PROBLEM

One must imagine the American corporation as a small iron ball, on a smooth level surface, surrounded by magnets. These magnets are the constituencies, or stakeholders, of the corporation. Their pulls, or interests, are occasionally diametrically opposed to each other, occasionally obliquely opposed, and almost never coincident. Management's job, under ordinary circumstances, is to keep them in balance. The history of the American corporation is a history of the motions of those magnets, shifting alignment, closing and strengthening, withdrawing and weakening. The interests of each, allowed to govern unchecked, would destroy the corporation and seriously compromise the interests of all. The process by which the corporation is preserved, often by the skin of its collective teeth, is called politics, and may involve legislation, regulation, or the accretion of a judicial tradition that balances the temporarily superior force. The major benchmarks in the history of the corporation—the development of the factory, the formation of cartels, the labor movement, the Great Depression, the sudden mobilization for war, the environmental movement, and now the hostile takeover phenomenon—are so many surges in the magnetic field, indicating a sudden strengthening in one of the constituencies vis-à-vis the others. At such surges, the political process intervenes to limit the damage and create a new equilibrium, not before damage is done, but, at least until now, in time to preserve the corporation's major functions for all parties. Thus, in response to the cartels, the antitrust laws were passed; labor unions were legitimated, stabilized, and limited by laws including the National Labor Relations Act; the environmental movement was similarly stabilized by regulations at federal, state, and local levels, the unpredictable civil rights movement by the affirmative action cases, and so forth. Each political/legal intervention grants to the surging constituency recognition—something it wants very much—a few of its demands, and the promise of consideration of future demands by an orderly process, in return for the promise to work within the present political and economic framework. Upon this process depends the future of American industry, at least as long as we choose to organize industry in corporate form.

The takeover phenomenon, "merger mania," is an owners' surge. It is not the first one in history; we will get back to parallels with the 1920s later in the chapter. Like the previous constituent surges, some of which produced sign-waving mobs at plant gates and threats of system-overturning violence, this one may not be as dangerous as it looks. The political process remaining intact, initial legislation to contain it while legitimating its major demands should be in place within a year. With the Indiana and Minnesota antitakeover legislation in place as I write this, Massachusetts and New Jersey expected soon and Delaware to follow, the process is already well underway at the state level. If history is any guide, the legislation will be changed several times before the system settles down again.

Why do these things happen? Largely because demographic or other deep structural changes (in this case, both) bring about changes in the absolute interests or relative strengths of the various factors. Tracking these changes may help to put the takeover madness in perspective, and perhaps supply guidance toward dealing with it.

First, the nature of the "owner" of the corporation has changed. When shareholders were individuals, most of them chose to buy into a company in large part because they believed in the enterprise's long-run potential for good returns, and were on that account willing to be patient through cycles and to support management's efforts to provide for the future by investments that would not immediately yield any return. To the extent that other factors were operating in the choice of portfolio, these factors tended to be personal friendship or identification with the company or its personnel, which would militate them more strongly against casual sale or sudden demands. When pension funds and universities started buying stock (instead of relying on bonds, their traditional repositories), we should have known we were in trouble. The manager of a fund has no attachments, emotional or otherwise, to the companies in the portfolio, but is interested only in increasing the absolute dollar amount in the fund. On that increase, or "performance," he is judged, and on it his job depends. Now these institutional funds, some of them pension funds but many more simply commercial ventures, own up to 70 percent of the outstanding stock of publicly held companies. While the managers were limited technically in the speed and accuracy with which they could change the portfolio, no real practical penalties attended this distinct change in interest—might as well stay in for the long term, for short-term dealings are not likely to bring higher returns. But with the advent of the computer, and the software designed to read trends and buy and sell in an instant, with the advent of fund managers increasingly willing to turn over stock at breakneck speed, and with the intensely competitive atmosphere that makes the conservative manager (rightly) fear for his job if he does not join the casino, the new "owners" of the corporation can and will snap from stock to stock on the promise of only short-term rapid advances. The takeover targets, as we shall see, are rich in such promises, and the disreputable professions that have sprung into existence to make the promises come true—raiding, risk arbitrage, junk-bond financing—draw from rich wells.[1]

The owners have changed, and so have the countervailing forces. For demographic reasons beyond the scope of this chapter, labor unions are no longer in a position to provide effective checks on owners. Customers have, at present, no say at all in these dealings; it will be interesting to see if the final settlement provides them with a voice. The nation, or national interest, seems to have snapped off its magnet and gone for a nap. Only the localities, and secondarily the states, seem to be aware of the damage being done to the economic fabric of America by this unrestrained greed, and are in a position to do something about it. That will be the sector to watch over the next months.

In what follows, we will trace briefly the debate over the economic benefit of unrestricted takeover activity, whether or not it is good for the economy, now or ever, and then turn our consideration to the more serious institutional and characterological fallout from this peculiar economic aberration.

ARE ALL THESE TAKEOVERS GOOD FOR BUSINESS?

Our first inquiry, then, must be a straightforward utilitarian analysis of the infamous takeover. We will confine our attentions to the "unsolicited" or "hostile" takeover, simply because it lends interest to this kind of analysis; for the characterization of hostility to apply, there must be at least some disagreement in this particular case about the costs and the benefits of the exercise.

To give the affirmative side first hearing, what are the supposed benefits of takeovers, or arguments for allowing the raiders to continue unchecked? The presumption of liberty operative in household-level market transactions, according to each the freedom to buy and sell at will, hardly applies in the buying and selling of companies. For good and sufficient reason, this area of the economy has been very closely regulated since 1929, and the operative presumption is that it should be regulated for the common good.[2] How do hostile takeovers serve the common good?

The arguments most often employed by the defenders of the raiders—the "Shark School," we might call them—is, as William Niskanen, chairman of the Cato Institute, put it, that "the market for corporate control"—that is, the tendency of raiders to try to buy out companies—"is exercising a healthy discipline on managers, whose interests often differ from those of the owners."[3] There are two points in this claim, both of which are worth examining. The first, and less interesting, is that managers as a class need some sort of discipline. Niskanen is not alone in this claim. Richard Darman of the U.S. Treasury also thinks that American business leaders, the managements of these target companies, are "bloated, risk-averse, inefficient and unimaginative,"[4] and T. Boone Pickens tags them with "regimentation, stifling of the entrepreneurial spirit, disregard for stockholders, and obsession with perquisites and power."[5] Michael Jensen, long the Dean of the Shark School, has consistently argued that the "takeover process penalizes incompetent or self-serving managers whose actions have lowered the market price of their corporation's stock,"[6] and James C. Miller, chairman of the Federal Trade Commission, has also argued that the takeover has a role as a "check on inefficient management," going on to comment that it "is no coincidence that calls for new regulation are coming increasingly from the management of potential takeover targets."[7] Possibly the most fervent of the Shark School, Henry G. Manne of George Mason University, regrets the current insider trading scandal largely because it might cramp the raiders' styles if they were implicated in insider trading. Manne says it would be worse yet "if the Boesky case could be used to justify additional regulations making tender offers even more difficult to mount. . . . The tender offer is the most important and beneficial financial invention of the 20th Century. Its very existence has probably added hundreds of billions of dollars to American capital values. Without it, noncontrolling shareholders in companies with widely diffused ownership would be nearly helpless in the face of managerial incompetence, self-dealing, or inattention to business."[8] That addition of "hundreds of billions of dollars to American capital values" means nothing except that all this churning has run up the stock market, which, in the absence of any real improvement in the condition of America's industry, is hardly reassuring. But the same belief in managerial incompetence apparently motivates the Reagan administration's opposition to any antitakeover legislation: according to Beryl Sprinkel, Chairman of the President's Council of Economic Advisors, the "administration believes hostile takeovers promote market efficiency by weeding out bad management."[9]

The weight of opinion is puzzling, given the complete absence of evidence for the belief expressed. A more likely explanation for the attractiveness of certain companies as takeover targets is that they are being managed very well indeed; that they have sold off unprofitable divisions, put profitable divisions on a much stronger footing, and that all of their operations now are likely to do very well—but the analysts who guide the stock market have not yet realized that, so the stock is "undervalued." That, at least, seems to be the case with Dayton Hudson, under attack as I write, and is likely the case with a good many other of the hapless targets.[10] Then it is the stock market, not the management, that is inefficient. But it is not the stock analysts who are "disciplined" by the hostile takeover. Very little independent evidence has been sought, or presented, that management of any target company in particular is incompetent, or more incompetent than other managements. Given the varied missions, cultures, and directions of corporate America, it is not really clear that there could even be one set of criteria for assessing competence in such a large class.

But the school asserts that there is one and only one criterion of competence, which brings us to the second and more interesting claim implicit in Niskanen's defense of the raid. The managers need to be "disciplined" because their interests may not coincide with those of the owners, the shareholders. Shareholder interests are the only interests that count, according to the school, and the only interest they have is (as above) seeing the price of the stock go up, so that they can sell it. The insertion of the question of whose interests shall count in a utilitarian analysis makes the issue one of a very small class in the study of ethics: only in more recent controversies in environmental studies, where questions concerning the countability of animals and ecosystems are sometimes raised, can we find a parallel.[11] In all other ethical issues, we count the interests of all and only those human beings whose interests are affected, in deciding whether that practice is beneficial. The queer results of the school's restrictive counting muddy the discourse in sometimes incomprehensible ways. At an extreme, the leaders of the school (Michael Jensen of Rochester, for example) simply announce that companies do not exist so shareholders are the only stakeholders there are. The "company," the entity you thought you were dealing with, is only a convenient term for the hired agents of the shareholders, agents who by definition may not consider others as stakeholders in any of their dealings.[12] More typically, the exclusion of all interests other than that of the owners is implicit and probably unconscious. In typical passages from an editorial condemning legal regulation of takeover activity, finance professor Irwin Friend first cites evidence that during the course of a takeover, there is a "marked increase in the stock price of the acquired companies—a benefit to shareholders," notes that there may be no increase in the price of the stock of the acquiring companies, balances costs and benefits to the two sets of shareholders, concludes that the benefit to the first set outweighs possible costs to the second set, and, with no further argument, goes on to introduce the next section with "Because of the evidence that takeovers have, as a whole, benefited the economy."[13] *No* evidence is presented that takeovers have benefited the economy, nor even that the class of all shareholders benefits in the long run. In this school of reasoning, only the shareholder of the moment counts, and his interests are only to be totted up on a deal-by-deal basis. In fact, the class is more restricted yet: Only the shareholders with instant access to the trading floor, who can tender their shares near the top of the stock's wild swing, benefit from the transactions. The target's shareholders who retain their shares—either because they are unaware of the tender offer, or because they have no access to the market at the crucial point in the deal, or because they hope the company will fight off the raid and continue as before—lose very badly. "Squeezed out at the back end," their stock loses its value and is redeemable only for junk bonds. So the consequences of this method of counting are uncertain at best; we cannot even say that the school properly calculates the interests of the people they choose to count. In any case, no convincing argument has been advanced that most of those impacted by the takeover activity should be left out of account.

Who, then, benefits when a company falls victim to a hostile takeover? Some of the shareholders of the target company surely benefit, as the escalating bids take the price of their shares well above where it would have been left to its own devices. Alarm at the possibility that these shareholders might miss out on these windfall gains if takeovers were banned tends to be attenuated by the realization that up to 70 percent of the shares of publicly held companies are held by huge institutional funds whose computer programs choose which stocks to buy and sell. But programs cannot really enjoy those profits, at least not in the time-honored ways—the gloating, the chortling at the misery of the defeated, the merry glass raised in celebration of one's profitable victory—so the damage they inflict is indeed a totally joyless affair for everyone concerned. Beyond this fraction of the previous owners of the target company, the major beneficiaries are the arbitrageurs who buy the stock at the rumor (or illegal foreknowledge) of takeover, the investment bankers who fund the raider, the raider himself, and their lawyers, consultants, and advisors.[14] With all due respect for those people, the number is just not very large.

Yet, if we actually start counting all the people affected by a typical hostile takeover, we come quickly to a conclusion that strains credulity: that there can be no reason at all for the controversy. For if we count all the injury that actually follows a takeover, we must condemn the practice with no room left over for discussion. Since the first popular journal articles on takeovers started to appear (Magnet's "Help! My Company Has Just Been Taken Over," for instance, in *Fortune* in 1984, and Lang's "Aftermath of a Merger" in *Northeast Magazine* the next year),[15] with their talk of suicides, unemployment, shattered careers, and families destroyed, followed up by more serious treatments of the effects of merger on the personnel of a company,[16] we have been on notice that just the costs to all employees were likely to outweigh the benefits to all the stockholders. Add to these the costs to the communities that hosted the doomed facilities of the acquired companies, especially the corporate headquarters, which often counted on those executives and their families for community leadership; costs to the creditors, who now find themselves holding notes for companies considerably less creditworthy than those they lent to; costs to the suppliers; costs to the retirees, whose pension funds are endangered; and the damaged far outnumber those who profit by hundreds to thousands, while the damage they suffer is far more significant than the limited monetary profit accruing to some shareholders.

But the utilitarian case for ending the takeover blitz is not limited to charting the effects of the raiders on the companies involved. Takeover activity inevitably initiates a reflex of equally dubious "shark defenses"—poison pills (which amount to shooting yourself in the foot so you will be less attractive to kidnappers), greenmail (a bribe to the raider, which benefits no one but the raider and hurts everyone else, including all of us who have to read about how much money he got), leveraged buyouts, and the frantic search for the "white knight," who often knights the company out of all they own anyway. The tales of companies "restructured" in the process of fighting off the raider compose a drumroll of death for that corporate competitiveness that we need to secure our economy against the Japanese: Union Carbide loading itself with debt after selling off its most profitable division,[17] Owens-Corning letting 480 of its 970 research employees go and slashing its research budget in half in the wake of restructuring,[18] and Goodyear Tire and Rubber cutting its research and development program by 7 percent after restructuring to fend off Sir James Goldsmith.[19] What happened to Phillips and the other oil companies after the runs made on them by T. Boone Pickens and Carl Icahn is now the stuff of legend.[20] The Shark

Defender School of Economics insists that all these cuts make the companies "more efficient" in the long run. More efficient at what? Not at developing new products. Efficient, it seems, only at raising the price of the stock. When the company retreats to its cyclically mature markets, it turns out plenty of cash to service its debts, and its stockholders may be very happy with it (operating income for Owens-Corning is expected to be up 80 percent in 1987, over 1985 levels, and the price of its stock is also up), but it is no longer able to do anything for the nation's economic future.

In the face of all these disasters, the greatest danger of takeovers is still the debt built up by raider or "successful" defender, threatening massive bankruptcies in the event of any economic downturn.[21] "The way our system runs," observes Andrew Sigler, CEO of Champion International, "a company can perform only in relation to the strength of its balance sheet. So the aggregate of all this leveraging is to diminish the strength of the entire economic system. In addition, this kind of game-playing imposes short-term attitudes and strategies on companies which are just the opposite of what is needed if this country is to remain competitive."[22] The "dangers of the proliferation of large-scale takeovers financed by excessive use of high-cost debt should be clear," warns investment banker Felix Rohatyn. "At a time when we should be trying to encourage long-term investment, this activity encourages speculation and short-term trading. At a time when we should be trying to strengthen our important industries to make them more competitive, this activity weakens many of our companies by stripping away their equity and replacing it with high-cost debt. Borrowing can promote growth when the borrowed funds are used by a company to make new investments in order to meet future market needs and to be more competitive. It is quite another story when leverage is created to pay out shareholders today at the expense of growth tomorrow."[23] It is this debt, and the accompanying explosion of stock values, that creates the ominous parallels between the raiders and the stock pools of the 1920s,[24] between the roaring market of the pre-Crash days and the "gossamer ladder" of today.[25]

The conclusion of all debate on the topic would seem to follow straightforwardly: the hostile takeover, the raid, the defenses, and the wild speculation accompanying the practices, should be ended immediately, by self-restraint if possible,[26] by legislation if necessary. Then where, in the economic debate, is the belief coming from that hostile takeovers are good for the economy and should be permitted to continue unfettered by restrictive legislation?

In the presence of belief without evidence—and claims and perspectives so skewed as to defy understanding—the sophisticated analyst turns his attention to the possibility that we may be dealing with religious belief. And of course we are: the religion of the Market, which has confessed since 1776 the belief that, left to their own devices, people seeking only to advance their own interests would increase without limit the wealth of their nations. In Adam Smith's description, the belief made sense; given the economic arrangements and financial transactions possible during the period of industrialization in the West, the belief worked out in practice as well as might be expected. Now we are confronted with a test of that faith—financial practices that strip the nation's wealth, turning it into instant cash for private parties, which are yet entirely consistent with the private interests of the parties capable of carrying on these practices. The "invisible hand" guides several million dollars worth of greenmail into Sir James Goldsmith's pocket. Nothing he does with it is likely to help us compete with the Japanese. What will be our response? A possible response, time-honored in religion, is renewed rigidity, and we find that response in the takeover issue: no seventeenth-century Jansenist tract can rival, in doctrinal rigor and callousness to human concerns, the twentieth-century Jensenist tracts on the divine rights of shareholders and the abysmal unworthiness of managers, workers, or any other claimants on a company's good faith.[27] Alternatively, do we abandon our faith in the free market, at least for this instance, and help the outraged legislators write good antitakeover legislation? Or have we covenanted forever with this mechanical deity, that no matter what it does to us, we will be its people?

We are unlikely to make much progress on the takeover issue until we can return all the issues to the realm of rationality—to a settled typology of claims (which definitional, which empirical, which moral), a settled method for gathering evidence for the empirical ones, and a settled standard of verification. If the claims that hostile takeovers are good for the economy are to have any plausibility whatsoever, in the face of overwhelming evidence of the misery they cause, we are going to have to agree on some way to test them and some acceptable way to calculate the test's results. Eliminating the interests of most of the citizens from consideration is not one of the acceptable ways.

INSTITUTIONS AND MORAL CHARACTER: THE INSIDER TRADING CONNECTION

In the preceding section, we argued utility: the greatest economic happiness of the greatest number in the long run, which does not seem, absent a religious faith in the free market that warps all seeming, to support the raiders' case for freedom. But utility functions are not all there is to morality, and unlike many economic practices, this particular surge seems to bring a train of ethical abuses in its wake. We cannot ignore the terrible dereliction of duty lacing the surface of the deals as they come to the light, like seams of coal on exposed faces of the mountain: raiders bending the law to make their conquest, arbitragers breaking the law for quick profit, company officials scrambling for golden parachutes in defiance of their fiduciary duties to shareholders, all with callous disregard for obligations built up over the years to employees, retirees, and the local community. And finally, focus of the most recent rash of articles, the question becomes one of virtue: where did all this unlimited greed come from? Why do people choose to live this way? Is there anything we can do about it short of canceling the free enterprise system? The shift from one mode of moral reasoning to another began when the insider trading scandal broke.

Now why should this be? After all, a hostile takeover attempt is a tender offer for stock in a company, not solicited by the company's board of directors, that when successful leaves the company in the control of the maker of the offer (heretofore referred to as the "raider.") Insider trading is a violation of the Securities and Exchange Act wherein a person legitimately or illegitimately privy to nonpublic information about a company uses that information to his own profit by trading in that company's stock. Logically, the two have nothing to do with each other. Opponents of antitakeover legislation insist that the two have nothing to do with each other. But everyone else knows that the two are intimately connected. The connections might be worth exploring, both to provide clarity and guidance for this issue and to supply an entering wedge to the whole issue of the relationship among institutions, activities, and the characters of the actors.

We may presuppose familiarity with the facts of last year's insider trading scandal. Dennis Levine, a mergers specialist with Drexel Burnham Lambert, sold to arbitrageur Ivan Boesky nonpublic information about companies about to become the subject of hostile tender offers, information he would legitimately have by virtue of his position and would be under an obligation not to reveal. Boesky traded on the information, got rich, and paid off Levine in suitcases full of cash. They got caught and started to talk about everyone else who was cheating. By the time Levine and Boesky finished implicating enough of Wall Street to keep themselves out of jail, there were many other arrests and indictments, some of them surely just, others probably not. Just to set the scale, Boesky's illicit profits—that portion of his profits directly attributable to his purchase of the private information—came to at least \$203 million.[28] The motivations of the illicit dealings are obvious, and deducible from ordinary practice. Once a likely takeover target has been identified, and a raider becomes interested in making a run at it, it is in the investment bank's interest to make sure that the deal goes through, and, hence, in its interest to nudge arbitrageurs in the direction of the target's stock to make sure large amounts of it are in friendly hands by the time the announcement is made and defensive tactics begin. It is in the raider's interest to get the arbitrageurs involved at an early date, and clearly in the arbitrager's interest to find out what stock is about to be sent through the roof by an announcement of a raid. So networks of information are formed—broad conspiracies of the merger people at the banks, the arbitrageurs, the raiders, and the swarms of lawyers that attend the deals and the dealers. The predictable result is a pattern of runups in the stock of companies put in play by the raiders, slightly before as well as after the raid. This pattern, obvious to casual observers for some time, can be seen in classic form in Boesky's trading patterns[29] and has been confirmed by a Securities and Exchange Commission (SEC) study of 172 successful tender offers.[30] The SEC study wondered out loud whether "illegal insider trading behavior could affect" the results, but reached no conclusions; *The Wall Street Journal* editorial on the report insisted that such runups were the result not of ill-gotten information, but just good clean rumors and "the ferreting out of valuable information as a sign of the efficient market."[31] Valuable information is information about raids: as I write this, the stock in Southland Corporation has just soared almost 15 percent of its value in very active trading, and "rumors have fanned investors' hopes by linking the Dallas-based company to such well-known corporate raiders as Samuel Belzberg, the Canadian investor, and the Dart Group Corporation."[32] Trading on inside information is very, very profitable, largely because it is grossly unfair, which is also why it is against the law.

As soon as the original insiders, including Boesky, were caught, speculation began. Why had they got themselves involved in lawbreaking? They were incredibly rich already and had easy access to everything that money can buy. In keeping with America's innate respect for the rich, they were also social lions, in positions of responsibility, trustees and directors of prestigious institutions. Why would they risk all that? What had happened?

An answer, probably the correct one, was worked out slowly by a series of analysts. In short, the greed just got out of hand. As is usual in such things, the symptoms showed up first in the youngest. A 1984 poll of over 180,000 college freshmen, taken by the Higher Education Research Institute at UCLA, showed that class to be more interested in making money than any class in the nineteen-year history of that survey.[33] In spring 1985, a feature article on student attitudes was appropriately titled "Students Hungry for the Good Life, Pocketful of Cash," and quoted one of the students interviewed: "Without a question, be as ruthless as you have to be, within a certain guideline of the law. . . . Stepping on people is human nature. I'm just going to step on someone to make it better for me. If there's a choice between me and him, it's going to be me. Why should I feel guilty? The opportunity is there; I would be a fool not to capitalize on it."[34] A year later, Dennis Levine and five other young men, all in their early to mid-thirties, were implicated in insider trading deals, and senior executives in the securities industry were wondering aloud "if the problem was associated with the 'yuppies' of Wall Street, whom they describe as overpaid and overly aggressive."[35] A few months later, Ivan Boesky was exposed, and the "youth" explanation went down the drain. Children, as we should know by now, will do exactly what they are told, exactly what their elders apparently approve. Greed is approved and rampant—"a greed of sheer, unmitigated purity, and a complete absense of any shame or any sense of propriety, ethics or guilt to keep the desire to acquire in check."[36] The greed has been praised,[37] condemned,[38] and psychoanalyzed,[39] but no one can fail to observe it.

Wall Street's next reaction was to condemn Boesky, Martin Siegel, and the others, for *their* greed, protesting that a few bad apples should not bring discredit on the whole profession. Such protests did not survive any comment; it is impossible to look at the takeover scene for more than a minute at a time without the greed of the inside traders blending into everyone else's. There is no way to condemn the insider trading without condemning the unproductive "caricature of capitalism" that the merger mania had produced, and the commentators from the popular press tended to do just that.[40] (The other way, of course, is to decide that since takeovers are beneficial to the economy, the laws against insider trading should be abolished, and the business press tends to that route).[41] Ultimately, the answer, as we should have known, was that the institutions had changed, permitting practices that would have been stopped by previous administrations, so the people who make money by their wits started pushing new kinds of deals for unheard of amounts of money, always looking to see if they would be stopped. When they were not, new companies sprang up to take advantage of the new possibilities, and old ones quickly formed new departments so they would not be left behind, and the fees went up again. With all the new people, and new kinds of enterprise in the field, there were no traditions in which to educate the youngsters, no boundaries to point out, no way of warning them, and, given the pace, no time to decide, even had there been a way of deciding, where those limits shall be. New practices, especially practices well outside the limits of the old ones, breed and reward new kinds of people; a new mentality takes over, old charts and compasses are discarded as new directions are adopted, and no one wakes up from the dream of limitlessness until the whole ship is on the rocks.[42] Charts that have hung in financial offices since the crash of 1929 still indicate the position of those rocks, but few of the newer offices hang those charts.[43]

Can Wall Street handle the problem alone? Probably not. Greed for money, as Plato pointed out in the *Republic*, cannot conceive its own limit, and Wall Street is even in theory incapable of adopting limits in the search for quick profits. So the businesspeople who write on these matters announce, regret, but finally accept, the greed that races like cancer through their enterprise, now terrified by it, now defending it desperately against those Washington ogres who seek to carve it out, perversely hugging it like some beloved disease.[44]

Where was the heart of the sin? It was in the evil dream that the capitalist society must let us make money, lots of money, without producing any wealth. The purpose of business is not to make a profit. The purpose of business is to convert resources into goods and services, within limits set down by the society, and it was simply a good eighteenth-century bet that the best way to get that job accomplished was to turn people loose to seek their own interests. The freedom of the individual was conditional upon conformity to a larger moral structure, as Smith explicitly urged; the freedom of the market was conditional upon that linkage holding true. It is true no longer, and the destruction of our industries, our financial soundness, and our children's souls seems to be the immediate result of our irresponsible refusal to take back the reins of the enterprise and bring it under rational control.

REGULATION, THE INSTITUTION, AND THE MORAL LIFE

"Ethics is a moral compass," argues Rohatyn. "It must be embedded early, at home, in grade school, in church. It is highly personal. I doubt it can be taught in college."[45] He is only partly right. There is a moral sense, a disposition to do the right thing and avoid the wrong, that is acquired early in childhood, if ever. But the great teacher of what is right and what is wrong is society itself, through its laws and institutions. There are facts of human nature which, by now, we ought to know better than we do. One is that human virtue is not a private matter, or privately created and maintained; it is the product of human institutions, maintained to that end and purpose, and human beings in turn are responsible for the creation and preservation of those institutions.[46] It is not true that you cannot legislate morality. Legislating it, one way or the other, is the only way you will ever get it. The institutional guardians who blandly claim that morality is not for the institution to set, do in fact set a morality—a moral climate of relativism, opportunism, and license to step on people, as our student so candidly put the matter. If we intend to do better, we are going to have to undertake as a people "to cultivate the best persons and the best in persons," as George Will said in his excellent and (I gather) unpopular book, *Statecraft as Soulcraft*.[47] Wall Street's greed is not inevitable, any more than the economic terrorism and criminality that flow from it. We are responsible for creating the institutions that, by legitimating their actions, create the people we sanctimoniously deplore, and responsible for doing something about them. There is no wisdom in accepting the dissolution of productive enterprise in the name of free-market myths, no virtue in steeling ourselves against the suffering of our citizens in the name of a doctrine no longer applicable, and no excuse for pretending that the evils that inhere in our institutions are beyond our control.

NOTES

1. Some of the flavor of these developments is caught (and some of the confusions caused by them exemplified) in Bruce Nussbaum and Judith Dobrzynski, "The Battle for Corporate Control," *Business Week*, May 18, 1987, pp. 102–9.

2. As A. A. Sommer, a Washington securities lawyer and former SEC commissioner, summed it up, it is absurd to argue that "such complex entities are simply commodities to be bought and sold like apples." Quoted in *The Wall Street Journal*, December 16, 1986, p. 37.

3. William Niskanen, Chairman of the Cato Institute, quoted in *Business Week*, November 24, 1986, p. 87.

4. See *The New York Times* editorial on the subject, November 24, 1986.

5. T. Boone Pickens, "How Big Business Stacks the Deck," *The New York Times*, Sunday, March 1, 1987.

6. Michael Jensen, "Takeovers: Folklore and Science," *Harvard Business Review* (November–December 1984): 109–21, quotation on p. 112.

7. James C. Miller, "Let's Reduce Regulations on Takeovers," op-ed in *The New York Times*, July 1, 1985. That sort of comment was enormously effective, given the ease of mounting an attack on any company at all, even the largest, in silencing attacks on the raiders. Any executive who spoke up was likely to find his company in play, probably permanently disabled from productive activity, within the week. The insider trading scandal has furnished these companies with some defense against the raiders, and

a counterattack seems to have begun. Bruce Ingersoll, "Executives Urge Curbs of Abuses in Takeover Bids," *The Wall Street Journal*, March 5, 1987, p. 62.

8. *The New York Times*, November 25, 1986, op-ed.

9. Beryl Sprinkel, quoted in *The Wall Street Journal*, June 24, 1987, p. 12.

10. See Isadore Barmash, "Dayton Hudson: Appealing Target," *The New York Times*, June 26, 1987, p. D1.

11. See, for example, Kenneth E. Goodpaster, "On Being Morally Considerable," *The Journal of Philosophy*, 75, no. 6 (1978): 308–25; Tom Regan, "The Case for Animal Rights," *In Defense of Animals*, ed. Peter Singer (Oxford: Basil Blackwell, Inc., 1985); Christopher Stone, *Should Trees Have Standing?—Toward Legal Rights for Natural Objects* (Los Altos, Calif.: William Kaufmann, Inc., 1974).

12. See, for an explicit statement of this position, Michael C. Jensen and William H. Meckling, "Theory of the Firm: Managerial Behavior, Agency Costs and Ownership Structure," *Journal of Financial Economics* 3(1976): 305–60, quotation on pp. 310–11.

13. Irwin Friend, "Resisting the Call for More Regulation," *The New York Times*, November 30, 1986, Business section, p. 2.

14. In the takeover of Revlon by Pantry Pride in the fall of 1985, the investment bankers' share alone came to over $100 million, legal fees to over $10 million, and the negotiated golden parachutes to $40 million. Added up, the costs of the takeover—not one penny of which went to shareholders—came close to 9 percent of the $1.83 billion deal. Daniel Hertzberg, "Advice in Revlon Brawl Wasn't Cheap," *The Wall Street Journal*, November 8, 1985, p. 6.

15. Myron Magnet, "Help! My Company Has Just Been Taken Over," *Fortune*, July 9, 1984, pp. 44–51; Joel Lang, "Aftermath of a Merger," *Northeast Magazine*, April 21, 1985, pp. 10–17.

16. See Stephen Prokesch, " 'People Trauma' in Mergers," *The New York Times*, November 19, 1985; "Do Mergers Really Work?" *Business Week*, June 3, 1985, pp. 88 ff.

17. Leslie Wayne, "Costs of Escaping a Takeover," *The New York Times*, January 20, 1986, p. D1.

18. Jack Willoughby, "What a Raider Hath Wrought," *Forbes*, March 23, 1987, p. 56 ff.

19. Ibid.

20. John Norell, president of a Phillips research subsidiary, wrote in a letter to the U.S. House Energy and Commerce Committee, "There is something fundamentally wrong in America that a $16 billion company who is financially strong and interested in long-range developments for itself, the country, and humanity on one day can then on the next day, after a run on it by Mr. T. Boone Pickens, be reduced to a debt-ridden, short term, and cost-cutting entity." John Norell, cited in Paul Hirsch, in *Pack Your Own Parachute* (Reading, Mass.: Addison Wesley, 1987), prologue.

21. "Especially if that downturn is accompanied," warns investment banker Felix Rohatyn, "by rising interest rates as a result of the flight of foreign capital from the U.S. Of the several financial time bombs ticking in our closet, this is potentially one of the largest and most dangerous." Felix G. Rohatyn, "The Blight on Wall Street," *The New York Review of Books*, January 17, 1987, pp. 3 ff. See also, for earlier warning, "Merger Tango," especially the interview with Felix Rohatyn, in *Time*, December 23, 1985; Leonard Silk, "The Peril Behind the Takeover Boom," *The New York Times*, December 29, 1985.

22. Andrew C. Sigler, "Looking Beyond the 'Aw-Shucks' Act"—the context was a debate between Sigler and T. Boone Pickens—*The New York Times*, March 1, 1987.

23. Rohatyn, "The Blight on Wall Street," 3ff.

24. Randall Smith and Linda Sandler, "Raiders' Activities Revive Memories of 1920s Pools," *The Wall Street Journal*, November 10, 1986, p. 47.

25. L. J. Davis, "The Next Panic: Fear and Trembling on Wall Street," *Harper's Magazine*, May 1987, pp. 35–45.

26. See Joseph G. Fogg, III, "Takeovers: Last Chance for Self-Restraint," *Harvard Business Review* (November-December 1985): 30 ff.

27. See Michael Jensen, "How to Detect a Prime Takeover Target," *The New York Times*, March 9, 1986, especially where he suggests that driving the company close to bankruptcy (through huge immediate payouts to stockholders) provides management with a nice crisis to "overcome resistance to retrenchment. . . . The crisis makes cutbacks, reassignments and layoffs more acceptable to employees" and provides good ways for the company to renege on other contractual obligations as well.

28. *The Wall Street Journal*, November 24, 1986, p. 2.

29. Fascinating graphs showing those patterns are to be found in *The New York Times*, November 23, 1986, Business section, p. 8.

30. *The New York Times*, March 11, 1987, p. D4.

31. *The Wall Street Journal*, March 19, 1987, p. 34.

32. *The New York Times*, June 17, 1987, p. D1. And as I revise this, Southland has been purchased (July 6, 1987). It could be argued that scholarly conferences on fast-breaking topics like this one are rather absurd.

33. Cited in "Students Hungry for the Good Life, Pocketful of Cash," *The Hartford Courant*, April 29, 1985, p. A10.

34. Ibid., A1.

35. James Sterngold, "On Wall Street, a Greedy New Breed," *The New York Times*, July 27, 1986, op-ed.

36. "Greed," unsigned editorial, *M*, October 1986, pp. 105–9.

37. By, among others, William Safire, "Ode to Greed," *The New York Times*, January 5, 1986, op-ed.

38. By, among others, Flora Lewis, "The Sanctity of Greed," *The New York Times*, April 20, 1987, op-ed.

39. By, among others, Daniel Goleman, "Explaining the Greed," *The New York Times*, February 22, 1987, p. D3.

40. For example, Richard Cohen, "Off-the-Wall-St. Reasoning About Greed," *New York Daily News*, February 23, 1987; and Richard Reeves, "Whither Ethics?" *Bridgeport Post*, February 20, 1987.

41. Henry G. Manne, "The Real Boesky-Case Issue," *The New York Times*, November 25, 1986; editorials in *The Wall Street Journal*, March 24, 1987, May 28, 1987, and passim.

42. One of the clearest expositions of this process on Wall Street is one of the earliest, Karen Arenson's, "How Wall Street Bred an Ivan Boesky," *The New York Times*, November 23, 1986.

43. For the extent of the parallels in the courses, 1920s and the present, see L. J. Davis, "The Next Panic." Michael Thomas, investment banker turned novelist, contends that the crash of 1929 is simply too far in the past to be effective as a deterrent. "You had a lot of people around on Wall Street when I went there in '61 who said, 'Never

again.' There was an establishment of older men who believed that experience counted for something, and whose experience had been altogether unhappy in a crash and depression that required a world war to solve, a solution that is probably not available today, if we get into trouble here. Those people are all dead now, and that kind of restraining membrane of memory just isn't here anymore.'' Michael Thomas, quoted in Duncan Christy, ''Michal Thomas on Wretched Excess,'' *M*, October 1986, pp. 110–11.

44. In an article entitled ''Regulation Club Won't Curb Wall Street Excesses,'' Michael Kinsley puzzles over the factors that may have led to Boesky's crimes, suggesting as a final candidate ''Reagan-era decadence and greed: Simple answer: Yes, there's too much of it about, although this also does not lend itself to a regulatory solution. Greed is inherent in human nature and essential to capitalism, of course. But the fever of selfishness and value-free wealth-worship that has swept the nation in the past few years is very real and not healthy.'' Read in order, the points in that paragraph are that greed (1) is very much present; (2) is bad; (3) should not be opposed by law; (4) is inevitable in any case; (5) is good; and (6) is bad. One gets the feeling that the author would like to see small, measured amounts of greed, just enough to keep the economy humming, never growing or shrinking, moderate greed at work in ethical people. But such self-limitation is not in the nature of the substance. Michael Kinsley, ''Regulation Club Won't Curb Wall Street Excesses,'' *The Wall Street Journal*, November 20, 1986, p. 35.

45. Felix G. Rohatyn, ''Ethics in America's Money Culture,'' *The New York Times*, June 3, 1987, op-ed.

46. Aristotle, *Politics*, Book I; *Nicomachean Ethics*, Book II.

47. George F. Will, *Statecraft as Soulcraft: What Government Does* (New York: Simon and Schuster, 1983).

Moral Issues in Corporate Takeovers

PAUL STEIDLMEIER

Takeovers are not new. In fact, they are a corollary of any definition of free enterprise. What is happening today, however, is unique in several respects. Takeovers seem to be the latest form of robbery, marked by insider trading and billions of dollars in golden parachutes and greenmail payoffs. While stockholders and the general public stand helplessly by, the big movers are fighting over the spoils. Rarely have the top echelons of corporate management and finance been so openly divided and willing to shed each other's blood. The rift in the ranks of the corporate elite has afforded the general public an unprecedented view of the inner workings of contemporary capitalism. The dramatic action is complex and is played out on two levels at once. The immediate action is about entrepreneurs who spin complex strategies of takeovers, and managers who marshall intricate maneuvers to outflank them. On another level, volatile and revolutionary changes are taking place in international capitalism. The result is that many of the leading roles and fundamental ground rules of modern business are being challenged.

In what follows I (1) clarify what is going on in a takeover; (2) discuss the economic and moral reasons proponents put forward; (3) analyze the responses of managers; and (4) evaluate the main components of a morally responsible policy.

WHAT HAPPENS IN A TAKEOVER

Takeovers are clouded by semantic confusion. Popular usage suggests that ownership of a company is being taken over right under the eyes of helpless and innocent shareholders by first cousins of the robber barons. That is imprecise. The most controversial issue has been management. Critics suggest that neither the target management nor the acquiring management safeguard the best interests of shareholders. A takeover is accomplished when an investment group gains enough shares of a stock to ensure that it can pick the management and set policy. This is typically done by buying up shares of the target company at a premium. Such a transaction is financed by a number of means, including junk bonds. A takeover is described as hostile when the current management wants to prevent it from happening. Contrarily, it is friendly when management is in favor of it.

By its nature a hostile takeover implies change and restructuring. Such a prospect makes present management, local communities, and the labor force apprehensive to say the least. On the other hand, market purists and the takeover investment groups argue for the changes in terms of improved economic performance. Stockholders are often split, depending upon their investment objectives and perception of how proposed restructuring will affect them.

ECONOMIC AND MORAL REASONS FOR TAKEOVERS

If one scans an information service such as *Predicasts* or a journal such as *Mergers and Acquisitions*, it is abundantly clear that mergers, acquisitions, and divestitures are a constant feature of the market system. Recent U.S. data on takeovers are summarized in table 4.1.[1]

In 1986 the number of tender offers stood at 197, up from 97 in 1982. Their value was $65.1 billion, a 17 percent decrease from 1985, but well above the 1982 figure of $25.8 billion. On the whole, 76.6 percent of takeovers that were initiated were successful. The failure rate for uncontested bids averaged 2.45 percent from 1978 to 1986. The failure rate for contested bids, however, stood at 48.8 percent; from 1983 to 1985 the average failure rate for contested bids was 68.9 percent.[2] The number of hostile offers declined from a high of 42 percent in 1982 to 26 percent in 1986. On an average, control of the company (rather than a mere stake) was the objective in 73 percent of tender offers. And 89.2 percent of offers were cash.

Takeovers are rationalized by proponents in terms of increasing economic efficiency. The focus is on management errors in strategic planning. In order to understand this rationale, it is important to review the main characteristics of corporate strategic planning in the preceding decades. The 1960s and 1970s marked a time of tremendous corporate structural change. Corporations grew through diversification and became conglomerates. In a sense it was also a "takeover period"; but, in general, large established companies were acquiring the smaller speciality companies. Many companies expanded into unrelated businesses. The underlying logic for such conglomerate diversification was based on portfolio analysis. The corporation was interested in maintaining steady earnings. Diversification provided it with a hedge against losses when one sector or industry had a downturn. But the reverse was also true. Higher profit levels were sometimes foregone in favor of maintaining a steady and safe level of growth

Table 4.1
Tender Offers: 1982–1986

	1982	1983	1984	1985	1986
Number of Offers	97	74	147	142	197
Number of Targets	76	60	125	116	181
Targets' $ Value	$25.8	$17.3	$58.6	$78.3	$65.1
% Completed Offers	73	78	80	76	76
% Hostile Offers	42	35	24	30	26
% of Offers Where Control Was at Stake	73	70	68	72	82
STATUS					
Completed	73%	78%	80%	76%	64%
Not Completed	27	22	20	24	20
Open	0	0	0	0	16
TARGET RESPONSE					
Friendly	43%	57%	63%	62%	69%
Hostile	42	35	24	30	26
Neutral	15	8	13	8	5
FORM OF OFFER					
Any-or-all	42%	64%	74%	73%	85%
Partial	37	16	17	23	12
Two-tier	21	20	9	4	3
CONTROL SOUGHT					
Stakehold	19%	10%	6%	9%	2%
Control	73	70	68	72	82
Lock-up	4	8	14	13	11
Mop-up	4	12	12	6	5
CASH/EXCHANGE					
Cash	88%	91%	91%	85%	91%
Exchange/Mixed	12	9	9	15	9
MARKET					
NYSE	37%	32%	33%	41%	38%
AMEX	16	8	12	8	21
OTC	43	50	49	40	33
Other	4	10	6	11	8

Source: Securities And Exchange Commission, *Monthly Statistics Review* 64, no. 2 (1987):6–9.

and income. To oversimplify, if a conglomerate had ten divisions, it was most likely at any given time that some would do well while others lagged behind or even incurred a loss. As long as a majority did well, steady profits could be assured. Some might even prove to be cash cows. Only rarely would all do well or all fail at the same time.

The management of such conglomerates posed some very difficult problems. In a (reported but yet unpublished) study of large diversified U.S. corporations from 1950 to the present, Harvard Business School Professor Michael Porter has concluded that the corporate strategy of many companies that diversified on the basis of a portfolio model has failed economic tests of performance.[3] It proved very difficult for management to remain aware of what was happening in all sectors of the corporation. It was far more difficult to be a leader or innovator in any sector. Not all diversification has failed, however. Those combinations based upon synergies of shared activities or skill transfer have had some success. It is the quasi-absolute allegiance to the portfolio rationale, which aimed to push cash from one business to another, that has proven in general to be weak. Adequate attention has not been paid to establishing and maintaining competitive advantage in an industry. Strange to say, product focus was lost, and corporate strategy became unmoored from primary business considerations.

Contemporary takeover entrepreneurs focus very much on what they call management's strategic mistakes in acquiring unrelated businesses which ended up as underperforming and/or undervalued. Takeover proponents claim that they can improve overall performance by getting rid of such assets and concentrating the business in a few well-chosen lines that promise high efficiency and return. Porter's study is important, for it provides an independent economic confirmation that corporate restructuring may be called for in today's milieu.

A second charge leveled by takeover proponents focuses on organizational inefficiency. They claim that corporate staffs are becoming bloated and inefficient bureaucracies. The term "corpocracy" has been coined to describe the bureaucratization of private enterprise. In their study of corpocracy Mark Green and John Berry estimate that corporate organizational inefficiency costs $862 billion a year, six times the amount of government waste estimated by the Grace Commission.[4] However tendentious such estimates may be, the traits of corpocracy are more telling: the prevalence of insensitiveness to employees, the encouragement of office politics over productivity, the fostering of secrecy over communication, the diffusion of responsibility through endless meetings, the production of paperwork paralysis, the neglect of potential markets, the encouragement of short-term thinking, the isolation of management from workers, the discouragement of innovation, and the avoidance of employees who rock the boat. If any of this is accurate, it is clear that capitalism has moved a long way from the ideals of Adam Smith. In such a situation overhead costs soar while innovativeness and the ability to move quickly suffer. It is not surprising, then, that proponents of takeovers propose large-scale reorganization with reductions in management and staff along with selling unproductive assets.

A third target of criticism upon which takeover advocates focus is the large amounts of cash that are devoted to senior management compensation and perquisites. This has opened managers to the charge that they are primarily out for themselves at the shareholders' expense. Raiders such as T. Boone Pickens and Carl Icahn have remarked many times that top management no longer thinks like shareholders.[5] Their interests and the shareholders' interests no longer coincide.

A fourth issue upon which takeover proponents focus is international competitive advantage. They see American industry heading down hill. Undersecretary of the Treasury Richard Darman, as well as former Commerce Secretary Malcolm Baldridge, joined the criticism of much of contemporary management for failing to apply and follow through on technology that they invented.[6] The nature of competitive advantage has changed dramatically in past years due to deregulation of many domestic industries, as well as sharply increased foreign competition. This increased competition is due to a number of factors: new cost-cutting technologies, lower labor costs, and intensity of sales efforts. Foreign competitors are not free of allegations of dumping.[7] In most industries, however, it would be difficult to maintain that their competitive advantage was due solely to dumping.

To restore the competitive edge of U.S. industry, takeover proponents primarily propose restructuring of production operations. Most often this means a leaner work force. They drive a hard economic logic of cost controls and input/output ratios. In addition, they call for tighter financial management and more efficacious sales efforts.

A fifth reason for takeovers is to expand capacity for production, distribution, and sales. At present it is frequently cheaper to buy than to build. This seems to be the logic operative in Chrysler's $3.5 billion takeover of American Motors, as well as in Emery Air Freight's bid for Purolator.[8] The takeover in this context is based upon synergies between related businesses and has good historical prospects for success.

A final reason advanced for takeovers is that comparatively low interest rates make takeovers, as well as leveraged buyouts by management, more attractive than ever. When low interest expense is coupled with a set of undervalued assets, the real costs for acquirers are greatly diminished. Takeover groups are criticized for junk-bond financing. Junk bonds are highly risky in comparison with other bond offerings. They are not for novice investors. They remain, however, a legitimate financial tool. More important, junk bonds are not the driving force behind takeovers.[9] In 1985 junk bonds financed $6.23 billion of all mergers and acquisitions, less than 5 percent of the $140 billion that figured in all mergers and acquisitions, and less than 10 percent of the $78 billion represented by takeover tender offers. All in all, 38.2 percent of junk bonds in 1985 went for mergers and acquisitions. Even though this trend seems to be increasing somewhat, the mode of financing is not the key issue.

The economic reasons for takeovers have a corollary in moral reasoning. Proponents of takeovers propose three dominant values: individual liberty, fiduciary duties to shareholders, and social utility. It is important to distinguish the morality of actions from the morality of intentions.

Viewing takeovers as a type of action, proponents argue that they can have good consequences for society. The fundamental rationale reiterates the basic free-market premise that individual liberty in economic decision making both protects the rights of the individual to seek his or her self-interest, and is in the long-term interest of society. With respect to contemporary takeover activity, proponents argue that the long-term results are in the best interests of society, for the U.S. economy will be healthier. Shareholders are also said to be better served by such a free market. During a takeover they may divest at a premium. If they hold their stocks, they will benefit in the long run by the improved economic performance of the company. Those taking over the company are themselves shareholders; their interests coincide with the other shareholders. In the end it is argued that a number of operating, financial, and tax benefits for both individuals and society may follow from a corporate takeover.

At the same time there is no doubt that takeovers can be like corporate earthquakes that frequently leave formerly standing companies as a pile of rubble. Only very strong institutions withstand the initial tremor and subsequent read-justments. A lot of attention has been focused on the intention of takeover groups. Do they really mean to increase the economic performance of the assets or are they opportunistically making a run at handsome greenmail payoffs? Major criticism comes when people suspect that those who take the company over do not intend to preserve and further it. Rather, they have in mind either to be paid greenmail or to strip the company of its valuable (undervalued) assets, pay off the bonds, pocket the difference, and get out. Those who believe in the likelihood of such a scenario not surprisingly see the takeover people as the first cousins of the robber barons.

It is only natural that an antitakeover coalition has emerged. Moral objections are based both on the (harmful) consequences of takeover actions as well as on the greedy and selfish motivation on those launching a takeover attempt. Opposition is composed of management, labor, and local communities. They are the ones in line to bear the costs of restructuring.

MANAGEMENT STRATEGIES TO FOIL TAKEOVERS

Management has developed a number of tools to discourage takeovers. In doing so they have spawned a new business vocabulary: poison pills, greenmail, white knights, and golden—as well as tin—parachutes. These tools have one thing in common: to make a takeover so costly that no one would attempt it. It is important to examine what management is doing and whose interest it serves. The same moral scrutiny regarding the intentions of management, as well as the consequences of its actions, applies.

Poison pills have been used increasingly by management to fend off aggressive takeovers. The definition of a poison pill is by no means uniform. In general, it involves the issuance of a pro rata dividend to common stockholders. This dividend comprises either stock or the rights to acquire stock of (1) the issuer ("flip-in" provisions); or (2) the acquiring persons ("flip-over" provisions) involved in a business combination with the issuer. In addition, poison pills may involve issuing stock with super voting rights, "back-end provisions" (which involve the right of shareholders to tender stock to the issuer for a specified securities package), and convertible preferred stock provisions.[10] The most important provision is that acquiring persons may be excluded from the exercise of such rights, even though they are stockholders. Poison pill rights cannot be exercised by stockholders unless triggered by specified events such as a merger, the commencement of a tender offer, or the acquisition of a specific percentage of the issuer's stock. Unless triggered, they are redeemable by the issuer at a nominal price. The intent of such pills is clear: management hopes to set up insurmountable barriers to hostile outside bidders who would purchase a company's shares. Stockholders are usually not consulted. In imposing prohibitive costs on outside bidders, poison pills effectively give management exclusive authority to decide whether an acquisition can proceed.

Defenders of poison pills say that they buy time. Without them the object of a takeover has only twenty business days following the beginning of a hostile tender offer in which to respond. Management argues that the additional time to negotiate is beneficial to shareholders in the long run. The Supreme Court of the state of Delaware upheld the legality of the pill in a 1985 decision, *Moran vs. Household International.*[11] In the past few years over 300 major American corporations have adopted the pill; not all have escaped takeover.

Opponents of the pill include both corporate raiders and large institutional investors, who argue that the pill actually works against shareholders. Rarely are they allowed to purchase more shares at a discount. Furthermore, the lethal effects of the pill prevent the stock from rising as it normally would in the course of a takeover and, thus, deprive shareholders of profits they could make by playing the market.

Frequently, in defending itself from a hostile bidder, management will turn to a "white knight."[12] A white knight is a friendly investor who will put away a large block of stock (at a discount price), but who will not pose a takeover threat. In its efforts to avoid being taken over by The Limited, Carter Hawley Hale Stores, Inc., turned to General Cinema, which invested $300 million in its stock in 1984. Eventually, in the face of a persistent bid by The Limited, Carter Hawley Hale had to come to an agreement with General Cinema. A white knight strategy does not necessarily save a company from restructuring, but it keeps it out of hostile hands, at least initially. (White knights do not always prove to be benevolent.)

Another device that management uses are golden parachutes (for managers) and tin parachutes (for labor).[13] A parachute affords the relevant party a hefty package of benefits in case of dismissal. Both labor and management find these parachutes very attractive, for they protect their own interests. Prospective raiders find them unattractive, for they impose increased costs. At the bottom line, it is the stockholder who pays the costs.

By far the most controversial strategy employed by management is the payment of greenmail. When Walt Disney productions bought back Saul Steinberg's shares in 1984, it effectively paid him a $60 million premium not to take over the company. Similarly, Gencorp offered $130 per share for 54 percent of its stock against an investor group offering $100; the investor group could net nearly $100 million.[14] In a 1964 ruling the Supreme Court of Delaware upheld the practice of buying back shares at a premium as long as the directors could show a "legitimate business reason" for doing so.[15] There is a great deal of controversy over what constitutes legitimate business reasons. Increasingly shareholders are demanding that they get a chance to vote on the matter.

In addition to these measures, a number of companies have turned to installing multiple-vote stock.[16] Such differential voting is sometimes tied to the length of time a stock is held. Usually it is a straightforward classification of types of common stock according to voting power. In a related move, some management groups are putting together their own takeovers by taking the company private in a leveraged buyout.[17] In either case management severely restricts those to whom it is accountable.

Finally a number of management groups are beginning to take a proactive stance to takeovers. They are scrutinizing their company profiles for items a raider would find attractive—large cash surplusses, undervalued assets to strip, overfunded pension funds, bloated staff—and taking the measures to correct them before anyone ever initiates a takeover offer.

Management claims to be guided by values of individual self-interest, distributive justice for those directly involved in the company (shareholders, workers, local communities), and overall social utility. They assume that the consequences of a takeover will be negative for all but the acquiring persons. On this basis they justify extraordinary means of greenmail, poison pills, and parachutes. These costs must be borne in order to protect the immediate interests of local communities, labor, and management, as well as the long-term interests of shareholders. They portray takeover groups as being after only their own self-interest while neglecting other stakeholders. Many shareholder groups object to these sorts of policies. They assert that they have adverse effects upon shareholders. Furthermore, management appears to be out for its own interests rather than for those of the shareholders.

COMPONENTS OF A MORALLY RESPONSIBLE POLICY

There is no clear answer to the question of whether takeovers are right or wrong. In Western market theory, the moral rationale of the market presupposes a social contract model. The social contract is based upon the dignity of the individual, which is expressed in terms of inalienable rights of life, liberty, and the pursuit of happiness. All persons count for one just by virtue of being a person. Each is to enjoy freedom of self-determination, fair opportunity, and due legal process. In the economic sphere all persons may own property; furthermore, they may allocate their resources for the purposes they wish, and exchange their resources or products accordingly. Each is entitled to the fruit of his or her labor. The market is a locus of mutual respect as well as mutual self-interest. Free individuals rationally come together to seek their self-interest. As they accumulate resources, allocate them, and exchange goods and services, their interaction is protected by property rights and mediated by fair, competitive prices. Mutual rights and duties are specified by mutual consent. The integrity of the system is based upon individual liberty and reason, as well as a *fair* competitive milieu, truthfulness, promise keeping, and a respect for the rights of others. In the instance of takeovers, there is considerable doubt that competition is fair; both takeover groups and entrenched management seem to abuse the power that their control of resources or official positions accord them.

When takeovers are viewed within the social contract framework, two principal questions come to the fore: first, whether the rights of all parties to the contract are protected and the fulfillment of corresponding duties ensured, and second, whether the legitimate interests of third parties are protected. Third parties are those who are not directly involved in the business contract but are affected by it. The legitimacy of a particular business contract is normally subject to the conditions of other legitimate business contracts, as well as of the prevailing social contract. In this way, stakeholders in a particular business transaction such as a takeover may be defined. In a takeover, both shareholders and acquiring persons enjoy specific property rights. In addition, however, there are contractual fiduciary responsibilities of managers to shareholders, as well as the legitimate claims of labor and local communities to be considered. The difficulty is to balance all of these claims. I take up two points. First, imbalances in market adjustments and, second, corporate governance.

Imbalances in Market Adjustments

Those in favor of takeovers argue market logic, primarily in terms of efficiency, competition, and shareholder profits. Their argument is both macro and long-term. It is macro because their focus is upon the competitiveness of U.S. industry in an increasingly tough international environment. They argue that companies that are the object of takeovers are sick and mismanaged. In the long run they are headed down the slope to extinction unless drastic measures are taken. The raiders come in, perform surgery, and help bring the U.S. industry back to health. It is extremely important to note that the premise is not to bring this or that company back to health exactly as it was. There is a process of restructuring involved. New management may dismantle parts or all of a company while simultaneously building up others. Assets do not vanish, but they take different forms and are managed in new ways.

Restructuring is necessarily long-term. Transitions are rarely smooth or balanced. Takeover groups are similar to bomber pilots who drop their weapons upon villages and factories from 30,000 feet. They do not see the carnage or hear the screams. Opponents of takeovers are those who are on the ground. They focus upon those who bear the short-term effects of the long-term process. In cost-cutting, for example, thousands of workers may lose their jobs, and the economies of local communities may be plunged to the brink of disaster. Furthermore, those who bear the costs of restructuring are not the same groups of people as those who will receive the benefits. In macro analysis a plant closed in Michigan is balanced out in the aggregate by one opened in Tennessee. On the micro level, however, those who lose out in Michigan are not those who gain in Tennessee.

In a case such as Sir James Goldsmith's attempted takeover of Goodyear, for example, Goldsmith's track record at Crown Zellerbach led people to believe that restructuring would be harsh. Three issues came together: a socially responsible layoff policy, plant closing and relocation policies, and management prerogatives. In the end the local community/labor/management coalition prevailed, but the amount of greenmail paid was staggering, and it made Sir James much richer than before.[18]

The heart of the controversy over the consequences of takeovers pits macro and long-term analysis against micro and short-term analysis. Increasingly, management has been willing to pay greenmail in order to prevail, at least for the moment.

Greenmail generally entails incurring large amounts of debt, as well as selling assets and internal restructuring in order to prevail. Goodyear ended up doing many of the things Sir James threatened to do. The result is that the interests of the local community, labor, and management are pitted against the shareholder. Soaring debt, falling investment, and curtailed research do not augur well for profits. In the case of Goodyear, debt rose from $2.6 billion to $5.3 billion. Planned investment fell from $300 million to $270 million, and research from $1.6 billion to $1 billion. Over $2 billion in assets were to be sold off. Sir James Goldsmith walked away with a $93 million profit. Stockholders have a hard time seeing themselves as winners. Their only real choice is to stick with management or sell their stock. Management blames Goldsmith's greed for their plight and claims to have done the best they could for shareholders and local communities. Many shareholders object that they should at least have a say in such an important decision. They are demanding shareholder approval for greenmail, poison pills, and parachutes. Furthermore, they object to the fact that takeover groups are offered premium prices not available to ordinary shareholders.[19] They are prevented from cashing in on the premium price takeover groups receive for their shares. They can either stick with the restructured company or sell their stock at the current market price. This apparent disparity between stockholder interests and those of management, labor, and the local community have raised a larger issue—corporate governance.

Corporate Governance

The shareholder is a property owner who does not have full control over his or her property. The weakest link in corporate governance today is found in the board of directors. In theory the board of directors is charged with securing the best interests of shareholders and monitoring the performance of managers.[20] Over the years an incestuous relationship has developed between top management and the board. In 75 percent of large companies, the CEO is also head of the board.[21] In most cases top management appoints the majority of members. For the most part, boards of directors simply rubber stamp what management decides. For some years there have been calls to make the boards more independent by placing more outsiders on them. The issue raised is the moral rectitude of management's intentions.

Shareholders have very little effective say. Annual meetings have not offered a fruitful venue for shareholders to communicate with each other, much less organize among themselves. Shareholders are routinely ignored in deciding important issues such as poison pills or greenmail. In addition, a number of corporations are interested in issuing nonvoting classes of common stock. Such a move is objectionable, for it would further insulate management from market forces of efficiency and competition. The only real power shareholders have is to sell off their shares.

It can no longer be assumed that management seeks the best interests of shareholders. Nor can it be assumed that the board of directors protects shareholders. In my opinion it is time for shareholders to gain control of the board. Other stakeholders, such as local communities, labor, suppliers, and consumers, should also be represented. Some suggest that if they want a say, they should also become shareholders. Be that as it may, such a change in the board would make management's task more difficult. That is exactly what is needed. The prescription is simple: (1) restore a shareholder's perspective, and (2) take explicit account of the claims of the various stakeholders in the business enterprise. The moral value espoused here is the effective liberty of stakeholders rather than the present hegemony of management and the board. Such a provision of liberty would resolve the distributional bias against shareholders and other stakeholders in decision making.

There is a very clear issue involved that goes far beyond takeovers. Company directors, investment bankers, and corporate raiders frequently set their own interests above those of company stockholders and other stakeholders. In theory, the market is not to be a zero-sum game. Empirically, the market can be both a short-term and micro zero-sum game, while it is at the same time a long-term and macro arena of mutual benefit. In market theory, both such market imperfections as well as externalities create a justification for public policy. Such realities are occasioned by a variety of reasons. Among them are the instability of business cycles, time lags in adjustments, disparities between those who receive the benefits and those who pay the costs, and power and greed that distort the fairness of the marketplace. In the case of takeovers, public policy is called for. It must be directed both toward the raiders as well as toward the managers. Rules are needed, not to eliminate the possibility of takeovers, but to make the process as fair as possible.

First, new laws are called for. Both the U.S. Congress and a number of state legislatures have been very active in this regard. One issue that is especially emphasized is what may be called the ethics of information. On the raider side of the ledger, immediate disclosure of a raider's stock position (rather than the current ten-day lag) is called for. Disclosure is presently required at 5 percent. It is worth considering a lower threshold (1 percent, for example). More important, all secret collusion between acquiring partners and the parking of shares must be curtailed. The possibility of ten secret partners each buying 4 percent and then acting in concert to mount a takeover must be prevented. Mandatory immediate disclosure at 1 percent level would be helpful. In addition, people are proposing changing margin requirements for trading, linking voting to a requirement that a stock be held for a minimum amount of time, altering the taxation of junk bonds, and installing debt ceilings. Such proposals are all debatable. For the market to be fair, the central issue is to change the rules regarding information.

The Securities and Exchange Commission (SEC) is charged, among other things, with ensuring the quality of market information. To do so, it needs additional staff and increased data processing potential.[22] In particular the SEC's EDGAR system (electronic data gathering, analysis, and retrieval) is essential for timely market surveillance and information. In addition, the monitoring of audit integrity and improvement of cooperative agreements with other countries are both essential measures.

Finally, the volatility of the world economy makes corporate restructuring increasingly likely. Labor and local communities must themselves begin to adopt proactive stances. How to do this is not clear in the economy in general, let alone in the case of takeovers. The point here is to bridge the gap between micro and macro perspectives. For their part, local communities would be healthier if they moved to diversify their economic base so as to reduce their risk in the face of market readjustments. Part of the responsibility of local government to society is precisely to build up a positive economic base by establishing a favorable business milieu. Labor, too, must begin to build into its policy the likelihood of job turnover rather than persisting in the quest for lifelong security. Job retraining and relocation seem to be a basic feature of modern business.

The takeover business is very complex. Responsible policy must necessarily focus upon the rectitude of individual behavior. At the same time steps must be taken to ensure the integrity of the fundamental rules of the game which guide the business system as a whole. Takeovers should not be eliminated, they should be made fair.

NOTES

1. Securities and Exchange Commission, *Monthly Statistics Review*, 64, no. 2 (1987): 6–9.

2. Donald V. Austin, and David W. Mandula, "Tender Offer Update: 1986," *Mergers and Acquisitions* (July/August 1986): 55–57.

3. Christopher Lorenz, "The Trouble with Takeovers," *Financial Times*, December 8, 1986, p. 14.

4. Mark Green and John Berry, "Takeovers—A Symptom of Corpocracy," *New York Times*, December 3, 1986, p. A31.

5. T. Boone Pickens, Jr., *Boone* (New York: Houghton Mifflin, 1987); idem, "How

Big Business Stacks the Deck,'' *New York Times*, March 1, 1987, p. F2; Steven Prokesch, ''America's Imperial Chief Executive,'' *New York Times*, October 12, 1986, pp. F1, F25.

6. ''Look Who's Bashing Corpocracy,'' *New York Times*, November 24, 1986, p. 18. Peter Kilborn, ''Treasury Official Assails 'Inefficient' Big Business,'' *New York Times*, November 8, 1986, pp. 1, 48.

7. Jerry K. Pearlman, ''Save the Lectures—Give Us Some Help,'' *New York Times*, December 14, 1986, p. F3.

8. Teri Agins, ''John Emery Looks for a Better Package,'' *Wall Street Journal*, April 2, 1987, p. 34; Leslie Wayne, ''Latest Corporate Takeovers Involve More Than Paper,'' *New York Times*, March 8, 1987, p. F1.

9. Michael S. Helfer and William D. Brighton, ''The Federal Reserve's Stand on Junk Bond Takeovers,'' *Mergers and Acquisitions* (July/August 1986): 48–54.

10. Suzanne S. Dawson, Robert J. Pence, and David S. Stone, ''Poison Pill Defensive Measure,'' *The Business Lawyer* 42, no. 2 (1987): 423–39.

11. Ibid., 423.

12. Isadore Barmash, ''Talking Deals—Carter's Ally Calls the Tune,'' *New York Times*, December 11, 1986, p. D2; Robert Williams, ''When You Can't Resist a Bear-Hug Look for a White Knight,'' *Journal of Accountancy* 162, no. 7 (1986): 86–93.

13. Alison Leigh Cowan, ''New Ploy: 'Tin Parachutes','' *New York Times*, March 19, 1987, p. D1, D8; David F. Larcher and Richard A. Lambert, ''Golden Parachutes, Executive Decision-Making and Shareholder Wealth,'' *Journal of Accounting and Economics* 7, no. 4 (1985): 179–204.

14. Robert J. Cole, ''1.6 Billion Buyback by Gencorp,'' *New York Times*, April 7, 1987, p. D1, D7.

15. Tamar Lewin, ''Business and the Law: Suits Aimed at Greenmail,'' *New York Times*, March 3, 1987, p. D2.

16. ''Failsafe Protection,'' *Mergers and Acquisitions* (November/December: 1986) 16–17.

17. Louis F. Lowenstein, ''No More Cozy Management Buyouts,'' *Harvard Business Review* 61, no. 1 (1986): 117–27.

18. Jonathan P. Hicks, ''Goodyear's Uneasy Aftermath,'' *New York Times*, December 5, 1986, p. D1, D2.

19. ''SEC's All-Holders Rule,'' *Mergers and Acquisitions* (November/December 1986): 15.

20. Louis F. Braiotta and A. A. Sommer, *The Essential Guide to Effective Corporate Board Committees* (Englewood Cliffs, N.J.: Prentice-Hall, 1987).

21. ''Corporate Boards,'' *The Economist*, December 20, 1986, p. 123–26; Idalene F. Kesner, Bart Victor, and Bruce T. Lamont, ''Board Composition and the Commission of Illegal Acts: An Investigation of Fortune 500 Companies,'' *Academy of Management Journal* 29, no. 4 (1986): 789–99; Idalene F. Kesner and Dan K. Dalton, ''Boards of Directors and the Checks and (Im)balances of Corporate Governance,'' *Business Horizons* 29, no. 10 (1986): 17–23; John D. Pawling, ''The Crisis of Corporate Boards—Accountability vs. Misplaced Loyalty,'' *Business Quarterly* 51, no. 6 (1986): 71–73.

22. Roger Oram, ''SEC Projects the Case for Defence,'' *Financial Times*, December 10, 1986, p. 6; Richard Wines, ''The Stock Watch System: Early Warning on Raiders,'' *Mergers And Acquisitions* (March/April 1987): 56–58.

II

ETHICAL ISSUES IN ORGANIZATIONAL TRANSFORMATIONS: CORPORATE, LABOR, AND GOVERNMENT VIEWS

— 5

Burial of the Golden Rule?

ROBERT E. MERCER

In preparing for the National Conference on Business Ethics, one of the toughest questions I encountered was: "Is this conference celebrating a resurgence of interest in ethics, or is it setting the headstone to mark the burial of the golden rule?" Today's business society is crowded with examples that chronicle the atrophy of ethical behavior. What we see around us reflects that the golden rule is being buried by an avalanche of greed, and the creation of real wealth is a forgotten goal. Is this what we are to expect of the "me" generation as it moves into leadership positions of what is becoming the "quick buck" society? It's easy to believe, today, that the golden rule is six feet under, because we are inundated with news that supports the theory of its passing. Each news story seems to be another signature on the death certificate. I get the impression that the media's new definition of *news* is, "All the sin, no matter how it fits." It's tough to advance a strong argument against such thinking since the reading and watching public seems drawn to these matters like moths to a flame. That flame of subversion, sex, and scandal is getting brighter, attracting more attention. I'm afraid it will become an obsession if we don't refocus and pay attention to some of the lesser lights that nevertheless are crucial to a high quality of life.

I strongly oppose burying the less sensational news matters having to do with the day-in, day-out pursuits of business large and small; people who exemplify the value of life's fundamentals; and fundamentals like family, a deity to worship, and allegiance to principle and country. I would even be so bold as to suggest that there are honest and principled people in our nation's capital who are busting their backsides for us. Individuals who are struggling against a tide of special interest rhetoric as they seek to make the right choices for their country and are struggling to represent the needs—if not always the perceived wants—of their constituents. Since martyrdom is no more popular today than it was in the day of Saint Paul or Joan of Arc, these honest and principled legislators need to hear from their constituents. These lawmakers need a word of encouragement from us—reassurance that their efforts are not in vain, reassurance of support and appreciation from the unseen majority.

What gets in the way of a revival—if not a resurrection—of the golden rule, is the litigious element in society, the lawsuit-happy folks who have our judicial system in snarls. That litigious element—primed and ready to pounce on the principles of honesty and fairness with the emotion and speed of a gunfighter—not only puts us on guard but diverts our behavior away from normal, human response. Never mind that this litigious element may be in the minority; we must remember that minority litigation can initiate sweeping changes.

If you need an example of minority influence launching broad changes in society, consider the skyjacking phenomenon. Skyjackers were a fraternity of incredibly small numbers. I doubt we had a dozen in this country. Yet today, *all* of us who travel by air are subjected to search-and-seizure rituals before boarding an airplane. Not so many years ago, everyone could board their airplane of choice with relaxed impunity. Today we pay a stiff price—and the cost of modern airport security is far-reaching—from the actual extra dollars built into the cost of our tickets, to the time delays and inconvenience we endure in quiet frustration. All this subdued agony, brought on by the action of a handful of people, is paralleled by yet another tableau showing how the lack of ethics by a few can encroach on the lives of the many.

Let us divert our attention to a similar scenario in the corporate world. To get into the mood, visualize a pack of sharks, swimming in relatively calm waters. Most of you have seen, *Jaws*, the movie, and you know a shark is defined as an emotionless *feeding* machine that just happens to live in a wet environment. Had you asked me, a year ago, what I thought of the prospect of fending off a shark attack, I'd have told you it sounds like about as much fun as hitting yourself in the head with a ball peen hammer. Then, I'd have changed the subject, because the idea didn't seem plausible. It turns out that we were shark bait after all, and about a year ago, Goodyear came face-to-face with a real hammerhead. Although this hammerhead carried all the markings of a shark, he was operating in the dry climate of Wall Street as well as the blue waters of the Atlantic, where he was hiding behind an obscure Cayman Islands Partnership. Our shark was a corporate raider.

It's interesting to note that *Fortune* magazine, in its current issue (September 28, 1987), rated all the sharks of the corporate takeover world. Our guy was given a top rating . . . a *four-fin* rating. Like a shark, he had no conscience and he traveled with a pack of razor-toothed friends hell-bent on ripping apart their prey in a feeding frenzy. And since that prey was—and still is—the corporations that form the economic base of this country, these sharks are chewing away at the free enterprise system. They've found a loophole in our net of laws and they're swimming through to grab corporate America by the backside. Our shark gathered a gang of co-conspirators into secret partnerships and offshore corporations, then launched an attack based on stealth and subterfuge.

I'll give you a single example of this subterfuge. I call it the nonoffer offer. It goes like this: Our raider writes a letter and reads it to me. It says he's going to issue a $49 tender offer for Goodyear stock. But he doesn't *mail* the letter; he just has his henchmen file it with the Securities and Exchange Commission (SEC), and then they tip off the news media. In the blink of an eye, our shareholders are reading about a $49 tender offer that never was *officially* offered. But the arbitrageurs pick up on it and suck up all the shares they can get from the institutional investors. You know the ones; their destinies are controlled by computers. Those computers see a dollar figure that triggers their "sell" signal, and suddenly your shares go from friendly hands to the mouths of the sharks. And you haven't had a chance to go to the institutions and say, "We're being raided? Don't sell your stock!" You haven't had the chance to say, "Wait up, guys . . . take a look at our program! You'll be better off with us than with those sharks." You don't have a chance to say that, because they've already sold out, and you haven't had time to put an offer on the street. By this time everyone is trying to get in on the feeding frenzy, and the price of your shares spikes up like a rocket launch. By the time you grab leather and put together a program to buy back those shares accumulated by your raider, along with a tender offer to your friendly shareholders, you find yourself deeper in debt than you ever imagined. Meanwhile, the shark swims away with enough of your backside to make sitting a painful experience. We're hoping to be able to sit comfortably again in a little over two years. We figure it will take that long to retire the indebtedness that cost Goodyear some 20,000 of its people, through layoffs, early-outs, plant closings, and the sale of assets.

Now that the smoke has cleared, we find Goodyear is also missing three of its plants, a profitable aerospace subsidiary, a five-star resort, a successful truck and auto wheel manufacturing company, extensive property holdings in Arizona, and much of our energy operations (which included a major independent oil company).

All this is a graphic demonstration of how a motive of greed fosters tunnel vision when it comes to a question of, "Shall I, or shall I not, do unto others as I would have them do unto me?" The only things that raiders can see at the end of their tunnel vision are the legal loopholes through which the real wealth of a national economy can be siphoned for their personal use. The raiding sharks claim that they are the greatest thing that ever happened to the stockholder and the economy. Those claims remind me of the recent Isuzu ads. As soon as you read the preposterous claims in big type, you start looking for the small line that says, "This man is lying." And then you chuckle, because you know it's all a joke. In the case of corporate raiders, there's no tag line in small type. The reality behind the raiders' screen of blue smoke is a rape of America's industrial base and a subversion of its ability to be world competitive. Ask yourself, "What products and services have these raiders created?'' Or, put the question another way: "What real wealth have they created that has added anything to the gross national product?'' If you need a definition of real wealth, call it the provision of services and the creation of goods, goods like bathtubs, automobiles, and tires, for example. The manufacture of goods and the providing of services creates wealth and adds to our gross national product. Swapping paper back and forth in a frenzy so you can sell out at the last minute and stash the money in a Swiss bank account creates no—I repeat, *no,*—real wealth in this country. The fact is corporate raiders are destroying wealth that millions of hard-working Americans have created over the last century. They are siphoning off wealth already created. Behind the banner of "enhanced shareholder value" the raiders are wreaking havoc across America, causing labor dislocation, forcing plant closings, and upsetting the economic balance of entire communities.

I don't see the golden rule—the foundation of ethical behavior—in this philosophy or its results. I see a lot of "Do unto others, and then *sell out!*" This is the kind of hollow thinking covered by the recently published book titled *The Complete Book of Wall Street Ethics.* Jay L. Walker is the author of this $6.95 volume, which opens with a page of quotes by Ivan Boesky. All the following pages—more than one hundred—are blank. Now here's an author who has a real way *without* words. The jacket cover tells us, "At last we see precisely what raced through the minds of some of Wall Street's top executives as they wrestled with some of the most important moral issues of our time." I submit that this book really hits the mark. But don't rush right out and buy a copy. Wait for the movie. It's sure to convince you that the sharks of the hostile takeover world have no comprehension of the golden rule. It's not part of their culture.

By the same token, there are lessons to be learned by everyone in today's takeover arena, and recently one of the smaller fish, an investment banking firm, found itself in an unexpected case of role reversal. This investment banking outfit, which had enjoyed synchronizing its swimming with the sharks in recent years, suddenly found itself under attack. And let me tell you, by all accounts, the cold fish in that outfit didn't take kindly to the prospect of someone having *their* tailfins for lunch. A couple more incidents like this, and the raiders may find enthusiasm waning among their cohorts in the investment community. But don't mistake my reasons for telling you this story. I'm not advocating an eye-for-an-eye. I wouldn't wish Goodyear's experiences with a hostile takeover attempt on anyone. But I am concerned about a growing public perception that anything's OK . . . if you can get away with it. I hope this conference will focus some discussion on the likelihood that the quick buck philosophy could undermine the ethics of corporate America. It is a philosophy that has moved some corporate managers to send conflicting signals down through the ranks of their fast-trackers. While calling for high moral standards, these leaders are demanding more and more in terms of profits. So, their lower-level guys cut corners. And just as bad, the lieutenants look the other way when their subordinates bend the rules. You can't tell me that these individuals do not carry those philosophies into higher positions if and when they are promoted. The obvious result: we are schooling successive generations of corporate leaders in progressively lower standards of ethics.

Speaking of low ethical standards, look at the role models served up for us by the prime-time television soap operas. There's J. R. Ewing, the no-scruples kingpin of the Ewing empire on *Dallas*; there's the very corrupt Alexis Colby of *Dynasty*; and they have equally nasty counterparts on *Falcon Crest* and *Knot's Landing*. These characters are to the *real* business world what the "Garbage Pail Kids" are to the original "Cabbage Patch" dolls. If the public draws its impression of business leaders from these caricatures, there's little wonder that people with damp ink on their diplomas already see Wall Street as the yellow brick road to riches.

I submit that several who recently followed that yellow brick road found no wizard's castle and no enduring pot of gold, nothing but a heap of trouble and two to ten years to think about it. Ethics in business today must extend far beyond the code that most companies allude to when questions of morality arise. These codes usually are a published philosophy that officers and employees are admonished to follow. At Goodyear, each person is asked not only to read our book of good behavior, but to sign a pledge of commitment. That pledge gives them an avenue of escape should they ever be asked to do something that sounds a bit shaky. It insists that they contact the chairman or our house counsel for advice.

Questions on ethics take on added importance to those of us operating in a global camp. Although Goodyear, for example, is chartered as an Ohio corporation, it must deal with the traditions, morals, and mores of cultures far different from what we call normal. Thus we base our conduct on the philosophy that ethics relates not just to other people, but to your government as well. Since we carry an Ohio charter, we follow the rule, "When in Rome . . . do as they do in Columbus." If the only way we can operate in a country is by greasing palms, we tell our people to keep their hands dry—and erase that country from our map. No one is questioning the need to abide by the laws of the land in which your corporation is chartered, but legislation is not the only yardstick for morally upright behavior. Corporate ethics has to be ingrained in the company's culture, and now we're back to the subject of teaching by example.

At Goodyear, that example dates back to 1915, when the company first began urging its employees to "protect our good name." For seventy-two years that slogan has been a reflection of our company's enduring concern for high moral standards. Through those years, we've found countless times when problems of ethics leave no question about the proper course of action. Questions of safety come to mind. When our safety committee is convened, it is not allowed to consider the cost of whatever the issue. The profit and loss (P&L) simply is *not* part of the discussion. After the decision has been made, we call in the hand-wringers who ask questions like, "My God! How are we going to pay for this?" These are times when the bottom line takes a back seat.

We find that some nonsafety issues fall into the same category, and I recall one case that demonstrates our teach-by-example philosophy. The driver of a Goodyear truck was at fault in a traffic accident in Washington, D.C. His truck hit a restored Volvo driven by a lady who had been widowed just two weeks earlier. Her late husband had spent a great deal of time restoring the car. The traditional knee-jerk procedures went into effect, and the widow was contacted by our insurance carrier. The contact was an impersonal knock on her door, by a guy who handed her a check for the Blue Book value of the old Volvo, $500. No consideration was given to the intrinsic or the sentimental value of the car. Fortunately, one of our guys happened to notice what had happened, and here's where the company's emphasis on ethics emerged. Our employee felt uncomfortable about the fairness of the settlement, so he contacted headquarters and explained the story. He was told to buy the lady a new Volvo. None of us knew the lady—or any information beyond the facts of the story as I've explained them to you—and it was all but forgotten when, two months later, I was approached by a congressman. He introduced himself, then continued to say that he was impressed with the Goodyear Tire and Rubber Company. He described us as a very human company, and I was compelled to ask how he had formed that opinion. He relayed the story of the wrecked Volvo and the widow, whose father, it turns out, had been a government official. And he added that the story had circulated across Capitol Hill with a great deal of positive reaction. I was delighted to find reinforcement for a decision based on fairness, not just on the bottom line. No one knows how far this example may have reached.

I'd like to think that such a case has far greater impact than the convenient platitudes we hear so often. It's easy to spout platitudes. It's easy to shout, "Do as I say, not as I do." But no one will. We need role models. The world needs positive examples of the golden rule in action, a pattern for those without a solid foundation of morality. We need these examples as ammunition to counteract today's uninvolvement syndrome. You remember when we all first became aware of disinvolvement. That was the day Kitty Genovese was attacked and murdered on a New York street while her neighbors stood mute and watched. There wasn't a Good Samaritan in the bunch. Not long ago someone attributed the death of the Good Samaritan philosophy—the golden rule—to a fear of backlash. Reprisal, in other words. We fear that the attacker we see, or the con man we overhear, or the pickpocket we witness, will get a lawyer, and *we* will find ourselves not heroes but defendants. So we back away from the morality of helping someone in need. We slink from the accident scene rather than trying to free a trapped victim.

Let me tell you about a nationwide program Goodyear started a few years back to honor unsung heroes of the highway, and how it has renewed my belief that the golden rule can be revived. This program, called the "Highway Hero" program, researches cases of truck drivers who have gone above and beyond the call of duty. These individuals have risked their lives and careers to rescue others, to avert danger, to right wrongs. Now I don't have to tell you that in many corners of our society the truck driver is not held in particularly high esteem. But I have nothing but the highest regard for the individuals I've gotten to know through this program, and they've left an indelible impression on me. That impression is: The true heroes of this world may be few, but they are unquestionably high examples of the golden rule in action. And they stand as role models all of us can look to for guidance when ethical questions materialize. I've asked these highway heroes, "Why did you stop to help get those people out of the burning car?" "Why did you dive into that swampy water *fifteen times* after the car sank out of sight?" "Why did you bother to get involved?" The answer given by Ronnie Stapleton of Beckley, West Virginia, was typical, but his words still ring in my memory. He said, "That could have been one of my kids in the burning car. I can only pray that if it *had* been one of my kids, somebody would have stopped to help. It's just the *right* thing to do." The golden rule. I was talking to a man who lived it. If he and others like him—in all walks of life—can be held up as role models, I can look at the future of our society with solid optimism. I see more than just a *glimmer* of gold in that old rule.

The Fast Buck—or Faith in the Future? The Ethics of Corporate Restructuring

EDWARD L. HENNESSY, JR.

I'm delighted to participate in Bentley's conference on business ethics. One famous commentator on ethics who took a rather dim view of the conduct of his fellow Americans was Mark Twain. He said, "Be good—and you will be lonesome." Maybe Twain was too pessimistic. However, it he were with us today, he'd probably think he could find ample justification for his views in the business world. He would certainly note practices like check kiting, money laundering, insider trading, and overcharging on government contracts. But I'll bet these misdeeds of *individuals* would interest him far less than the harmful actions of certain *organizations* that are having a much greater impact on our society.

The organizations I'm thinking of are wolf packs of corporate raiders, investor groups, and banks. And the actions are restructurings that aim not at building or managing companies, but at making quick money by breaking up and liquidating companies and pieces of companies. Such methods of doing business are making a few people rich—and a lot of people unhappy. For this reason, those who take the low road in restructuring seek to justify it on high moral grounds. In fact, they're promoting their own version of business ethics—a view that glorifies trading for instant profits in the marketplace. Their new ethics draws on Adam Smith's familiar idea that truly competitive markets deliver the best economic result, both for sellers and buyers. But it elevates this notion into an eleventh commandment of economic conduct that goes something like this: Business people must *always* be governed in their decision making by cost/benefit conditions of efficient markets. This is necessary, not only to achieve success for themselves and their companies, but also to maximize wealth in the economy and deliver the highest possible welfare to the nation.

The loudest preachers of the new ethics, of course, are the raiders themselves. But in the same pulpit we find a group of economists who lionize raiders and praise their redistribution efforts for being almost as public-spirited as those of the Internal Revenue Service (IRS). A number of young investment bankers are also strong believers in the efficient trading ethic. According to a recent article in *Fortune*, these bankers can make a virtue even of putting their client companies into play—as long as this deal-making pumps the stock market up enough to advance what they call the public interest.

In this chapter I'd like to take a critical look at this new ethics of efficient trading. In my view, such deals maximize short-term wealth at the expense of long-term wealth. This is why they are actually damaging to business and to our economy. I'd also like to discuss the approach to restructuring that I believe really does benefit the nation. I think our businesses must emphasize building for long-term growth through such means as research investment, programs that develop human resources, and mergers that create value by establishing new forms of cooperation among operations. In talking about the ethics of restructuring, I will give much more emphasis to practice than to principles. Obviously, I'm a business manager concerned with making operating decisions that have the best results for my company and for the economy. Therefore, concepts of business ethics have the most meaning for me when they are seen as part of this everyday activity.

According to Harvard economist Michael Jensen, we owe a great debt of gratitude to the raiders. The restructurings they have caused have added billions of dollars to the stock market. And all this new value placed on restructured companies is equivalent to resources liberated from the control of wasteful managers—resources now able to move more quickly to their highest-valued uses.

But how about the long term? Does this deal-making result in a strengthening of America's future productivity? To hear Jensen tell it, the deals usually siphon resources *away* from companies whose investments in research and other future-oriented activities are weak and unpromising. But, in fact, traders put companies into play simply because they're undervalued enough to generate big stock market gains. And undervalued companies may or may not be the ones with weak future-oriented programs.

Take T. Boone Pickens' recent move on Boeing. Like much of the aerospace industry, Boeing is undervalued. And the company has $3 billion in cash on hand that is earmarked for development programs. These are the ingredients Pickens has so often cooked into a stock buyback feast for himself and Mesa Petroleum. If he did it again, he could once more be a hero mining gold for shareholders. But this time his liquidation of the target company's long-term programs wouldn't earn him much applause—unless he could convince us that the 747 is just as expendable as new oil discoveries.

If *all* undervalued companies are fair game for raiders, what are the prospects for future-oriented programs in our economy? The impact of the raiders might be compared to that of a bad storm that causes devastation near its center and less intense but very widespread destruction at its outer reaches. At ground zero we find the remains of firms like AMF, Scovill, and Continental Group that have been broken up or stripped of assets by the raiders. Many of these firms used to be healthy. And a number of them had strong potential for growth because of cooperative activities established among their various operations. These are the important long-term programs that are lost to the economy when raiders dismember whole companies.

Farther from the center of the storm, we find a larger group of companies that have been badly damaged by the raiders, but have escaped in one piece. Firms like Unocal and Phillips Petroleum have taken on billions of dollars in debt to outbid the raiders and save their organizations from breakup. Many such companies are forced by high interest costs and low credit ratings to devote most of their resources to controlling this debt. So they greatly reduce their investment in capital projects, research and development (R&D), and other long-term programs.

On the outskirts of the storm are hundreds of companies that feel the force of the raiders as a threat rather than an actual attack. But these companies, no less than the others, are rushing to take defensive actions that are self-destructive. Because their stock is undervalued, these firms are vulnerable. If they are raided, they can expect no support for strategic programs from their institutional owners. Their only protection is getting stock prices up. So these companies give most of their attention to maximizing current profits and buying their own stock. They, too, bow down before the efficient trading principle and defer or liquidate long-term programs.

In fact, some managements are ruled by Wall Street not just in their financial planning, but even in deciding what new businesses to enter—or how to give a new look to old businesses with smoke-and-mirror tricks. They rush to deck themselves out in the latest product fashions touted by analysts. And if hula hoops or seedless grapes make no lasting contribution to the economy, what do they care?

As for the many companies that are adopting Wall Street's short-term financial perspective, I agree with Peter Drucker that they're creating big problems for America—that we're placing ourselves at a dangerous disadvantage in the competition with Japan and other highly productive nations. Amazing as it may seem, the battle between raiders and companies is sometimes said to be a Darwinian struggle that assists the evolution of business by creating organizations that are ever more efficient, more competitive, and more fit for survival. Actually, what we're seeing is the *reverse* of evolution. Our "liberating" of resources from managerial control has become so indiscriminate that we're undoing the very process of building for the future which business depends on. We're headed back down the Darwinian slope toward *lower* forms of organization—as deal after deal leaves more and more of our operations either reduced to fragments or liquidated into money.

Thus, business must work to build awareness that deal-making for fast bucks is wrongheaded and dangerous. We must stress the point that business people cannot contribute to the good of society by concentrating on near-term profits alone. Even more important is the need to increase competitiveness and profitability over the long term.

What does this mean for restructuring activities? We must replace the ethics of efficient trading with an approach that emphasizes productive building. Say a company acquires another firm whose operations have sound strategies and promising long-term programs. The acquirer should preserve these programs and continue to build on them. The combined companies can create new value by collaborating in a number of ways: one or both of the firms may gain better market coverage, better technical support for R&D projects, or an improved use of physical resources.

We have built our own company largely through restructuring of this kind. In mergers with Bendix Corporation and The Signal Companies, we acquired the large aerospace and automative equipment operations that now represent roughly 70 percent of our business. Technology is one key area where we've been building new value by emphasizing cooperation among these acquired businesses and our traditional chemical operations. Many of the advanced materials developed by our chemical labs are being used—or will be used—in the sophisticated products made by our aerospace and automotive operations.

Now, I'm under no illusion that my productive building approach is as easy to sell as deal-making. Obviously, a program that works against our short-term interests will be slow to win converts, especially in a nation now on the leading edge in federal debt, trade debt, corporate debt, consumer debt, farm debt—and probably even broken piggy banks. Nonetheless, I think we must make a strong effort to put across this distinction between right and wrong kinds of restructuring activity.

It may seem surprising that so many people have missed the distinction, have bought the raiders' line that deal-making is good for America. But it's easy to miscalculate the value of a restructuring deal. When you do the cost/benefit analysis of deals only on a case-by-case basis, you can reach conclusions that wider experience tells us are wrong.

This is the problem with the deals that liquidate long-term operations of undervalued companies. If considered one at a time, such deals seem to generate net gains for the economy—mainly because the stock market is very limited in its ability to assess the future. But if we consider liquidating development programs at *all* undervalued companies, it's clear such action would destroy a good part of our economy.

Another ethical issue that needs to be considered is whether restructuring practices are fair or unfair to *people*. The raiders don't offer much guidance here, since the companies and people they target are viewed as nothing more than assets priced by the marketplace. This idea was popular with employers in Victorian factories. But it has not stood the test of time with any wider following.

Don't think we're going to win friends and influence people by rediscovering it now—no matter how many sacks of fan mail the raiders get from the arbitrageurs.

In an effort to counter the raiders, some business managers have advocated a "stakeholder" view of the corporation that emphasizes our links with employees, customers, suppliers, and local communities. According to this idea, all these stakeholders have valid claims against corporations. And in making decisions about how corporate resources should be deployed in restructuring moves, companies must weigh the interests of these stakeholders one against the other. This means, of course, that the interests of shareholders will no longer be favored in all cases. For example, according to one chief executive quoted recently in a major business publication, his company's 40,000 employees have much deeper and more important stakes in the firm than shareholders.

I think such a response reveals a misconception of the proper role of the corporation. I believe the primary purpose of corporations is the traditionally recognized one of producing wealth for shareholders and for the economy. That's not to say we should ignore the concerns of other groups. But managers who give priority to other stakeholders are exceeding their mandate. They are transforming themselves from businesspeople into public officials or pastors. And let's face it, most business leaders aren't qualified by experience for these other responsibilities. When we try to take on a do-gooder role, most people don't think we look the part. The raiders say our concern about employees or local communities is just a show aimed at saving our own jobs. And right now the raiders seem to be playing to fuller houses than we are.

Still, I believe businesspeople really mean it when they stress the fact that corporations must acknowledge the interests of all their stakeholders—and when they say these interests should not be at the mercy of every pirate that sails over the horizon. In fact, this is my own view. But I'm convinced that employee and other stakeholder interests can be defended on a sound *business* basis, even though they may not be line items on the P&L.

For example, if a company is to survive and prosper over the long term, it needs employees who are both versatile and dedicated. So to make sure that we develop such employees, we do more than offer competitive wages, salaries, and employee benefits. We also offer work that is diversified, continually changing, and increasing in complexity. We create company cultures that foster a sense of community. We bring people together in programs that grant public recognition for service, promotions, and special achievements like improving productivity or inventing patent-winning technology. And we encourage greater employee participation in decision making about job procedures and workplace rules.

Only by doing these things can we stimulate the creativity and gain the committed support we need to ensure our productivity and profitability over time. If we choose to deny the larger human and social impact of the corporation, if we try to reduce a company to the bare essentials of a commercial transaction, we will end up with a work force that is less capable and less dedicated over the long run. And we will also cause *society* to be indifferent—if not completely hostile—to the interests of corporations and their shareholders.

Let me sum up what I've been saying here. Businesspeople must look beyond the present when evaluating restructuring deals. They must calculate the costs and benefits with a view to the larger consequences. When they do this, they will concentrate on productive building—not on making the fast buck today. They will emphasize development efforts in technology and marketing, mergers that create new value, and programs aimed at improving our human capital.

Businesses that take this approach can rightly say they are serving society as they pursue their own interests. For they will be increasing productivity and generating wealth on a continuing basis. Whether you're talking about mergers and acquisitions or everyday operations, this is the *only* final purpose of business that can qualify as genuinely ethical.

In one of his books, Peter Drucker describes a disagreement between two famous economists over what economic activity is the most important. Adam Smith, with his focus on traders in efficient markets, gave the first place to maximizing economic gain. But the French economist Jean Say gave priority to risk-taking that releases capital from the unproductive past and invests it in making a better future. He even coined a new word, "entrepreneur," to describe the businessperson who undertakes such investment.

Clearly, in today's business world—with its rapid changes in technology and markets—risk-taking must be ranked as more important than maximizing immediate gain. Today the great need of business and our economy is for entrepreneurs who will commit resources to an unknown future. And the great danger is that we may fail to take such risks—that selfishness or short-sightedness may keep us from building productivity for tomorrow.

Ethics of Organizational Transformation in Takeovers, Plant Closings, and Cooperative Ventures

WILLIAM C. NORRIS

It is a pleasure to participate in this conference. From the spectrum of business practices falling under the umbrella of organizational transformation, I have chosen to focus my chapter on the categories of hostile takeovers, friendly mergers, plant closings, and large-scale technological cooperation.

Before proceeding with the review of the selected categories, I should make four statements as background. First, for the most part, ethics is currently being relegated to a back seat in these transformations as many corporate executives are being pressured to change their practices radically to become more competitive. Those changes reflect diminishing concern for employees, communities, and national interests. While this drive for competitiveness appears to be paying off at the moment, it will be self-defeating in the long run unless ethics has a prominent role.

Second, it is difficult to exaggerate the seriousness of the declining competitive position of the United States in world markets, with its adverse economic and social consequences. The 1985 report of the President's Commission on Industrial Competitiveness provided a good perspective of the foreign competitive challenge which cuts across the breadth of American industry. It warned that our ability to compete was eroding, and that we were losing world market share in industry after industry, including seven out of ten high technology industries. Further, it should be noted that nine of the ten fastest growing U.S. industries have been in high technology areas and currently constitute 43 percent of the total value of U.S. manufactured exports.

Unfortunately, the trends flagged by the president's commission have continued. According to the Department of Commerce, the United States recorded its first worldwide trade deficit in electronics in 1986, going from a $1.3 billion surplus in 1985 to almost a $1.9 billion deficit last year. At the same time, a report prepared for the Joint Economic Committee of Congress predicted that when all the figures are in, 1986 will produce the first full-year high technology trade deficit since this category was first identified.

Loss of market leadership in high tech industries is not restricted solely to reduced trade and loss of jobs in high tech companies. Adverse effects are also felt widely in other sectors because high tech products, such as microcomputers, are used to improve performance and quality and lower costs of products, processes, and services in other industries. Hence, other industries can be placed at a severe competitive disadvantage if they do not have the same access to the most advanced high tech products as their foreign competitors.

Improving this dismal situation is a gargantuan task, requiring many actions; however, the most important is a vast increase in innovation. Let us be reminded that innovation is the process of getting new products and services on the market or improving existing ones. It often starts with research, which is followed by development, manufacturing, and marketing. Innovation is also the source of most jobs.

My third statement is that there is a considerable commonality of meaning and, at the same time, ambiguity in the use of such terms as ethics in business, morality in business, corporate responsibility, and social responsibility; however, I believe that each of these concepts form the underpinnings of a broader notion of social justice—I also believe that most agree that this broader concept of social justice communicates best what we want most for our country.

Further, because of the complex interrelationships in our society, any one sector—even business, with its vast resources—is severely handicapped and cannot be nearly as effective as it might be in furthering social justice unless there is cooperation with other sectors.

The single, most effective way to promote social justice is to create more jobs, especially better-paying jobs—or put another way, the source of social injustices, be it poverty, child abuse, alcoholism, or crime, high correlates to the denial of the right to a decent job. Unfortunately, there are a large number of people in that category, including the handicapped and disadvantaged in both urban and rural areas. Rural poverty is increasing, and an urban underclass is growing. Both are contributing to the development of a two-tiered society.

As with improving competitiveness, the single, most important action for improving the availability of jobs is a vast increase in innovation. Such effort is only affordable if we increase the efficiency of the creation and application of technology through broadly based technological cooperation.

My fourth and last statement is that business can best promote social justice not with acts of charity, but by fostering innovation through certain types of cooperation and other actions which increase competitiveness and, at the same time, promote job creation. Such an approach should be welcomed by corporate executives, most of whom have a social conscience and would like to serve the common interest if they can achieve that goal in consonance with business objectives.

TECHNOLOGICAL COOPERATION

With that background, I will now review large-scale technological cooperation. Unfortunately, neither the need nor desirability of a massive expansion in large-scale cooperation is widely understood; however, there is a gradual awakening to the merit of cooperation in general as evidenced by the growing number of joint ventures between two companies to develop, manufacture, and market products, and by small-scale cooperative research programs among industry, universities, and state government

While there have only been a few large-scale cooperative efforts involving a number of companies, universities, and government, such efforts are critically important as the best way to develop base technologies which can be widely used by individual companies for creating new products, services, and processes or improving existing ones.

MCC

The outstanding example of large-scale technological cooperation is MCC, the Microelectronics and Computer Technology Corporation. It was established four years ago and is located in Austin, Texas. Initially, there were eleven member companies from the U.S. computer and semiconductor industries. This number has grown to twenty.

MCC is a cooperative effort to develop base technologies for use in microelectronics and computing by members and licensees who will each add their own value and continue to compete with products and services which employ those base technologies, but which are of their individual conception and design, for use in their freely selected markets.

It is already clear that MCC will have enormous benefits in more efficient development of technology. For example, each dollar that Control Data invests in MCC research programs produces research results of interests to the company with an average cost of five dollars. Other MCC members are realizing similar returns. The importance of sharing extremely scarce scientific and engineering talent cannot be overemphasized in an environment where our education system is failing to produce sufficient quantity and quality of technologists. Equally important, technology created by MCC will be licensed on reasonable terms to others, including small companies.

I should also note that MCC has received substantial support from the state of Texas, and twenty-five universities are participating in the research and development effort. Participation by the federal government is expected in the future.

The last and obvious point is that every industry needs one or more cooperative efforts of this type. A five-to-one leverage in creating base technologies across the board in this country would provide a much-needed boost to innovation to make us more competitive.

However, progress in expanding such cooperation is pitifully slow in comparison to what is needed and feasible, partly because of lack of understanding of the need and benefits. Additional reasons include the long time span to produce results, current tight budgets in both the public and private sectors, and the pressure on corporations for quarter-to-quarter earnings increases. These realities made it difficult to establish MCC four years ago and even more difficult to get other large-scale cooperative efforts started today.

MTDI

To help respond to that need, the Midwest Technology Development Institute (MTDI) was established in 1985 by nine midwestern states. A principal objective of MTDI is promoting cooperative technology development through the establishment of a series of industry, university, and government consortia, each focusing on a single area of technology.

Thus far, three fields have been selected for the establishment of technology development consortia:

• rural development
• advanced ceramics and composites
• advanced manufacturing

These consortia are in various stages of implementation. The consortia for rural development, called the Rural Enterprise Partnership, is in operation, and four industry-university-government cooperative projects are underway. The advanced ceramics and composites partnership is ready to launch, and the planning for the cooperative effort in advanced manufacturing will be completed in about six months.

While these three consortia represent important progress, as noted earlier, many more are needed. Thus, it behooves corporations to expand their participation in such large-scale technological cooperation. The basic concept is sound, feasible, and fair for all parties, and offers the best chance for enhancing U.S. competitiveness in critically important industries.

As mentioned earlier, there are difficulties in getting large-scale cooperative efforts started, not the least of which is the unrelenting pressure for quarterly earnings improvement; therefore, federal tax credits should be made available during the early years to help offset the cost until technology results begin to flow, providing the basis for new products and services.

Furthermore, for years business has been saying, "Get the government off our backs and we'll perform even better." Consistent with that position then, business assumes greater responsibility for providing an adequate number of jobs. This responsibility can be fulfilled to an important extent by helping create the new technology to undergird innovation. Consequently, participation in large-scale cooperation is not only good business; it also promotes social justice.

COMMUNITY LEVEL COOPERATION

Another very important form of cooperation is at the community level among all sectors in order to:

1. Help build a much greater understanding of, and support for, the need for a massive, nationwide surge in innovation;
2. Provide more effective assistance to small business because that sector is a major source of innovation and creates most of the new jobs; and interrelated,
3. Facilitate cooperation between large and small businesses.

In order for community level cooperation to be most successful in achieving these and other objectives, a new institution, called an innovation network, is needed.

It consists of three major elements: cooperation office, seed capital fund, and business center. Let me describe how an innovation network functions in providing assistance to small companies to get started and operate profitably.

Cooperation Office

The cooperation office is the pivotal element of the network. It is a nonprofit, community-based organization financed by state and local government, private contributions, client fees, and funds generated by investments in client companies.

The permanent staff is small, but the cooperation office draws on a volunteer advisory panel of scientists, engineers, marketing specialists, and executives for the specific expertise required to help entrepreneurs prepare and evaluate business plans. Because these plans are expertly conceived, the chances of receiving adequate financing and achieving economic viability are substantially increased.

Seed Capital

Equity financing is often not available for new companies during their initial formation and early development stages from banks, venture capital funds, and other conventional sources because of the higher risks involved. Therefore, a source of seed capital is needed.

The best type of seed fund is a consortium of state and local government and private investors, where the government investments are subordinated and state tax credits are available to the private investors. This approach balances the interests of the public and private sectors. The private investor receives an attractive return with reasonable risk, and the government receives a somewhat smaller one. However, the difference is more than made up by tax revenues the government collects from the increased number of people employed and from the expanded economic activity that results.

Business Center

A business center provides various combinations of consulting services, shared laboratory, manufacturing, and office facilities, and other services to facilitate the startup and growth of small businesses. Economies of scale make it possible to provide occupants of the center with needed facilities of much higher quality and considerably lower cost than any would be capable of obtaining or providing for itself.

Large Company Participation

Cooperation between large and small business is facilitated by the innovation network. Such cooperation can be very rewarding to both parties. Small companies are handicapped by insufficient management and professional expertise, inadequate availability of technology, and scarcity of capital. At the same time, most of the technology, management, and professional expertise and capital resources are found in big business—and are often underused.

By making available its underused technology and ideas, and by offering its professional and management assistance to a small company, a large company can realize additional income from past investment—also, large companies can gain more economical access to new products and markets through equity investments in and R&D contracts with small companies.

Such actions accentuate the strongest attributes of both large and small enterprise. Small companies, which are inherently more creative and flexible and have lower overhead, can frequently develop new markets, products, and services sooner for less cost; whereas larger companies, with greater resources, can provide efficiencies in marketing and production. All types of companies—not just manufacturing companies, but also banks, insurance companies, retail companies, utilities, law firms, public accounting branch offices, and so on—can participate successfully.

A number of years ago, Control Data started a cooperative program with small businesses, which included one or more of the following actions:

- transfer of selected technologies
- equity investment
- R&D contracts

During that time, Control Data has developed one or more of such relationships with seventy companies. Over all, the results have been good. Similar activities by a few other large companies could be cited; however, the point is that the potential for the practice is much greater than is being realized.

Replication

An innovation network, consisting of the three major elements I've just described, is being replicated in a number of places. The most progress is being made in the states of Illinois, South Carolina, and Minnesota. Illinois is in the process of implementing eight networks, while South Carolina is establishing seven, and Minnesota, four.

While considerable progress has been made, it is far short of what is required to provide enough decent jobs in the future. However, strong initiatives by companies, as proposed, would help get the needed action by other sectors.

In summary, benefits for companies participating in community-level cooperation includes potential for acquiring new products and markets and making profitable, long-term investments. At the same time, jobs are created. Additionally, the community, with the establishment of an innovation network, is in a better position to manage its own destiny by having the means to diversify its business base and reduce dependency on any one plant where employment might be drastically reduced, or the plant closed or moved. This advantage for both communities and companies will be considered further when plant closings are reviewed.

HOSTILE TAKEOVERS

Next, let me review hostile takeovers, which are a major detractor from innovation. One reason is the extensive social injustice caused mainly by employee trauma from job losses and career disruptions.

In spite of the urgent need for more industrial innovation, hostile takeovers and the threat of hostile takeovers only impede such efforts. They cause dissipation of the most important part of the innovation resources in target companies—skilled personnel—and they undermine teamwork.

Experience shows that a high percentage of senior executives leave after a takeover. For example, a survey in 1984 by Lamallie Associates, an executive search company, concluded that approximately 50 percent of senior managers leave within a year after their companies are taken over, and 75 percent will probably leave within three years.

Increased turnover is not confined to members of senior management, but occurs at all levels of management and in other areas. This is caused by the excessive trauma that is inflicted, starting with a fear of job loss and/or a career path being in jeopardy.

The initial phase of a hostile takeover is unnecessarily nerve-wracking because of lack of information or credibility of assurances about the aggressor's plans. There are always company commitments to employees, both implied and stated, relating to job responsibilities and career paths. Employees expect them to be fulfilled; yet they understand that due to competition, adverse economic conditions, and other factors not under the complete control of management, some may not be fully met.

However, when a raider engages in an unnecessary and unilateral takeover, it causes abrogation of many commitments in the target company that inflict cold-blooded and unjust human injury—cold-blooded because the aggressor knows that employee injuries will be caused; and unjust because they could have been avoided either by achieving the takeover objectives in another way or by recognizing that the objective of "I want it and therefore I shall have it" is not necessarily legitimate.

For many employees, fear of job loss is replaced by forced departure due to changed plans, overlap in positions between the target and acquiring company, or the elimination of jobs to achieve savings to help pay for the cost of the takeover. For those employees who have the option of continuing employment, there is a widespread feeling of disgust and resentment over being victimized. A divisive "us versus them" attitude often develops as well. As a consequence, those employees who can find other acceptable employment leave. Many of those who stay are disillusioned and feel less commitment and loyalty to their companies. For example, a recent survey by *Industry Week* magazine showed that nearly 60 percent are less loyal to their employers than five years ago, and the major cause is takeover mania.

Lack of commitment and loyalty, along with distrust, creates an adverse climate for teamwork, which is essential for timely and efficient results in innovation. Not only is such teamwork required among executives and R&D technologists to design the best products, but teamwork on the factory floor is necessary for the lowest-cost, highest-quality output.

In sharp contrast to employee disruptions in this country is Japan, where hostile takeovers rarely are attempted. Companies are looked upon more as permanent institutions, and a strong consensus prevails that one company does not have the unilateral right to buy another one. As a result, hostile takeover attempts are viewed with public contempt. Such reactions, along with the focus of lifetime employment by large Japanese companies and other factors, contribute to an environment of harmony and cooperation in Japanese companies. The adverse implications on competitiveness of the contrasting turmoil of fear, distrust, and disgust in U.S. companies stirred up by takeovers is easy to grasp by anyone with a sense of objectivity.

Another detractor from our ability to compete is the decreased availability of funds for R&D after a hostile takeover. Because of the substantial increase in debt to finance takeovers, higher interest costs undercut investment in R&D, as well as other parts of the innovation cycle.

Additionally, the threat of hostile takeovers detracts from innovation, especially the long term R&D component, as corporations tend to favor short-term innovation investments at the expense of the long term in order to maintain quarter-to-quarter earnings growth that is needed to maximize company stock prices to make the company less attractive as a target for a raider.

The adverse impacts of hostile takeovers are not limited to target companies and their employees. Communities and states in which these companies are located invariably experience economic damage. Jobs are lost, tax revenues are reduced, unemployment costs rise, and eventually welfare cost increases begin.

Nor does it stop there. Like a pebble dropped in a pond, the ripples expand. When jobs are lost or transferred, the merchants, professionals, and businesses dependent upon employee spending experience the loss as well. Real estate values fall; construction falls off. There occurs, in essence, a *"reverse* economic multiplier effect.''

Experience shows that charities and civic organizations also suffer. Raiders have yet to demonstrate a commitment to charitable giving. But it is not just corporate financial support—the loss of an independent firm translates into a loss of personal time contributions and leadership provided by the company's employees.

For too long, the debate over hostile takeovers has focused on traditional notions about the rights of shareholders and bidders and the efficient operation of markets—as though all that was involved was the routine sale of a chattel or piece of land. But much more is involved, and social justice is being trampled, helping create the environment that spawned Ivan Boesky and others of his ilk. In addition to these crooks, a much larger number of unscrupulous characters within investment banking and on its fringes are operating short of illegality, but in shady ways.

There is growing support for federal legislation to constrain hostile takeovers. I've been an advocate of it for twenty years, although I'm not convinced that it would be the best solution, because it is unlikely that sufficient legislation will be enacted. The best answer is public disgust, which would make hostile takeovers so socially unacceptable that they wouldn't occur. However, U.S. society will continue to suffer further widespread injustice from hostile takeovers until business, labor, academia, government, and church organizations do much more to articulate their adverse consequences, which would build a strong public antipathy.

I won't take the time to express my views on legislation to constrain hostile takeovers, except to note that the most important provision would be the requirement for a social impact analysis in any contemplated takeover. I'll elaborate on that right now.

FRIENDLY MERGERS

My strong belief about the destructive aspects of hostile takeovers does not infer that I am against all mergers. Quite the contrary, friendly mergers are an essential part of our American system. However, they, too, can cause unacceptable social harm unless a concerted effort is made to address it.

In order to minimize employee trauma and other adverse effects, every company should adopt a policy that requires a social impact analysis to be made at the earliest stage in any contemplated acquisition. Social injury that cannot be eliminated is cause for rejection.

Briefly, the social impact analysis requires a statement of the reasons for the acquisition, development of five-year business plans under which the resulting business combination would be operated, and an analysis of the effect on all constituents, including employees, the communities in which plants are located, suppliers, and customers. In addition, an assessment is made of the effects on the innovation capabilities of the acquired company.

Control Data has such a policy. It was adopted ten years ago and has served the company well. Since good business practice mandates that thorough planning take place before an acquisition is made, virtually no cost is added by considering social effects. Furthermore, experience shows that severe adverse social impacts as a result of an acquisition can be very costly in dollars, or tarnished public image, or both.

Hence, a policy requiring social impact analysis is good business in the broadest sense, being both profit- and society-oriented. Executives welcome such a policy as a means of responding to their social conscience without being exposed to the criticism of being softheaded by those who either fail to see or don't want to see the merits of taking social factors into reasonable account in business decisions.

PLANT CLOSINGS

The last category of organizational transformation to review is plant closings and plant relocations. Of course, they will often result from a hostile takeover, or even a friendly merger, in the absence of adequate advance planning. On the other hand, a closing, relocation, or drastic reduction in employment may be unavoidable, even in carefully considered plans for an acquisition, consolidation, or divestiture that is necessary to improve productivity, market access, or some other compelling economic reason. In that event, I believe that in the interest of good business and social justice, the corporate owner has three major responsibilities:

1. Provide as much advance notice as possible to the employees and community;
2. Provide employees who will lose their jobs with reasonable severance compensation and assistance in finding alternative employment;
3. Assist the community in developing alternative sources of jobs.

I believe that as a general rule, in the event of a plant closing or relocation, companies should provide advance notice. Thoughtful people are currently debating just how much notice should be required.

The amount of severance pay is the same as paid under other circumstances of work-force reduction. A preferred approach to assistance for developing alternate sources of employment is the innovation network and the capability it provides a community to diversify its business base. The point is simply that if a community doesn't have a network, then a company making a drastic reduction in employment or closing or moving a plant should encourage the community to establish one and provide assistance. This can be done in a number of ways, such as investing in the seed capital fund and making the plant, or part of the plant, available as a business center at the lowest reasonable cost.

A better approach is for companies with branch plants to encourage and assist communities to establish innovation networks before a serious employment reduction problem arises. As noted earlier, participation in innovation network activities can be profitable, long-term investments. At the same time, there is the opportunity to make clear to the community that:

1. The presence of the plant provides great economic benefits—for example, one measure is that every year, each job is worth around $20,000 because of taxes paid, sustained economic activity resulting from the payroll dollars flowing into the community, and more;
2. The company may not be able to operate the plant indefinitely due to changing markets, advancing technologies, or other factors;
3. The community should anticipate the possibility of that event and prepare for it by establishing an innovation network.

With that approach, a company can be in the position of being thanked for the great contribution it made during the years it operated the plant rather than being castigated for a drastic reduction in employment. Or worse, it could be subject to plant-closing legislation, with the inference that it must be forced to do what is right, at possibly onerous costs. How ironic in view of the tremendous benefits enjoyed by communities from the jobs! No one is more to blame for this misconception than business itself.

CONCLUSION

Much more can be said about plant closings; however, it is time to end this chapter. In concluding, I want to emphasize that becoming "lean and mean competitors" through restructuring is not enough. Progress in expanding innovation is the key to meeting the aspirations of our society. Achieving efficiency in innovation requires teamwork—among executives, researchers, product engineers, and those on the factory floor. On the other hand, teamwork is undermined when loyalty bonds between companies and their employees are destroyed and replaced by distrust as a result of injustices inflicted by restructuring.

Consequently, companies should think and act in terms of social justice that fosters innovation. This would remove impediments to teamwork and create a corporate culture which would strongly inspire ethical behavior in other ways. I believe that most executives have a conscience; however, without some encouragement and a structure to make compliance as free as possible from internal and external counterpressures, most will not respond in accordance with conscience dictates.

As I look about and see the growing gap between the rich and the poor, the black people who are generally worse off than ten years ago, and the emergence of an underclass, I'm reminded of the arson and riots which swept through my home town of Minneapolis and sixty-eight other cities in America in 1967. Before that tragic occurrence, it was widely believed that such an event wouldn't happen in our beautiful city, but it did, in a depressed area on the north side. The cause was mainly lack of decent jobs and lack of opportunity to participate in the good life that the vast majority in the city enjoyed.

At that time I said, "You can't do business in a society that is burning, and Control Data should do its part to help eliminate the root cause by putting jobs there." The Company did that in north Minneapolis and in six other poverty-stricken areas cooperatively with the federal government, cities, and communities. It was a rewarding program for both the communities and Control Data. The communities benefited from the jobs, and the plants were profitable and competitive. Also, Control Data employees worldwide were enormously proud of the program, and our customers, especially those overseas, applauded our efforts.

Today, because of advancing technology and changing markets, only two of those plants are still operated by Control Data. However, the company was able to find buyers for the other five, and employment levels have been maintained. In addition, innovation networks are being established with assistance by Control Data in three of the communities.

The poverty plant program is further evidence that business can assume responsibility for jobs without conflicting with its first priority of making a profit. In fact, it's clear that unless business—that sector of society which provides most of the jobs and has most of the resources to create them—assumes a greater initiative for providing jobs, our quality of living will continue to deteriorate. At the same time, there is the risk of a repeat of the violence that swept through our cities only two decades ago, or something worse. Extensive cooperation to expand innovation vastly, along with other actions to promote social justice, provides the greatest hope for America's future.

8

What is a Corporation's Responsibility in the U.S. Today?

ANDREW SIGLER

For quite a while I've been involved with the general issue of corporate responsibility, or with what we might refer to as concerns about acceptable behavior
within a company. I have also been involved with the specific issue of takeovers.
I will explain what I believe without expanding too much, because all of these
are reasonably complicated subjects, any one of which I could spend quite a bit
of time discussing.

I think it's important first of all to lay your prejudices out. I've spent all my
time, business time, with one company. It is a resource-based, large process
industry. For all sorts of reasons, we have facilities in places where trees grow;
that is, we're essentially rural, with a little bit more emphasis on the South, but
we do have fairly major operations in the upper Midwest, Canada, and elsewhere.
When I joined the company, it was a very paternalistic, family-owned corporation, and it still is a very typical thing to have a whole family, maybe even
three generations, working in a mill. Therefore, by the combination of the family
aspect and the rural atmosphere, I come from a culture that is very involved
with community and the individuals that work for it; sometimes this is good and
sometimes bad, but that's the way it is.

I've also been involved in the Business Roundtable for quite a period of time.
I was involved in 1981 when I chaired the operation, which I think made the
first public statement of what corporations are responsible for. The Business
Roundtable tried to get away from this thing that says, "I am responsible for
maximizing the return of my shareholders," which is outdated, oversimplified,
and maybe even a crutch to justify lots of things. I'll mention a little bit more
about shareholders later. We had a whole series of constituencies: customers,
employees, communities, suppliers, society, and shareholders. If you're going
to run a corporation intelligently today, you have to deal with all of these. I

have a difficult time specifying what our responsibility is to all of these, but the fact of the matter is you can't continue to operate unless you deal with all of them, and deal with them in a way that's acceptable. If you don't do that with your customers, you're out of business. If you don't do that with your employees, you're out of business. And particularly in a company like ours, where we have been involved in the pollution and environmental areas in about every way you can name, if you don't deal with the community and suppliers in an acceptable way, you're out of business.

With all of that said, if there is no profitable bottom line, there is nothing else. I stole that line from Thornton Bradshaw, who used it many years ago when he was president of Atlantic Richfield; if there is no bottom line there is nothing else. So, in an oversimplified way, I'd say corporate responsibility today is to perform. We have to perform successfully. I'll say a little bit more about how to define that performance—because I think it's very complicated—but if we don't perform then we're all in trouble.

Whether you like them or not, large corporations run the ballgame. That is the economic drive of our society. Who buys high tech? Do you buy high tech? I buy high tech, a lot of it. A big, old, dumb processing business buys high tech. The drive for new investment, the recycling of old mills, the entrepreneurial spirit: all of that comes from corporations, whether you like it or not. Investment bankers make money; they don't create anything. And I guess the major point that I want to make is that corporations are people. They are people put together in ways so that they perform, some much better than others. And they have to be treated as rather tender institutions. I don't think any of us believe that humans are totally motivated by pay; although certainly if you read the October 5, 1987 *Forbes* cover article, "The Richest Man in the World; and 95 Also-rans," you would see that greed seems to have become the ultimate motivation. We are obsessed with lists of who has the most money. But corporations are people and have to be dealt with as people, and if they're not—if they're dealt with as assets and chips—it doesn't work very well.

I personally am totally outraged at what raiders do to companies. In the guise of routing out "entrenched management," they have lunched off our economic system as no human beings have ever lunched off anything in proportion to personal money made in the last five years. Maybe one day when Alexander sacked the Persian city he made as much money, in proportion to what has been made today, but I doubt it. The raiders put companies into play for short-term profits. We have yet to have a merger in the takeover area where management is thrown out, and new management comes in and runs it happily into the sunset. That's the theory we like to argue about, but that's not what happens, and what I want to try and do is talk a little bit about the "why's."

Companies that are taken over have so much debt that they either have to be liquidated or unwound in a major way. Scovill, Continental Group, Uniroyal—these are the companies that I can almost see from my office. You've already seen a lot of examples, so I won't say much about them. In my opinion, the raiders, the investment bankers, and the lawyers have dressed up their personal greed by claiming to do the Lord's work: throw out inefficient and entrenched management, and so on. I think the aggregate of their actions has been very destructive, and it has had the effect of corroding the national economic strength for the better part of the last six years.

Ethics? They lie about their intentions, they hurt the little people. They don't hurt me; if someone tried to take over Champion and we either were taken over or made one of those deals—which I'll address later—I personally could probably make between $50 and $100 million. It's the little guy who gets it in the neck, not me. They lie about their intentions, they lie about performance, and they claim to be doing it in a way to help society, by throwing out entrenched management. If anyone wants to ask about the entrenched management issue, I'm not sure what that means, but I'd be glad to argue about it.

I have a tough time with the issue of greed. I have a tough time with the idea that greed is the only thing that counts in this society. What's that television show, *Lifestyles of the Rich and Famous*? If we've really come to that, and those are our values, I think we've got terrible problems.

You can't argue hostile takeovers in theory; you've got to know how they work, and you've got to know how, in detail, the game is played. One of the problems is that the whole subject is generally described in horrible jargon that we've all created. Let me run through some points regarding one example, but I'm certainly not trying to describe the whole area.

First of all, takeovers wouldn't be possible without the pension money. We've gone from practically nothing to approaching $2 trillion. The pension money owns American equity today; it owns somewhere approaching two-thirds of all the equity on the New York Stock Exchange. It owns somewhere around 75 percent of Champion. It is totally short-term driven. It is valued on its return. The computer churns, monthly and weekly. Probably a third of my shareholders don't know they own my stock. It's called "index," it's called "futures," it's called "buying programs." When the market moves ninety points, when it crosses the line, the computers come in, and they drive it up, and they drive it down. And the money is what makes it work. The money establishes the price of stock.

Stock is priced today on a formula of what the current earnings or expectations of earnings in the next quarter are. Period. Assets and other factors aren't considered. Short-term pressures set the price. This also involves the buying of junk bonds, but I won't go into that. The game is to take advantage of the difference between the market value of the stock of a company and the market value of the assets of the company. When the Dow Jones Industrial average is around 1300, this is much easier to do. But in a cyclical company that is dealing with a price/earnings ratio of nine, on a cyclical down with 6.5 million acres and all of those things . . . plus this money is available to be loaned to people to buy assets. You borrow all the money, you go in and sell the assets, and you make what's in between. That's a takeover, that's how it's played. There are all sorts of variations, but that's how the game is played.

T. Boone Pickens and Newmont are a classic example. They buy stock and they proclaim, they make noise, they say they're going to take over, and all the stock churns; the short-term opportunists take advantage and buy. Within a week 60 to 70 percent of the rest—and with Newmont there's the South African ownership—is bought by short-term opportunists. The company is "in play," and certain things have to happen. We used to have greenmail, straight out. Now we have leveraged buybacks. That's greenmail, except you give it to everybody. That's what happened in this case. They bought back so much stock, they made $200 million, and they prorate that—that's greenmail. Then there are LBOs, leveraged buyouts, where the management decides "*I* might as well make it instead of *him* making it." But management LBOs usually begin with management having only 1 percent. Yet this is the same deal, played the same way, but someone else heads it. And today it's a thing called restructuring, with an equity stub, and it's fairly clever—and that's how I could make all that money.

Whether it is an actual takeover or not, you end up with a totally neutered company. It can't do anything. It has so much debt it must sell off assets. I heard on the news about a company that recently got a lot of fanfare, and in a spinoff it bought a magazine publishing company. I'm in the business of selling paper, so I listen to things like this. The magazine publishing company was an arm of CBS. They sold the whole chunk of their magazines to the *Los Angeles Times*. You've got to sell off, you've got to liquidate, because you can't handle it any more.

So, in effect, we are extracting equity. Now there's a theory that says it doesn't make any difference. Equity on a balance sheet is what powers this economic system. If someone wants to ask me, we could get into an argument about money chasing and whether or not it's efficient, but the fact is, once it comes out of here it doesn't go back to the place where it can be productive.

I guess there's a useful role for M&As, mergers and acquisitions. If you study the 1960s, when the theory was that anybody could manage anything, and you talk about synergism, then I think we all proved that you can't manage everything. And so, M&As have had some value. But I get into real trouble with my associates when I say mergers and acquisitions don't have value, and what we're doing now is absolute madness. It has forced a short-term attitude on us, and it's caused companies not to do all the things that we really get paid to do in terms of performance: long-term investment, creation of jobs, creation of wealth, and R&D. All these kinds of things that we're supposed to do to keep this country strong, we haven't done.

How do you protect yourself? You screw up your balance sheet, that's how you protect yourself. You louse it up so they can't play the game on you. Instead of running at a normal rate of debt, you run at a *lot* of debt. You do the negative kind of things, so that the game can't be played. Is anyone doing that? Sure.

The takeover process has been stopped to some extent by state law. I think

New York State has the most intelligent approach to it. In effect, their law doesn't allow the liquidation game to be played. If you buy, you've got to hold, or you're taxed heavily; and if you sell, the law requires you to go to a board of directors, and if it's declared hostile, then you can't play the sell-off deal. I happen to believe that directors in general do a reasonably good job. I think we are getting legislation, and we should listen to what Congressman Edward Markey has to say today, since he heads the House Subcommittee on Telecommunications and Finance. But let me raise a couple of issues that I think are important questions in this area.

Who owns American corporations? Who's going to act as the old theoretical owner? It's a terrible problem; I don't know the answer. We can't let management not have pressure, but should an equity index fund, for example, the one owned by the State of New York, the largest individual group I think, $40 billion, $50 billion—should such a fund apply the pressure? I met some people from SUNY. Their money would be in that fund. It's a major shareholder of mine, and it's indexed. Who owns? Who is supposed to have a say? Who am I supposed to please? Now, if you really want to know the issue, then know how pension funds work. If you have a defined benefit program, what that fund does doesn't make any difference, but what the corporation does is what makes the difference. It's the corporation's money, it's not the person's money. Very complicated ingredients here. But who are the owners? Who are my owners? A computer? Just think of how many shares of Champion got bought and sold by a computer on an index or to pay off the futures ordered yesterday between 3:42 P.M. and 4:30 P.M. Who are my owners? Whom do I ask what they want me to do? I think we have to find a different way of grading companies and evaluating them, not necessarily as an investment. But today all we do is on the basis of short-term performance, and there is intense pressure to perform.

Now, the thing that I think bothers me most of all is that while all this is going on, the world is feeling its oats. We've come to the point where Europe and, in an amazing way, the Far Eastern countries have understood what world business competition requires. We are watching the globalization of industry, and we are being left behind. We are not only being left behind because of the kind of pressures that make people unable to take advantage of the kind of long-term investments. We are also left behind because if you're over there, you might as well come buy somebody here, if you're Hanson Trust or somebody. We can't go and buy anybody over there, but its a heck of a lot easier for them to do it here.

While all this is going on, I think we are coming out of this, probably in our lifetime, with the reputation of being a second-rate economic factor. And if you think a society based on service will work, look what's happening with how the Japanese are dealing with the financial service business. Do you really think if they win the economic war of creating economic value, they're going to use U.S. banks and U.S. investment bankers? So, I think the implications of this are pretty scary.

To sum up, I think corporations have very complicated and broad responsibilities. Whether we like it or not, the corporations are the structure that we've put in place to create jobs, to create wealth, basically to support, manage, and direct the economic system. You don't have to love them—they're very difficult to love—but you'd better understand what's going on in today's world, because we are destroying things in ways that I think imperil the future of the country.

9

Corporate Restructuring: Perspectives of Organized Labor

DANIEL W. SHERRICK

Allow me to express the United Auto Workers Union's thanks for the opportunity to present the views of a trade union at a conference on the topic of the ethics of corporate restructuring. As I'm sure will come as no surprise, the UAW believes that it is a crime that the interests of workers, their families, and their communities are so systematically excluded from most of the debate on the question of corporate takeovers, mergers and acquisitions, and restructurings; unfortunately from the perspective of workers and their unions, that debate has thus far largely involved interests identified with shareholders, raiders, corporate managers, and financial institutions. While each of those constituencies is no doubt entitled to express its opinion on the debate, conspicuously absent from most of these debates is any analysis of the impact of the recent orgy of corporate restructuring on those whose very livelihood often hangs in the balance: the workers, their families, and their communities. The UAW is therefore particularly pleased to be invited to speak on this important subject.

Let me state at the outset that one of my central theses is that the dislocations, uncertainties, and disruptions caused by corporate restructurings have tremendous social costs. I would like to illustrate this by way of example. Recently, a large corporation defended a takeover attempt by engaging in various types of restructurings and recapitalizations. In part, this defensive strategy involved selling off some of the corporation's most profitable divisions and subsidiaries. One of these divisions is involved in the manufacture of aerospace equipment. The employees of that division are represented by the UAW. Within the space of a few days, I received calls from the local union president at each of this division's facilities. In each phone call, the story was the same: we've heard rumors in the plant that we're being sold. We're getting bombarded with questions from the membership about whether this is true and what will happen if we're sold. Will we keep the same contract? Will our jobs still be there? What will happen to our pension fund? Will the retiree health care benefits still be there? Should people eligible for retirement retire now or wait to see what happens?

Of course, the local management officials at each plant were almost as much in the dark about the situation as the workers. The labor relations staff—those with whom the local union has the most direct contact and on whom the local generally relies for information—were completely uninformed.

I described to the local leadership the legal rights of a work force unfortunate enough to be the victim of an asset sale. Legally, asset purchasers are not bound by the contractual promises made by the former owners; only a contractual obligation in the form of a successorship clause in the collective bargaining agreement will provide protection. Even so, successorship clauses are generally held to be enforceable only against the former owner—and generally will not create an obligation on the part of the asset purchaser to live up to the promises made by the former owner. Further, enforcing such obligations generally involves lengthy litigation.

Vested pension rights are protected to some extent by federal pension law, but workers in their fifties—not yet eligible for a livable pension benefit and facing a very difficult time finding alternative employment—are often devastated after having given twenty or twenty-five years of their adult lives to a single company. Finally, and of increasing importance in recent years, company-paid retiree health care benefits will sometimes be jeopardized by such transformations. Unions like the UAW and the Steelworkers have very aggressively pursued litigation to enforce retirees' rights to these important benefits with tremendous success. Still, such litigation is costly and time-consuming, always depends on the nature of the particular contractual promises made, and often results in a temporary lapse in coverage before the court finally orders the benefit continued. Finally, even if retiree health or successorship litigation is successful, the seller always has the option of filing for bankruptcy and evading these obligations altogether while the banks and other secured lenders fight over the shell corporation remaining. As you can imagine, hearing me describe these legal realities only increased the feeling of powerlessness which these employees were already feeling because of the lack of information regarding their particular situation.

Fortunately, in this situation, I was able to contact appropriate officials at corporate headquarters and demand that they release to the union those portions of any sales agreement dealing with employee matters. Their first response, of course, was that the negotiations with the buyer were still in progress and nothing could be released immediately. This response only served to increase the anxiety already being felt by the individuals involved. They knew their plant was being sold, but I couldn't tell them to whom, for what purpose, or with what result.

Finally, just a few days before the news hit the newspapers, I received a copy of some portions of the sales agreement from the attorneys for the company. As it turns out, those documents showed that the buyer was assuming all the contractual obligations of the seller, that the pension plan was being continued in effect, and that retiree health benefits would continue to be paid.

By the time we got that news, though, the membership was so disheartened, so distrustful, and so cynical that they never completely recovered. They had lived with months of uncertainty, months of the company's refusal to provide information, and months of knowing that tremendous change was in the works that might threaten their jobs. Most of the locals asked that I personally visit their plants to explain in person the provisions of the sales agreement to the local union leadership. When I went, I saw a group of people demoralized by uncertainty and powerlessness, and hostile to management—both the former and the future management.

Unlike many situations, the news I brought was good—the work force would retain its jobs, the collective bargaining agreement would remain in effect, and the pensions and retiree health benefits were protected. Even so, the employees were bitter, and it will take the new owners years to generate the kind of trust and mutual respect that had existed between management and labor in the plant prior to the transition.

The transition, of course, extracted other costs from the business. The new owner was significantly smaller than the former owner and was forced to borrow most of the money to finance the purchase. The new owner, therefore, will likely be forced to cut back on investments in new machinery and equipment and may attempt to cut back on labor costs in order to generate sufficient cash flow to service the massive debt incurred as a result of the purchase.

Let me hasten to add that the example I have just described represents the *best* situation from the workers' point of view. With increasing frequency, asset purchasers tear up collective bargaining agreements, break promises made by former owners, hire entirely new work forces, or close plants and generate wholesale layoffs. In those situations, of course, the union is forced to fight for the rights of the employees, often through litigation. In those situations, the social costs are even more apparent and devastating. My point in discussing the example I chose, though, was to point out that even in the smoothest transitions the relationship between the employer and employees is damaged, and the workers inevitably come to realize their own powerlessness. They see decisions being made that vitally affect their livelihood and their family, and—often after having worked loyally for a company for most of their lives—they are forced to stand by and watch while bankers, corporate adventurers, investment bankers, and corporate raiders decide to rape their employer for the sake of closing the deal.

The current frenzy of takeover and restructuring activity is also doing tremendous damage on a macroeconomic scale. Formerly healthy companies are cutting back on new investment, research and development, modernization efforts, and employee compensation at precisely the time when business in the United States is most in need of a long-term perspective. Scarce capital resources are being diverted from these useful functions to address extremely short-term concerns arising from the capital markets themselves. The threat of a takeover, apparently driving many investment and disinvestment decisions today, forces a company to allocate resources to maximize short-term earnings and prop up share prices. This effort necessarily diverts attention and resources from another, more important, consideration: the long-term health of the company as determined by its ability to compete in the product market by maintaining modern facilities, conducting research and development, and maintaining stable employee relations.

This continuing explosion of merger and acquisition activity represents a tremendous threat to the health and well-being of the U.S. economy. According to *Business Week* magazine, U.S. companies spent nearly $200 billion in 1986 on corporate mergers, acquisitions, and restructurings, more than three times the amount spent in 1983, just three years earlier. In 1984 and 1985 alone, total corporate debt rose by almost $400 billion. By the beginning of 1987, total corporate debt exceeded total corporate net worth by 12 percent. According to Felix Rohatyn, a partner at the Lazard Freres investment banking firm, since the 1982 recession the percentage of cash flow spent servicing debt has increased, making corporations far more vulnerable. During the 1976–79 recovery the cost averaged 27 percent of cash flow but since 1982 the cost has increased to 50 percent.

This tremendous increase in corporate debt will have several predictable results. It will siphon off a staggering portion of cash flow—cash which would otherwise be available to enable the corporation to make business decisions necessary to compete successfully in the product market. It will make the new debt-laden corporation extremely vulnerable to a decrease in sales caused by recession or routine market fluctuation. The important cushioning effect which equity served—by allowing a company to weather cyclical downturns without risking default on loans or pressure to make precipitous decisions to raise cash by selling off assets—is diminished whenever the debt-equity ratio is skewed by the excessive leveraging which accompanies so many of these corporate transformations.

I have already touched on some of the other social costs involved in the current wave of takeover activity: the increasing feeling of powerlessness which it causes in work forces unfortunate enough to be victims of such a transformation. I would also just like to mention briefly two other side effects of the current situation. First, the transaction costs of these activities alone are staggering. Investment bankers, attorneys, and lending institutions all charge a hefty fee for their services. Often these transaction costs alone will consume 5 percent or more of the total value of the business being sold, restructured, or recapitalized. Skewing things even further, these fees are often contingent on the transaction being consummated. The interests of the professionals charged with responsibility for monitoring the transaction is therefore often to push the transaction to consummation even if the stock price reaches levels disproportionate to the future earnings capability of the company involved.

Second, the presence of this takeover activity has had impact on the decision-making process of corporations potentially subject to the raider's pursuit. Increasingly, of course, all corporate management have come to see themselves as potential takeover targets. To defend against such potential takeovers, corporate management is forced to make decisions based not on the best long-term business strategy but rather on extremely short-term objectives such as propping up stock price, incurring new debt in order to become a less attractive target, or buying back the companies own stock in order to go private and prevent raiding activity. Absent from these strategies is any consideration for the long-term health of the company. When American businesses are facing perhaps their greatest challenge in terms of overseas competition, decisions are being made based on the chaotic machinations of the capital markets and not on the basis of maximizing the ability of American industry to compete in the increasingly efficient world market. I submit that this trend is doing irreparable damage to the U.S. economy and is crippling our ability to remain competitive in the world marketplace.

Apologists for the current wave of takeover activity tend to rely on the rhetoric of the free market to justify the current situation. The market for corporate control, they say, should be fluid in order to allow efficient managements to displace so-called "entrenched" management. Battles for corporate control, therefore, should be subject only to the constraints imposed by the capital markets themselves; tampering with those market forces will only introduce inefficiencies. This argument, I believe, ignores several crucial facts.

First, what we are seeing today is not merely an extension of previous behavior in the capital markets. Rather, we are seeing every day new heights reached in the ability to leverage companies, the creation of new financing instruments such as junk bonds backed only by speculative projected future earnings, and new levels of corporate adventurism and ego-driven battles for corporate control. The free market argument simply does not address the aberrational nature of the current climate. Presumably, capital markets have been largely subject to free market forces for most of this century. Why, then, have the past four years seen such an exponential rise in this activity, with its attendant debt and leverage explosion?

Second, the free market defense of the current situation ignores the macro-economic social costs of the current trend. These costs—worker powerlessness, skewed debt-equity ratios, unacceptable vulnerability to economic slump, transaction costs, and erosion of our industrial base—are staggering when considered in the aggregate. In any particular transaction, however, presumably rational businesspeople and bankers are deciding that—for that transaction alone—the economics make sense. Much like the corporation that makes a "rational" business decision to pollute a river rather than spend the money for decontaminating its by-products, the investment bankers—driven by a desire to close a deal—will decide that a leveraged buyout can be consummated despite the tremendous new debt burden that will result. As noted, the side effect of this new debt burden all too often prevents the company from making an adequate investment in tangible things such as new equipment. In both the pollution and the takeover examples, society is left with an unacceptable result: intolerable pollution or damaging the overall health of the economy caused by excessive leverage.

We learned gradually over the past two decades that pollution was an "externality," the cost of which business—in the absence of legislation—would simply pass on to society as a whole. Without legislation limiting a corporation's ability to impose its waste on our environment, business had no incentive to behave responsibly toward our physical environment. Similarly, the current wave of corporate transformations is imposing a tremendous social cost, a cost that is currently borne by society as a whole in the form of unemployment, lost competitiveness, dislocation, and the inability to modernize the corporate infrastructure. These social costs, I submit, must be "internalized."

The success of a takeover must be judged not solely by its consummation, its success in displacing current management, or the ability of the new company—by selling assets, skimping on new investment, and cutting wages—to pay off the senior debt over the five-year period after the transaction. Instead, the success or usefulness of takeover activity must also be judged by its overall impact on the economy, its effect on workers, their families, and their communities, and the continuing ability of the company to remain healthy in the long term. Judged by these standards, I submit, most corporate takeovers are dismal failures.

Before moving on, I would like to speculate briefly on some of the causes of the current wave of takeover activity. Obviously, the increasing willingness of regulatory authorities such as the SEC to remain passive in the face of this activity is a crucial factor. Also, the rapid creation of new financing instruments such as junk bonds and the increasing presence of large pools of capital willing to engage in speculative purchase of non-investment-grade paper is a necessary ingredient to the present situation. Perhaps most important, the fact that these transactions—whether consummated or not—cause disruptions and divert capital based on strategic responses such as greenmail obviously creates an irresistible temptation for adventurism designed not to acquire corporate control, but simply to force a defensive strategy and divert large amounts of money into the hands of the takeover artist and his or her investment bankers. As Felix Rohatyn explained to the Senate Committee on Banking, Housing and Urban Affairs, a symbiotic relationship has developed between arbitrageurs and raiders, both of whom are managing large pools of money and looking for rapid returns. The basic purpose of their relationship is to destabalize, sell and break-up large corporations.

Obviously, the current wave of takeover activity could not occur without the presence of these financial mechanisms and incentives. I would like to speculate, however, that there may be another dynamic occurring that is helping to fuel the current activity. The past ten years have seen incredibly rapid growth in sheer number of people employed by institutions such as investment banks, large law firms, and financial institutions. This new generation of financial and legal professionals was largely schooled in a liberal arts tradition during the affluent 1960s and 1970s. None has experienced an extended period of social dislocation or hardship such as the Great Depression, and few have experienced personal financial need. This new class of professional financial manipulators has come to view the capital markets of this country as their personal property. They seek to make their mark on the world, but not by inventing new production methods or successfully managing long-term business operations. Rather, they measure their success by the ability to manipulate ever-increasing amounts of capital, by the powerful thrill of closing a deal, or by successfully skimming off large amounts of money during the course of a transaction itself. The driving psychological force motivating this new class of financial manipulators is extremely short-term in perspective and is apparently willing to tolerate long-term damage both economic and social.

Before closing, I would like to comment briefly on the ethical implications of the current wave of takeovers and battles for corporate control. While I must admit that I am not really familiar with the scholarship now emerging on the topic of business ethics more generally, I assume that any analysis of ethical implications of business conduct must start with the observation that, as a rule, capitalism does not single out ethical conduct for reward. Rather, the market economy is designed to reward efficiency. To the extent that a business decision is driven by ethical—as opposed to purely efficient—considerations, then, that decision may introduce inefficiencies, and, presumably, should not be rewarded but rather discouraged by a pure market economy.

Now, it seems to me that there may be two ways in which business decisions which are ethics-driven may be justified in the ordinary situation. First, entry barriers to various business enterprises create a tolerance for business decisions that are not pure efficiency-driven. Thus, the manager of a business may make an ethics-based decision not to cut off the health care benefits of a widowed spouse of a longtime employee without fear that that decision alone will create the opportunity for a competitor to usurp the market position of the business. Of course, this tolerance for "inefficiencies" has its limits, which depend on various market factors. But, in the ordinary conduct of a long-term business, the basic goodwill of the individual managers is allowed some room to express itself.

Second, again in the context of a long-term relatively stable business environment, the ethical decision may also be the efficient decision. The company that treats its employees, their families, and their communities with responsibility and respect may create loyalty, goodwill, and mutual respect, which will pay for itself.

Unfortunately, it seems to me that neither of these processes is really applicable to the takeover environment. In that environment, there are essentially no entry barriers—anyone with enough cash can instantly become an equal player. Also, as I have already discussed, long-term considerations such as creation of loyalty or goodwill are simply absent. Even the financial institution—which judges a proposed transaction by analyzing whether the various layers of debt can be serviced over a relatively short period—is unlikely to be persuaded much by a claim that the raider will make ethical decisions during or after the transaction, and thereby generate loyalty and goodwill. Certainly, for the raider, for the incumbent management, and for the shareholder, the presence or absence of long-term loyalty and goodwill is simply not an issue. All those players make decisions based on a simple calculus of share price, potential changes in share price, potential future earnings, and the short-term gains that could be realized by restructuring the company by breaking it up and selling it piecemeal.

Of the two motivations or justifications for ethical business behavior that I have been able to identify, therefore, it seems that neither is likely to influence the decision-making process of the players in the takeover game. It seems, therefore, that no amount of injection of ethics into the debate surrounding this issue will have an appreciable impact on the current rate at which this destructive activity is occurring.

Of course, when individuals allow their behavior to continue to have socially damaging consequences, and education or injection of ethical standards alone does not seem likely to alter that course of behavior, the only way to prevent such socially damaging behavior is legislation. As we learned with pollution fifteen or twenty years ago, the only way to force businesses to take into account the social costs of their behavior—and to internalize the social costs of business decision making—is to prohibit the most abusive practices or make them so costly as to discourage their continuation by legislation.

There are currently several legislative initiatives pending to regulate the take-over process. Quite properly, some of these directly address the socially dislo-cating results that such activity often entails. The UAW supports these initiatives to curb such abuses and believes that the health and well-being of American society and American industry must be protected from the excesses of the current wave of takeover activity.

The Economics and Ethics of Adjusting to a New Competitive Environment: Mergers and Takeovers

DAVID T. SCHEFFMAN

The idea of a two-day conference on the Ethics of Organizational Transformation is fascinating. However, it seems to me that a more appropriate topic might have been: "The Ethics of Adjusting to a New Competitive Environment." Let me explain.

Focusing on the adverse circumstances that sometimes accompany organizational transformations makes it easy to mistake their real cause. Mergers, takeovers, and restructurings do not arise in a vacuum. These business decisions, like others, arise from businesses' need to respond to changes in their competitive environment.

Let me begin by placing recent merger and acquisition activity in an economic and historical context. First, remember that mergers and acquisitions are simply two of many types of transactions by which assets are bought and sold in our economy. Companies buy new and used machinery and other capital equipment, and they hire and fire employees and managers. Sometimes they find it more profitable to buy a whole company rather than putting the pieces together themselves. Mergers and acquisitions, then, are just one method by which corporate assets are acquired by those who value them most highly and can put them to the best use. As economic columnist Robert Samuelson points out, "Anything that shifts investment to more profitable uses—or spurs efficiency—improves our collective welfare."[1] Often the most efficient way—and sometimes the only way—to spur such socially beneficial shifts is by a merger or takeover.

To understand what is driving the recent activity in corporate transformations, recall what has been happening over the past twenty years in our economy. If we were to summarize the American economy over that period in one word, that would would be *change*. We have experienced double-digit inflation, astronomical interest rates, and their painful cure. Oil prices skyrocketed and crashed. A great technological revolution began and is continuing—in computers, telecommunications, bioengineering, and many other areas. Americans have moved to the Sun Belt and have grown older. Our industries have become more exposed to foreign competition than ever before. Finally, much of the capital and management infrastructure of the American economy has been replaced or modified. And some of our largest industries are involved in a basic rethinking of how to produce and sell their products. (The automobile industry is one prominent example.) All these changes in our economy have produced a dramatic transformation of the competitive environment we face. In a fundamental sense, the merger and acquisition activity we have seen in recent years is not a cause of change or instability in our economy. Rather, mergers and acquisitions are one of our economy's reactions to the changing competitive environment.

Now, what about the extent of merger and acquisition activity in recent years? Filings of mergers and acquisitions with the Federal Trade Commission (FTC) under the Hart Scott Rodino Act have been up significantly in the past few years. However, the Hart Scott Rodino Act has only been in force since 1977. The number of mergers, although up in recent years, is not high relative to some earlier periods in this century. Looking at a longer history of merger activity gives us a different picture. For example, *Mergerstat* reports about 2,500 transactions in 1985, and about 3,400 transactions in 1986. (To give some perspective to these transaction numbers, there are over 1 million corporations with a net asset value over $500,000 in our economy.) The average of *Mergerstat*-reported transactions for the period 1968–86 was 3,400, about the same number as in 1986. And there were 6,100 transactions in 1969—almost two and one-half times the number in 1985—and almost twice as much as the tax law change-driven merger activity in 1986. Prior to the 1960s we find that the major merger waves in our economy occurred at the turn of the century and in the 1920s. Merger activity in those periods dwarfs the present period.

Although we are not near record numbers in merger activity, what is unusual about the mergers and acquisitions of the mid- to late 1980s is the size and visibility of some of the transactions, particularly hostile takeovers. Although much ink has been spilled on hostile takeovers, W. T. Grimm & Company's statistics show that in 1986, a record year, forty were attempted, and only fifteen were successful. Consider now the size of some of the recent mergers and takeovers, and how that relates to changing economic conditions. Some of the recent mergers have been very large, even accounting for the fact that the dollar size of our economy has grown more than five times in the past twenty years. But viewed in terms of the world economy, we get a different perspective—one that is relevant, given that our economy is increasingly integrated into a very competitive world economy. Although the Chevron/Gulf Oil merger was one of the largest in history, keep in mind that Saudi Arabia is now the largest independent player in the world oil market—and Saudi Arabia has proven oil reserves about fifty times larger than those of Chevron and Gulf. In considering the automobile industry, remember that during the 1980s Japan has been the largest producer of automobiles in the world. U.S. producers, more than ever before, are competing in a market larger than the United States alone, and one response has been mergers that have resulted in larger U.S. producers.

But the increasing importance of foreign competitors is but one of the driving forces behind mergers and acquisitions. There are many others. For example, about 25 percent of the mergers during 1982–84 took place in recently deregulated industries.[2] Airlines are perhaps the best-known example. Before 1979, the government was the manager of the airline cartel, setting prices and preventing entry. With deregulation, the airlines had to compete—a new environment for them. Texas Air was an obscure intrastate carrier at the time of deregulation. As an intrastate carrier it operated in a nonregulated environment. This experience in a competitive environment gave it an advantage when interstate airlines were deregulated. Through merger, Texas Air was able to transfer this knowledge and experience to other air carriers, such as Continental.

Employment in the airline industry is up—but wage levels have fallen. But this is not caused by mergers and takeovers. Rather, the increased competition resulting from deregulation has caused the carriers to cut fares, so that they can no longer afford the inefficiencies formerly tolerated under regulation. And American consumers have been the beneficiaries. It has been estimated that consumers save about $10 billion a year from the lower fares arising from deregulation.

Deregulation is also behind a good deal of the merger and acquisition activity in the petroleum, natural gas, transportation, insurance, and financial industries. As with airlines, we have seen the effects of deregulation: some consolidation, much more competition, and significantly lower prices.

Technological change has also been an important factor behind other mergers and acquisitions. Consider, for example, the changes in ownership and management of the three major television networks, which have recently received a lot of attention. The advent of satellites and cable television has dramatically increased the competitive pressures faced by the major networks. It is hardly surprising that now the networks pay closer attention to the bottom line. They are facing an evolving competitive environment in which they are becoming simply three players among many.

Therefore, there have been a number of basic changes in our economy that have transformed our competitive environment. Foreign competition, deregulation, and technological change are just three. The change in competitive conditions has stimulated mergers and takeovers. Now, what does the evidence show about the efficiency of the mergers and takeovers that have occurred? Have they facilitated our adjustment to changed conditions and benefited our economy?

As I have explained, mergers, takeovers, and restructurings are but three of many reactions of businesses to changed competitive conditions. But some would have us believe that these reactions to competitive change are like a fever that arises from what they would term the disease of competitive change. And, like the treatment of a fever, they would have us enact policies they would characterize as analogous to giving the patient a rest and aspirin—by increasing the regulation of corporate transformations. But there are important economic and ethical reasons why such policies should not be adopted. Even if we liken competitive change to a disease (rather than an expansion of opportunities), it is not a disease that will just go away with time like a cold. The well-being of our whole economy is tied to our productivity. If we restrict businesses' ability to make changes that improve productivity, all of us lose from a less efficient, less competitive economy. There is solid evidence that mergers and takeovers have resulted in a more efficient economy.

There have been a number of takeovers or attempted takeovers that have stimulated major corporate restructurings, and, as a result, have dramatically increased the value of the affected corporate assets. I have already discussed a few examples of industries in which mergers and takeovers have increased competitiveness and benefited consumers and our economy. And sometimes a takeover or attempted takeover has shown that the value of a particular corporation is much larger if it is broken up. What is happening in these transactions is that the corporation, prior to takeover, was not structured to operate efficiently in the current competitive environment.

How can that happen? Corporations can become highly bureaucratic with entrenched management. Necessary changes can become difficult to make without substantial pressure from the outside. H. Ross Perot's dialogue in 1987 with General Motors is a vivid example. Sometimes that pressure takes the form of a hostile takeover, where a raider tries to go around the management to make a deal directly with the shareholders. Mergers and acquisitions are one method by which corporate management is changed, disciplined, or given guidance. It is not surprising that one of the groups most vocal in its condemnation of takeovers is current managers—their jobs are often at stake.

Besides the examples in the financial press, there is a great deal of scientific evidence bearing on the issue of the efficiency of mergers and takeovers. There has probably been no topic more examined in recent years by economists. The Council of Economic Advisors summarized the evidence in 1985 and concluded: "There is powerful evidence that takeovers as a group are beneficial."[3] And the evidence for mergers is the same. Mergers and takeovers can improve efficiency, transfer scarce resources to higher valued uses, and stimulate effective corporate management. They can also help firms to recapitalize so that their financial structures are more in line with prevailing market conditions.

Exhaustive studies using stock market evidence find that the value of target firms' stock rises substantially as a result of takeovers. Michael Jensen and Richard Ruback surveyed thirteen studies examining the effects of mergers and tender offers which occurred during the 1960s and 1970s.[4] These studies indicate that during this time period the shareholders of successfully acquired target firms earned premiums which ranged from 16 to 30 percent.

A more recent study written by the Office of the Chief Economist (OCE) of the Securities and Exchange Commission studied all tender offers, including over-the-counter targets, which occurred between January 1981 and December 1984.[5] The OCE study found that the shareholders of the 225 successfully acquired targets studied earned premiums of 52.3 percent. The stock market studies have also indicated that the shareholders of bidding firms have also gained from tender offers, although these gains are much smaller than those earned by target firms' shareholders. Gregg Jarrell and Annette Poulsen studied 663 successful tender offers which occurred during the period from 1962 through 1985.[6] Over this period, bidders realized small, but statistically significant gains of approximately 2 percent. Since the acquiring firms are, on average, four to five times larger than the target firms, this smaller gain translates into a 8 to 10 percent average return on the assets of the target firms accruing to the bidding firms.

These percentage increases in shareholder returns represent tremendous increases in real wealth in the economy. According to a recent study by SEC Commissioner Joseph Grundfest and his associate Bernard Black, between 1981 and 1986 shareholder wealth increased due to takeover activity by a minimum of $167 billion measured in nominal dollars, $184 billion measured in constant 1987 dollars, and $209 billion based on the assumption that gains are reinvested at the three-month T-bill rate.[7] Moreover, these numbers actually underestimate the true shareholder gains from takeovers because they do not include increases in value attributable to changes in behavior and firm structure that result from real or perceived takeover threats. Grundfest and Black believe that these gains may well exceed the directly observable gains.

Conversely, there is substantial evidence that target shareholders lose significantly when their managers defeat tender offers. Studies by Paul Asquith, Michael Bradley, and Jarrell find that when target managers successfully defeat a tender offer, target shareholders suffer losses of 15 to 52 percent.[8]

What about the effect of mergers and takeovers on jobs? Opponents of takeovers often assert that the benefits accruing to target shareholders in the form of high premiums come largely at the expense of labor. Andrei Shleifer and Lawrence Summers have recently articulated this view in a rigorous theory focusing on implicit long-term contracts between labor and incumbent (target) management.[9] Raiders are viewed as exploiting these implicit contracts by using the threat of bankruptcy and other pressure tactics to force significant wage concessions and by firing employees who had previously been promised lifetime employment by the now displaced target management. This activity, in theory, can be socially inefficient because it can ruin the market for these implicit long-run labor contracts, and force labor and management to use less efficient contracting devices. As examples of this type of labor exploitation, Shleifer and Summers refer to the takeovers by Frank Lorenzo in the airline industry.

Despite the popularity of the view that takeovers adversely affect wages and employment, the "labor exploitation" theory has not been widely tested, and very little empirical evidence of the effects of takeovers on labor exists. Nevertheless, in one recent study, Charles Brown and James Medoff present some statistical evidence on the effects on wages and employment of acquisitions that took place in Michigan, and their results tend to refute this theory.[10] They find, on average, that both wages and employment rise for firms involved in acquisitions. They conclude that "the common perception of acquisitions providing the occasion to slash wages and/or employment finds little support" from their data. While these results are not consistent with the Shleifer/Summers theory, the experience of firms in Michigan is not necessarily indicative of the United States as a whole. For example, Brown and Medoff's sample contains few large mergers. Moreover, Brown and Medoff do not distinguish between friendly and hostile acquisitions, so it is not clear if they are studying the same phenomena that the Shleifer/Summers theory is describing.

Glenn Yago and Gelvin Stevenson recently examined the effects of acquisitions in New Jersey.[11] They found that less than 2 percent of the total jobs lost from plant closings in New Jersey were associated with corporate acquisitions. Of course, the fact that only a small percentage of layoffs were associated with takeovers does not imply that only a small percentage of takeovers were associated with layoffs. Nevertheless, Yago and Stevenson conclude that there "is no evidence that the change in ownership had anything to do with these reductions in employment." As with Brown and Medoff, Yago and Stevenson do not distinguish between hostile and friendly takeovers, and much of their discussion of the positive effects of acquisitions on wages and employment appears to be based on examples of friendly acquisitions.

So the evidence indicates that mergers and takeovers benefit shareholders, increase efficiency, and do not, on net, result in lost jobs. So why should we worry about mergers and takeovers? One reason would be if a merger results in the remaining producers in an industry being sufficiently shielded from competition that they can raise prices to the detriment of the economy—that merger is illegal under the antitrust laws. The job of the FTC and Department of Justice is to block such mergers.

Mergers of significant size must be reported to the government prior to their consummation. We investigate all mergers that raise a potential competitive problem. If our examination of competitive conditions and efficiencies indicates that a merger will make the industry less competitive, the commission or the Department of Justice act to see that the merger does not proceed. The antitrust authorities are not the only regulators of merger activity in our economy. The Securities and Exchange Commission, the states, and the courts all have a significant regulatory presence.[12]

But antitrust and securities regulation problems are not the main source of public concerns about mergers and acquisitions. The real political issue is that mergers and takeovers can result in politically visible changes in the affected corporations. Jobs can be lost in particular plants in particular localities in particular congressional districts. Indeed, plants are sometimes closed. Costs are imposed on workers and managers. Why are these costs worth it? Why not just avoid these costs by stopping mergers and takeovers? One reason is that shareholders of acquired companies would lose. The evidence on this is beyond dispute.[13] But why should government policy be directed at protecting the shareholders who gain from takeovers and not the managers and workers who may lose? It is important to recognize that the maximization of shareholder wealth is not just an end in itself. The maximization of shareholder wealth is important because it indicates that the underlying corporate assets are employed in their most valuable, most efficient uses. By forcing management to employ corporate assets efficiently, takeovers not only benefit shareholders, but also benefit consumers and the economy as a whole. The efficient management of society's resources insures that the real cost of the goods and services purchased by consumers is as low as possible. In this sense, competition in capital markets for the control of corporate assets, like competition in product markets, acts to maximize consumer welfare. Moreover, the shareholders that gain directly from takeovers do not merely represent a small number of very wealthy investors. Millions of small investors of all social ranks invest in publicly traded firms; furthermore, many individuals who have never purchased a share of stock have much of their wealth tied to stock investments. Both blue-collar laborers and corporate executives who have money invested in a pension fund or a life insurance policy are indirect investors in the stock market.

We do not hear managers arguing that takeovers are bad because they might lose their jobs, however. Rather, the rhetoric is usually about sacrificing long-term objectives for the short-term bottom line. If only, they tell us, they could stop worrying about corporate raiders, they could get about the business of making their companies more competitive. What is conveniently overlooked in the rhetoric is the possibility that the current managers may not be the right ones for the current competitive environment. Or that their corporate plan may no longer be competitive. These possibilities have been shown to be realities in a number of the takeovers and attempted takeovers in recent years.

I do not mean to imply that managers that need to be replaced are necessarily bad managers. Management expertise is often specific to particular competitive conditions. For example, some managers are good at marketing products in an environment in which competitors sell products of similar quality. But they may not always be good at changing their company's production process to confront the challenge of new competitors who produce superior quality products. This, in my opinion, is one of the biggest problems U.S. industries have had in adjusting to increased foreign competition—particularly from the Japanese. Remember, one of the biggest books of recent years was *In Search of Excellence*, whose theme was that American firms need to focus more on providing quality products and service to their customers.

Managers are not the only people affected by mergers and takeovers—as I have already noted, employees are also affected. Sometimes a merger or takeover results in lower wages or lost jobs. Adjusting to a more competitive environment is always painful. But we will not get more competitive by resisting making the changes necessary to compete. And sometimes, to get more competitive, workers have to change, or plants have to move. And when that happens, consumers and the whole economy gains.

Of course, not all mergers and takeovers will turn out to be successful. As with any market activity—the introduction of new products, research and development, investments in capital—not all mergers and takeovers will attain the objectives and benefits contemplated. But the market, although it will make mistakes, is the proven best picker of winners. And it never shelters losers for long.

Permit me an analogy that I think illustrates the process of competitive change. Not too many years ago, the United States was so dominant in basketball that it could almost walk through the Olympic competition. But in recent years other countries have caught up. And worse yet, we lost to the Russians. No one suggested the way to remain competitive would be to shelter our players from foreign or domestic competition, and to go on as if nothing had changed. Instead, we scheduled foreign teams more often. We had tougher tryouts, and looked even harder for the best players and coaches. We paid more attention to how effective the team would be, rather than how talented the individual players were. And we trained longer and more intensively. Those are costs we have had to bear to remain competitive. The result is that we play better basketball in international competition. And we still usually win. We will never again win as easily as in the past. That is as true in automobiles and computer chips as it is in basketball. But, as would have happened in basketball, if we do not allow the necessary adjustments to take place, other countries will pass us by.

We rely on private voluntary participation in athletics and in the U.S. Olympic program to insure that we remain as competitive as possible in basketball and other Olympic sports. Who do we rely on to insure that mergers and acquisitions are increasing our competitiveness and the well-being of consumers? The antitrust laws, enforced by the FTC and Department of Justice, insure that anticompetitive mergers are not allowed to proceed. But, as in basketball, our reliance on free markets is the fundamental basis of our national strength. The biggest economic advantage we have over our foreign competitors is not our natural resources or work force. Rather, it lies in our ability to adapt and change in response to changes in the world economy, because free markets adapt most quickly and efficiently to changing competitive circumstances. Our record over the past few years, in terms of growth of output and employment and the prices paid by consumers, is a record to be envied by all other countries. And this is partly because we have allowed our markets to adjust to new competitive realities.

So mergers, takeovers, and restructurings are not a fever arising from the disease of changed competitive conditions—they are part of the medicine for dealing with the so-called disease. And if we do not take the medicine, the health of our economy will be weakened.

Now let me explore (as a nonexpert) what I see as some of the important ethical issues that arise from the way society deals with these calls for increased government involvement in mergers, takeovers, and restructurings. No system of ethics is ever developed in a vacuum, and so the ethics governing how society deals with mergers, takeovers, and restructurings will reflect wider ethical principles in society as a whole.

I presume that there is broad agreement that the private use of coercion to obtain someone else's property is theft. However, for some reason, it has apparently now become accepted in our society that it is ethical, sometimes even noble, for one group to use the coercive power of the government, in essence, to steal the property of another group. And one of the most common forms of this activity these days is to get the government to shelter you from the winds of competitive change by making other groups bear those costs.

Let me try to make as clear as I can what I think is the central ethical issue here. It is certainly ethical for society to consider helping displaced workers. Where the important ethical issue arises is in the sort of relief that society provides and who pays for it. The most commonly proposed types of relief advocated for the dislocations arising from mergers, takeovers, and restructurings would impose the costs directly on the shareholders of the firms involved. For example, restrictions on takeovers enacted by either managements of individual firms or by statute by the federal and state governments have been shown to reduce the value of the shares of companies that might be takeover targets by billions of dollars. And prevent plant closings or requiring substantial advance notice of closings will have the same effect.

Consider the following hypothetical situation. Shareholders buy into a public company in 1985. For the next two years, theft by the managers and workers becomes widespread. The value of the company's stock plummets. Then, a so-called raider sees an opportunity to make money by taking over the firm and replacing those managers and workers who are the cause of the firm's problems. He offers to buy stock from the shareholders at a price above the depressed current price. Should society bail out the thieving managers and workers? Of course not. Society as a whole should not use its resources to insulate such managers and workers from the market's punishment for their misdeeds. And it would be particularly inappropriate to make the shareholders pay the costs of keeping bad managers and workers in place—the shareholders, after all, have already paid for the bad managers' and workers' actions through the depressed value of the company's stock.

Thieving managers and workers are not usually the cause of poor performance. So now consider a different hypothetical situation. The managers and workers have gotten a little fat and lazy because the competitive environment has been relaxed. Now there is a change in the competitive environment, and the firm begins to lose market share. Again, the shareholders of the firm lose, as the increasingly poor earnings reports are reflected in the price of the company's stock. Then, a raider sees an opportunity to cut fat and improve the firm's performance. And the fat-cutting costs some managers and workers their jobs. Should society do something to help them? Maybe. But should we make the shareholders, who have already paid for the firm's worsened performance through the depressed price of the company stock, pay more? Would that be fair? I cannot see how.

But the response of managers who are potential targets of takeovers has been to run to federal and state governments to ask for legal protection against take-overs they find to be hostile—to them. In essence, they want the government to make their shareholders pay more than they have already paid for the managers' failings.

Let me conclude with some general questions about the ethical issues I see here. Why is it fair to protect inefficient firms and managers at the expense of their shareholders? Especially since the shareholders have already paid for the inefficiency in the depressed value of their investment. And why is it fair for all of us to bear the costs of a less competitive economy? Why is there so little criticism of federal and state legislators who pass laws that protect entrenched management? Economics columnist Robert Samuelson points out, "The assumption is that a company's existing management has an inalienable right to control its destiny. Why?"[14] Well, I have an answer to Robert Samuelson's query—it is now considered ethical in our society for one group to go to the government and receive benefits extracted from another group, almost independent of the ethical merits of such a transfer. It comes down to who has the political power, and who is most clever in clothing their special interests in public interest rhetoric. But shareholders are much less politically visible than displaced workers and managers. More important, consumers who as a group benefit significantly from efficient mergers and takeovers, do not have much of a voice in the rhetoric about the perils of takeovers.

Managers threatened by takeovers are not the worst of the special interest pleaders. They are just among the newest in an increasingly long line of those who openly seek to use the government to benefit themselves at the expense of the public at large. Is it business ethics that is the main ethical problem in our society? I think not. I suggest that if we really want to understand the important ethical problems in our society, then we should look to an ethical climate that condones using the government for what often amounts to theft.

NOTES

The opinions expressed are those of Dr. Scheffman, not necessarily those of the Federal Trade Commission or individual commissioners. The author thanks Larry Schumann for helpful comments.

1. Robert Samuelson,"Healthy Hostility," *Washington Post*, May 1, 1985, p. F6; Samuelson, "A Ghastly Antitakeover Idea," *Washington Post*, December 23, 1987, p. F1.
2. U.S. Council of Economic Advisors, *Economic Report of the President, 1985*, pp. 194–95.
3. Ibid., 198–99.

4. Michael Jensen and Richard Ruback, "The Market For Corporate Control," *Journal of Financial Economics* 11 (1983), 5–50.

5. Office of the Chief Economist, Securities and Exchange Commission, *The Economics of Any-or-All, Partial, and Two-Tier Tender Offers*, 1985.

6. Gregg Jarrell and Annette Poulsen, "Bidder Returns," Securities and Exchange Commission working paper, 1987.

7. Joseph A. Grundfest and Bernard S. Black, Securities and Exchange Commission, *Stock Market Profits from Takeover Activity Between 1981 and 1986: $167 Billion is a Lot of Money*, (Washington, D.C.: U.S. Government Printing Office, 1987).

8. Paul Asquith, "Merger Bids, Uncertainty, and Stockholder Returns," *Journal of Financial Economics* 11 (April 1983): 51–83; Michael Bradley, Anand Desai, and E. Han Kim, "The Rationale Behind Interfirm Tender Offers: Information or Synergy?" *Journal of Financial Economics* 11 (April 1983): 183–206; and Gregg Jarrell, "The Wealth Effects of Litigation by Targets: Do Interests Diverge in a Merge?" *Journal of Law and Economics* 28 (April 1985): 131–77. For a further discussion of these papers and the issue of managerial opposition to takeovers, see Frank H. Easterbrook and Gregg Jarrell, "Do Targets Gain From Defeating Tender Offers?" *New York University Law Review* (May 1984).

9. Andrei Shleifer and Lawrence Summers, "Hostile Takeovers as Breaches of Trust," National Bureau of Economic Research, presented at the Conference on the Economic Effects of Mergers and Acquisitions, Key Largo, Fla., February 1987.

10. Charles Brown and James Medoff, "The Impact of Firm Acquisitions on Labor," National Bureau of Economic Research, presented at the Conference on the Economic Effects of Mergers and Acquisitions, February 1987.

11. Glenn Yago and Gelvin Stevenson, "Mergers and Acquisitions in the New Jersey Economy" (Washington, D.C.: Securities Industry Association, 1986).

12. And the economic evidence indicates that those regulations often impose substantial costs on merger and takeover activity. For example, a recent FTC report examining the effects of takeover regulations passed in New York in 1985 found that its sample of ninety-four firms studied suffered an average decline in value of approximately 1 percent as a result of the regulations (Paul Schumann, "State Regulation of Takeovers and Shareholder Wealth: The Effects of New York's 1985 Takeover Statutes" [Washington, D.C.: Federal Trade Commission, Bureau of Economics, 1987]).

13. See Michael Jensen and Richard Ruback, "The Market for Corporate Control: The Scientific Evidence," *Journal of Financial Economics* 11 (1983): 5–50, and Gregg Jarrell, James Brickley, and Jeffrey Netter, "The Market for Corporate Control: Evidence since 1980," *Journal of Law Economics* 28 (April 1985): 131–77.

14. Robert Samuelson, "Boesky: Takeover Taint?" *Washington Post*, November 26, 1986, p. B2.

11

Takeover Reform: A View from Congress

EDWARD J. MARKEY

I am pleased to be able to discuss tender offer reform and some of the other finance and securities issues that will face us during the 100th Congress.

I am Chairman of the House Subcommittee on Telecommunications and Finance, and our subcommittee has primary jurisdiction over the Federal Communications Commission, on the one hand, and the Securities and Exchange Commission, on the other. Our jurisdiction runs from "fairness" over the airwaves, to "fairness" on Wall Street. Thus, on one side of our jurisdiction, we hold hearings on "dial-a-porn," while on the other side, we investigate Dennis Levine's calls to his stockbroker, or as Levine used to call it, "Dialing for Dollars."

These are remarkably challenging times in the history of our capital and securities markets. First, Wall Street right now is coping with the biggest spate of scandals in its history. Through it all, the integrity of and confidence in our markets must somehow be safeguarded. The small American investors remain the lifeblood of our market system. If they lose confidence in our markets, they take pension funds, mutual funds, and IRA investments with them. Our markets need these strong domestic sources of investment, and our subcommittee will do everything within its power to preserve market integrity and investor confidence.

Second, our economy is in the midst of a takeover binge that is unprecedented in our history. These takeovers, both the hostile kind from the outside, and the leveraged buyouts from the inside, have been fueled by a five-year-old bull market and by historically high levels of junk-bond-based corporate debt.

Third, the globalization of our securities markets has become a reality. Twenty-four-hour tracking is commonplace along the Tokyo-London-New York belt. As a result, new challenges are presented in protecting the interests of U.S. investors abroad and in monitoring and assessing the impact of foreign investment in U.S. markets.

Fourth, new trading techniques, such as program trading, and new trading instruments are being developed at an astonishing pace. As a result, our subcommittee, as overseer of the securities markets, must separate the wheat from the chaff by determining whether any of these innovative techniques or instruments present intolerable risks to our markets.

Fifth, incident to globalization, the 1980s have seen U.S. commercial banks head offshore to purchase substantial interests in foreign securities firms. Through those firms, banking interests engage in trading and underwriting activities from which they are barred in the United States by the Glass-Steagall Act. I am concerned that this fifty-four-year-old law, fashioned in different times and not designed for a world economy, might cause a nonstrategic outflow of U.S. dollars abroad and inhibit the growth of diversified financial services in the United States to the detriment of both our international competitiveness and, ultimately, our consumers.

I have already commenced a series of hearings on this issue. So far, we have heard from Alan Greenspan, Chairman of the Federal Reserve Board; David Ruder, Chairman of the Securities and Exchange Commission (SEC); William Seidman, Chairman of the Federal Deposit Insurance Corporation (FDIC); and Robert Clarke, the Comptroller of the Currency. We also heard from representatives of the commercial banking and securities industries.

One of the problems with any discussion of Glass-Steagall is that it elicits strong emotions from all sides, and this sometimes inhibits progress in the debate. The questions typically posed are emotionally charged and predict dire consequences if the wrong turn is taken. For example, by preserving the Glass-Steagall barriers, are we really presiding over the demise of the banking industry and ceding America's position of prominence in the world's capital markets? Conversely, by acting to lift restrictions on securities activities by banks, will we really be inviting a second Great Depression?

In order to quiet the Cassandras, I have set out a very precise list of questions regarding the current roles and practices of, and interrelationships between, the banking and securities industries. The questions I have posed leave no room for fluff or posturing. I requested the Chairmen of the Federal Reserve Board, the SEC, and the FDIC, along with Comptroller Clarke and Treasury Secretary Baker, to respond to these questions and to provide a blueprint for reform of our financial services industry. These responses will give us a basis for determining whether change is required and, if so, what form that change should take.

My principal goals in this area will be to further the interests of the domestic consumers, both individuals and corporations, who buy the products generated by our financial services industry and, second, to enhance our nation's international competitiveness. But I feel strongly that these goals must be accomplished at no expense to the overall integrity of our financial system.

As you can see, the subcommittee is at the vortex of the major and constantly changing financial issues of our day. These are not esoteric issues of mere academic interest. Every one of them has significant long-term implications for our economy, and immediate implications for the lives and the personal economies of our people.

For example, one of the most heralded events of recent months has been the dramatic decline in the Dow Jones Industrial Average. On August 25, 1987, the Dow hit a record level—2722. Since that time, the Dow has fallen more than 350 points to the 2350 level, and, very significantly, more than 275 of those points were lost during the past nine trading days.

On October 6, 1987, the Dow set a record loss for one day—down 91 1/2 points. This staggering loss, however, is already old news, because on Wednesday of this week the Dow dropped 95 1/2 points to set still another record. Such instability in our securities markets is of critical importance to our subcommittee and, in the interest of the investing public, we need to come to grips quickly with this increasing volatility.

Therefore, the day after last week's ninety-one-point drop, I wrote a letter to the Chairman of the SEC. I asked the commission to undertake a study of the factors that caused that decline, and to assess the market's current degree of stability.

It seems that whenever we experience a severe downdraft in the market, the papers are awash the next day with comments from brokers, market technicians, and economists suggesting that the previous day's "correction" was "technical," or that it was an overreaction of a jittery market to fears of higher domestic inflation or West German interest rate increases. Others point out that even a ninety-one-point drop is not significant in overall percentage terms because the Dow is at its highest levels in history. Last week every broker or market analyst with a pocket calculator couldn't wait to punch out the statistic that a ninety-one-point drop was only 3.5 percent of the Dow whereas on Black Tuesday in 1929, the Dow lost a full 12 percent of its value.

Well, who's kidding whom? As the Dow has reached its highest trading levels in history, it has begun to suffer increased intraday and end-of-day volatility. Rises and falls of 40, 50, 60, and now even 80 and 90 points are not uncommon. And my concern for maintaining stability in our securities markets is not met merely because the Dow has lost, in percentage terms, less than the value it lost on Black Tuesday. That should not be our yardstick! Indeed, I believe that in absolute terms, the volatility in the market is increasingly so great that the sheer magnitude of these numbers, coupled with the market's ever-increasing velocity as a result of program trading, could trigger an investor response that could, in turn, create a near free-fall situation.[1] As I told the Chairman of the SEC, "In such a situation, investors will hardly be assuaged by the refrain of market apologists who urge that the initial stages of the decline were modest in percentage terms.''

America's securities markets have been called the fairest, most liquid, and most efficient in the world. I want to ensure that they stay that way. Therefore, whenever I see factors at work that could impair the integrity of those markets, our subcommittee will scrutinize those factors to the nth degree.

For example, during this summer, the subcommittee held hearings on virtually all aspects of program trading, including index trading and risk arbitrage. We heard from the foremost experts in the United States on these innovative new trading techniques. Almost to the person, they assured the subcommittee that computer-generated index trading and risk arbitrage do not contribute to market volatility and do not impair the market's integrity. Well, after assessing all of that testimony, I frankly remain unconvinced that program trading might not some day play an important role in a rapid and uncontrolled market decline. Our securities markets are too precious to be allowed to run on automatic pilot, and I intend to push and probe every step of the way to make sure that their integrity is protected.

My concerns about the stability of our markets have also led me to question the potential effects on those markets of foreign investment. Might sudden declines in particular foreign markets precipitate similar declines in our own markets?

In the last five years, foreign investment in the United States has doubled— to $850 billion. As a result, more and more activity affecting the structural integrity of our markets falls outside of our supervision and control.

For example, the Tokyo stock market is even more "go-go" than our own. In Japan, stocks are selling at an average of seventy-five to eighty times earnings, compared with twenty times earnings for companies on the New York Stock Exchange. Recently the Nikkei average—the Tokyo Exchange's equivalent of our Dow—crossed the 27,000 barrier for the first time.

Earlier this year, Nippon Tel & Tel issued a new offering on the Tokyo Exchange at *$7,775* a *share*. Its recent price was over *$20,000* a *share*, more than 250 times earnings. At that price, that company's value exceeds that of the entire West German stock market.

The interrelationship among world markets led me to wonder if, for example, the Tokyo market were to plunge from those dizzying heights, would the foreign interest in American stocks also crash? I take some solace from the fact that the Tokyo market has not joined the Dow in this most recent decline, but due to heavy Japanese investment in the United States, I am not certain that the converse would be true. Therefore, during the coming months we will be examining the potential impact of foreign investment on our U.S. markets.

Amid this whirlwind of activity, the principal focus of my subcommittee's attention during the past several months has been takeover reform. At least in this area, our attention is rewarded by some of the most colorful terms, and colorful characters, in the business world today.

One of my favorites among the new terms is "deal junkies." Deal junkies are usually lawyers or investment bankers or arbitrageurs who start to sweat if they go more than two days between takeover battles. Their financial instincts are extremely refined, but their vision is sometimes only as lofty as the next day's stock price.

Then there are the arbitrageurs, who have been around for centuries. The early currency traders were arbitrageurs. But today arbs have new-found notoriety. Everyone knows what an "arb" is today. Can you imagine what a blood-curdling feeling it must be for the board of directors of a target corporation to hear the cry, "The arbs are in!"

Even Carl Icahn has a healthy respect for arbitrageurs. Icahn once told his wife, "If I ever need a transplant, get me the heart of an arb because I'll know it's never been used!"

And you have to remember who Icahn is. During the midst of the TWA takeover, when tempers were getting hot, someone told Icahn that he wasn't going to make a lot of friends with his attitude. To which Icahn said, "If you want a friend, get a dog!"

These Wall Street warriors did not invent takeovers, but they have dramatically changed the order of battle. What is new in takeovers today is the size, hostility, the amount of debt created, and the destructive implications for corporations. Yet, these struggles for control are fought with such intensity—such urgency— that there is little time to think about their real economic value or their place in the national interest.

No matter what you think of raiders, arbitrageurs, or hostile takeovers, they are all today an accepted part of the American corporate landscape. During recent years, abuses have crept into the takeover process that was established by the Williams Act. In order to address these abuses, on April 27, 1987, John Dingell and I introduced H.R. 2172, the Tender Offer Reform Act of 1987.

Before I tell you about some of the more important provisions of this bill, I'd like to set our deliberations in context. Just days before introduction of our bill, the Supreme Court handed down a decision in the *CTS* case. In *CTS*, the Supreme Court held that Indiana's statute, which required a disinterested shareholder's vote to vest voting rights in an acquiror's control block and extended the tender offer period to fifty days, was constitutional.

Many legal authorities predicted that the *CTS* case would stampede other states to adopt similar laws. All eyes turned to Delaware expecting to see a statute passed in the mere blink of an eye. But Delaware slammed on the brakes and decided to sit and think about things for awhile. Apparently, the best business minds in the country couldn't decide whether the Indiana statute actually slowed down hostile takeovers or speeded them up. Others suspected that target corporations would lose access to most of the weapons in their defensive arsenal if laws were passed that provided for a shareholder vote to deal with changes in corporate control.

Even today the business community is still digesting the impact of the *CTS* decision. However, the one benefit of all this confusion is that a lot of questions are being asked about the role of the states in the tender offer process, and we will be addressing those questions in our deliberations on this bill.

Now let me review with you some of the key provisions of H.R. 2172. First of all, the bill has something of a populist flair insofar as it deals with problems and terms that have become familiar to people who are not corporate raiders or investment bankers or takeover lawyers. Greenmail, poison pills, golden parachutes, ten-day windows—these are all addressed by the bill.

For example, the bill restricts the availability of greenmail payments. It prohibits a company from purchasing its securities at a price above the average market price of the securities during the thirty preceding trading days, from any person who has held more than 3 percent of its shares for less than two years. Greenmail would be permitted only if a majority of the shareholders approve or if the company makes an equal offer to all other shareholders.

The bill also deals with golden parachutes. It prohibits a company, during a tender offer, from entering into or amending agreements that increase the current or future compensation of any officer or director. The prohibition does not apply to routine compensation agreements made in the normal course of business. This provision is an extension of recent amendments to the tax code that discourage golden parachutes by increasing the tax imposed on them.

The bill also deals with poison pills, lock-ups, and tin parachutes. It provides that a corporation cannot establish or implement, during the proxy or tender offer time period, *without shareholder approval*, poison pills, tin parachutes, or lock-ups. The bill requires shareholder approval for any defensive tactic that provides for severance pay or other lump-sum payment to a large number of corporate officers or employees, when that payment is activated by a change in corporate control.

The bill would make it unlawful for any broker or dealer to trade any stock that has fewer or greater than one vote per share. One of the difficulties we will face in the coming months will be to develop a one share/one vote standard for corporate democracy that will operate in conjunction with an Indiana-type statute.

The bill closes the infamous ten-day window by requiring anyone who acquires more than 5 percent of a company to announce the acquisition publicly and to repeat the filing to the commission and to each exchange on which the company is traded within twenty-four hours. The acquiror is then precluded from acquiring additional securities of the same class for two business days after the acquisition. We may move to tighten this thirteen(d) filing period even further. The bill, also in Section 4, seeks to make certain that these filing requirements extend to groups acting in concert to acquire shares in a company. This new provision is designed specifically to prevent teams of raiders, bankers, and others from acting in a concerted manner to purchase more than 5 percent of a company without making the requisite disclosures. The SEC has implicated Ivan Boesky, Boyd Jefferies, and others in such schemes.

The bill requires that tender offers remain open for at least sixty calendar days, rather than the present twenty business days. In addition, Section 7 of the bill requires bidders to provide an "executive summary"—in clear language—of the terms and conditions of the offer, in addition to the usual tender offer materials received by shareholders. There is a feeling that today's tender offer disclosure documents are rather incomprehensible given the complexity of many of these transactions. This section would simply require a concise statement in plain English of the price, terms, and key conditions of the offer, including financing arrangements.

The bill prohibits, in Section 11, "market sweeps." If you make a tender offer and terminate it, you are precluded from acquiring securities of the class you tendered for, for a period of thirty days, except by a new tender offer. The bill essentially requires a thirty-day cooling-off period.

The bill also prohibits, in Section 13, "creeping tender offers." If you acquire 10 percent of a company, and if you want to acquire more, you must do so by tender offer.

And last, but certainly not least in importance, the bill provides for easier access to proxy materials. It gives free and equal access to the corporate proxy machinery to holders of 3 percent of a company's shares, or more than $500,000 of the corporation's voting securities (whichever is higher) for the purposes of nominating candidates for election to the board of directors.

We have gone to great lengths during the hearing process to make certain that all legitimate points of view were represented at our hearings. We have heard from acquirors such as T. Boone Pickens and Harold Simmons. We have heard from corporate management, from the principal takeover lawyers and investment bankers, from institutional investors, from representatives of the states and federal government, from shareholder groups, from labor, and from others.

By listening to and assessing these diverse points of view, we have been educated further. We have learned, for example, that there may be issues that the original bill should have addressed, but did not—issues such as confidential voting, corporate debt, leveraged buyouts and long-term versus short-term economic considerations in contests for corporate control. These are issues that we are considering now, and we may soon determine that they merit inclusion in the bill.

In case you haven't noticed, Congress is not always able to act immediately to solve particular problems or abuses. The process can be painfully slow. As we engage in that process, therefore, we must be certain that the problems we are addressing have not become yesterday's news, while new, emerging concerns go unnoticed. One can become fixated on the abuses that have developed with regard to hostile takeovers, and lose sight of the larger picture of which those abuses are only a small corner.

Let me put this concern in practical context. Earlier this year, we got Dennis Levine out of jail for a day to come to Washington to testify in a closed session before Congress. He met privately with me the night before the hearing. Levine told me how the large investment banks conspire with corporate raiders to put company after company into play.

In a typical scenario, the mergers and acquisitions (M&A) department of an investment bank will focus on a company that might make a convincing target. Its share price might be low because of a cyclical downturn; management might have lost a key employee; the company might make a commodity that is under pressure from imports. It might have a lot of cash on its books, or simply have underused debt capacity. There is an almost endless stream of factors that can be used to convince a company that it is a viable target.

The M&A department will then approach the prospective target with an offer to serve as its defensive advisor. If the company accepts, it means a large defensive restructuring fee for the investment bankers and the lawyers. If the company spurns the proposal, the investment banker "shops" the company as a potential target among the raider community. Once someone finds the company attractive and has accumulated a sufficient amount of stock, the investment banker and the lawyers leap onto the offensive side of the fray.

The raiders, for their part, are always ready to put a target into play because there is virtually no downside for them. It reminds me of when Darrell Royal was the football coach at Texas. Royal used to say, "When you put the ball into the air, three things can happen, and two of them are bad." Well, when a raider puts a company into play, three things can happen, and all of them are good! The bidder can get the company. He can be greenmailed out of the action at a hefty profit. Or, he can tender his shares to a white knight at a substantial profit. So, assuming the raider has a sufficient position in the stock so that his profits will cover his legal and financial advisor expenses, there is no downside to putting someone into play.

Now Congress could probably address a large portion of this problem by closing the 13(d) window, by tightening the definition of "group," and maybe by giving the SEC additional enforcement authority. Indeed, we will probably do all of that and more. But to stop there would be myopic. Rather, it is critical that we examine the outgrowths of these abuses and make every effort to try to address the broad economy-wide problems they create.

For example, in recent years, our economy has seen an enormous number of corporate restructurings. One of the principal reasons for these restructurings is to fend off hostile takeovers. Today, companies are loathe to be caught with extra cash in their coffers, even if it might be wise to keep such funds on hand for a rainy day, such as a recession or a market sector slump.

Similarly, times have changed in America with respect to borrowing. There was a time in this country when it was a very positive corporate development to have underused debt capacity. It meant that you would have easier access to funds in an emergency. Now, if a company is so well managed as to have underused debt capacity on its books, that company is a natural takeover target.

As a result, many otherwise strong companies have leveraged themselves to the hilt to look totally unattractive in the takeover market. And what is going to happen to those companies during the next recession or downturn? In my judgment, we are setting ourselves up for business failure after business failure, and some of our previously strong public companies will be the W. T. Grants of the late 1980s and early 1990s.

Let me offer one case that I have followed rather closely. In order to avoid falling prey earlier this year to British publisher Robert Maxwell, Harcourt Brace Jovanovich undertook a significant corporate restructuring at a cost of $3 billion in additional debt. Now does anyone really believe that Harcourt Brace is going to be a more vital company as a result of loading up with this new debt? Subsequent events lead me to believe that Harcourt Brace preserved its independence at a very significant cost.

First, Harcourt Brace's restructuring *tripled* the company's debt. It is now highly vulnerable to economic downturns and interest rate increases. It has drastically reduced its margin for error.

Second, Harcourt Brace recently announced its second quarter earnings—a loss of $70.8 million. Last year, Harcourt Brace reported net income of $10.9 million for this same quarter. But here is the key figure: revenues for the second quarter this year were nearly $100 million *more* than for the same quarter last year!

So we have revenues increasing from $312 million to $409 million, yet whereas last year Harcourt Brace reported net *income* of $10.9, this year they reported a net *loss* of $70.8 million. The difference is probably interest on the debt.

Then, a few days after Harcourt Brace issued its second quarter report, it quietly put its magazine division on the market. Harcourt Brace was reportedly seeking $400 million for the sale of this unit to help service its debt.

Finally, earlier this week, the *Wall Street Journal* reported that Harcourt Brace had nearly completed the sale of its business publications unit and its school supply company. And although the buyer was not named, the *Journal* article speculated that it could be a management team lead by Harcourt's vice chairman and an investment bank.

And that leads to another type of problem that can arise from this takeover mania. It seems that corporate managers have learned something from the raiders and have tried to get in on the spoils themselves. The rise in leveraged buyouts (LBOs) in recent years has been nothing short of phenomenal. And again the abuses in this field have also been noteworthy.

Take the Metromedia LBO as just one example. In December, 1983, Metromedia's chairman proposed taking Metromedia private by means of an LBO. The management group offered to pay shareholders in the neighborhood of $720 million for the company. The prospectus included two "fairness" letters from Lehman Brothers and Bear, Stearns attesting to the fact that the price to be paid to shareholders was fair. I should note parenthetically that, according to a subsequent article in *Barron's*, Lehman Brothers was paid $750,000 for its two-page opinion, with another $3.25 million to be paid if the deal was consummated on the terms it endorsed. Bear, Stearns was paid $500,000 for its opinion, along with another $2 million if the deal went through on its recommended terms.

Well, the deal did go through, but here is the interesting part. Within twenty-four months, the management group sold off a portion of Metromedia's assets—TV stations, cellular systems, the Harlem Globetrotters, and the Ice Capades—for almost $4.65 billion. Thus, they paid the shareholders $720 million for a company that two years later turned out to be worth at least six times that amount, with significant additional assets remaining in the original company.

Metromedia is not an isolated case. Indeed, abuses with regard to LBOs have become almost as pervasive as with hostile takeovers. My subcommittee is currently reviewing filings made with the SEC under Rule 13e–3 by companies in going private situations to determine whether all material facts in the transactions were disclosed. In addition, in our SEC oversight capacity, we are determining what additional enforcement or penalty provisions may be necessary to assist the commission in enforcing violations of this rule.

Is there a unifying theme to all of this? I think there is. Earlier I mentioned the need to maintain the integrity of our markets. Well, now I would expand that to say that we must also maintain integrity *in* our markets. Congress is not interested in decreasing market activity, but rather in increasing market integrity.

Whether we are examining the work of an outside raider or an inside raider, whether a hostile takeover or an LBO, we must be certain that the *process* has integrity; that shareholders are not cheated, and that our nation's future is not mortgaged. We need both moral integrity and fiscal integrity. Otherwise, shareholders and deal-makers alike will be content with their short-term paper profits while the rest of the world is running our financial affairs, providing us with credit for imported automobiles and computers, and writing down our debt.

The United States presently has over $7 trillion in debt on its books. Our consumer debt of $1 trillion and our public debt of $2 trillion are far outpaced by our corporate debt of $4 trillion. And in this era of proliferating junk-bonds, the quality of much of this corporate debt has deteriorated. Remember that the overwhelming majority of junk bonds were issued during prosperous economic times. They have never had to endure a serious economic downturn or a period of steadily rising interest rates.

Moreover, much of this debt is of questionable economic usefulness. It is not plant and equipment debt, or research and development debt. As a nation we still spend far less on these components than, for example, Japan or West Germany. Rather it is LBO debt and defensive recapitalization debt. As John Shad, former Chairman of the SEC, said, "The more leveraged takeovers and buyouts today, the more bankruptcies tomorrow."

Alfred Malabre of the *Wall Street Journal* has just written a book entitled *Beyond Our Means*. In it he makes the interesting observation that as a country we underinvest in new plants and technologies while we overinvest in quick gratification. He points out that Americans live in the most wonderful houses in all the world, but have some of the most rusted and outdated factories.

We all know people who live only for today. They get what they can, while they can, however they can, with no thought to the future. This is a bad philosophy for an individual, and a disastrous one for a nation. As Chairman of our subcommittee, I hope always to keep in view important short-term goals, but will never permit immediate economic gratification to obscure the best long-term interests of our citizens and our economy.

NOTE

1. On October 19, 1987, four days after these remarks were delivered, the Dow Jones Industrial average plummeted 508 points.

III

ETHICAL ASPECTS OF STRATEGIES AND TACTICS IN MERGERS AND TAKEOVERS

12

Ethics and Transformation Tactics: Human Resource Considerations in Mergers and Acquisitions

ANTHONY F. BUONO
JAMES L. BOWDITCH

Mergers, acquisitions, and related downsizing and divestiture activities have been front-page headlines for so long that our society almost takes them for granted. The statistics are staggering. In 1985, over 3,000 mergers and acquisitions involving U.S. firms were announced for a total value of almost $180 billion (McLeod, 1986). In 1986 alone, there were over 4,200 mergers and acquisitions with an estimated value of approximately $200 billion. This pace continued unabated as the first quarter of 1987 witnessed over 900 mergers worth in excess of $32 billion (*Mergers & Acquisitions*, 1987a, 1987b). The level of activity has been so high and constant that approximately 10 percent of the work force—roughly 12 million people—are estimated to have been directly involved in a merger, acquisition, or related downsizing or divestiture (Kay, 1987).

Perhaps more startling is the fact that while we have come to expect small and medium-sized firms to be involved in both friendly mergers and hostile takeovers, corporate giants have increasingly gotten into the act. "Megamergers" that affect major segments of the work force are beginning to be commonplace: consider Texas Air's acquisition of Eastern Airlines, Continental Airlines, and the now-defunct People's Express; Chrysler and AMC's merger; Burroughs and Sperry's combination into UNISYS; and General Electric's acquisition of RCA. Hostile takeover threats of large corporations dominate the business news as well, as exemplified by Revlon's ongoing courtship of Gillette, and T. Boone Pickens' well-documented forays.

THE HUMAN SIDE OF MERGERS AND ACQUISITIONS

While it seems that contemporary management has placed its faith in corporate growth, renewal, and strategic redirection through merger and acquisition, increasing criticism has focused on the human costs associated with such transformations (cf. Buono et al., 1988; Marks & Mirvis, 1985; Norris, 1986; Schweiger et al., 1987). Indeed, mergers and acquisitions can sufficiently transform the organizational structures, systems, processes, cultures, and employment prospects of one or both of the firms that people often feel stressed, angry, disoriented, frustrated, confused, and even frightened. On a personal level, these feelings can lead to a sense of loss, psychosomatic difficulties, marital discord, and, at the extreme, suicide (cf. Magnet, 1984; Robino & DeMeuse, 1985; Schweiger et al., 1987). On an organizational level, these feelings are often manifested in lowered commitment and productivity, increased dissatisfaction and disloyalty, high turnover among key managers, leadership and power struggles between those managers who stay, sabotage, and, in general, a rise in dysfunctional work-related behaviors at all levels of the hierarchy (Buono & Bowditch, 1987, 1989; Bastien, 1987; O'Boyle, 1985; Pappanastos et al., 1987; Pritchett, 1985).

Although much of this human turmoil may be inevitable as organizations struggle to adapt to increasingly competitive environments, the difficulties involved in such large-scale transformations are frequently intensified by questionable management tactics and decisions during the merger and acquisition process. Rather than being the well-planned, carefully calculated strategic acts they are portrayed to be, mergers and acquisitions are often described as having a life of their own, with shifting periods of waiting and frenzied activities, a sense of escalating momentum, cascading minor changes, rising tensions and conflicts, and stressful uncertainties (Buono et al., 1985, 1988; Jemison & Sitkin, 1986b; Marks & Mirvis, 1985). Yet, a growing body of research suggests that many firms underestimate the problems and overestimate the potential benefits involved (*Business Week*, 1985; Lubatkin, 1983; Michel & Shaked, 1985).

In an effort to gain control of such a frenetic situation, managers often develop a crisis mentality which creates a type of merger myopia, a nearsightedness to merger-related problems that affects virtually all decisions (Mangum, 1984; Marks & Mirvis, 1985). As a result, many actions and decisions concerning employees that would normally be dealt with in fairer, more thoughtful ways are unexplored as managers become entrenched with a particular solution to their problems. While this orientation gives managers and executives the illusion that they are in control of the underlying process, early merger strategies are usually overly simplistic, one-sided, and dysfunctional to both employees and the overall success of the combination (Buono & Bowditch, 1989; Jemison & Sitkin, 1986a, 1986b; Marks & Mirvis, 1986).

Although many of the human problems associated with mergers and acquisitions—fears and uncertainties, stresses and tensions—cannot be eliminated or totally prevented from disrupting organizational performance, managers can influence both the integration process and consolidation outcomes. Based on a review of the literature (cf. Gillis & Casey, 1985; Halbouty, 1985; Haspeslagh & Jemison, 1987; Jemison & Sitkin, 1986b; Marks & Mirvis, 1985; Richman,

1984) as well as our own research (Bowditch & Buono, 1987; Buono & Bowditch, 1987, 1989; Buono et al., 1985, 1988), five key concerns and dilemmas—each with a strong ethical component—seem to capture much of the current tension underlying the human side of mergers and acquisitions:

1. the notion of *competing claims*, the reality that mergers involve multiple parties, each with their own interests and needs;
2. *secrecy versus deception* in communication in terms of the managed release of information in an open, honest, and timely manner, or the controlled release of information to distort the truth and manipulate people;
3. the distinction between *coercion and participation* in terms of the extent to which people are forced into certain situations or provided with a true opportunity to take part in discussions and decisions;
4. how the processes underlying *grief, loss, and termination* are handled;
5. the *level of respect* for organizational members and other key constituents as individuals.

This chapter attempts to clarify our understanding of some of the ethical dilemmas and problems associated with managing organizational transformations by analyzing two large-scale organizational combinations: (1) a horizontal merger between two mutual savings banks; and (2) a conglomerate acquisition and divestiture through a leveraged management buyout (LBO) of a food retailer. By using the five issues noted above, we will delve into implications for managing the employee dimension of mergers and acquisitions in a humanistic and ethical manner.

THE BANK MERGER

In August 1981, Urban Bank and Suburban Bank, two medium-sized savings banks located in the Northeast, formally began a "friendly" merger of "equals." Because of instability in the thrift industry, the merger was part of a strategic effort to create a stronger, more competitive institution. Although the plan was initially applauded by members of both banks, within a matter of months following the merger employee commitment to the combination drastically declined, job satisfaction and related attitudes plummeted, and overall productivity and profitability deteriorated. What had initially seemed to be a "perfect marriage" quickly became a virtual battleground between warring camps.

Characteristics of the Banks

Before the merger, Urban Bank was the fourth largest savings bank in the state, with an asset base of $600 million. The main office, which was located in the heart of a major metropolitan city, was supported by a network of thirteen branches and 325 full-time employees. Due to its urban setting and the location of its branches, the institution served a largely blue-collar clientele. It operated with a divisional structure and was rather bureaucratic in nature, with clearly defined and bounded jobs at all levels.

Suburban Bank was the fifth largest savings bank in the state, with approximately $500 million in assets and 275 employees. In contrast to Urban Bank, the institution's headquarters and all branches were in relatively prosperous, suburban areas. Its customer base was largely professional and white-collar. The bank operated with a centrally controlled functional organization, but individual jobs were more loosely defined, especially at the managerial and professional levels. While there was a complete file of job descriptions of all employees at Urban Bank, for example, the expressed policy at Suburban Bank was that employees should do what was needed, especially at the professional level, for the success of the bank.

THE CONGLOMERATE ACQUISITION AND DIVESTITURE

Within an eighteen-month period, Coop Foods went through three changes in ownership. After being an autonomous component of a conglomerate empire for fifteen years, the company was acquired by a larger conglomerate and then divested through a management leveraged buyout. Yet, despite this rapid and, at times, unstable period of change, employee attitudes remained relatively constant, and productivity and profitability improved substantially.

Characteristics of the Companies

Unlike most supermarket chains, Coop Foods was initially part of an agricultural cooperative in the northeastern part of the United States. In 1944 the company incorporated and separated its retail stores from the cooperative. Over the next three decades, the company developed a chain of retail grocery stores, supported by a wholesale grocery distribution corporation.

In 1971 Coop Foods was acquired by Aero Corporation, a diversified conglomerate with interests in aerospace, defense, and industrial products that wanted to expand into food and drug retailing. The conglomerate allowed Coop Foods to operate as an autonomous unit, essentially as it had prior to the acquisition, without any disruptive, internal reorganization. The parent company would benefit from the cash generated by the supermarket chain, and Coop would have access to the corporation's financial and computer resources. Under the ownership of Aero Corporation, Coop Foods became one of the largest food retail chains in the Northeast. During this period, the company, employing over 7,200 employees, had grown to ninety retail stores, sixty-eight franchise stores, and supplier relations with 220 independent markets.

In 1984 Aero Corporation was acquired by TransCo, another conglomerate involved in commercial products, consumer products, and railroad activities, with an emerging interest in aerospace technology. TransCo wanted to complement its growing aerospace program with Aero's well-established unit known for its sophisticated landing gear. Coop Foods was considered to be too far removed from the strategic focus of TransCo and was divested less than one year later through a leveraged buyout by the supermarket chain's top management team and an investment banking firm.

STUDY DESIGN

A multimethod field approach employed in a longitudinal (bank merger: 1979–86) and cross-sectional (conglomerate acquisition: 1987) design was used to gather data on the precombination organizations, the transformation process, and the post-transformation experience. Information on the organizations was obtained through in-depth interviews with organizational members, observations, and archival data gathered throughout the study period. Lengthy interviews with the Chief Executive Officers (CEOs), upper-level managers, and employees throughout each organization focused on such items as: (1) personal descriptions of the organization, (2) organizational history, (3) types of people working at the firm, (4) type of place the organization is to work at, (5) management style before and after the transformation, (6) policy and procedural changes, (7) the transformation process itself, (8) outcomes of the transformation, and (9) general facets of organizational life. Following grounded theory (Glaser & Strauss, 1967) and phenomenological approaches to organizational research (see Sanders, 1982), transcripts of the interviews were examined for concepts and themes that could characterize the organizations. These emergent hypotheses were then tested in discussions with members of the research team and the firms to develop shared perceptions of each organization's culture and the transformation process.

Organizational climate surveys with the populations and stratified random samples of the different organizations were also undertaken. The surveys focused on employee perceptions about various facets of organizational life, including the transformations, organizational commitment, job satisfaction, interpersonal relations, job security and advancement, organizational policies, management and supervisory behavior, and compensation. A complete discussion of the underlying methodology (Bowditch & Buono, 1982) and study design (Buono et al., 1985, 1988; Buono & Bowditch, 1989) is available for interested readers.

COMPARATIVE ANALYSIS OF THE TWO TRANSFORMATIONS

Using a stakeholder perspective (e.g., Freeman, 1984), the analysis focuses on employee-related issues that confronted the banks and the supermarket chain during the transformation process. In both cases, different ethical models—a utilitarian perspective, theory of rights, theory of justice—were pitted against each other in an attempt to resolve the dilemmas raised by the organizational change and to justify a chosen course of action.

Competing Claims

Although it has long been recognized that mergers and acquisitions involve multiple parties with their own competing and, at times, conflicting interests, historically this conflict has been framed in terms of the investment of the acquiring and acquired firm's stockholders (Gillis & Casey, 1985). The traditional business gospel is that a company is essentially a piece of private property owned by those who hold its stock. Accordingly, firms have sacrosanct and inviolable obligations to these individuals. Employees are viewed as servants of the firm, functioning as technical instruments in production, marketing, finance, and so forth (Buono & Nichols, 1985; Freeman & Reed, 1983). Under this model, the idea of legitimate competing claims is largely viewed in terms of the interests of the two stockholder groups (ethical egoism). Corporate officials are duty-bound to define and pursue the best interests of these individuals (see Richman, 1984). Even the contemporary understanding of stockholders as investors rather than owners retains these distinctions.

A more recent perspective, by contrast, argues that many groups in society—employees, customers, suppliers, local communities, interest groups, regulators—are materially involved with the corporation through different types of transactions. In this stakeholder model corporations are viewed as having responsibilities to these claimant groups that often go beyond the immediate interests of stockholders. Employees are regarded as persons with a wide range of legitimate needs in which the corporation must take an interest. Stockholders continue to occupy a place of prominence, but their interests and desires are no longer absolutely decisive for the determination of corporate conduct (Buono & Nichols, 1985; Freeman, 1984). With respect to merger and acquisition decisions, the stakeholder model suggests that a utilitarian orientation (the greatest good for the greatest number of stakeholders; see Richman, 1984) should help to resolve the difficulties posed by competing claims.

In many instances, however, the greatest good is difficult to determine. The bank merger, for example, was complicated by extreme cultural differences across the organizations. Although these banks were approximately equal-sized mutual savings banks operating in the same Standard Metropolitan Statistical Area (SMSA) and appeared to have similar characteristics on paper, each employee group as well as customers, competitors, and bank regulators saw the banks as being quite different. Members of Urban Bank perceived the institution to be quite people-oriented, an egalitarian but rather bureaucratic type of organization whose CEO and upper-level managers encouraged a participative management style. Suburban Bank, by contrast, was characterized as more task-oriented, an authoritarian workplace whose CEO was the key source of power and decision making. In fact, at the time of the merger the state banking commissioner described the two banks as being "as different as you could possibly get—Urban Bank very collegial and consensual and Suburban Bank totally autocratic."

Although the employees described the organizational cultures of these two banks as almost extreme types, a comparison of quality of work life surveys (1979–80) taken in the two institutions *prior to* any merger-related discussions indicates that both employee groups were quite accepting of their respective organizations (see Table 12.1). While there were some differences in levels of premerger satisfaction (e.g., training effectiveness, job challenge), similar portions of employees reported pride in working for their bank, and satisfaction with its systems of compensation and advancement, the context of their work, and interpersonal relations on the job. Despite the different realities of organizational life in the two banks, the conditions had existed for an extended period of time, shaped and were shaped by quite divergent values and beliefs, and were viewed as "the way things should be" (Buono et al., 1985).

While the combination was to be a merger of equals, each employee group felt that *their* culture and orientation was better than the other. In their minds, each of these stakeholders felt that they had a legitimate claim that the culture of Merged Bank should be closer to their organization's rather than to the merger partner's. Yet, despite these competing perceived rights, upper-level management overlooked the differences in both merger planning and integration. The cultural differences were sufficiently strong, however, that they undermined attempts to resolve potential operating difficulties and facilitate interaction between employees from both banks, and contributed to drastic declines in employee satisfaction and commitment following the merger (see Table 12.1).

In this instance, the issue is not whether the different employee groups were right or wrong in their attempt to support their culture at the expense of the other. Rather, the key point concerns the way in which management attempted the cultural integration in dealing with the collision of different philosophies, values, and styles. Indeed, rather than recognize the legitimacy of different cultural orientations and values, there was little concern by either CEO for the views of his employees. As the CEO of Suburban Bank, who became Chief Operating Officer (COO) of Merged Bank, repeated on a number of occasions, "I don't give a damn what they [the employees] think. If they don't like it, [expletive deleted] them." In this situation, however, the theories of rights and justice (cf. Cavanagh, 1984; Velasquez et al., 1983) underscore the legitimacy and importance of the employees' perspectives. Yet, the CEOs of the merger partners dismissed these beliefs and attitudes as insignificant compared to the greater good they felt would come from the merger.

In the supermarket acquisition, by contrast, instead of attempting to blend the different cultures, the conglomerate followed a cultural pluralism orientation (see American Bankers Association and Ernst & Whinney, 1985). Both Aero and TransCo allowed maximum flexibility in letting Coop Foods operate autonomously, permitting cultural diversity to exist within a shared strategy for growth. When attempting a fully integrated, horizontal merger such at the bank consolidation, of course, there is a much higher probability of culturally oriented competing claims than would tend to be found in a conglomerate acquisition

Table 12.1
Organizational Climate Comparison: Urban vs. Suburban Banks, Pre- and Postmerger Periods

PERCENT FAVORABLE

| | 1979-80 PRE-MERGER SITUATION | | 1982 POST MERGER | | | | 1984 POST MERGER | | | |
| | | | MERGED BANK | PRIOR AFFILIATION | | | MERGED BANK | PRIOR AFFILIATION | | |
	Urban	Suburb		Urban	Suburb	New		Urban	Suburb	New
Number of subjects	325	188	100	45	45	10	140	50	50	40
SELECTED ITEMS										
ORGANIZATIONAL COMMITMENT										
Sense of Pride	90%	86%	46%	34%	50%	78%	74%	68%	80%	76%
Good Customer Service	75	na	43	30	44	83	73	68	80	75
JOB RELATED										
Overall Job Satisfaction	73	na	54	49	52	89	75	78	76	67
Job Challenge	72	54	56	64	43	66	74	77	79	59
Satisfactory Work Hours	84	86	92	90	90	94	90	93	94	79
Amount of Work Reasonable	72	60	77	71	81	83	84	81	82	87
Job Worthwhile and Important	87	na	79	86	86	78	88	89	92	83
JOB SECURITY & ADVANCEMENT										
Job Secure if Performed Well	91	89	58	46	64	77	74	64	74	89
Say What I Think Without Fear	58	61	54	64	36	72	57	45	66	63

	1	2	3	4	5	6	7	8	9	10
Advancement Opportunity	71	72	41	37	37	72	58	58	57	59
Promotions Deserved	50	55	37	37	28	73	36	30	65	40
COMPENSATION & BENEFITS										
Paid Fairly	43	39	48	53	42	50	50	49	52	44
Good Benefits	86	86	88	86	90	83	82	73	98	72
SUPERVISOR RELATIONS										
Supervisor is Fair	83	90	79	79	81	56	88	86	86	91
Available when Needed	75	na	82	77	85	83	87	92	84	83
Capable of Doing Job	na	93	84	85	82	78	91	93	90	87
Lets me Know What's Expected	79	76	78	79	72	72	90	90	91	87
Ensures Employees are Well Trained	64	73	66	61	63	78	73	65	86	76
MANAGEMENT										
Employee Oriented	72	74	38	32	36	72	40	32	46	46
Opportunity to Interact with Management	47	74	36	29	39	50	47	49	52	43
Training Effectiveness	50	73	44	38	41	77	62	57	64	67
ORGANIZATIONAL COOPERATION										
Departmental Cooperation	44	48	31	27	27	67	57	52	54	66
Co-workers do their Share	73	74	77	76	73	72	81	81	79	86
Good Communication	36	67	27	17	29	61	46	41	47	52

na = not available

Table 12.2
Coop Foods: Organizational Climate Comparison

| Number of Subjects = 278 | PERCENT FAVORABLE | | |
Selected Items	Aero Era	TransCo Era	Coop Era
ORGANIZATIONAL COMMITMENT			
Sense of Pride	96%	82%	84%
Pleasant Place to Work	80	74	77
Expect Long Career	69	64	68
Productivity High	69	70	73
JOB RELATED			
Satisfied with Job	77	74	78
Doing Something Important	84	85	88
Job Challenging	76	78	76
Amount of Work Reasonable	69	65	58
Advancement Opportunity	51	43	44
Enough People to do Job	53	48	40
High Rate/Turnover	43	52	51
JOB SECURITY			
Say What I Think without fear	55	51	55
Job Secure if Performed Well	86	84	86
Promotions Deserved	43	36	39
COMPENSATION & BENEFITS			
Paid Fairly	55	51	42
Salary Administration Fair	33	33	31
Good Benefits	90	84	87
SUPERVISOR RELATIONS			
Managers are Approachable	62	60	63
Know Who to Approach with Problem	88	87	88
Supervisor Listens	70	70	72
Know Where I Stand	79	77	75
Management Aware of Problems with job	45	50	37
WORKING CONDITIONS			
Work Space OK	60	54	48
Equipment Satisfactory	56	57	47

Table 12.2 Continued

ORGANIZATIONAL COOPERATION			
Employees do Their Share	59	57	58
Cooperation Between Workers	59	57	61
Cooperation Between Offices	60	59	62
Co-workers Help When Needed	60	60	62
Mgmt., Keeps me Informed of Changes	61	55	62
ORGANIZATIONAL TRANSFORMATION			
Top Management Improve QWL	54	40	53
Changes in Ownership/Good	..	24	60
Expectations of Changes Accurate	66	68	62

(Diven, 1984). However, the fact that TransCo did not attempt to change Coop's culture was continually mentioned by the supermarket's employees as a significant determinant of their relatively stable levels of satisfaction and commitment following the acquisition (see Table 12.2).

Potential conflicts of interest can also emerge from competing claims in merger and acquisition situations. In the bank merger, for example, questions were raised concerning the extent to which the self-perceived career needs of the CEOs disproportionately influenced the merger decision. Urban Bank's CEO, nearing retirement, wanted to exert more influence on industry-wide issues and felt that being part of a larger institution would afford him the opportunity to be more visible at the national level. Suburban Bank's CEO, by contrast, wanted to be in control of a larger, more influential bank. The merger, which created a dual top management structure, provided both individuals with their desired opportunities.

Following the consolidation, Urban Bank's CEO assumed the role of CEO but was rarely around the institution, instead devoting his time and energies to national industry association activities. Suburban Bank's CEO became Chief Operating Officer (COO) and assumed control of all internal decisions. While these were the preferred activities for both individuals, extending back to their presidency of the premerger banks, employees felt that each CEO was more interested in fulfilling his own agenda (egoism) than in doing what was good for the overall bank (utilitarianism). Many employees, for example, reported that their former president had "sold them out," which further contributed to lowered commitment and satisfaction after the merger (Table 12.1).

In sharp contrast, the top management team at Coop Foods underscored—both publicly and privately—the important role played by the supermarket's employees. While they had an obvious interest in obtaining control over the company through the leveraged buyout from TransCo, employees did not perceive any hidden agenda on top management's part as they did in the bank merger. Coop's executives made themselves available to their employees, and, although not completely successful, attempted a "management by walking around" strategy. The overall effectiveness of their efforts, however, is reflected in the profitability of the venture. Despite a period of relatively high inflation, interest rates, and unemployment, the company was consistently able to increase sales and earnings. The bank, by contrast, took longer than other banks merging during the same period to become profitable (Buono et al., 1987). While such financial comparisons cannot be solely attributed to differences in employee attitudes and behaviors, especially in service-oriented organizations such attitudes and behaviors do have a significant effect on performance outcomes (e.g., Schneider, 1980).

Secrecy versus Deception

When faced with a merger or acquisition, basic questions emerge in managers' minds concerning the nature and timing of communication to employees. Although it has been suggested that merger negotiations be carried out in secret to minimize uncertainty among organizational members (Graves, 1981), most research indicates that the creation of formal, internal communication mechanisms as early as possible may limit much of the anxiety otherwise fueled by rumors, the grapevine, or even outside news reports (Buono et al., 1987; Marks, 1982).

Legal and operational realities, however, raise some difficulties. First, Security and Exchange Commission (SEC) guidelines limit what can be told—even to employees—about merger or acquisition plans. Second, since the actual details of a merger have to be worked out over a period of several months or even years after the combination, management rarely has accurate answers to employee questions. Thus, on one level, communication concerning what is about to transpire is constrained by both legal and operational restrictions.

In many instances, however, managers attempt to use such constraints to deceive and manipulate employees. The standard approach to merger communication is for management to inform employees that little will actually change in the day-to-day operation of the company, even when it is known that major changes will probably occur. In the bank merger, for example, both CEOs publicly assured their employees that they would be secure in their membership in the merged bank. Leading up to and immediately after the combination, they repeated their statements that there would not be any merger-related layoffs as long as people did their jobs well.

In mid-December, just four months after the legal merger, however, a series of staff reductions at all levels was announced: 5 percent immediately, 13 percent by April, and 18 percent by October. The layoffs, which became known as the "Christmas massacre," resulted in a profound and widespread distrust of the new leadership and bank (see Table 12.1). Yet, even in the wake of the turmoil and dissatisfaction created by the "massacre," the Chief Operating Officer of Merged Bank (ex-CEO of Suburban Bank) argued that he would use the same tactic again, in order to "gain time and momentum" for the merger. This tactic seems to be more the rule than the exception, as exemplified by the recent firing of the top management team of another bank *one day* after an acquisition, even though some of them had been given personal assurances that their jobs were secure (Bailey, 1987).

In the supermarket, by contrast, a concerted effort was made to ensure that all communications were as accurate and honest as possible. With the support of TransCo, a series of well-timed memos and bulletins were sent out to keep people officially informed. Additionally, managers actively used the office grapevine to "keep people informed every step of the way." While management did not have all the answers and employees still wondered exactly how and when things were going to change and how they would be affected, most people reported that the acquisition was "handled with care" and that they appreciated the "accurate grapevine."

Coercion versus Participation

While most premerger statements and discussions about postmerger integration emphasize the importance of participation in bringing about organizational change, studies have indicated that the process is usually tightly controlled by top management (cf. Barmash, 1971; Buono et al., 1988; Sales & Mirvis, 1984). Merger-related restructuring, for example, is argued to be typically *done to* rather than *done by* employees. Due to chaotic events and bursts of activity, the potential for enlightened management of people and the change process is often lost in the shuffle (Kanter & Seggerman, 1986).

In the mergers and acquisitions under study, there was a sharp contrast between participative and coercive orientations during the combinations. Shortly after the bank merger, Merged Bank's COO returned from a trip late in the day to find a number of prior Urban Bank officers leaving "on time," which infuriated him. He decided that due to the changing competitive circumstances in the thrift industry, if Merged Bank were to survive, it would be necessary to impose Suburban Bank's task-oriented culture on it. As he suggested to the researchers, "old habits die hard." His subsequent efforts to "weed out" key Urban Bank officers and managers and to make the organization "more competitive" and "more in tune with the (financially volatile) times" were interpreted by many organizational members as threats and evidence that he wanted to "use up" people. While both merger partner employees expressed dissatisfaction following the merger, the significance of his efforts is reflected in that in virtually all instances, Urban Bank employees were significantly less favorable in their responses on the postmerger climate surveys than Suburban Bank members (Tables 12.1 and 12.3).

The ramifications of such dissatisfaction are reflected in a whistleblowing

Table 12.3

Merger Questions by Former Bank of Employment, 1982 Postmerger Survey

PERCENT FAVORABLE

ITEM	Urban Bank	Suburban Bank
All things considered, the merger should not have taken place.	47%	28% **
My former bank's philosophy is the dominant one since the merger.	26	37 *
There has been an improvement of policies and procedures in the new (merged bank) compared to those in my pre-merger bank.	20	38 **
There is a lingering feeling of resentment between the employees of the merger partners.	78	57 *
There is a lot of friction between former Urban Bank and former Suburban Bank employees.	64	36 **
The atmosphere at the bank is becoming similar to "the good old days".	10	22 **
My department has been strengthened by the merger.	24	53 *
I feel that employee benefits have improved as a result of the merger.	66	83 *
A majority of the employees have come to accept the merger as a necessary and worthwhile step.	36	58 *
Most people are afraid to open up with their feelings about the merger.	74	37 **

** $p < .01$
* $p < .05$

incident that took place three years after the merger. In the fall of 1984, the COO sent a memo to his senior executives to elicit their support for the industry's political action committees (PACs). Although the COO argued that the memo was "never intended as a threat," it was leaked to the press, and the local papers reported that employees were "fearful they'll lose their jobs if they don't (contribute)." The incident led to a probe by the FBI and the Justice Department, and the bank admitted to violating federal law and paid a $17,000 fine.

Yet, perhaps most interestingly from an employee perspective is the fact that the practice in question was fairly common to both banks prior to the merger. As one of the managers explained, "[Urban Bank CEO] used to make the same type of plea at our staff meetings. [Suburban Bank CEO] did the same thing at one of our meetings. The dollars were real low, so he followed it up with the memo. That's when people felt they had him. It was on paper." Thus, the underlying reason for the whistleblowing appears to have been generated by a sense of cultural revenge for the coercive way in which the postmerger integration process was managed (Buono & Bowditch, 1987).

Throughout the changes in ownership of Coop Foods, in contrast, a specific attempt was made to involve employees in the transformation. During both the TransCo acquisition and the leveraged buyout, for example, Coop maintained an advisory council of employees that had been in place since 1976. While employees argued that the success of the council was "dependent on the people in it," it was acknowledged as an important vehicle for communication during the changes. Virtually all the supermarket's officers underscored its importance during the transition both as a sounding board and as a way of providing mutual assistance and guidance between employees and management.

Coop Foods, of course, did not have to integrate itself operationally with a similar firm. TransCo and Coop, however, chose a much more participative change strategy compared to the more coercive tactics employed in the bank merger. As exemplified by the attitudinal, operational, and financial outcomes in the present study, as well as other research (e.g., Nurick, 1985; Sashkin, 1984), such participative methods are related to more favorable organizational climates and productivity than coercive approaches.

Management of Grief, Loss, and Termination

During a merger, employees typically experience conflicting emotions ranging from shock, anger, disbelief, and helplessness to hope, excitement, and great expectations for the future (Bowditch & Buono, 1987; Marks & Mirvis, 1985; Schweiger et al., 1987). Depending on how the acquisition unfolds and the experiences of employees, of course, individual reactions can vary widely. However, following a merger there is typically a mourning or grief period similar to that experienced when a family member dies (cf. Fried, 1963; Sinetar, 1981), as the dissolution of familiar work surroundings and the slow and steady exit of friends and associates signals the "end of what was."

In the bank merger, for example, people became quite nostalgic about their prior bank affiliations during the initial aftermath period. Interview and survey data (see Table 12.3) indicate that employees displayed an active dislike of their merger partner counterparts, the "other bank's" managers, and its policies and cultural orientations. Frequently mentioned complaints by respondents from *both* merger partners were a loss of family atmosphere, freedom, camaraderie and accessibility to management, a disruption of social ties and communication patterns, and decreased cohesion and organizational commitment.

According to psychological theorists (e.g., Janis et al., 1969), the idealization of the lost entity is a typical grief reaction and part of the process of "working through" the loss. Especially in contested mergers and acquisitions, employees have been found to behave in ways similar to reactions to death and dying— denial, anger, bargaining, and eventual acceptance (Marks & Mirvis, 1986). As part of this reaction, people may display a general depressive tone and somatic symptoms, experience a sense of helplessness, and express both direct and displaced anger (Fried, 1963).

From a managerial perspective, it is important to assist employees in dealing with such feelings because employees' residual anger can persist for years following a merger (Levinson, 1970). Since the management decision to enter into the merger or acquisition precipitated the loss and resulting grief, however, top managers also have an ethical responsibility to reduce the turmoil they brought about. Reports of successful acquisitions and transformation efforts (e.g., Bice, 1988) underscore the importance of carefully planned and thoughtful intervention. In the bank merger under study, however, no such attention or intervention was attempted.

The way in which employee terminations and staff reductions are handled also send clear signals about management's values to the employees. Yet, research suggests that most people involved in a merger or acquisition feel that termination decisions are handled in an arbitrary and ineffective manner (Schweiger et al., 1987). In the bank merger, the "Christmas Massacre" and what were reported as cavalier ways of dismissing employees further fueled dissatisfaction with the merged institution and its management, and precipitated a rise in voluntary turnover (Buono et al., 1987). In a similar situation, organizational members at North Carolina National Bank (NCNB) nicknamed the institution "No Care National Bank" after "heads rolled" following an interstate acquisition—within one year only one of the merger partner's department heads was still employed. With the next acquisition, about one-half of the top 300 officers left NCNB within eighteen months (Heylar, 1986).

Interestingly, it does not appear to be staff reductions and layoffs per se that create dissatisfaction and bitterness, but rather the way in which these terminations are handled (Schweiger et al., 1987). During TransCo's takeover of Coop Foods, for example, a number of middle managers were let go for performance reasons. Although no promises concerning managerial job security were made by TransCo, these terminations initially fueled apprehension and anxiety on the part of many employees. However, it was also clear to most people that the terminations were based on performance factors rather than arbitrary standards or cultural differences, and were largely accepted. In such instances, it is still important for the organization to aid those being terminated with outplacement assistance, counseling, and related job search and support services.

Respect for Employees as Individuals

Historically, the relationship between employer and employee has been governed by the employment-at-will doctrine: the employment contract is terminable at will be either party at any time and for any reason. Although this perspective has been challenged by public policy questions based upon the greater social good it has led to the rather simplistic view that employees only have those rights that they negotiate with their employer (Elliston et al., 1985). Employees and employers, however, are not mere abstractions, and, as individuals, organizational members have a moral right to be treated with respect and dignity (DeGeorge, 1986). Yet, in large-scale change efforts, employees are often viewed as mere replaceable parts in the overall production or service process. As a result, the respect and dignity they might normally be given are neglected for the greater good that is projected to come from the transformation.

In the bank merger, for example, top management continually asserted a utilitarian view that while there might be "some pain for certain individuals," the overall success of the institution was dependent on the success of the consolidation. The lack of respect for employees as individuals (theory of rights) is exemplified in such tactics as deceiving them about job security after the merger, ignoring their personal rights and cultural orientations during the integration period, using coercive strategies to force change, and so forth.

While these decisions may have been made with such admirable ends in mind as creating a stronger bank to serve the local community or securer jobs for the employees who remain, it is in the firm's enlightened self-interest to be open and progressive in its dealings with organizational members (Buono & Nichols, 1985). Research indicates that mergers have less than a 50–50 chance of being successful (*Business Week*, 1985; Louis, 1982; Pritchett, 1985), and much of that failure is increasingly attributed to mismanagement of the firms' human resources (Buono et al., 1988; Marks & Mirvis, 1986; Robino & DeMeuse, 1985; Schweiger et al., 1987). By ignoring the rights of organizational members or questions of justice in dealing with them, managers precipitate unrest, increased dissatisfaction and alienation, and lowered commitment and work efforts. As exemplified by the supermarket acquisition and buyout, in contrast, by attending to these issues the result can be more favorable employee attitudes, work efforts, and ultimately productivity and profitability outcomes.

CONCLUSION

Mergers and acquisitions between two previously autonomous companies involve an enormous adjustment to change within a relatively condensed time period. Organizational combinations, by their basic nature, generate high levels of stress, conflict, tension, and uncertainty in the lives of employees at all levels of the hierarchy. Indeed, the myriad issues and traumas raised by such transformations are sufficiently severe that regardless of how thoughtfully or carefully employee-related concerns are handled, some turmoil and displacement are inevitable (O'Boyle & Russell, 1984; Pappanastos et al., 1987).

The five issues presented in this paper—the notion of competing claims, secrecy versus deception, coercion versus participation, the management of grief, loss, and termination, and respect for organizational members—however, appear to capture much of the tension underlying the human side of mergers and acquisitions. By illustrating how these issues were dealt with in two organizational combinations, we have attempted to show how underlying management decisions and tactics influence employee attitudes and behaviors, and, ultimately, the overall operational and financial outcomes of the transformation. There were, of course, some major differences in the two consolidations. The banks were involved in a horizontal merger, requiring a much greater degree of operational integration, cultural change, and reduction in force than the conglomerate acquisition or leveraged buyout of the supermarket chain. At the same time, it is clear that the rights of organizational members did not have to be violated as extensively as they were in the bank merger. Such actions create unnecessary costs for both the individuals involved and the organizations.

In dealing with these issues, it is important for management to be wary of getting caught up in a utilitarian interpretation of the transformation as leading to the greatest good for the greatest number of stakeholders at the expense of the organizations' employees. An ethical position with respect to bringing about such change also entails treating employees in fair and just ways, and ensuring that their rights as individuals are upheld. The dilemma managers face is the need to balance the demands of a utilitarian view of creating social good (ends) with the process of achieving those ends (means). If such large-scale transformations are to be successful—operationally and financially, as well as ethically—both the end goals of the change effort and the process of implementation must be characterized by a high degree of ethical integrity. While this may indeed place a significant burden on corporate managers in their dual role as strategist and change agent, the reality of increasing employee and other stakeholder pressures on such transformations necessitates such a posture.

WORKS CITED

American Bankers Association and Ernst & Whinney. *Implementing Mergers and Acquisitions in the Financial Services Industry: From Handshake to Hands On.* Washington, D.C.: American Bankers Association, 1985.

Bailey, D. M. "Home Owners Fires 4 Top Officers at Union Warren." *Boston Globe*, October 7, 1987, p. 71.

Barmash, I. *Welcome to Our Conglomerate—You're Fired.* New York: Dell Publishing, 1971.

Bastien, D. T. "Common Patterns of Behavior and Communication in Corporate Mergers and Acquisitions." *Human Resource Management* 26, no. 1 (1987): 17–33.

Bice, M. O. "The Transformation of Lutheran Health Systems." In *Corporate Transformation: Revitalizing Organizations for a Competitive World*, R. H. Kilmann, T. J. Covin & Associates. San Francisco: Jossey-Bass, 1988, 435–50.

Bowditch, J. L., and A. F. Buono. *Quality of Work Life Assessment: A Survey Based Approach.* Boston: Auburn House, 1982.

———. *Great Expectations: When the Hopes for a Better Life Following a Merger Turn Sour.* Paper presented at the 47th Annual Meeting of the Academy of Management. New Orleans, Louisiana, August 1987.

Buono, A. F. and J. L. Bowditch. *The Human Side of Mergers and Acquisitions*. San Francisco: Jossey-Bass, 1989.

———. "Mergers and Countercultural Tensions: Employee Resistance to Organizational Culture Change Efforts." *Proceedings of the Eastern Academy of Management* (1987): 105–8.

Buono, A. F., J. L. Bowditch, and J. W. Lewis. "The Cultural Dynamics of a Transformation: The Case of a Bank Merger." In *Corporate Transformations: Revitalizing Organizations for a Competitive World*, R. H. Kilmann, T. J. Covin & Associates. San Francisco: Jossey-Bass, 1988, 497–522.

———. "When Cultures Collide: The Anatomy of a Merger." *Human Relations* 38, no. 5 (1985): 477–500.

Buono, A. F., J. L. Bowditch, and A. J. Nurick. "The Hidden Costs of Organizational Mergers." In *Psychologie du Travail et Nouveaux Milieux de Travail*, A. Larocque, et al (eds.). Quebec: University of Quebec Press, 1987, 313–33.

Buono, A. F. and L. T. Nichols. *Corporate Policy, Values and Social Responsibility*. New York: Praeger, 1985.

Cavanagh, G. *American Business Values*. 2nd ed. Englewood Cliffs, N.J.: Prentice-Hall, 1984.

DeGeorge, R. T. *Business Ethics*. 2nd ed. New York: Macmillan, 1986.

Diven, D. L. "Organizational Planning: The Neglected Factor in Merger and Acquisition Strategy." *Managerial Planning* (July/August 1984): 4–8, 12.

Elliston, F., J. Keenan, P. Lockhart, and J. Van Schaick. *Whistleblowing: Managing Dissent in the Workplace*. New York: Praeger, 1985.

Freeman, R. E. *Strategic Management: A Stakeholder Approach*. Boston: Pitman, 1984.

Freeman, R. E. and D.L. Reed. "Stockholders and Stakeholders: A New Perspective on Corporate Governance." *California Management Review* 25, (1983): 88–106.

Fried, M. "Grieving for a Lost Home." In *The Urban Condition*, L. J. Duhl (ed.). New York: Basic Books, 1963, 151–71.

Gillis, J. G. and K.L. Casey. "Ethical Considerations in Takeovers." *Financial Analysts Journal* 41, no. 2 (1985): 10–12, 18.

Glaser, B. G. and A. L. Strauss. *Discovery of Grounded Theory: Strategies for Qualitative Research*. Chicago: Aldine, 1967.

Graves, D. "Individual Reactions to a Merger of Two Small Firms of Brokers in the Reinsurance Industry." *Journal of Management Studies* 18, no. 1 (1981): 89–113.

Halbouty, M. T. "The Hostile Takeover of Free Enterprise: Respect for Human Dignity." *Vital Speeches* 51, no. 20 (1985): 613–16.

Haspeslagh, P. C. and D. B. Jemison. "Acquisitions—Myths and Reality." *Sloan Management Review* (Winter 1987): 53–58.

Heylar, J. "Regional Trend: In the Merger Mania of Interstate Banking, Style and Ego are Key." *Wall Street Journal*, December 18, 1986, pp. 1, 10.

Janis, I. L., G. F. Mahl, J. Kagan, and R. R. Holt. *Personality*. New York: Harcourt, Brace & World, 1969.

Jemison, D. B. and S. B. Sitkin. "Acquisitions: The Process Can Be the Problem." *Harvard Business Review* 64, no. 2 (1986a): 107–16.

———. "Corporate Acquisitions: A Process Perspective." *Academy of Management Review* 11, no. 1 (1986b): 145–63.

Kanter, R. M. and T. K. Seggerman. "Managing Mergers, Acquisitions and Divestitures." *Management Review* (October, 1986): 16–17.

Kay, M. *The Impact of Mergers, Acquisitions and Downsizings.* Speech presented at a meeting of the New England Society of Applied Psychologists. Chestnut Hill, Mass., September 1987.

Levinson, H. "A Psychologist Diagnoses Merger Failures." *Harvard Business Review* 48, no. 2 (1970): 139–47.

Lubatkin, M. "Mergers and the Performance of the Acquiring Firm." *Academy of Management Review* 8, no. 2 (1983): 218–25.

McLeod, D. "Mergers Create Human Resource Problems." *Business Insurance*, April 21, 1986, p. 30.

Magnet, M. "Help! My Company Has Just Been Taken Over." *Fortune*, July 9, 1984, pp. 44–51.

Mangum, W. T. "In the Merger Hurricane, Keep an Eye on the Human Side of Change," *Data Management* (Summer 1984): 26–29.

Marks, M. L. "Merging Human Resources: A Review of the Literature." *Mergers & Acquisitions* (Summer 1982): 38–44.

Marks, M. L. and P. H. Mirvis. "The Merger Syndrome." *Psychology Today* (October 1986): 36–42.

———. "Merger Syndrome: Stress and Uncertainty." *Mergers & Acquisitions.* (Summer 1985): 50–55.

Michel, A. and I. Shaked. "Evaluating Merger Performance." *California Management Review* 27, no. 3 (1985): 109–18.

Norris, W. C. "Takeover and Justice." *U.S. News & World Report*, November 24, 1986, p. 83.

Nurick, A. J. *Participation in Organizational Change: The TVA Experiment.* New York: Praeger, 1985.

O'Boyle, T. F. "Loyalty Ebbs at Many Companies as Employees Grow Disillusioned." *Wall Street Journal*, July 11, 1985, p. 27.

O'Boyle, T. F. and M. Russell. "Troubled Marriage: Steel Giants' Merger Brings Headaches, J&L and Republic Find." *Wall Street Journal*, November 30, 1984, pp. 1, 20.

Pappanastos, J. S., L. T. Hillman, and P. A. Cole. "The Human Resource Side of Mergers." *Business* (July/September, 1987): 3–11.

Pritchett, P. *After the Merger: Managing the Shockwaves.* Homewood, Ill.: Dow Jones-Irwin, 1985.

Prokesch, Steven and Teresa Carson. "Do Mergers Really Work?" *Business Week*, June 3, 1985, 83–100.

"Quarterly Profile." *Mergers & Acquisitions* 21, no. 4 (1987a): 71.

"Quarterly Profile." *Mergers & Acquisitions* 22, no. 1 (1987b): 95.

Richman, J. D. "Merger Decision Making: An Ethical Analysis and Recommendations." *California Management Review* 27, no. 1 (1984): 177–84.

Robino, D. & K. DeMeuse. "Corporate Mergers and Acquisitions: Their Impact on HRM." *Personnel Administrator* 30, no. 11 (1985): 33–44.

Sales, A. and P. Mirvis. "When Cultures Collide: Issues in Acquisition." In *Managing Organizational Transitions*, J. R. Kimberly and R. E. Quinn (eds.). Homewood, Ill.: Richard D. Irwin, 1984, 107–33.

Sanders, P."Phenomenology: A New Way of Viewing Organizational Research." *Academy of Management Review* 1, no. 2 (1987): 353–60.

Sashkin, M. "Participative Management is an Ethical Imperative." *Organizational Dynamics* (Spring 1984): 5–22.

Schneider, B. "Employee and Customer Perceptions of Service in Banks." *Administrative Science Quarterly* 25, no. 2 (1980): 252–67.

Schweiger, D. M., J. M. Ivancevich, and F. R. Power. "Executive Actions for Managing Human Resources Before and After Acquisition." *Academy of Management Executive* 1, no. 2 (1987): 127–38.

Sinetar, M. "Mergers, Morale and Productivity." *Personnel Journal* (November 1981): 863–67.

Velasquez, M., G. Cavanagh, and D. Moberg. "Organizational Statesmanship and Dirty Politics: Ethical Guidelines for the Organizational Politician." *Organizational Dynamics* (Fall 1983): 68–78.

Understanding Target Management's Role When Facing an Unsolicited Takeover Attempt

PETER LINNEMAN
ELIZABETH CALLISON

The role of target management in the face of a hostile tender offer is a subject of much controversy. No other corporate transaction illuminates so clearly potential conflicts of interest between management and shareholders as when a bidder suddenly appears with the intention of acquiring the firm. All actions by target management have the potential for conflict of interest, and there are no simple methods to discriminate actions that are in shareholders' best interests from those that are not. Defensive tactics increase the costs of an acquisition and thus lower the probability that a bidder will appear at all. Some analysts argue that when faced with an unsolicitated offer, target management should remain passive. Others argue that bidders in hostile takeovers are robbing target shareholders and harming the long-term interests of the corporation. In this view, target management has an obligation to take defensive actions in order to protect shareholder interests.

The responses of target management to unsolicited offers run the gamut from passivity, to gut reactions that the bidder (in cahoots with arbitrageurs) is robbing the shareholders, to creating devices that place target shareholders in a better bargaining position, to the erection of impenetrable barriers that prevent control from changing hands. We argue that the two extremes, passivity and impenetrable barriers, are inappropriate. Also, shareholders, the press, and the regulators should be wary of knee-jerk reactions and attacks on bidders' motives. Rather, reactions that provide information to shareholders so that they can evaluate the offer and/or improve the bargaining power of the shareholder class are legitimate activities of target management.

SCENARIO

Management believes that the current stock price of $25 per share is too low. They feel that the discount rate the market applies to the firm's earnings stream is too high, reflecting the short-term nature of modern shareholders. They believe that their company is worth $40 per share and continually try to convince the investment community of this undervaluation.

Over a two-month period, the stock price moves up to $30 per share on fairly heavy volume. Management thinks that the market has recognized the under-valuation of the company and that a correction is underway. Suddenly, an un-solicited offer is received for $36 per share. Management's joy turns to terror as they realize that the recent stock price appreciation is part of the normal runup associated with tender offers.

The appropriate reaction of management under this scenario is unclear. On the one hand, the $36 offer represents a 44 percent premium over the stock price two months before. If they reject (and fight) the offer and it is withdrawn, the share price may fall back to $25. Shareholders will be unhappy, lawsuits charging management entrenchment will no doubt be filed, and management's own wealth (to the extent that they own shares and options) will fall. On the other hand, accepting the $36 offer means accepting an offer below the $40 they believe the company is worth. This, in actuality (if not legally), violates management's fiduciary duty to the shareholders. Further, there is a substantial probability that if they reject the offer, a higher bid will be forthcoming, either from a third party or from the original offerer.

Management must make its decisions in the face of imperfect information. For example, there is no guarantee that management is correct in its valuation of the company at $40 per share. Similarly, there is no guarantee that a superior offer will be forthcoming.

The potential for conflict of interest serves to magnify the problem, as man-agement's interests may not be synchronous with those of shareholders. Spe-cifically, an unsolicited offer raises the possibility that management personnel will lose their jobs. No managers want to lose their jobs, or they would have resigned prior to the offer. While management rarely overtly "rapes" share-holders, it may mistakenly evaluate its own importance and overcompensate itself at shareholder expense. Also, management may be too busy implementing business plans made earlier to take the time, or have the objectivity, to recognize that these plans may not currently be value-maximizing.

PASSIVE RESPONSE

A strategy of total management passivity, recommended by some analysts, avoids the potential for conflicting interests, as it leaves the decision completely to shareholders. However, this solution is clearly nonsensical. It cannot be the case that when faced with the ultimate decision about the financial fate of their investments, shareholders do not benefit from the use of their fiduciary agent—management. Shareholders have compensated management handsomely to provide fiduciary advice and management skills, and clearly this situation is one in which professional advice is required. This "Alice in Wonderland" thinking would similarly suggest that lawyers be kept on retainer but never used (as their fees are based on efforts, which can be padded) and that people should consult physicians but not undergo the recommended procedures (doctors are paid for services rendered and hence may prescribe them to generate fees). In all cases in which one relies on a professional for advice, there is potential for conflicts of interest. Shareholders as a class retain professional management for both advice and daily oversight of the firm. The fact that there is a potential for conflicts of interest in the face of an unsolicited offer does not indicate that the management should not give advice. Rather, it indicates that shareholders should consider management's advice with a healthy degree of skepticism. However, shareholders need the help of their well-paid fiduciaries in order to obtain the best deal possible.

GUT RESPONSES

Target management frequently reacts to unsolicited offers by attacking the motives of the bidder in undertaking the offer, and of shareholders for considering tendering. These gut responses come in four garden varieties. Shareholders, the press, and regulators should look hard at these attacks. In doing so, they will quickly discover that these are knee-jerk reactions with no substantive basis.

One common attack focuses on the plans of the bidder with respect to the future of the company. Target management claims that the raider, pejorative for a bidder, is not creating real value, but is simply "busting up" the company. The image created is that the raider buys the target just for the fun of dynamiting its productive facilities. Of course, the "bustup" is generally nothing more than divesting the firm of some divisions to buyers who will continue to operate them separately. There is no magic formula that dictates which business lines and divisions belong under the umbrella of a particular company. The market determines corporate structure and allows resources to flow to their most productive uses. Far from destroying productive assets, the "bustup" bidder profits by selling the divisions to an owner that intends to increase productivity. Thus, "bustup" bidders serve the function of allocating assets to more productive owners. It is telling that frequently the typical buyer in these "bustups" is the incumbent management of the division.

A second variety of gut reactions is to claim that the bidder is simply out to make money. This is indeed a strange complaint. Bidders legally buy and sell stocks (and assets), depending upon their confidence in management abilities, market conditions, and expectations for the future. If the bidder makes money, it is because there is money to be made in reallocating resources to more productive uses. Since all investors buy shares to make money, the only difference between raiders and average investors in this regard is the number of zeroes involved in the transaction, not the fundamental objective.

A third variety of gut reaction is to chastise shareholders for their short-term orientation. Management claims that this short-term focus makes the company vulnerable to takeovers and robs the economy of farsighted management. This claim is both hollow and misdirected. First, there is no systematic evidence to support the claim that takeovers represent situations in which long-run management is replaced by those who sacrifice long-run profits. Further, if shareholders wish to focus on the short-run gains, it is their right to do so. They are allowed to determine the time horizon for their investments and to buy and sell shares accordingly. If, in fact, shareholders have shorter time horizons than management claims to have, it may be because management has not delivered in the past. The story that profits will be forthcoming in the future has been told too often and, just as crying wolf diminishes the response to the plea, shareholders may simply choose to ignore such self-serving proclamations. It is too easy for management to claim that the future will yield high profits in order to excuse bad decisions made currently.

Finally, it is frequently argued that the shareholders who tender to the unsolicited bid are not real shareholders, but rather arbitrageurs ("arbs") who are not interested in the company's future. Management further argues that it is answerable only to real shareholders, and not arbs. Such an argument is fundamentally unsound. When an arb buys a share of the target, it buys all of the rights and obligations associated with that share. Just like any other shareholder, the arb purchases the right to future cash flows associated with the share, the right to sell the share, and the right to vote. As long as the arb legally obtains the shares, management has a fiduciary duty to act in the interest of the arb, just like any other shareholder.

The intellectual bankruptcy associated with drawing distinctions among types of shareholders in terms of management responsibility is made clear when one realizes that institutions, such as Goldman Sachs or Salomon Brothers, own shares for a variety of separate departments. For example, shares in a company may be owned as part of their own account, for pension fund clients, in trust accounts for clients, and for its risk arbitrage desk. Is this institution a real shareholder in the first three cases but not in the last? In each of these cases the shares are controlled by the same institution. Target management wishes to define this institution as a real shareholder only when it is convenient to do so, yet clearly it is a real shareholder in all cases.

If taken to its logical extreme, the argument that arbs are not real shareholders means that if arbitrageur owned 100 percent of the outstanding stock, management would be free to run the company in whatever fashion they please because arbitrageurs are not real shareholders. Such a conclusion is clearly at odds with our concept of corporate governance and the rights of shareholders.

STRATEGIC RESPONSES

Some defensive managerial responses have valid purposes, regardless of their end result. Others are clearly self-serving and should be forbidden for the welfare of target shareholders. The key to understanding the difference between defensive tactics that can be in the shareholders' best interests and those that are solely self-serving, is whether the tactic precludes the opportunity to tender shares. Those that circumvent the process by effectively eliminating the bidder only serve management interests at the expense of target shareholders. Other defensive tactics that release information about the target that has heretofore been private or that enhance the bargaining power of shareholders may be in the best interests of shareholders.

IMPENETRABLE BARRIERS

Impenetrable barriers to the successful completion of an unsolicited tender offer can be erected by target management. These barriers prevent the bidder's offer from reaching target shareholders. Because these defensive tactics reduce shareholder options, they can only be construed as entrenching. Four defensive tactics in current use reflect such managerial entrenchment. Any potential gains to shareholders are clearly outweighed by the harm to shareholders.

The first such defensive tactic is the repurchase of shares at a substantial premium, held by a legitimate unsolicited bidder. Since these repurchases remove, rather than create, competition for the company's shares, they cannot serve to enhance shareholder value. The only exceptions to this view are when the bidder is a pure nuisance, or if a forthcoming superior bid is contingent upon the absence of the unsolicited bidder as a shareholder. While such cases may exist in theory, a review of actual situations reveals that the bidders whose shares are repurchased are serious pursuers of the target and are a nuisance to target management in the same way that a conscience is a nuisance to a sinner. Further, superior bids for the target that are contingent on the absence of the unsolicited bidder do not seem to be the explanation for any such repurchases.

Press, politicians, and target management have labeled such repurchases greenmail and have likened the behavior of the bidder to that of a blackmailer. In fact, few analogies could be farther from the truth. Blackmail is the price the perpetrator extracts for silence about some indiscretion in the victim's ancient past. Greenmail, on the other hand, begins with a public proclamation about the bidder's belief that target management is poor, and hence greenmail cannot buy secrecy. A further key distinction between blackmail and greenmail lies in the source of the funds. The victim of blackmail draws upon personal funds, while target management removes the threat with shareholder funds. Finally, the bidder who receives greenmail, contrary to popular opinion, is not engaging in criminal-like activity. It is the offerer of greenmail who is acting negligently. In fact, if the bidder is a public company, then fiduciary duty to its shareholders may require that the bidder accept a greenmail payment.

The second defensive tactic that reveals an attempt to entrench management is the introduction of a dual capital structure with disparate voting rights among shareholders in the face of an unsolicited bid. It is important to realize that dual capitalization structures are legitimate when not implemented to remove the possibility of an acquisition. In these cases, the two classes of common stock are part of an optimal capital structure that depends on the prices available on different categories of debt and equity instruments. This is particularly true when the structure is announced at the time of the initial public offering, with the superior voting rights held by the founder of the company. At the initial offering, all purchasers of the shares know exactly what voting rights they are buying and who holds the voting control. However, when dual capital structures are implemented after a class of shareholders is already in place, whether there is immediate danger from an unsolicited bid or only a general threat, there are severe problems of conflicts of interest. If the plan calls for shareholders to reduce their control by creating a second class of superior shares controlled by management (with provisions rationally leading most shareholders to select the inferior voting shares), entrenchment occurs. In these cases, the supposed value-enhancing opportunities were neglected until the threat of takeover. A review of the plans that have been adopted in these circumstances shows that the control of the common shareholders at the time of the recapitalization substantially decreases, while the control of incumbent management increases commensurately. This restructuring virtually assures the failure of the unsolicited offer. It is indeed ironic that dual capitalization structures are sometimes used by the same management teams that attack two-tiered bids because they feel that two-tiered offers do not treat all shareholders equally.

A third defensive tactic that unambiguously harms target shareholders is a management buyout proposal formed to compete with an unsolicited bid. An attempt by target management to buy the company after the appearance of an unsolicited offer, although creating the appearance of competition, serves to stifle an outside bidding contest. After all, what white knight can be expected to compete with the bidder without management support?

Management buyout bids instituted in response to an unsolicited offer present unresolvable conflicts of interest. On the one hand, management's fiduciary duty requires it to obtain the best offer for target shareholders. On the other hand, as a bidder, management profits by offering the lowest acceptable price to shareholders. Management cannot act as a fiduciary agent (a role for which they have already been handsomely compensated) while at the same time attempting to structure their own bid (which they hope will be enormously profitable). Structurally, these conflicts are solved by setting up a group of outside directors to represent shareholders' interests. That is, the current solution to the problem is to eliminate management from the shareholder advisory process. However, this is an abrogation of duty by management, as shareholders have already contracted (and paid for) their services. Shareholders cannot be adequately served if at the moment of truth, management refuses to give its expert advice on the value of the company based upon information obtained over the years at shareholder expense. As noted earlier, passive response by management is nonsensical, and removing themselves from the fray through submitting an offer and then leaving the advising to outside directors is equally perverse.

It may be possible for management-led buyout offers to overcome the inherent conflicts between fiduciary duty and personal wealth maximization through the reliance on outside directors and financial advisors. However, the limited time frame created by an unsolicited offer clearly makes this impossible. In the offer time period, outside directors must simultaneously figure out operational and financial details best known to the management, evaluate and react to the un-solicited bidder, evaluate and react to the target management's bid, and carry out their normal employment responsibilities. This is far too much to expect realistically from outside directors within the short time period triggered by an unsolicited offer.

The use of incremental bidding tactics by a management buyout team further indicates the violation of fiduciary responsibility. When the management team first offers $38 and then two days later $40, only to raise the final offer to $41, it is hard to see how they can be acting in shareholders' best interests. If $41 is the fair price, how can they have bid only $38 only a few days earlier? Had they won at $38, shareholders would have been cheated. Further, who can believe that $41 is the right price, the maximum price that shareholders should receive? Since outside bidders bear no fiduciary loyalty to target company shareholders, the use of incremental bidding tactics by outsiders is perfectly legitimate, and may be a fiduciarily responsible tactic in terms of the bidder's shareholders. However, target management should never be allowed the luxury of an incre-mental bidding strategy.

The final, and most recent, defensive tactic that clearly violates shareholders' best interests is the lobbying of state legislatures to pass laws forbidding an unsolicited takeover attempt for that particular target. Examples of this type of behavior have become common. For example, Washington State, at the urging of Boeing, the state's largest employer, passed legislation that imposes a five-year ban on the sale of assets to pay off debt for any company with more than 20,000 employees that is taken over in a hostile bid. The political power wielded by large firms in states whose economic base depends on their employment is enormous. The abuse of this power to coerce the state legislators to enact laws that entrench managements of large companies by making its acquisition im-possible is clearly a violation of fiduciary duty to shareholders (although within the company's constitutional right to petition the government). In many cases, these laws are written in such a fashion that they only apply to the firm which argues for the passage. For example, Boeing is currently the only company in Washington that qualifies. Basically these laws are state-sanctioned management protections at the expense of shareholders.

The common theme in the four strategic responses analyzed is that they put up impenetrable barriers to an unsolicited bidder. In doing so, they remove the shareholders' right to sell their shares to whomever they please. Removing this opportunity can only entrench management and disenfranchise the shareholders.

NON-PREEMPTIVE DEFENSES

Other defensive tactics have more ambiguous effects on shareholder welfare. These defenses generally serve to alter the terms on which the bidder can approach the shareholder but do not necessarily prevent the approach, as such they may benefit or harm shareholders. Some management teams may adopt them for entrenchment under the guise of value-enhancing tactics. These tactics include fair-price amendments, super-majority rules, pacman defenses, and shareholders' rights plans.

For example, shareholders' rights plans (often referred to as poison pills) may be designed either to make the target unpalatable or to cause the raider to raise and restructure the offer. Since the adoption of a shareholders' rights plan generally adds uncertainty and causes delays in the bidding process, the use of this strategic device may increase the likelihood of creating a competitive bidding situation. Further, they reduce the likelihood of two-tiered offers and increase the likelihood of a negotiated deal. However, excessive rights plans can clearly insulate target management from acting in the interests of shareholders. It is interesting to note that shareholders' rights plans have not kept numerous companies from falling prey to unsolicited bidders. However, the designers of these rights plans never claimed that these plans are designed to render companies takeover-proof. Instead, they have stated that these plans are designed to eliminate potentially abusive two-tiered unsolicited bids.

In a similar manner, the fabled pacman defense may reflect target management's intention to retain their jobs at all costs. Alternatively, it may simply represent an unstated agreement with the bidder's intention to combine the companies, but a strong disagreement about which management team should be in command of the combined firm. Since the latter situation is one which commonly arises in friendly merger negotiations, it may be that the pacman strategy simply works out this fundamental problem in the pages of the *Wall Street Journal*, rather than behind the closed doors of a boardroom.

CONCLUSION

What, then, is a target management to do when confronted with an unsolicited takeover attempt? Passivity is not appropriate. Gut responses may buy time but serve to antagonize all parties. Other management responses can either serve to entrench the management or to enhance shareholder value. However, the erection of impenetrable barriers that prevent an offer from reaching the shareholders serves only to entrench. These defenses are thus a violation of management's fiduciary duty.

We have carefully observed, and even played a very minor role, in the merger wars of the past decade. We have heard, and sometimes believed, the justifications for all defensive actions taken by target management. As a result of these observations, we believe that target management should play an active role when faced with an unsolicited offer. However, while wide discretion should be given to management regarding ways to represent shareholders, we must always remember that not all defensive tactics serve shareholders' interests and, in particular, the four mentioned earlier never do.

How to Preserve and Build Your Managerial Core During Corporate Restructuring

HERBERT W. JARVIS
ROBERT F. PEARSE

ECONOMIC ASPECTS OF MERGERS, ACQUISITIONS, AND LEVERAGED BUYOUTS

According to data published in *Mergers and Acquisitions*, the total dollar value of corporate mergers, acquisitions, and leveraged buyouts during the past ten years is in excess of $700 billion.[1] In 1986 alone, the value was over $190 billion. The number of mergers rose from 1,209 in 1977 to 4,024 in 1986.

The same data indicate that 34.3 percent of the mergers and acquisitions involved divestitures; 21.4 percent were leveraged buyouts. Combining these figures reveals that over 55 percent of mergers and acquisitions during the last ten years involved significant restructuring. Such restructuring has a direct impact on each organization's managerial core. We define the managerial core as that group of managers whose skills and motivations are essential to operations.

The merger and acquisitions business has become so significant that *Business Week* refers to it as "corpocracy." The article states, "The restructuring of Corporate America could well generate the kind of social and political heat that normally goes with a severe economic crisis."[2]

Deal-makers tend to present themselves as being altruistically concerned with enhancing stockholder value through the divestment and restructuring that follow a merger and acquisition or leveraged buyout. For the record, it should be noted that those involved in such activities usually come away with a significant profit for themselves and their associates. A recent *New York Times* article, "Shaking Billions From Beatrice," indicates how significant this type of profit can be.[3] For service fees, Kohlberg, Kravis, Roberts & Co. received $45 million. In addition, a projected profit from their investment could be as high as $2.4 billion. Drexel Burnham Lambert got $86 million plus $810 million in projected profits.

The third largest profit maker, Donald P. Kelley, received a projected $277 million profit on his investment, plus significant fees.

The *Times* quotes Jim Hightower (Texas agriculture commissioner) as saying, "Kolberg Kravis now controlled the nation's largest food conglomerate, but couldn't make a biscuit if someone kneaded the dough."[4] Kravis justifies the large fees earned by investment bankers, lawyers, and other specialists in terms of the enormous risks involved.

Golden parachute payments by BCI Holdings to former Beatrice executives included William W. Granger, Jr. (Chairman for four months), $6.4 million; Anthony Luiso (Executive Vice President), $3.48 million; and David E. Lipson (Executive Vice President), $4.27 million.

HOW SUCCESSFUL HAVE MERGERS AND ACQUISITIONS BEEN?

There is more than one way to define success in this field. One author cites comparisons on the basis of earnings per share. According to this definition of success, he indicates that acquisitions have only a 50–50 chance of being successful. In a random sample of ten companies engaged in acquisitions, not one achieved the *Fortune 500* 13.82 median return on investment.[5]

P. Haspeslagh and D. Jemison state that the raider "captures value," while the builder "creates value."[6] To capture short-term value, the raider often engages in such activities as asset stripping and excessive leveraging. In addition, his policies are frequently determined by short-term tax considerations. Essentially, he is willing to mortgage potential future value for short-term gain.

The raider's strategy is to acquire a corporation and enhance shareholder value by selling off assets, reducing debt, and cutting costs. He expects to make a one-time profit for his efforts and risks. He does not intend to stay and run the company over a long period of time. He achieves the goal of a "lean and mean" organization by aggressive cost cutting, maximizing cash flow to pay off debt, and then moves on. The raider is successful when he has completed this process.

The collaborative builder, in contrast, creates value on a long-term basis by producing operating profits that will satisfy stockholder expectations over a long period of time. To become highly cost-effective in today's environment, the builder, like the raider, has to create a "lean and mean" organization. The heart of his organization is a managerial core that is committed to helping him run a productive and competitive corporation. The builder is successful when the organization reaches this level of productivity and competitiveness.

This chapter will deal primarily with the differences in approaches to the managerial core group used by the raider and the builder during restructuring. The voluntary merger is a special situation. It uses collaborative building strategies to blend two managerial cores into one new "lean and mean" corporation.

THE VOLUNTARY MERGER APPROACH TO THE
MANAGERIAL CORE

In a voluntary "merger of equals," the newly evolved organization takes the best human resource strengths available from both merged organizations. Combining the best people from both organizations and eliminating redundancy creates the synergistic saving.

Selecting the new CEO involves both performance and political considerations. In successful voluntary mergers, the CEO both provides personal leadership competence (relative to the organizational mission) and is also politically acceptable to all key constituencies. The next key managerial core decisions involve combining the two old boards of directors into one new board. Allocating responsibilities to a new set of managers usually involves matching the new organizational mission with individual talent. Key factors in making core manager assignments include age, experience, and performance reputation.

Even in the friendliest voluntary merger, restructuring the managerial core can't be accomplished without some individuals experiencing stress dislocations and disappointments. Some managers are bound to be frustrated, even bitter, at the impact of the new arrangements on their career status and opportunities. Old premerger subgroup loyalties continue to exist for a time. It takes time for employees to perceive and respond, to give up their old subgroup identification and see themselves as members of a new managerial core team. The intensive use of "what's fair" business ethics treatment is particularly important in minimizing intergroup transition problems.

CREATING A "LEAN AND MEAN" ORGANIZATION
THROUGH RESTRUCTURING

Restructuring is a primary cost-reduction tool used by both the raider and the builder to streamline operations after mergers, acquisitions and leveraged buyouts. It typically involves both divestiture of divisions and downsizing corporate staff.

A recent *Fortune* article indicates that effective restructuring can make U.S. corporations competitive again.

Seven corporations, representing a cross section of the Fortune 500, offer compelling testimony that restructuring can indeed lower break even points substantially and lead to a doubling or even tripling of earnings. The seven are Ford Motor Co., Ralston Purina, Eastman Kodak, Champion International, Hanson Industries, Cyprus Minerals, and Navistar International.[7]

A recent *Business Week* article states that America's new "leanest and meanest" corporations give us our best hope for competing successfully in world markets.

such companies are representative of a new hard nosed approach to business in the U.S. They have cut costs to the bone, selling marginal businesses, closing inefficient plants, slashing personnel. But these companies have gone much further to boost productivity. They have become innovators in product development, marketing and distribution, constantly discovering ways to do the job better and cheaper. They are also willing to spend money to make money.[8]

The builder uses many of the same techniques as these successfully restructured corporations. He sees restructuring, creating a new high-productivity climate, and building a "lean and mean" organization as necessary to survive and grow in a strongly competitive market. N. Tichy and M.A. Devanna, in their recent book, *The Transformational Leader*, cite a number of collaborative building approaches to improving corporate performance.[9]

THE RAIDER AND THE COLLABORATIVE BUILDER HAVE DIFFERENT TIME FRAMES

The raider and the collaborative builder have many similar goals. The major difference in their approach to handling the managerial core during restructuring results from their different time frames. Although *what* each does is similar, *how* they go about doing it is quite different. While both honor *integrity* in the sense of honoring legal contracts, the raider's short time frame does not require application of the "what's fair" business ethic.

The builder has a significantly longer time frame. To change a low-performance corporate culture into a high-performance one requires careful building over a longer period. Preserving and building a productivity-oriented managerial core is the key to building a competitive business that returns stockholder value over time.

THE RAIDER'S APPROACH TO THE MANAGERIAL CORE

The raider usually brings in or keeps a relatively small group of proven performers as his core management. They know how to work with him and are willing to implement his methods. The raider intends to provide profits and value not only to shareholders but also to key core managers and to himself. In effect, he says to members of the managerial core, "I expect to make a lot of money on this deal, and I am willing to put in my own money to demonstrate my confidence. I also expect you to put your money into the deal as a sign of your confidence both in yourself and in me. I'm willing to give you a piece of the action (profits and equity appreciation) if you produce according to my satisfaction. If I don't make it, you won't make it. Don't ask me for an employment contract." The raider feels that managerial core members who ask for an employment contract lack confidence both in themselves and in him. Given this blunt "produce or perish" challenge, managers who sign on have a clear understanding of requirements and rewards.

The raider drops those members of management he thinks he doesn't need. This variation of the survival of the fittest breeds managers who are committed to follow and adopt the raider's philosophy. Like the gladiators of old, those who survive become skillful at their trade. Those who don't survive fall by the wayside.

THE BUILDER'S APPROACH TO THE MANAGERIAL CORE

Both the raider and the collaborative builder have to divest, downsize, and restructure to achieve a "lean and mean" organization. Typically, restructuring involves eliminating layers of management. Both the raider and the builder end up with significant reductions in layers. A typical organization, for example, might reduce from seven layers to four.

How the builder does the restructuring is very crucial for the long-term success of his organization. In addition to practicing integrity by honoring legal contracts, the builder practices the "what's fair" business ethic because he is convinced that members of the managerial core will accept the inevitable dislocations of restructuring better if they feel they and others have been treated fairly. His philosophy is pragmatic rather than utopian. He communicates by both deeds and actions that the "what's fair" ethic will be the cornerstone of his effort to preserve and build a restructured management team.

CEO actions in managerial layoffs and reassignments need to be seen as both necessary and equitable. A number of factors are important in developing an equitable treatment climate during layoffs. Relative ability, past contribution, capacity to relocate, and severance pay to bridge the economic loss need to be put into the "what's fair" decision. Managers in the same general categories should be treated as uniformly as possible to avoid perceptions of inequity.

A feeling that numbers of the management core are not personally benefiting at the expense of loyal long-service employees during restructuring is very important. Managers and rank-and-file employees can accept unpleasant changes if these changes are perceived as being both necessary and fairly handled. Respecting beliefs about what is fair and acting accordingly brings both positive motivation and a willingness to produce in terms of new standards of performance.

The new organization's managerial structure should closely relate to new corporate goals. In restructuring, the existing managers will generally fall into one of three categories: essential, temporarily necessary, and redundant.

Members of the *essential* group can be reassured about their future relatively easily. They can be given employment contracts, performance incentives, and challenging work assignments. The collaborative building message to this group is: "Don't jump ship. We consider you essential members of our managerial core. Here is how you can contribute to the new, 'lean and mean' organization." It is important that members of this group be made part of the company's ongoing decision-making process. Their involvement and participation help to create commitment. This commitment results in both productivity and job satisfaction.

Those managers who are redundant should be notified early and terminated. Top management should establish a termination program in which the manager's level of management, length of service, and past performance are considered. When emotional and financial support is provided appropriately as part of a career transition system, it is easier to build support for the new emerging corporate culture. The managerial core group that needs and deserves the most careful treatment are the temporarily necessary. These managers are asked to devote a significant period of time (usually six to eighteen months) to serving the new organization. They must do this knowing they will be terminated later. Their full-time employment will not permit them to answer ads or take interviews. When their assignment is over, they should be provided with special outplacement and other career relocation services. This should be in addition to a generous severance arrangement. Top management tries to position them so they are able to move on to opportunities outside the corporation with a minimum of separation trauma. Providing reasonable secretarial assistance, phone service, and office space, where necessary, is often helpful as a way to gain their continued contribution.

IMPACT OF RESTRUCTURING ON THE MANAGERIAL CORE

In its special report, "Managers Without a Company," *Fortune* discusses the human impact of restructuring on affected managers. The article states:

For most who get the ax in corporate retrenchments, generous severance packages can't compensate for the grief and humiliation. For most of those left behind at the office, life becomes filled with anxiety as they wait for the ax to fall again.[10]

A recent series of articles in the *Personnel Administrator* is devoted to developing effective approaches to restructuring and downsizing in order to avoid negative impact on managers and nonmanagerial employees. One article states,

The key to success seems to be a strategic plan that validates the cuts and makes decisive eliminations. Job cuts must appear sensible even to those most painfully affected. Communication of the rationale soothes hurt feelings, regardless of how generous the severance settlements may be. And it gives remaining employees a clear sign regarding how their performance and future contributions to the company will be linked to their own success.[11]

USING THE PRODUCTIVITY GRAPH TO CHANGE THE CORPORATE CULTURE

Necessary changes during restructuring raise employee anxiety levels throughout the organization. Expectations and assumptions that existed in the old cor-

Figure 14.1
The Productivity Graph: Restructuring Corporate Culture

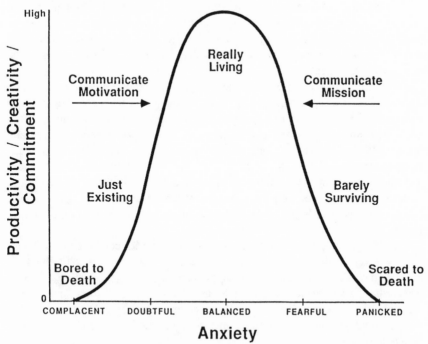

porate culture are often shattered. Sharply increased anxiety based on uncertainty causes managers to question job security, compensation policy, performance standards, and even the basic mission of the company.

To optimize productivity, commitment, and creativity, both the raider and the builder must deal with core manager anxiety. A method of converting managerial anxiety into productivity is depicted in the ''Productivity Graph'' (see Figure 14.1).[12] The horizontal axis indicates that employee anxiety levels can be placed in one of three broad categories from almost none to extremely high. At the low end, employees are complacent. The Complacents are convinced that their job is absolutely secure. They generally lack interest or commitment. This type of employee or manager is typically found in the benevolently paternalistic company. Often these are the old-line bureaucracies where compliant mediocrity has been rewarded for loyal, unimaginative conformity to bureaucratic performance norms. These corporate cultures offer high job security and do not reward productivity beyond a low average output. The prevailing employee/manager attitude is, ''What I do doesn't really matter. I'll conform, do what I'm told, and no more.'' Unless they undergo a radical change in attitude, not many managers of this type survive in a ''lean and mean'' organization. Those who do survive have to change their value system and old behavior patterns. They also have to respond to incentives tied to performance. The new culture requires them to live with a higher level of anxiety because they have lower job security. Their compensation is based on productivity rather than on bureaucratic conformity. They must emotionally accept the fact that the corporate culture has changed. They either meet the new standards or leave.

At the high-anxiety end of the horizontal line is a second group of managers, the Panicked. During a takeover or restructuring, many managers fall into this category. They overreact to rumors and perceive the culture change as being laden with uncertainties and fear of job loss. High anxiety drains energy and results in low productivity. Their relative immobilization is often due to a lack of understanding of their job status. They also feel helpless and lost because they do not understand the new corporate mission, or because they have not been involved in the decision-making process. Emotionally, these managers feel, ''I don't know what's going on, where I fit in, or where the corporation is going.''

The third group, the Balanced, are those managerial core members whose anxiety level is above that of the Complacents and below that of the Panicked. They have enough anxiety to be energized into productive behavior when roles, assignments, and rewards are made clear. Yet they are not immobilized with overanxiety as the Panicked managers are. They are capable of becoming performance-oriented members of the new ''lean and mean'' organization.

The raider quickly creates a core management group by bringing in his proven key manager team from outside. He enlarges this core by selecting those he needs from within the corporation. He often does this within a few days of gaining corporate control. All core members understand and accept his mission of capturing value or they are terminated.

The builder generally moves more deliberately. He provides an incentive to existing managers who help the restructuring succeed. Since his long-term goal is to create value, he builds by looking first within the core to find those who will help him implement change. His ''what's fair'' approach helps lower anxiety even in the Redundant group who are terminated.

In both the raider and builder approaches, effective incentives and communications will either restore or increase productivity as the new ''lean and mean'' corporate culture evolves. The builder can use the ''Productivity Graph'' as a corporate culture change tool during restructuring.

He first estimates the levels and types of anxieties that exists within the organization. Then he sets up planned communications and incentive programs designed to bring the organization into the Really Living portion of the graph. Effectively done, this results in a new ''lean and mean'' high performance corporate culture.

HOW COST-EFFECTIVE IS THE "WHAT'S FAIR" BUSINESS ETHICS APPROACH TO RESTRUCTURING?

The builder's "what's fair" approach generally costs more in up-front investment in developing a "lean and mean" high-performance team culture than does the raider's approach. In fact, the "what's fair" ethics approach is not even relevant to the raider's strategy. His total focus is on eliminating leveraged debt, enhancing his own and shareholder equity, and developing positive cash flow.

The builder invests time and money in a "what's fair" approach to restructuring. Building a high-performance growth organization requires developing managerial core commitment and dedication. The builder's "lean and mean" team produces the long-term financial results that shareholders expect.

In terms of final cost, nothing is more cost-effective than productivity. By using "what's fair" ethics, plus lowering manager/employee anxiety (as illustrated in the "Productivity Graph"), the builder enables employees at all levels to produce in the restructured organization. The builder's initial investment in building the managerial core is repaid many times over in long-term performance results.

NOTES

1. "1986 Profile," *Mergers & Acquisitions* (May/June 1987): 57.
2. "Deal Mania," *Business Week* Special Report, November 24, 1986, p. 75.
3. "Shaking Billions from Beatrice," *New York Times* Sunday, September 6, 1987, p. 7F.
4. Ibid., 8F.
5. P. Pritchett, *After the Merger: Managing the Shockwaves* (Homewood, Ill.: Dow Jones-Irwin, 1985), p. 9.
6. P. Haspeslagh and D. Jemison, "Acquisitions—Myths and Reality," *Sloan Management Review* (Winter 1987): 54–55
7. "Old-Line Industry Shapes Up," *Fortune*, April 27, 1987, p. 23.
8. "America's Leanest and Meanest," *Business Week*, October 5, 1987, p. 78.
9. N. Tichy and M.A. Devanna, *The Transformational Leader* (New York: Wiley, 1986).
10. F. Kessler, "Managers Without a Company," *Fortune*, October 28, 1985, p. 51.
11. Special section on Restructuring, Downsizing Strategies, and Outplacement, *Personnel Administrator* (February 1987): 45–64 (quotation on p. 64—"Downsizing Strategies").
12. The "Productivity Graph" model is adapted from an illustration presented by Judith Bardwick while lecturing at an R.I.T. Executive Seminar on her book, *The Plateauing Trap* (New York: Amacom, 1986).

___ 15 _____

Tender Offers: An Ethical Perspective

JOHN R. BOATRIGHT

More and more people are concerned with the hostile takeover as a moral issue. It deeply offends the sense of justice of a great many Americans.
—Peter F. Drucker
"To End the Raiding Roulette Game"[1]

INTRODUCTION

The increasing pace of mergers and acquisitions in recent years has focused attention on some very troubling questions about the justification of takeovers and the morality of certain takeover practices. The hostile takeover in particular has struck some observers as a complete abandonment of morality in the free enterprise system, and even those who take a more sanguine view are troubled by the excesses of takeover activity and the damage it does to American business.[2]

The moral problems raised by takeovers are much too tangled and complex for a single chapter, and so I have chosen to limit the scope to some of the problems involved in one particular practice, namely tender offers. My reason for choosing this subject is that a tender offer is the most commonly used technique in hostile takeovers, and these unwelcome assaults occasion the sharpest tactics and consequent charges of foul play. In addition, tender offers are governed by federal law as part of the regulation of the securities market, while questionable defensive tactics and most other aspects of takeovers are within the province of state laws concerning corporate governance. The subject of tender offers, therefore, can be treated in relative isolation from some of the other moral problems posed by mergers and acquisitions.

As a means for acquiring corporate control, tender offers have not occasioned as much concern as the desirability of takeovers in general or the defensive strategies that have been devised to counter them. It is common for hostile takeovers to be decried along with such colorful tactics as poison pills, shark repellents, golden parachutes, and the like, but rarely do we hear of tender offers themselves being criticized. Like any financial practice, however, there is a potential for abuse, which must be curbed by appropriate regulation. And the use of tender offers in place of other means for acquiring control of a corporation raises some substantial problems about the rights of stockholders and their role in corporate governance.

In this chapter I am mainly concerned with what can be morally objectionable about tender offers which would warrant their regulation. Some of the objections are obvious and are addressed by existing legislation and proposals for reform, but there are some which are less obvious and have not been adequately addressed.

AN OVERVIEW OF TENDER OFFERS

A tender offer is an offer to purchase shares of stock in a corporation in return for cash or certain securities. The price or value of the securities usually represents a substantial premium over the price at which the stock is trading at the time. The purpose of a tender offer is to enable the bidder, which may be a single investor, a group of investors, or another firm, to gain a large block of shares quickly, usually when this cannot be done by open market purchases. There are many reasons for purchasing a large block of stock, but most commonly the purpose is to acquire control of a corporation or to merge it with another. A tender offer is called hostile or unfriendly when it is made directly to the stock-holders without consulting the management of the target company.

Much of the alleged unfairness of tender offers arises from their use in swift well-organized raids, which catch the management of target companies unaware. In particular, the now illegal "Saturday night special"—in which an offer is made over a weekend when the stock market is closed and the company is not prepared to respond—seems to give the aggressors an unfair advantage by allowing time and the lack of information to work to their advantage. The management of a company has a fiduciary responsibility to make a response that best serves the interests of the stockholders. If the offer represents the best value, the management has no rightful choice but to recommend its acceptance, but if it is not a good value, the managers of a company have a corresponding obligation not only to counsel against it but to take other legal defensive measures in an effort to thwart the takeover. It takes both time and information to assess a tender offer adequately and to respond in a responsible way.

The stockholders who must decide whether to tender their shares labor under the same disadvantages and more. Will they realize a greater return by keeping the stock or selling? What is the value of any securities offered as payment? What are the plans of the aggressor? Will a better offer be made? In addition to the necessity of answering these questions quickly and without sufficient knowledge, stockholders are also subject to other forces. Partial offers for only a fixed number of shares put great pressure on stockholders to tender quickly or run the risk of not being able to sell at the premium price, and two-tier offers in which one price is set for a fixed number of shares and a different price (usually lower) for the balance of the shares to be purchased create an incentive to tender early to get the higher price. In some cases, however, the offer is increased, or there is a better offer by a competitor—which is sometimes the company itself, offering to buy back its own stock—or a white knight come to save the company from an aggressor.

The beneficiaries of the premium on tendered shares are often large investors, including arbitrageurs, who have access to information more quickly and have the resources to develop large positions in a target company purely for speculative purposes. In the case of partial or two-tier offers, there is the possibility that such investors could provide all the wanted shares at least on the first tier, which would deprive smaller investors of the opportunity to sell at a premium and perhaps force them to settle for a lower second-tier price. The owners of stock held in a street name may never even learn of a tender offer, which may not only prevent them from participating, but also open the way for brokerage firms to take advantage of such accounts.[3] Some large stockholders may be in a position to demand greenmail, whereby a company offers to buy back a portion of its own stock, usually from an aggressor, in order to thwart a takeover bid. In one instance, though, a company made a tender offer for its own stock that *excluded* a large investor.[4]

Perhaps the most frequent instances of questionable conduct since the passage of legislation curbing the major abuses of tender offers have been attempts to evade the law by exploiting the lack of a precise definition.[5] The definition of a tender offer became an issue, for example, in the attempted takeover of Becton, Dickinson by Sun Oil Company, when the resulting court suit turned on whether private purchases of 34 percent of Becton, Dickinson stock from six individuals and thirty-three institutional investors in an organized blitz that was completed within an hour constituted a tender offer. A federal district judge ruled that it did, and Sun's takeover bid failed.[6] Another question is whether self-tenders should come under the laws regulating tender offers. The SEC charged that the stock repurchase plan used by Carter Hawley Hale Stores to resist a hostile takeover was a thinly disguised tender offer, but the SEC lost this case in court.

More recently, several prominent takeovers have featured open-market purchases after the withdrawal of tender offers. Hanson Trust Plc., for example, purchased 25 percent of SCM stock from just six larger holders within two hours of canceling a tender offer, which led the SEC to charge that the tender offer was used to entice arbitrageurs to amass large blocks of stock, which could be bought on the open market after the termination of the tender offer.[7] In the resulting suit, *SCM Corp. v. Hanson Trust Plc.*, the SEC position was again rejected, which has left great uncertainty as to what constitutes a tender offer.[8]

There are several other troubling aspects of tender offers, which I shall mention but not pursue any further. One concerns the source of the cash or the kinds of securities that are used as payment. In a leveraged buyout the payment is made by borrowing against the assets or the anticipated profits of the company taken over. The use of so-called junk bonds to finance takeovers has been viewed by many as a threat to the soundness of the securities markets. Finally, the largest award to date in a suit involving a tender offer is the $10.5 billion settlement awarded to Pennzoil for damages when Texaco upset the "handshake" agreement between Pennzoil and Getty Oil Company. The issue here is mainly when has an agreement been made, and the only likely result will be to ensure that there is a signed contract before an announcement is made.[9]

THE WILLIAMS ACT

The main piece of legislation regulating tender offers is the Williams Act of 1968.[10] Before 1968 tender offers were largely unregulated except by stretching existing laws to cover them, with less than satisfactory results.[11] The stated purpose of this act is to protect investors by imposing time limits, disclosure requirements, and certain other rules for making tender offers when a bid is made to obtain control of a corporation.[12] It also protects target companies by putting an end to the abuses of the "Saturday night special."

Under Section 14(d) of the Williams Act, a tender offer must be accompanied by a statement filed with the SEC and with the target company detailing the terms of the offer, the nature and source of the financing, information on the bidder, and the bidder's plans in the event of a successful takeover. Section 13(d) requires a similar statement within ten days from anyone who acquires 5 percent (originally 10 percent) of a company's stock. Such information alerts stockholders and target companies to an impending takeover attempt and provides the basis for an orderly response.

Critics of these provisions have pointed out, however, that given the speed with which stock can be purchased, the ten-day window allows an aggressor to continue buying and perhaps gain a controlling interest before a statement must be filed. The act does not prevent several buyers acting in concert to acquire less than 5 percent each, and when large blocks of stock are accumulated by arbitrageurs in anticipation of a bid, it is possible to buy from them directly without a tender offer, as occurred in the Hanson takeover of SCM. Proposals have been made to prevent this by reducing the filing period from ten to five days and by prohibiting purchases in excess of 5 percent until after the disclosure statement is filed.[13]

The Williams Act deals with limited and two-tier offers and the equal treatment of stockholders by requiring proration of all shares tendered during a specified period. Thus, if more shares are tendered than the bidder has offered to buy, then the same percentage of each stockholder's shares tendered during the period of offering must be purchased. Any tender offer must be open for a period of twenty business days (originally ten calendar days) in order to allow stockholders time to learn about and evaluate it. Those who tender their stock also have fifteen days in which to change their minds, which allows the acceptance of any better offer. A provision of Section 14(d) known as the "best price rule" explicitly requires the bidder in a tender offer to pay any increased consideration to all tendering shareholders.

None of these provisions is without complications. When stock is tendered in a proration pool, the stockholder has little way of knowing what portion will be accepted. Any stock tendered cannot be used for other purposes, and the longer the proration period, the longer use of the stock is tied up in the tender offer. Since each new offer or change in a previous offer creates a new proration pool, there is the possibility of multiple proration pools, which have the potential for manipulation.[14] The grace period allows for precisely timed counteroffers, which gives the second bidder an advantage, and since this bidder is often a white knight, the SEC holds that this advantage tips the balance in favor of the target company.[15]

A potentially important provision, Section 14(e) of the Williams Act, prohibits "any fraudulent, deceptive, or manipulative acts or practices." Prohibitions on fraud and deception are common features in the regulation of commercial transactions, but the word "manipulation" introduces a distinctively ethical element which is not clearly defined. The courts have been reticent, however, to construe "manipulation" very broadly. So far, most of the suits based on 14(e) have dealt with defensive measures and in particular with lockups and "crown jewel" options.[16] With one notable exception, namely the Mobil-Marathon case, the decisions in these suits have not found various defensive tactics to be manipulative under the Williams Act. In a landmark decision, the Federal District Court of Maryland held in the case *Martin-Marietta v. Bendix* that since the Williams Act is purely a disclosure requirement, there can be no manipulation as long as the proper disclosures are made. In the words of one observer, "So long as you tell all, there can be no 'manipulation'."[17]

CAN TENDER OFFERS BE COERCIVE?

The purpose of regulating tender offers, according to the SEC Advisory Committee on Tender Offers, is "to protect the interests of shareholders and the integrity and efficiency of the capital markets."[18] No mention is made of the other parties involved except to say: "Takeover regulation should not favor either the acquirer or the target company but should aim to achieve a reasonable balance." The report also states that takeover regulation should not be used either to promote or to deter takeovers. These last two points can be combined by saying that in the battle for corporate control, tender offer laws should be completely neutral between the competing parties and between alternative outcomes. I argue later that it is not possible to separate the interests of stockholders from questions about the justice of the competition or of alternative outcomes nor to avoid these questions about justice in devising a regulatory scheme. But

I want to focus first on the ostensible aim of protecting the interests of stockholders.

Embedded in the legal structure of our economic system is the principle that each person is the best judge of his or her own interests. A libertarian defender of voluntary transactions, in particular, would sanction any offer and a response to it on the grounds that all of the parties involved ought to be at liberty to decide for themselves. A person's interests are harmed if that person is made worse off in some way, but there can be nothing unjust, according to the libertarian view, if the harm results from a purely voluntary transaction. Being made worse off by force or fraud, on the other hand, cannot be justified in this way, for even if there is agreement, it cannot be wholly voluntary. Accepting a tender offer, however, generally makes the stockholder not worse but better off, since the bid typically involves a substantial premium. What can be wrong with merely offering to buy a portion of a person's stock holdings, especially at a price above the current trading level, as long as there is no force or fraud?

I argue that tender offers can be morally objectionable for being coercive. The possibility of coercive offers is an important and widely discussed topic about which there is considerable controversy. Among legal scholars there is concern that the immense power of government to withhold benefits can serve to secure compliance almost as effectively as the threat of punishment. Offering child support payments to an unmarried mother on the condition that she not live with a man, for example, might be regarded as a form of coercion, even though the technique of control is a benefit and not the threat of some harm. Some philosophers, on the other hand, deny the possibility of coercive offers on the ground that supposed offers are disguised threats rather than true offers.[19]

The coercive potential of tender offers arises, I believe, from the possibility of what economists call a "trader's surplus." In an economic transaction, both parties may be assumed to emerge better off, but one party may be comparatively better off than the other as a result of superior bargaining power. Every trader has a minimum transfer price for any good, which is the lowest price at which a good is willingly traded, and a trade will be made at any price above the minimum. A trader with superior bargaining power, however, may be able to frame the choice situation in such a way that in the resulting trade what he receives is well above the minimum transfer price for what he gives up, while the poor bargainer gains something that is only slightly above the minimum transfer price for what is given in trade.

It is a fact of economic life that people have unequal bargaining positions for a wide variety of reasons, and this inequality may be used to drive a hard bargain without inviting a charge of coercion. A hard bargain need not be unjust. Often the difference in bargaining strength results from factors that cannot be easily altered without giving up something of moral value. The housing market, for example, is subject to fluctuations that give an advantage at one time to buyers and at another to sellers. The forces at work are largely beyond the control of individuals in the housing market, and insofar as they could be controlled—say by a price control board—greater injustice might result. A free market in housing, moveover, benefits and harms the typical homeowner in roughly equal measure over a lifetime of buying and selling, so that the overall result is just.

Without the safeguards of the Williams Act, tender offers may involve unequal bargaining positions without the justifying condition that it cannot be easily altered without giving up something of moral value. If the choice is to tender immediately or risk the possibility of not realizing the premium reflected in the offer, then a stockholder may voluntarily but reluctantly choose to sell. The reluctance arises from the fact that the stockholder is not being allowed to make a fully rational decision in which all relevant information is duly considered. The choice that the stockholder would like to have includes access to adequate information and sufficient time to evaluate the offer carefully, as well as the opportunity to consider all possible competing offers.

We cannot always be presented with the choices we would like to have, but tender offers could easily be made on more agreeable terms, which allow the stockholder to make a decision less reluctantly without requiring the offerer to make any significant sacrifice. Control over the timing of an offer and over access to vital information may confer a significant advantage that influences the outcome, but such factors are easily altered. Moreover, taking this control away would not seem to violate any right of the offerer nor subvert any desirable social goal. A different outcome may not be to the advantage of the offerer, and in this respect something of value has been lost. But it remains to be shown that the offerer *ought* to have this advantage and that what has been lost has *moral* value. The solicited stockholder, on the other hand does, lose something of value—namely the opportunity to make a rational decision, although it is open to question whether this is a matter of right.

Unregulated tender offers thus have a potential for coercion in a definition offered by Daniel Lyons.[20] In Lyon's definition, an offer is coercive when a person is "rationally reluctant" to trade on certain terms and recognizes that easier terms would be offered were it not for the possibility of trading on the other terms.[21] The Williams Act limits the possibility of trading on terms that greatly favor the offerer and gives easier terms which eases the legitimate reluctance of the stockholder to respond.

PARTIAL AND TWO-TIER OFFERS

Most of the proposals for changing the present regulatory structure of tender offers concern fine tuning the delicate balance of commonly recognized competing interests and concerns. The use of partial and two-tier offers, however, raises some special problems, which have largely gone unnoticed. One arises from the fact that shares of stock that are tendered in a proration pool typically will be accepted only in some fraction, which cannot be known beforehand. The stockholder would presumably benefit from the premium on the accepted shares, but the transfer of corporate control that may result from a successful tender offer could adversely affect the value of the stock that is not accepted. Thus, the stockholder could end up comparatively worse off as a result of accepting the tender offer. The problem is not avoided by knowing the amount of stock that will be accepted or by refusing to tender. In the latter case, the stockholder could be even worse off by forgoing the benefit of the premium.

Consider the following hypothetical case: Stockholder S owns 100 shares of the ABC Corporation currently trading at $10 for a portfolio value of $1,000. A tender offer of $15 a share is made by the XYZ Corporation for a fixed number of shares. S thinks that the management of XYZ cannot run ABC as efficiently and that the total investment of S in the merged ABCXYZ Corporation will be worth less than the value of S's stock in ABC that is not accepted in the tender offer. Suppose that S tenders all 100 shares, of which ten are accepted, and that after the merger S is issued ninety shares of ABCXYZ stock with a market value of $9 each. S has $150 in hand for the accepted shares and $810 in the stock of the new corporation for a total of $960. S has lost $40 in the series of transactions.

If a greater percentage of shares had been accepted in the proration pool, say 20 percent, then S would have assets valued at $1,020 and would come out $20 ahead. Knowing the percentage, however, would not alter the decision on whether to tender, for regardless of the percentage accepted, S's only choice is to tender. By not tendering in a successful takeover bid, S would end up with 100 shares of ABCXYZ valued at $9 for a total of $900, which is the worst possible alternative.[22]

This case is an instance of the well-known lesson contained in the prisoners' dilemma. The ideal solution would be for all stockholders to cooperate and refuse to tender, but without an opportunity for this kind of cooperation, the rational choice for each individual stockholder could only be to tender in order to minimize the loss. The power to impose a prisoners' dilemma choice situation on others confers a great advantage, which can often be used to coerce. Stockholders could face a choice little different from the gunman who says, "Give me your money or your life." The corporate raider may be in a position to say instead, "Tender and lose, or don't tender and lose more."

Cooperation to make a rational choice is often impossible, and sometimes the denial of the possibility of cooperation can be justified. However, partial and two-tier offers are both avoidable and unjustifiable. Voting by stockholders at meetings or in proxy contests, which was the most commonly used method in hostile takeovers before tender offers, offers a practical alternative to a prisoners' dilemma choice situation. Each stockholder votes purely on the basis of self-interest, but self-interest in such a case is usually identical to the best interests of the firm. More important, all stockholders share proportionately in the benefits offered by the settlement in a successful takeover. No one is forced to make a choice in a prisoners' dilemma situation in which the effective consequences of that choice depend on the choices made by others.

This problem of partial tender offers is also shared by two-tier offers, for the two kinds of offers are functionally equivalent. After a successful partial offer, the outstanding stock can still be purchased on the open market at its currently traded value. Thus, a partial offer can be viewed as a two-tier offer in which the second-tier price is the market value. If a second-tier offer is for only a fixed number of shares, then the entire tender offer is obviously a partial one. Even if the second-tier price is for all outstanding shares, the fact that the first tier is for a fixed number creates a potential for the same kind of loss that can result from partial offers (though the likelihood is less, since the second-tier price is usually above the market value). When the compensation in a tender offer is not in cash but in securities, such as the stock of the acquiring company or stock in a new merged entity, it may make little difference whether a stockholder tenders or not. The value of the stock held by the investor is now heavily dependent on the performance of the acquiring company, and in the event of a merger, the investor's stock will be converted to that of the new entity. It is possible in a successful takeover for those who tender and those who do not to end up with identical holdings.

WHY SHOULD TENDER OFFERS BE REGULATED?

Even if tender offers can be coercive, it does not follow that the law ought to be used to prevent them or to rectify the distributional consequences of their use. The libertarian view in particular holds that the law should be used only to facilitate voluntary agreements and not to impose some other conception of justice on the terms of transactions or on the outcome. Alternatively, it might be held that in regulating tender offers something of moral value is given up to which the offerer has a right, and that is the opportunity to enter into any purely voluntary agreements. There is a fatal flaw in this libertarian view, which has been pointed out by Anthony Kronman in connection with contract law.[23] Economic transactions are held to be justified by libertarians as long as they are the result of purely voluntary agreements, but the voluntary nature of agreements is diminished to the extent that one party takes unfair advantage of another. Libertarians commonly recognize transactions involving force and fraud as unjust, despite the agreement of the parties, for agreement under such circumstances is not purely voluntary. Even when there is no force or fraud, an agreement may still not be completely voluntary, as when a person takes unfair advantage of superior knowledge or of another's financial distress. Kronman's point is that the word "voluntary" has a normative content, and that, as a result, the libertarian position is incomplete and must be supplemented by some additional principle of justice, which can demarcate instances of unfair advantage-taking.[24]

What could serve as an additional principle of justice to supplement the libertarian view? Kronman suggests two likely candidates. One is the well-known utilitarian principle, and the other is a vaguely Rawlsian principle that he calls "Paretianism." Under a Paretian principle, a rule restricting advantage-taking is just when everyone is better off with the rule than without. Regardless of which principle is chosen, however, consideration must be given to more than just the interest of the stockholder solicited in a tender offer. In any given tender offer, there are identifiable shareholders the protection of whose interest may be the purpose of a particular rule, but the rule itself must be adopted with a view to serving the interests of all affected parties by maximizing aggregate welfare (utilitarianism) or by making everyone better off (Paretianism).

The Paretian principle would require us to consider all parties who are potential participants in a tender offer. A bidder in one takeover attempt could be a target in another, so that a rule on tender offers must be such that the person in question would be better off on balance with that rule than without it. Imagine a financier who through a series of hostile takeovers, which were made possible by favorable tender offer laws, loses his empire to an even sharper operator who takes advantage of the same legislation. On balance, is the financier better or worse off as a result of that particular set of tender offer laws? Once the question is framed in this way, it becomes clear that the interests of those connected with the target company, a group that includes its stockholder, management, and other employees, as well as everyone else who is affected in some way, must be considered as actual or potential stockholders.

It is even more evident that under the utilitarian principle the interests of all parties must be considered in determining the rules for regulating tender offers. One way of making the point is by observing that in drafting tender offer legislation, the aim cannot be to protect stockholders from all harm. It is not all interests that ought to be protected but only some that an investor has a right to have protected. Which ones are these? In a famous passage in his essay *Utilitarianism*, John Stuart Mill gives this answer: "To have a right, then is, I conceive, to have something which society ought to defend me in the possession of. If the objector goes on to ask why it ought, I can give him no other reason than general utility." For investors to have a right that their interests be protected, there must, in Mill's view, be some good to the whole of society that justifies that right.

I conclude, then, that on none of the ethical positions considered is there any reason not to use the law to impose morally desirable restrictions on the use of tender offers. Indeed, such restrictions are unavoidable, for the law takes a stand on the balance of competing interests as much by its silence as by what it says. Furthermore, the regulation of tender offers cannot consider only the interests of the stockholder while professing neutrality between the competing parties and between alternative outcomes. There may be good reasons for protecting the interests of the stockholders who are recipients of a tender offer, but *these* reasons cannot relate only to the interests of the particular investors in question. They must include in some way the interests of a wide range of parties, which in turn cannot be separated from the question of whether takeovers are good or bad for the economy as a whole.

STOCKHOLDER RIGHTS AND CORPORATE GOVERNANCE

The stockholder interests that the law regulating tenders offers is designed to protect seem to include only financial interests. Such a narrow view does not encompass the full range of interests that a stockholder may have, and, in particular, it neglects the rights that stock ownership confers in the governance of a corporation. By law, stockholders are the owners of a corporation and the persons ultimately responsible for its operation. The right that the law confers— to participate in decisions about the management and disposition of corporate assets—is also a part of the interests of a stockholder which deserves legal protection.

Any decision regarding a takeover must be made by the stockholders, either by voting their shares of stock in a stockholders' meeting or a proxy contest, or by selling them in a tender offer. By selling in a tender offer, however, a stockholder may be making a decision that is personally advantageous but not in the best interests of the company. A principle of American law states that a corporation is a juridical person with its own interests, which may not be identical with those of stockholders or any of its other members.[25] Managers and directors have a fiduciary responsibility to a firm for the prudent stewardship of its assets, but the shareholders have no similar responsibility to anyone and are free to make decisions solely for their own benefit.

The traditional justification for such a system of corporate governance is an extension of Adam Smith's "invisible hand" argument, to the effect that stock-holders in promoting their own interest will also promote the interest of the firm, as well as that of society as a whole. In this view, there is no need for stockholders to have a fiduciary responsibility for the interest of a firm as distinct from their own interest, because it is unlikely that the two would ever diverge. While there could be a conflict of interest for a manager or a director of a firm—and hence a need for a fiduciary responsibility—no such conflict could exist between the interests of the firm and those of its nominal owners.

There are good reasons to question this justification, however, in an age in which the market is dominated by professional managers of institutional investment funds and speculators. The former have a fiduciary responsibility to their own constituencies to realize a high rate of return and could even incur personal liability for failing to take full advantage of an investment opportunity. It would be very difficult for an account manager, whose career depends on each quarter's results, to have any great regard for the long-run health of the companies whose stock is in the portfolio at the moment. There would certainly be no cause for hesitation on the part of arbitrageurs and other speculators who are in the market only for the gains to be made from such corporate raids. Even an individual investor who might do better to hold onto a stock is often unable to resist the immediate gain of a tempting tender offer.

The use of tender offers in takeover bids thus raises some disturbing questions about whether the interests of a corporation are adequately protected. When takeovers can be effected by the decision of those stockholders who accept a tender offer for their own economic gain, there is no one left to represent the interests of the firm. In a thoughtful commentary, A. A. Sommer, Jr., points out that state laws have generally required that mergers and sales of substantial corporate assets be approved not only by a specified percentage of stockholders but also by the directors as an exercise of their fiduciary responsibility.[26] Such requirements serve to ensure that some consideration will be given in takeovers to the interests of the corporation as distinct from those of the stockholders. The underlying principle is that decisions about corporate control are of such importance that they require, in Sommer's words, "the intervention of a judgment untainted by the narrow economic interests of the shareholders."[27]

From the point of view of individual stockholders, a right of stock ownership, namely effective decision-making power on the management and disposition of corporate assets, is imperiled by the use of tender offers in takeover attempts. In stockholder meetings and proxy contests there is the opportunity to propose and weigh alternatives with the assurance that all those who vote have a stake in the outcome. The response to a tender offer is a kind of vote, but one in which there is scarcely any debate over the merits of the alternatives, and those who vote by selling their shares have no further stake in the outcome. Peter Drucker has compared tender offers to bribes.[28] Surely an offer to bribe a sufficient number of stockholders in a vote to oust the incumbent management of a company would be regarded as unethical. But how would such a bribe differ from offering a premium in order to entice shareholders to sell some of their stock and the voting rights that go along with it? Sellers are compensated not only for their investment in the stock but also for the loss of their voting rights. It is not those who are "bribed" in a tender offer who are harmed, but those who retain their shares and find that their right to participate in decisions about corporate governance is significantly diminished.

CONCLUSION

The major provisions of the Williams Act are consistent with the claim in this chapter that tender offers can be coercive and ought to be regulated in order to alleviate the unnecessary hard bargaining that would make a stockholder rationally reluctant to trade even on apparently favorable terms. Much can be done to refine the law to achieve its aim. The SEC Advisory Committee on Tender Offers submitted a list of fifty recommendations, most of which deal with very specific details. Few have been adopted, however, due to the present antiregulatory mood in government. Especially urgent are reforms to inhibit large investors from acting in concert to effect a takeover without a formal tender offer. One proposal from the SEC Advisory Committee is to require that purchases of stock in excess of 20 percent be made by a tender offer, except for purchases directly from the issuer.

Other possibilities for reform include eliminating or sharply restricting hostile partial and two-tier offers, which would go a long way toward eliminating the possibilities for coercion and unequal treatment of stockholders. Aggressors would have to be prepared to assume full responsibility for a company taken over. The same result is achieved in the British system by requiring any entity that acquires more than 30 percent of a company to make an offer to buy all of the remaining shares at the highest price it paid. A commissioner of the SEC, Charles L. Marinaccio, has proposed that partial tender offers be permitted only with the approval of the board of directors of the target company, since this tactic is largely responsible for making extortion by greenmail possible.[29]

It has been suggested that the problem of protecting stockholder rights in corporate governance could be addressed by requiring that takeovers be approved by a majority of the independent directors of the target company.[30] A different kind of independent voice is provided by an Indiana law, which denies voting rights to those who acquire a certain percentage of a company's shares until voting rights are approved by a majority of preexisting disinterested stockholders (which excludes the incumbent management). The constitutionality of the Indiana law was recently upheld by the Supreme Court, thus reversing a longstanding position that the Williams Act preempts state antitakeover legislation.[31] An entirely different approach is taken by the British system in which a voluntary Panel on Takeovers and Mergers advises all parties in a takeover attempt. One drawback of the British system, however, is that the decisions of the panel are not legally binding.[32]

These possibilities for reform are put forth only as suggestions for further exploration. The regulation of tender offers must inevitably be a very complex enterprise in which a large number of interests and concerns must be carefully balanced, and the construction of a regulatory scheme must involve the efforts of legislators, legal and financial experts, economists, business leaders, and also, I believe, philosophers who can offer a vital ethical perspective.

NOTES

1. Peter F. Drucker, "To End the Raiding Roulette Game," *Across the Board*, April 1986, p. 39.

2. See for example Michel T. Halbouty, "The Hostile Takeover of Free Enterprise," *Vital Speeches*, August 1, 1986, pp. 613–16.

3. One way of doing this is by "short-tendering," which involves increasing the amount of stock tendered in a proration pool by borrowing shares from idle accounts. For one example see Robert McGough, "Autopsy Report on a Tender Offer," *Forbes*, April 9, 1985, pp. 56–58. In the case described it is estimated that investors who failed to tender in a financial restructuring plan by Phillips Petroleum Company lost $162 million.

4. The case is Unocal's self-tender, which excluded T. Boone Pickens. The SEC intervened on the grounds that this violated the equal treatment principle, but Unocal's position was upheld by the U.S. District Court of California and the Delaware Supreme Court, largely on the grounds that self-tenders fall under state jurisdiction as part of the

laws regulating corporate governance and hence are outside the scope of federal legislation. Laura Jereski, "Empty Gesture," *Forbes*, November 4, 1985, p. 66.

5. Congress declined to offer a precise definition in order to make legislation flexible enough "to deal effectively with transactions, not envisioned or imagined in 1968." Letter from Sen. William Proxmire to the Chairman of the SEC, in *Securities and Exchange Commission Report on Tender Offer Laws* (Washington, D.C.: U.S. Government Printing Office, 1980), 3. For an attempt to define a tender offer, see Thomas J. Andre, Jr., "Unconventional Offers under the Williams Act: The Case for Judicial Restraint," *Journal of Corporation Law* (Summer 1986). The SEC has proposed a definition of a tender offer, Securities Exchange Act Release No. 16385, November 29, 1985 (44 FR 70349), but a better solution in the view of the commission is tightening the disclosure requirements of the Williams Act.

6. A full account of the Sun Oil bid for Becton, Dickinson is contained in Richard Phalon, *The Takeover Barons of Wall Street* (New York: G. P. Putnams's Sons, 1981).

7. Paula Dwyer, "The SEC Pounces on 'Creeping' Tender Offers," *Business Week*, October 7, 1985, p. 83.

8. Laura Jereski, "The Quick-Draw Takeover," *Forbes*, November 4, 1985, p. 71.

9. David Pauly, "Merger Ethics, Anyone?" *Newsweek*, December 9, 1985, pp. 46–47.

10. Public Law 90–439; 82 Stat. 454. The Williams Act is an amendment to the Securities Exchange Act of 1934.

11. See Hugh L. Sowards and James S. Mofsky, "Corporate Take-Over Bids: Gap in Federal Securities Regulation," *St. John's Law Review* 41 (1967): 499–523.

12. Speech by Sen. Harrison Williams, 113 *Congressional Record* 854.

13. *Securities and Exchange Commission Report on Tender Offer Laws*, pp. 55–56, 84–85. Advisory Committee on Tender Offers, Report of Recommendations (July 8, 1983).

14. These points are made by Peter Brennan, "SEC Rule 14d–8 and Two-Tier Offers," in Marc I. Steinberg, *Tender Offers: Developments and Commentaries* (Westport, Conn.: Continuum, 1986), 114–15.

15. See Linda C. Quinn and David B. H. Martin, Jr., "The SEC Advisory Committee and Its Aftermath: A New Chapter in Change-of-Control Regulation," in Steinberg, *Tender Offers*, 17–18.

16. For a discussion of the history of the Section 14(e) litigation, see the comments by Ralph Ferrara, in Steinberg, *Tender Offers*, 315–18.

17. Ralph Ferrara in Steinberg, *Tender Offers*, 318.

18. SEC Advisory Committee on Tender Offers, Report of Recommendations (July 8, 1983). Reprinted in Quinn and Martin, "The SEC Advisory Committee on Tender Offers and Its Aftermath."

19. On the standard analysis of coercion offered by Robert Nozick, for example, a threat must be made with the intention of carrying it out, and seeming instances of coercive offers are explained away as departures from moral or customary expectations. Thus, in Nozick's example of the wicked slave owner who offers not to administer the usual daily beating in return for complying with some request, a threat is still being made, since a daily beating is not a moral or customary norm. Nozick, "Coercion," in Sidney Morgenbesser, Patrick Suppes, and Morton White, eds., *Philosophy, Science and Method* (New York: St. Martin's Press, 1969), 440–72. Virginia Held rejects this standard analysis and argues that some offers can be coercive, especially if the inducements are high

enough. Held, "Coercion and Coercive Offers," in J. Roland Pennock and John W. Chapman, eds., *Coercion* (Chicago: Aldine-Atherton, 1972), 49–62. Held's position is criticized by Michael D. Bayles, "Coercive Offers and Public Benefits," *The Personalist* 55 (1974): 139–44. The controversy is further explored by Don VanDeVeer, "Coercion, Seduction, and Rights," *The Personalist* 58 (1977): 374–81, and Theodore Benditt, "Threats and Offers," *The Personalist* 58 (1977): 382–84. For another criticism of Nozick, see Harry Frankfurt, "Coercion and Moral Responsibility," in Ted Honderich, ed., *Essays on Freedom of Action* (London: Routledge and Kegan Paul, 1973), 63–86.

20. Daniel Lyons, "Welcome Threats and Coercive Offers," *Philosophy* 50 (1975): 425–436. The analysis of tender offers in the preceding paragraphs owes a great deal to Lyon's article.

21. The precise formula which Lyons gives is: (1) P knows that Q is rationally reluctant to give *y* to P for *x*; and (2) Either Q knows that he has a right to *x* from P on easier terms, or Q knows that P would have given *x* to Q on easier terms, if the chance had not arisen to trade *x* for *y*. Lyons, "Welcome Threats and Coercive Offers," 436. For further thoughts on this formula, see Daniel Lyons, "The Last Word on Coercive Offers . . . (?)," *Philosophy Research Archives* 8 (1982): 393–414.

22. Another solution would be for S to sell all the stock at the announcement of a tender offer and at least be no worse off. This is no real solution, however, if the stock is undervalued by the market (which is likely if the company is a takeover target), for S would still lose the difference between the real value and the market price.

23. Anthony Kronman, "Contract Law and Distributive Justice," *The Yale Law Journal* 89 (1980): 472–79.

24. Robert Nozick recognizes this point but argues that what is needed is not a further principle of justice but an accounting of what rights we have, for whether the voluntariness of our actions is diminished by the actions of others depends on whether they acted within their rights. Robert Nozick, *Anarchy, State, and Utopia* (New York: Basic Books, 1974), 262. This position still seems to admit the incompleteness of the libertarian view. There cannot simply be a right to engage in voluntary transactions without limits.

25. This point is well made by A. A. Sommer, Jr., "Hostile Tender Offers: Time for a Review of Fundamentals," in Steinberg, *Tender Offers*, 264.

26. Ibid.

27. Ibid., 266.

28. Drucker, "To End the Raiding Roulette Game," 34.

29. Charles L. Marinnacio, "Forcing Corporate Raiders to Walk the Plank," *Business and Society Review* (Spring 1985): 27–28.

30. Made by Representative Peter J. Rodino, Jr., to the National Association of Manufacturers Issue Briefing Breakfast, March 3, 1984. Cited by Sommer, "Hostile Tender Offers," 269. Sommer also cites a point made by John J. Huber, Director of the SEC's Division of Corporation Finance, that the Rodino proposal would also place on directors "a heavier burden of justifying their actions in a takeover contest, thereby denying them the awesome protections afforded by the business judgment rule." Sommer, "Hostile Tender Offers," 269.

31. *CTS Corp. v. Dynamics Corp.*, No. 86–71 and 86–97.

32. For a discussion of the merits of the British system see Deborah A. DeMott, "Current Issues in Tender Offer Regulation: Lessons from the British," *New York University Law Review* 58 (1983): 945–1029.

__ 16 _____

Stakeholder Welfare, Managerial Ethics, and Management Buyouts

ROBERT F. BRUNER
LYNN SHARP PAINE

What is happening is, in my estimation, serious, unfair, and sometimes disgraceful, a perversion of the whole process of public financing, and a course that inevitably is going to make the individual shareholder even more hostile to American corporate mores and securities markets than he already is.[1]

> A. A. Sommer, Former SEC Commissioner

Any time people talk about enhancing shareholder value, they're using words of terror to a bondholder. . . . [Companies with] sleepy management were a bondholder's dream. You knew they wouldn't embark on anything reckless.[2]

> Margaret Patell, Investment Manager

A lot of us feel that we got took.[3]

> Hourly Employee, Dan River, Inc.

What has happened with the merger and acquisition movement, the leveraged buyout movement, the hostile takeover movement, all those related developments, is that nothing . . . is based on what is better for society. . . . The real test is wholly financially driven.[4]

> Joseph Auerbach, Professor

The critics of corporate restructuring, and particularly leveraged buyouts, are legion. Almost every clientele of the firm—outgoing stockholders, creditors, employees—has something bad to say. The exception is management and their fellow investors, who profit enormously from these complex transactions, and for better or worse, they choose to remain silent.

The prime criticism of management buyouts (MBOs) is that managers exploit other stakeholders on behalf of their own interest. The most loudly voiced criticism comes from shareholders, who ask whether they are getting the managerial loyalty to which they are legally entitled. But employees and creditors, too, complain that buyouts hurt them and benefit management. While management has no legal duty to operate a business in the interests of employees and creditors, critics argue that they have a moral duty to do so, and that MBOs violate that duty. In essence, the charge is that management buyouts involve a breach of managerial ethics. Some critics even recommend that buyouts be banned.

We write neither to praise MBOs nor to bury them. Rather, our objectives are to examine management's responsibilities to stockholders, creditors, and employees, and to suggest an approach for assessing MBOs that takes these responsibilities fully into account. We provide a framework for identifying buyouts that satisfy management's responsibilities. This framework can help boards and managers protect the interests of corporate stakeholders and diminish the frequency of management abuses that have led critics to condemn buyouts across the board.

An appraisal of buyouts is timely. The value of firms going private has risen dramatically: from $636 million in 1979[5] to $40.9 billion in 1986.[6] This reflects a rise not only in the number of MBOs annually, but also an increase in their average size. For instance, Beatrice Foods went private in 1985 at a cost of $6.2 billion. The rising tide of MBOs has been accompanied by increasing debate over the propriety of the actions of the stewards of stakeholders' interests, mainly boards of directors.

In the next section, we describe the management buyout and discuss two levels of criticism of buyouts. In the section following that, after briefly discussing contending conceptions of management's responsibilities, we argue that, under certain conditions, buyouts are compatible with both conceptions. We close with a discussion of some implications for managers and their boards.

THE PROBLEM

Management Buyouts

A management buyout is the purchase of a company's assets by its own managers, who typically finance the transaction with a large proportion of debt—hence the alternative name, "leveraged buyout." The buyouts of greatest concern involve public companies which are taken private—hence another common name, "going private" transactions. Management is almost always assisted in the transaction by a buyout promoter, who provides advice on structuring the transaction as well as equity capital.

To participate in these transactions, managers usually commit most if not all their personal wealth to help provide the equity capital. In addition, they may personally guarantee the debt of the new firm, which is often many times the size of their own net worth.

In general, management buyouts are enormously profitable for the equity investors. For instance, John Puth, the President of Vapor Corporation, took the company private in 1972 and public again in 1976. He received a $2.1 million profit on an initial investment of $175,000.[7] The value these transactions create may come from several sources:

1. *Operating efficiencies.* Some researchers argue that the enormous risks assumed by, and incentives given to, management prompt them to operate the firm more efficiently.[8]

2. *Tax efficiencies.* The interest on the loans in the management buyout is paid from pretax income. Thus, the interest expense reduces the firm's tax expense. This is called a "tax shield." Another tax shield is depreciation expense. When the assets of a firm are sold, the buyer is allowed by the IRS to allocate the purchase premium to depreciable assets, which are written off over time. There are many more arcane ways to save tax expense arising from the nature of the buyout, but the pattern should be clear: equity owners gain by reducing a firm's tax exposure.

3. *Financing efficiencies.* Although tax and operating efficiencies may explain in part the ability of the firm to borrow heavily, they don't tell the whole story. Management buyouts reduce agency costs, in other words, the risk that after the transaction managers will expropriate the wealth of the owners of the firm. This is because (a) after the MBO the managers *are* the owners of the firm; (b) managers have bound themselves explicitly to delivering the cash flow of the firm to the providers of the capital; and (c) if they fail to service the debt, they suffer substantial penalties (for example, the loss of their personal wealth and bankruptcy).

Problems with Buyouts

Criticisms of buyouts may be divided into two general categories. The first concerns the legitimacy of gains from these efficiencies. At whose expense are these gains achieved? The second category concerns the allocation of gains. Assuming that buyouts present opportunities for legitimate gains, to whom do they belong?

Critics concerned with the source of gains argue that they come at the expense of important stakeholders like employees and creditors. For example, operating efficiencies are sometimes achieved at the expense of employees who are laid off in the process of liquidating unprofitable divisions. Levi Strauss & Co. went private to preserve "important values and traditions." Yet in the year that followed, the company sold or discontinued several product lines, thereby reducing employment levels.[9]

Other gains may come at the expense of creditors. It is often wrongly supposed that "creditors" refers to large financial institutions such as banks. But in reality, firms can have numerous classes of creditors, including individual investors who hold long-term bonds and suppliers who extend trade credit.

As a general rule, a leveraged buyout pays off all preexisting debt. But this does not mean that creditors are unaffected by the MBO. An MBO can have the following effects on creditors:

1. *Create investment risk.* Some types of creditors loan money with the goal of funding some future obligation with the proceeds of that investment. This is explicitly the behavior of life insurance companies, though there is evidence that individual investors behave this way as well (for example, anticipate the cost of a college education or retirement). Prepayment of a loan may mean that the investor would be unable to reinvest the principal at the same rate of return and be unable to meet the future funding target.[10]

2. *Impair creditworthiness.* Some creditors, namely the trade suppliers, do not depart with the MBO. These creditors are usually asked to continue supplying on the same credit terms even though they are in fact making riskier loans than they were before the MBO. Though the incidence of bankruptcy of MBO companies is relatively small, the collapses of Enduro Stainless, Inc., Thatcher Glass, Brentano's, and Havatampa emphasize the basic fact of increased credit risk.

Still other gains come at the expense of the public sector, whose tax coffers are reduced in proportion as a buyout reduces the corporate tax bill.

Other critics worry not so much about the sources of gains in buyouts but about their allocation. The primary change is that management captures for itself gains that properly belong to shareholders or other buyout participants, such as employees whose pension assets may be used to finance the buyout.

A close reading of the recent history of MBOs reveals instances in which it appears that managers exploited their fiduciary position for their own self-interest. Managers may, for example, fail to deliver fair value for the company to the selling shareholders. Though we defer a definition of "fair value" until the next section, one might posit that in an open and competitive market, what is fair is whatever a buyer is willing to pay. Yet in the following cases, management attempted to take the company private at a price to shareholders *lower* than competitive market values:

1. *Multimedia, Inc.* Management rejected the bid of $1.02 billion from Lorimar in favor of a leveraged buyout plan calling for a purchase price of $825 million. Later, under pressure, management withdrew its MBO proposal and proceeded with a recapitalization plan that would deliver $890 million to shareholders, still less than Lorimar's offer.[11]

2. *Fuqua Industries.* Management rejected an offer of $25 per share for the company in favor of an MBO proposal at $20 per share. Shareholders filed eleven separate lawsuits in an attempt to block the transaction. Later, under pressure, management withdrew the MBO offer.[12]

3. *Woodward and Lothrop.* Alfred Taubman offered to finance a management buyout of the company at $59 per share and cut management in for 20 percent of the company. Heirs of the department store's founders were outraged and sought another buyer, who offered $64 per share.[13]

4. *Beatrice Foods.* A shareholder lawsuit claimed that the MBO offer was "hundreds of dollars too low" and that managers were motivated to promote the buyout because

it would accelerate golden parachute agreements which provided for $50 to $60 million in severance benefits to sixty executives.[14]

5. *Stanwood Corporation.* Insiders who owned 48 percent of the stock proposed to take the company private at a bid price barely greater than its historical stock price, and its quick liquidation value based on inventories and land.[15]

6. *Jim Walter Corporation.* Management rejected an offer of $2.8 billion for the company in favor of an MBO proposal for $2.44 billion.[16]

While there may be considerations that could justify management's actions in these cases, it is arresting that a nontrivial number of the most prominent MBOs is the focus of claims that managers are underpaying for their corporations' assets.

Instances in which management appears to be unfairly appropriating opportunities for gain from employees may also be cited. When employee pension funds are used to finance buyouts, management has been known to attempt to sell shares to employees at inequitably high prices,[17] or to limit the voting rights on shares owned by employees.[18]

Management's position in the transaction and its control over employee pension fund assets provide opportunities for the buyout team to underpay, and thus, in effect, to expropriate gains from selling shareholders and participating employees. As noted earlier, opportunities for management to benefit at shareholders' expense have led some critics to conclude that buyouts should be banned.[19] Others advocate a mandated bidding period to ensure that management does not underpay relative to competitive bidders.[20]

In summary, buyouts raise numerous questions about managerial conduct. Evaluating these criticisms and formulating an appropriate response require a framework for understanding management's responsibilities.

EVALUATING BUYOUTS: THE BEST ALTERNATIVE STANDARD

Management's Responsibilities

The most widely discussed contending views of management's responsibilities may be termed the "stockholder" and "stakeholder" views.[21] In the stockholder view, management is a fiduciary for the firm's shareholders. As fiduciary, management is obligated to put forth its best efforts to promote shareholders' interests, usually intepreted as their financial interests. Not only must management act affirmatively to promote shareholder interests, it must refrain from doing anything that would injure the shareholders or deprive them of profits which are lawfully available to them. A particularly important aspect of fiduciary duty is management's responsibility not to benefit itself at the expense of shareholders.

Proponents of the stockholder view differ in their recognition of constraints on management's obligation to promote shareholders' interests. Milton Friedman, for example, regards the law as imposing limits on this obligation.[22] Daniel

Fischel, by contrast, suggests that obedience to law is required only if it is profitable.[23] According to Fischel, if obedience would be unprofitable, management should violate the law and pay the required damages or penalties. Despite differences among proponents of the stockholder view, the central shared belief is that the interests of stakeholders other than shareholders is not a proper object of management's concern.

The stakeholder view is more difficult to express succinctly, since there are several possible interpretations. The gist, however, is that management has a responsibility to promote, and refrain from harming, the interests of all the corporation's stakeholders—shareholders as well as other stakeholders such as employees, creditors, suppliers, customers, and the general public. This responsibility sometimes requires management to refrain from acting in ways that would be legally permissible and profitable for shareholders on the grounds that doing so would harm the legitimate (though not legally protected) interests of other stakeholders.

In the stakeholder view, the interests of a broad range of corporate constituents are proper objects of management's attention.[24] The stakeholder view does not mandate that management is obliged to take any particular actions to advance the interests of a given constituent, but only that generally these interests ought to be taken into account in some fashion. Most discussions of the stakeholder view are vague as to the precise weight and import to be given to the interests of differing stakeholder groups, but one might give the stakeholder view a strong, moderate, or weak interpretation.

The strong interpretation would hold that management may act only in ways that promote *all* stakeholders' interests. A more moderate version would require management to conduct business in ways that promote the interests of stakeholders considered in the aggregate. The moderate version would permit management decisions that the strong version would prohibit, since the moderate version takes into account the number of stakeholders involved and the seriousness of the interests affected. The moderate version permits trade-offs among stakeholder groups, while the strong version apparently would not. A weak version, which is actually consistent with the stockholder view, would advocate careful consideration of all stakeholder interests as part of the process of determining what strategies, policies, and actions would best promote shareholders' interests.

Evaluating these contending views is outside the scope of this chapter. Our point is that there are circumstances in which management buyouts are consistent with management's responsibilities as conceived under either view. The essence of our argument is that the degree to which management fulfills its responsibilities to each stakeholder group must be assessed by reference to alternative available outcomes. Whether stockholders, employees, or creditors are better off or worse off after a buyout is an inadequate basis for evaluating management's conduct. The critical question is whether a buyout is the best available alternative for a stakeholder group.

Buyouts and the Stockholder View of Management Responsibilities. From the stockholder point of view, the crux of the criticism of buyouts is that management gains at the expense of shareholders. The central question in the debate is this: Who is entitled to the gains created in buyouts? In other words, what is a fair price for a buyout? Managers who take their companies private might like to think the gains should be theirs as a reward for the additional risks incurred. But such an allocation of gains ignores management's fiduciary responsibility to shareholders. As a fiduciary, management is obligated to put forth its best efforts for the corporation and most especially, not to benefit at its expense. Managers are obligated to eliminate operating inefficiencies and to exploit unused debt capacity in ways that benefit the corporation's owners rather than themselves. To the extent that management's buyout profits come from eliminating inefficiencies that could have been eliminated without going private, management is expropriating shareholder wealth. To the extent that a buyout permits managers to exploit opportunities for gain created by their own management failures, a buyout may encourage lax management.

A buyout represents a classic opportunity for unethical self-dealing, since management, in a sense, sits on both sides of the bargaining table. As part of the buyout group, management occupies the position of the purchaser seeking to buy the corporation's assets at the lowest possible price. At the same time management has a fiduciary obligation to promote the interests of shareholders. This potential conflict between self-interest and duty inherent in the situation makes buyout negotiations suspect and raises special questions of fair price. The negotiating process cannot be relied on to yield a fair price, since buyer and seller do not stand in an arm's-length relationship. Indeed, as fiduciary, management is privy to confidential information and an understanding of a company's problems and potential far beyond that of outsiders.

What standard of fairness should be applied in self-dealing transactions? Traditionally, the law has answered that a transaction is fair if it is at least as advantageous as a hypothetical transaction with an unrelated third party in a reasonably competitive market.[25] The hypothetical arm's-length standard, however, is too narrow. It does not fully acknowledge the fiduciary duty of the corporate officer or director. A transaction may be fair by an arm's-length bargaining standard while at the same time not in the interests of the corporation. For example, the price of a parcel of real estate being sold by an officer to the corporation may be fair in an arm's-length sense, but buying real estate may not be in the corporation's best interests.[26] Deciding whether a real estate purchase is in the corporation's interest involves looking beyond similar transactions to alternative ways to satisfy the corporate objectives at stake. Purchasing property is only one way of acquiring additional space, for example, if space acquisition is the objective in question. In a self-dealing transaction the obligation of the fiduciary is to promote the corporation's interests in the broader sense, and not merely to act as an unrelated third party.

If the obligation of managers is to put forth their best efforts on behalf of shareholders, fair price in self-dealing transactions should be tied to the available course of action most consistent with this obligation. Elsewhere we argue that the standard of fair price in a buyout should be the value shareholders could obtain if they synthesized the buyout on their own by borrowing heavily, re-purchasing a large percentage of shares, increasing the shareholdings of man-agers, and even selling plant and equipment and then leasing them back.[27] A synthetic buyout, in practice called a "leveraged recapitalization," is an alter-native with which a buyout must always be compared.

The synthetic MBO standard of fair price is more appropriate than competitive market standards, since it incorporates recognition of management's fiduciary duty. A synthetic MBO offers some measure of what management could do to increase share price short of going private, and this represents some measure of what management owes shareholders. This standard establishes the floor from which buyout prices should be negotiated. A buyout at any price above this floor is not unfair to shareholders. Provided that management pays shareholders a fair price, there should be no objection to management's taking a company private under the stockholder view of management's responsibilities.

Buyouts and the Stakeholder View of Management Responsibilities. Fair price alone would not provide ethical clearance for a buyout on a stakeholder view of management responsibilities. As discussed earlier, stakeholders other than shareholders must also be taken into account. The strong and moderate versions of the stakeholder view require management to do its best for all stakeholders and not to benefit at their expense. In assessing management's conduct under the stakeholder standard, whether the standard is interpreted weakly or strongly, the question is not whether any class of stakeholders gains or loses in a buyout, but how the class fares in a buyout as compared with other alternatives. What is the stakeholder's position compared to what it would be under other likely scenarios?

Whether management is doing its best for stakeholders, be they shareholders or other stakeholders, depends upon the available alternatives. The possibilities for comparison depend upon a particular firm's situation. Typically, however, the alternatives to an MBO include a synthetic MBO or leveraged recapitalization as already discussed, or carrying on business as usual with the risk of a takeover—hostile or friendly. Our assumption is that the firm has unused debt capacity and is thus a possible takeover candidate.

The matrix in Table 16.1 provides a framework for assessing the effects of various alternatives on three key stakeholder groups frequently discussed in the buyout debate: stockholders, employees, and creditors. (A complete analysis of a particular buyout would include other stakeholders as well.)

Adopting a policy of carrying on business as usual would in many cases deny existing shareholders and possibly existing employees the opportunity to partic-ipate in *any* of the gains from restructuring through the MBO. In addition, such a policy would virtually guarantee that such restructuring would be carried out by outsiders to the firm—whether in the form of friendly or hostile takeover—

Table 16.1
Strategic Alternatives and Hypothetical Outcome for Stakeholders

	Do Nothing (Takeover)	Liquidate	Leveraged Recap.	MBO
Stakeholders				
Stockholders	*	*	*	*
Employees	Bad	Worst	Fair/Poor	Best
Creditors	Fair	Fair	Worst	Good

*Ranking of outcomes for stockholders is impossible a priori without more detailed information. Under the assumptions of this example, any restructuring will benefit stockholders to some degree.

and might cost stakeholders some of the implicit control they have over the restructuring via the responsibilities of existing management.

Compared to a hostile takeover, an MBO will be in most cases at least as advantageous for employees. In addition, MBOs sometimes offer employees enhanced job security and equity participation in the buyout. Indeed, employees are more likely to receive equity in an actual buyout than in a leveraged recapitalization, and, for that reason, an MBO may be the most attractive option for employees. As a defense against Carl Icahn's hostile tender offer for Dan River in 1984, management executed a buyout financed in part by an employee stock ownership plan. In effect, the rank-and-file employees were allowed to participate in the buyout as investors.

Creditors, too, will prefer a buyout to a leveraged recapitalization in many cases. A buyout provides creditors an opportunity to renegotiate terms, whereas a leveraged recapitalization does not. As a result of a synthetic MBO, a creditor may see his high grade bonds decline in quality to junk. When Allegis, Inc., announced a leveraged recapitalization in May 1987, its stock price rose by about 20 percent, but its bond and note prices fell by 4 percent. When Colt Industries announced a recapitalization in July 1986, prices of some of its bonds fell by 20 percent. Such losses in market value are devastating to creditors.

We do not wish to argue that buyouts are always best for stakeholders, but merely that they can be. Whether a buyout is, in fact, preferable for a given class of stakeholders depends upon the particulars of the transaction—how it is financed, how the new company will be structured—as well as the available alternatives. But it is clear that under some circumstances a buyout can be best for key stakeholders, whether we adopt the strong, moderate, or weak interpretation of the stakeholder thesis. The stakeholders at Weirton Steel would have no company today if MBOs were prohibited. The Weirton Division of National Steel Corporation was due to be liquidated in 1980 on grounds of inefficiency. Six years later, Weirton is one of the more efficient steel producers in the United States and is financially healthy.

CONCLUSION

A close look at many recent buyouts indicates that managers have in some cases violated their responsibilities to shareholders and other stakeholders. The existence of managerial greed in these cases, however, should not obscure the intrinsic nature of buyouts and the potential benefits they may offer many classes of corporate stakeholders. Contrary to popular opinion, management buyouts per se are not ethically objectionable.[28] Certainly, management members of the buyout team may face a conflict between their personal interests and their responsibilities to shareholders and other stakeholders. But this conflict can be managed so that it does not result in unethical conduct.

We have suggested in broad terms an approach for assessing whether a buyout is consistent with management's responsibilities, on both a stockholder and stakeholder view of those responsibilities. A clear conception of their responsibilities is essential for conscientious managers who may be tapped by outside investors for participation in a buyout or who may believe that a buyout offers the best hope of avoiding a hostile takeover. A clear conception of management's responsibilities is equally important for directors charged with assessing buyout proposals, especially in cases where management may attempt to take advantage of its position to the detriment of other stakeholders.

Widespread recognition of the "best alternative" standard for evaluating MBO proposals is critical for forestalling the possible adverse consequences of the managerial conflict of interest present in MBOs. Essential also is adequate disclosure of information about the buyout and alternatives such as the synthetic MBO. One implication of our analysis is that management buyout proposals should include more extensive disclosure than is commonly provided or required.[29] Boards, for example, could require the buyout team to submit information about the effects of the buyout, as compared with other feasible alternatives, for various stakeholder groups.

With appropriate standards and information, it is possible to determine how wealth is created and allocated in an MBO and to compare it with other strategic alternatives. With the consequences of a proposed MBO clearly defined, boards can make informed decisions about corporate restructurings and ensure that management satisfies its responsibilities to the corporation's stakeholders.

NOTES

The authors thank R. Edward Freeman, James E. Heard, and Dennis Logue for their comments on previous drafts and gratefully acknowledge the financial support of the

Olsson Center for Applied Ethics, The Colgate Darden Graduate School of Business Administration, University of Virginia.

1. A. A. Sommer, "Going Private: A Lesson in Corporate Responsibility," address at Notre Dame Law School, reprinted in *Securities Regulation Law Journal* (BNA) No. 278 (November 20, 1974), D-1.

2. G. Anders, " 'Recapitalizations' Are a Bonanza for Some, But Bondholders Can Take a Terrific Beating," *Wall Street Journal*, June 1, 1987.

3. P. Engardio, "At Dan River, 'A Lot of Us Feel that We Got Took' ", *Business Week*, April 15, 1985, p. 97.

4. Quoted in R. Howard, ed., "Corporate Takeovers: Are the Raiders Right?," *HBS Bulletin* (February 1987): 48.

5. W. T. Grimm & Co., News Release, Doremus and Company, Chicago, January 12, 1984, p. 2.

6. "1986 Profile," *Mergers & Acquisitions* (May/June 1987): 71.

7. N. Wallner, "Leveraged Buyouts: A Review of the State of the Art, Part II," *Mergers & Acquisitions* (Winter 1980): 24.

8. See, for example, H. DeAngelo, L. DeAngelo, and E. M. Rice, "Going Private: Minority Freezeouts and Stockholder Wealth," *Journal of Law and Economics* 27 (1984): 367; F. H. Easterbrook and D. R. Fischel, "Corporate Control Transactions," *Yale Law Journal* 91 (1982): 698–737. However, others argue that these operating efficiencies are not material. See, for example, Louis Lowenstein, "No More Cozy Management Buyouts," *Harvard Business Review* (January/February 1986): 147–56.

9. The CEO said, "Maintaining employment for the sake of employment isn't paternalistic, it's irresponsible if it jeopardizes the welfare of all employees." M. Beauchamp, "Tight Fit," *Forbes*, August 11, 1986, p. 94–95.

10. Of course the opposite situation could also obtain. If yields to maturity in the credit markets are higher than the coupon rate on the company's debt, then creditors could actually *welcome* the prepayment, because it would mean that they could reinvest their funds at a higher yield.

11. S. Kilman, "Multimedia Inc. Approves Offer of $890 Million," *Wall Street Journal*, April 9, 1985.

12. J. Montgomery, "Fuqua Suspends Four Executives in Merger Row," *Wall Street Journal*, August 14, 1981, p. 5. Also, J. Montgomery and R. E. Rustin, "J. B. Fuqua's Plan to Take Company Private Attracts Lawsuits and a Leveraged Buyout," *Wall Street Journal*, August 17, 1981, p. 17.

13. P. J. Regan, "Management Responsibility in Attempted Takeovers," *Financial Analysts Journal* (September/October 1984): 16.

14. R. Johnson, "Beatrice Holders File Suit to Block Leveraged Buyout," *Wall Street Journal*, November 19, 1985, p. 45.

15. L. R. Rublin, "Buyout or Sell-out? Are Shareholders Getting a Raw Deal?" *Barron's*, November 18, 1985, pp. 15–16.

16. L. P. Cohen, "Jim Walter Sets Buy-Out Pact for $2.44 Billion," *Wall Street Journal*, August 14, 1987, p. 3.

17. Scott and Fetzer managers proposed an MBO in which management would get 20 percent of the company for an investment of $9 million and in which the employee stock option plan (ESOP) would get 41 percent for $182 million—suggesting that managers would get one-half as much equity while only putting up one-twentieth as much of the

cash. The MBO was prevented by the Department of Labor, whose approval was required for the ESOP-based transaction. L. J. Tell "ESOPs and LBOs," *Barron's*, November 18, 1985, p. 77.

18. Dan River Inc. went private with an ESOP to avoid takeover by Carl Icahn. The ESOP acquired 70 percent of the company with an investment of $110 million in Class A common stock at a price of $22.50 per share. Managers and an investor paid $4.3 million to buy 30 percent of the company in Class B common stock at $2.06 per share. The Class B common was indexed to float at $22 per share less than the Class A common and was junior to the Class A in liquidation. The Class A common had limited voting rights, however, and it could vote only on merger or sale of the company. And until the ESOP claims are allocated, the ESOP stock will be voted by the trustee as directed by management. The voting rights of Class B stock are unrestricted.

19. For example, Victor Brudney and Marvin A. Chirelstein, "A Restatement of Corporate Freezeouts," *The Yale Law Journal* 87 (1978): 1365–70.

20. Lowenstein, "No More Cozy Management Buyouts," 1147–56.

21. Whether managers and boards of directors *should* concern themselves with the welfare of stakeholders other than equity owners continues to be a vigorously debated question. See, for instance, R. Edward Freeman and William W. Evan, *Stakeholder Capitalism*, (forthcoming), for the pro-stakeholder view. The stockholder-only view is represented in the writings of Milton Friedman, *Capitalism and Freedom* (Chicago: University of Chicago Press, 1962).

22. Milton Friedman, "The Social Responsibility of Business Is to Increase Its Profits," *New York Times Magazine*, September 13, 1970.

23. Daniel R. Fischel, "The Corporate Governance Movement," *Vanderbilt Law Review* 35 (November 1982): 1271.

24. See, for instance, Tad Tuleja, *Beyond the Bottom Line* (New York: Facts on File Publications, 1985) for a discussion of different stakeholder groups.

25. Robert C. Clark, "Agency Costs versus Fiduciary Duties," in *Principals and Agents: The Structure of Business*, ed. John W. Pratt and Richard J. Zeckhauser (Boston: Harvard Business School Press, 1985), p. 74.

26. Example from the American Law Institute's *Principles of Corporate Governance: Analysis and Recommendations*, Tentative Draft No. 5, "Duty of Fair Dealing," April 1986, Comment to §5.02(a)(2)(A), pp. 34–35.

27. Robert F. Bruner and Lynn Sharp Paine, "Management Buyouts and Managerial Ethics," *California Management Review* 30 (Winter 1988).

28. Benjamin J. Stein, "Going Private is Unethical," *Fortune*, November 11, 1985, p. 169.

29. See Bruner and Paine, "Management Buyouts and Managerial Ethics," for a proposal that disclosure requirements under the federal securities laws should be expanded to include disclosure of the values that could be created for shareholders by a synthetic MBO. Current law requires a reasonably detailed discussion of the factors upon which a buyout is judged to be fair. The authors suggest that the synthetic MBO standard should be among the factors included in the discussion.

Corporate Restructuring and Employee Interests: The Tin Parachute

DIANA C. ROBERTSON

Shareholder interests dominate the management of U.S. corporations. Management theorists as well as corporate managers increasingly advocate a stakeholder approach to management, perhaps in reaction to the current imbalance between attention given to shareholders and that paid to other major stakeholders. Employee interests, in particular, have received more and more emphasis from senior management, and have attracted the attention of authors like Peters and Waterman, but are slow to gain a stronghold in the corporate boardroom.[1] At the same time, management concern about productivity in the United States over the past few years indicates that attention to employees as stakeholders is imperative.

This chapter focuses on a very recent and quite dramatic exception to the imbalance between shareholder and employee interests: a severance package dubbed the "tin parachute." The tin parachute covers all employees and, like its executive counterpart, the golder parachute, is activated in the event of a takeover. Dollar amounts for each employee are more modest than those accorded to executives, but the mechanics of the two plans are similar.

It is interesting to note that European countries have handled this issue very differently. The "employment at will" concept, which so permeates the thinking of both employers and employees in U.S. companies, is virtually nonexistent. Instead Europeans tend to believe that once a person has worked at a job for a period of time, he or she has acquired a right to that job, a right that resembles a property right. In Europe when ownership of businesses is transferred, employees retain all of the rights held under the first employer. In the United States, in a takeover situation, the existing employment relationship with its accompanying rights is nullified under the new ownership. The tin parachute represents an attempt to align more closely with the European model of employment, where the employee retains certain rights regardless of the identity of the employer.

This approach is consistent with the erosion of the employment at will philosophy reflected in recent court decisions favoring plaintiffs who were fired at will, and in recently enacted state laws protecting employee rights, including, for example, laws shielding whistleblowers from dismissal. Under a specified set of circumstances, the tin parachute can constitute an implicit employment contract similar to the European view of employment, and to the principle increasingly upheld in the U.S. courts—that seniority on a job or with a company may imply an unwritten employment contract.

This chapter will first discuss the controversial mechanism known as the golden parachute and its justification to both board members and shareholders. Parallels between golden and tin parachutes will be drawn. Second, various motivations behind corporate adoption of the tin parachute are outlined. Is it primarily a poison pill to ward off a hostile takeover attempt or a socially responsible corporate policy assuring employees of job protection? Third, the incidence and features of existing tin parachutes are delineated. These include who is covered and for how long, and detail the exact nature of the change of control of the company, which must take place in order to activate the parachute. Fourth, the social responsibility of the tin parachute to both employees and shareholders is analyzed. Finally, the future of the tin parachute is assessed and its probable impact on corporate restructuring evaluated. Will it be effective in fending off hostile takeover attempts? If it is effective, will the tin parachute be upheld in court cases involving potential shareholder suits?

GOLDEN PARACHUTES

The golden parachute as executive security has become increasingly commonplace in this era of takeovers and corporate restructuring. A 1984 law that levied a tax on these expensive parting gifts failed to suppress their popularity. In fact, golden parachutes actually doubled among Fortune 100 industrialists from 1983 to 1985. That increase continued unabated. As of April 1987, 46 percent of major companies surveyed include golden parachute arrangements for their executives.[2] Defenders claim that such severance packages enable executives to make more objective decisions in a takeover situation—decisions that best represent the interests of company shareholders. Golden parachutes encourage key executives to remain with the company through the critical transition period as the change in control takes place. Additionally, as more and more companies institute golden parachutes, those firms without them will be at a disadvantage in attracting and retaining the most competent and marketable executives.

Detractors, on the other hand, consider the amounts of money involved to be excessive and are not convinced that shareholders' interests are the driving force behind golden parachutes. The controversy includes the question of who in the corporation should instigate and approve the severance packages. This was reflected in the contradictory claims of key principals in the Bendix-Martin Mar-ietta-Allied merger. William Agee, the chief executive of Bendix, exercised his $4 million bailout agreement as his company was taken over by Allied. Agee, who is frequently asked to justify this arrangement, has replied that while he did not request a golden parachute, he was grateful that the outside board had given him one. A member of that outside board contradicts Agee by stating that the golden parachutes were initiated by management, and, in fact, the amounts involved were reduced by the directors. The defensiveness of senior executives exemplified in the Bendix incident is not unusual. Critics view golden parachutes as executives' means of saving themselves and bailing out of a company whose interests run a poor second to the executives' personal needs.

Another major limitation of golden parachutes is that while they are certainly attractive for the few executives who enjoy their privileges, their elitist nature ignores the needs of the majority of the company's employees. In the case of the golden parachute, the individuals benefiting are handpicked (perhaps by their own hand), whereas the tin parachute typically is nondiscriminatory and covers all employees.

RATIONALE FOR THE TIN PARACHUTE

First and foremost in most executives' minds is the potential value of the tin parachute as a poison pill. The acquiring company would be required to honor the terms of the compensation program, an obligation that management believes will be prohibitively expensive. Intuitively, the prospect of paying out millions of dollars to employees as a necessary cost of the takeover would seem to give pause to any potential acquirer.

However, closer examination of the construction of the tin parachute reveals that this anticipated scenario probably will not take place. Nearly all tin para-chutes are double-triggered, that is, it takes two sets of conditions to activate them. The first is a change in control—the actual takeover situation. Second, the acquiring company must discharge the employee. It can be assumed that the acquiring company probably would not engage in massive layoffs. The cost of paying those employees who are terminated could be considered relatively im-material in proportion to the overall takeover costs.

A second incentive for adoption of the tin parachute is as justification for the golden parachute. A company whose executives wish to negotiate generous bailouts for themselves may present the board of directors with a comprehensive plan which masks their true agenda. Alternatively, companies that already have golden parachutes may feel pressure from disgruntled employees who question their own lack of job security in the face of staggering amounts of protection for senior executives.

The third motivation for implementing tin parachutes is both to boost employee morale before a takeover, and to protect employee jobs after a takeover. When a company is perceived as a takeover target, employee morale and productivity typically drop. When takeover rumors begin, employees are concerned about the likelihood of being fired and about their prospects for new employment. The existence of a tin parachute means that employees don't have to be thinking about rewriting their resumes, or how they will finance their chidren's educations. Instead they can focus on job performance, knowing that the tin parachute reduces the probability that they will be fired. Also, if they are fired, the tin parachute provides a financial cushion that allows them adequate time to secure other employment.

FEATURES OF TIN PARACHUTES

A difficulty in documenting the incidence of the adoption of tin parachutes is the reluctance on the part of many companies to disclose their existence. The tin parachute, unlike its golden counterpart, is not required by law to be disclosed in proxy filings or other publicly available documents. Companies are reluctant to signal their concern about a takeover or admit their vulnerability as a target.

Firms are caught in the bind of wanting their employees to know about the tin parachute, but not wanting to broadcast the program to the investment community. Thus, most companies have avoided mentioning tin parachutes in the press and will respond to inquiries only when the resultant information remains confidential. One such confidential survey conducted in June 1987 indicates that 7 percent of the major companies responding have tin parachutes in place, most of which had been implemented in the preceding year.[3]

Information from these firms and the half dozen companies which have publicized their tin parachutes shows that the majority of the parachutes are remarkably similar, but that companies also have devised some interesting variations. For example, most tin parachutes cover all full-time employees. But some companies limit coverage to corporate staff, and others set a minimum length-of-service requirement for eligibility.

There are many differing concepts of what constitutes a change in control, with a strong trend existing toward using multiple definitions. A common yardstick is an acquisition of a certain percentage of the company's stock, ranging from 20 percent upwards. A 20 percent threshold can present problems, however. First, in some companies where major shareholders own large blocks of stock, an acquisition of 20 percent could happen unintentionally. A second definition is change in the composition of the board of directors, with most companies requiring a majority of the directors to change. A third measure of change in control is an SEC filing under the Securities Exchange Act of 1934. Finally, liquidation, sale, merger, or consolidation are considered to constitute change in control.

Nearly all the companies define termination to include constructive discharge as well as involuntary termination. Demotion, decrease in pay, and relocation all constitute constructive discharge. The most common window period—that is, the period of time after the takeover for which the tin parachute remains operable—is two years. Most companies do not reduce the amount of severance paid if the employee obtains subsequent employment during the window period.

A typical change-in-control agreement, either golden or tin, specifies severance payment as some multiple of annual or monthly compensation. The formula for tin parachutes also may include length of service and the amount of pay granted under other severance conditions.

Some examples of the features of well-publicized tin parachutes illustrate the ways in which firms have tailored the plans to suit their individual needs. Herman Miller's employees with two to five years of service receive one year's pay and bonus; those with more than five years get two and one-half times total compensation. Diamond Shamrock provides one month's base pay for each year of service with a minimum of three months and a maximum of twenty-four. Mobil Corporation employs a two-tier plan. Its top 800 managers are entitled to two years of compensation, if they are terminated in the first year after takeover. The remainder of the company's employees would get twice their usual severance benefits. America West Airlines grants between 50 percent and 250 percent of annual pay, including bonus and profit sharing. Accuray Corporation provides compensation and benefits for the number of months equal to years served, and includes special benefits for older workers.[4]

THE SOCIAL RESPONSIBILITY OF TIN PARACHUTES

There are three points to be made about tin parachutes that may render them controversial in terms of their social responsibility. All three points hinge on the company's intent in designing and implementing the tin parachute. First, is the tin parachute meant to be a poison pill? Second, is the tin parachute meant to protect employee interests or to justify the golden parachute, or both? Finally, is the tin parachute meant to be activated only in a hostile takeover, or will it also operate in a friendly takeover, including a management-led buyout? (See Table 17.1.)

Another overriding concern is the question of whether or not the tin parachute favors employee interests to the detriment of shareholder interests. It is not clear from current knowledge that it does. But if it does, how does that affect the perception of its social responsibility?

Is the Tin Parachute Meant to be a Poison Pill?

Only one company is known to employ a single-trigger tin parachute. That company is Herman Miller, Inc., a Michigan-based manufacturer of office furniture. A change in control is the only condition needed to activate its tin parachute. If such a takeover happens, every Herman Miller employee can collect the tin parachute if fired or if he or she quits voluntarily. The plan is clearly meant to be a poison pill, to protect the company from takeover, not to protect the employees' jobs.[5] The double-trigger nature of most tin parachutes reduces

Table 17.1
The Tin Parachute as Socially Responsible

PRO	CON
Double trigger nature of most parachutes renders them in-effective as poison pills. Cost is immaterial to acquiring firm.	Parachute is designed solely as a poison pill.
Knowledge about tin parachute raises employee morale. Employees know their jobs are protected, regardless of firm ownership.	Parachute is implemented only to justify extremely generous golden parachutes. Employees are aware that tin parachutes are "convenient" to senior management's agenda.
Parachute's intent is to protect employees; no distinction is made between friendly and hostile takeover situations.	Parachute may not be activated if takeover is friendly (includes management-led buyout).

their effectiveness as poison pills and supports the contention that the intent of the tin parachute is to protect employee interests.

Herman Miller is also unusual in its stipulation that the tin parachute only operates in a hostile takeover. Most firms do not distinguish between a friendly and hostile takeover. One problem is definitional. It is difficult to specify in advance the characteristics of a hostile takeover. Point of view influences judgment. The acquiring company may consider the takeover friendly, while the acquired firm sees it as hostile. Also, friendly negotiations can turn to hostile ones, and less obviously, hostile takeovers have been known to turn friendly. The fact that the tin parachute opens in a friendly takeover, including a management-led leveraged buyout, again argues for its intent to protect employees, not to act as poison pill.

Whose Interests Are Served?

No executive is going to state that tin parachutes were adopted only to make golden parachutes more palatable; it is impossible to assess empirically how much the justification of golden parachutes plays a part in implementing tin parachutes. Utilitarians argue that the outcome or effects of the tin parachute, the protection of employees, should be used as a measure of the plan's social responsibility, regardless of the intent of the instigators.

A final consideration is serving employee versus shareholder interests. If the tin parachute acts to boost employee morale and productivity, shareholder interests are also served. If the costs of activating the parachute are relatively immaterial in proportion to the total takeover costs, shareholder interests are not compromised. If the tin parachute did subtract from shareholders' profits, it is not clear that this renders the plan less socially responsible. Many human resources programs are costly to the firm, but these expenditures are not examined from a shareholder versus employee point of view. Why should the tin parachute be singled out for this type of analysis?

FUTURE OF TIN PARACHUTES

The biggest question yet to be answered is how tin parachutes will be activated. Accuray received an unsolicited $35-a-share cash offer from Combustion Engineering, Inc., in December 1986. After a period of negotiation, including a counterbid from Hercules, Inc., of $40, Accuray accepted an offer from Combustion of $45. The tin parachutes were not opened in this instance because this was considered to be a friendly takeover.

A second example of tin parachutes figuring in a takeover bid is that of T. Boone Pickens' 1985 attempt to acquire Diamond Shamrock. Pickens made the deal contingent upon the invalidation of the poison pill, including the tin parachute. Diamond Shamrock refused.[6] It is not certain how much of a role the existence of the parachute played in the failure of that deal to reach completion. To date there are no known instances of raiders backing off when they learned of the existence of such a defense.

Another major unresolved question is that of how the tin parachute will stand up in court if challenged by irate shareholders. If it is part of a package designed to fend off a hostile change of control, and still proves ineffective, then it may be singled out by shareholders.

Overall, the firm's cost-benefit analysis in adopting the tin parachute is quite favorable. The initial costs of design, communication, and implementation are not high. The tin parachute is a clever means of protecting employee interests even beyond the tenure of present management. Just as the incidence of the more controversial golden parachute has grown rapidly, tin parachutes should take hold over the next five years. The diffusion may be accelerated or curtailed depending on the circumstances in which the first tin parachutes are actually activated.

CONCLUSION

This chapter outlines the features of and motivations for corporate tin parachutes. Studies indicate that the incidence of such plans is increasing. If companies become less reticent about discussing their tin parachutes, more detailed study of the motivation for such plans and corporate decision-making processes about their adoption can be conducted. The diffusion of the tin parachute from company to company and within industries can also be traced.

Whatever a corporation's intent in adopting a tin parachute, the outcome for the employees is favorable. Perhaps the tin parachute is a prototype for programs which benefit employees and also protect the firm as a whole. Certainly, the tin parachute represents an important step for U.S. corporations toward the European model of the protection of employee rights.

NOTES

1. Thomas J. Peters and Robert H. Waterman, Jr., *In Search of Excellence* (New York: Harper & Row, 1982).

2. Hewitt Associates, *Survey of Employment Contracts, Change-in-Control Arrangements, and Incentive Plan Provisions*, Company report, June 1987.

3. Ibid.

4. Alison Leigh Cowan, "New Ploy: 'Tin Parachutes' ", *New York Times*, March 19, 1987.

5. Joani Nelson-Horchler, "A Catchall Parachute," *Industry Week*, February 9, 1987.

6. Conversation with John LaGreca, Diamond Shamrock, April 1987.

Demanagerialization of U.S. Industry: Corporate Restructuring, Mergers and Acquisitions, and Displacement of Managerial Level Employees

S. PRAKASH SETHI
BHARAT B. BHALLA

DEMANAGERIALIZATION OF THE U.S. INDUSTRY

A disquieting management revolution is sweeping the United States. One of its foremost manifestations is the widespread displacement of white-collar workers, primarily professionals and mid-level managers from the ranks of American corporate organizations. We call this trend "demanagerialization" of corporate America. Demanagerialization is one of the by-products of the industrial restructuring being affected by mergers, acquisitions, and leveraged buyouts. The drive toward restructuring and downsizing of U.S. industry has been caused by three sets of factors:

1. A number of corporate managements had become too insulated from market factors and had failed to respond to changing competitive forces in the external environment. Their low-producing assets offered other, more aggressive, entrepreneurs an opportunity to wrest control of the enterprise.
2. A desire for making large investment fees and easy returns on asset sales has turned hordes of investment bankers and arbitrageurs into corporate raiders—the corporate version of ambulance chasers.
3. Many corporate managers have joined the bandwagon of downsizing, restructuring, and even going back to basics, if for no other reason than self-preservation and seeking safety in numbers. In the process, the long-term interests of American industrial and business strength have been seriously undermined. The ascendency of financial asset manipulation as the prime corporate game has accelerated the trend toward deindustrialization rather than contributing to building our competitive strength.

Another corollary of this trend, and the one that is the focus of this chapter, is the predominant concern of the new "instant" owners to improving the immediate returns on corporate assets. This has been necessitated to pay off huge debts assumed during the takeover of acquired companies and to provide high economic returns to the risk-takers and holders of junk bonds. In the process, the long-term interests of the corporation, as an organic entity, often receive short shrift. If history of past waves of mergers and acquisitions is any guide, most of these mergers will also fail to stand the test of the market.[1] The ultimate losers will be those very constituencies that have the most stake in the corporation's survival, and least opportunity to make a fast buck and a quick exit.

The advocates of this trend liken the process to ridding the corporation of bloated bureaucracies, staff, and specialist superstructures. The restructured corporation is supposedly turned into a "lean and mean operating machine," capable of meeting the new competitive challenge. There are indeed cases where such a course of action is necessary if a corporation is to survive. However, we feel that, more often than not, it is the direct result of a corporation's need to meet the immediate demands of its new owners—financial operators—and is often done at the expense of a corporation's long-term interests. The newspapers are replete with daily stories of thousands of junior and mid-level, and often senior, managers being laid-off and involuntarily retired by a substantial number of corporations that are among the largest in the United States. Apart from the legal aspects of alleged age discrimination in such involuntary retirements, we believe this trend has some potentially harmful micro and macro implications for the American business in particular, and for American society in general. Furthermore, it would be fallacious to view all these people as mere liabilities or costs that must be avoided and minimized to the maximum possible extent. In the race toward downsizing, we have failed to take into account the human assets that are being sacrificed and the potential damage that such a loss would do to a corporation's ability to compete in a changing global competitive environment. These are the people who, with their long-term loyalty to the organization and knowledge of its workings, provide the necessary management depth—which enables the corporate organizations to cope with changes in their external environment.

Let us look at the two significant changes in the world economic environment and how U.S. industry has responded to these changes. The first change is the internationalization of the world economy. The world has become truly a global village. The new entrants from the Asian countries, including Japan, South Korea, and Taiwan, into the international competitive arena have radically altered the competitive mix. U.S. industry, which long had a preemptive advantage in the world market, now finds itself competing with similar industries from other countries. This competition is not limited to its overseas markets alone. U.S. industry is feeling the pinch in its home market as well.[2]

Moreover, world competition is not merely a matter of price competition based on relative cost advantage. It is a competition based both on quality-cum-price and structural-institutional rigidities. U.S. industry is finding it hard to compete, both at home and abroad, with foreign producers who offer quality products at competitive prices, and often provide a greater variety of products.[3]

U.S. industry's response to world competition has been somewhat myopic and defensive. It viewed world competition as a short-term problem in production economy. It has ignored the fundamental change in the competitive mix and in technology that have altered the production economies on the one hand, and consumer expectations on the other. The result has been a growing risk in business, long-term commitment to markets, and a need for tremendous agility in altering product mix to meet consumer expectations. U.S. industry, in its attempt to maintain its competitive edge, primarily in its home market, searched for alternate ways to produce goods at lower cost. This strategy initiated the process of U.S. deindustrialization through contracting out and moving production to low-cost, offshore locations and deliberate underutilization or even outright closing of high-cost, local production units in various industries. In our own estimation, roughly 30 percent of all the marketable goods sold by U.S. industry in the local market are produced by its overseas subsidiaries and affiliates. This does not account for the foreign-made parts which are used in the locally assembled products. The impact of this deindustrialization process is evident both in the displacement of local labor force and a perennial burden on the U.S. balance of payments.

The pace of deindustrialization does not seem to slow down. Recently, Xerox Corporation announced the elimination of approximately 800 managerial and professional jobs at its U.S. marketing group. The decision saved Xerox $40 million.[4] On April 25, 1988, Chrysler Corporation announced its decision to close down its K-car production line in the United States, moving it to Mexico. This move offshore is likely to eliminate over 5,000 jobs within the next two years.[5] General Motors plans to achieve an additional cost saving of $2 billion in 1988, by reducing its worldwide employment by 15,000 employees.[6] Honeywell, which has restructured itself as Honeywell-Bull by joining with Groupe Corporation Bell of France and NEC of Japan, is planning to reduce its existing production capacity and cut management-level employees. The impact of the changes is a loss of 1,600 jobs in the United States.[7]

The deindustrialization process is causing a steady displacement of labor, particularly the blue-collar workers, in basic and certain consumer goods industries. The unionized labor force in these industries is seeking job security, while at the same time trying not to give up many of the financial gains achieved through collective bargaining in previous years. Companies have responded by investing in automation, moving production overseas, and, whenever possible, through outright closure of existing facilities. However, these changes have neither been well-thought-out nor well-implemented. The result is that American business finds itself in a no-win situation at home. It is saddled with higher costs and outmoded production facilities when compared with its foreign competitors.

The second significant change is the internationalization of technology and technology dispersion. American manufacturers have been losing the technological edge that they had enjoyed following World War II. The technological superiority of U.S. industry is being challenged at every level. Although the

United States still has an edge in technological innovation, other OECD (Organisation for Economic Co-Operation and Development) nations, particularly Japan and West Germany, have surpassed the United States in many technological areas particularly in the area of technological applications to mass-produced quality goods sold in various markets, including the United States, at competitive prices.

We believe U.S. industry is again misreading the signals for future trends. It considers the growing gap in the process and production technology as a natural phenomenon. It is widely believed that the U.S. economy is sliding from an industrial society to a postindustrial society or a service society in which knowledge-based and ancillary industries will replace manufacturing. Hence, the current decline in U.S. productivity growth is natural and inevitable.

Thus, instead of concentrating its efforts on rejuvenating the industrial base through long-term investments that improve process and production technologies, U.S. industry has favored restructuring which yields short-term profits. The industrial restructuring is based on the strategy of mass-scale harvesting of marginal operations and regrouping of residual profitable assets into new or existing business units or entities. The restructuring process, evident in the shrinking size and scope of the U.S. industrial base, has two distinct characteristics:

1. Restructuring has accelerated deindustrialization by treating maturing industries and low-margin operations as orphans. This will continue to have serious employment implications for blue-collar workers and mounting burden on society either to retrain them or to provide them with honorable means of subsistence.
2. Restructuring is causing a consolidation of the remaining productive assets into potentially profitable packages via takeovers, mergers, acquisitions, and leverage buyouts.

This trend continues. The results of this consolidation process are visible in the outright elimination of many companies, including certain well-known names like Bendix, Continental Group, Inc., General Foods, Getty Oil, RCA, and Sperry, from the U.S. industrial landscape. The human dimension of industrial restructuring is apparent in the displacement of thousands of blue-collar workers. What is not generally realized is that the process has also resulted in a loss of thousands of white-collar jobs. For the future of U.S. industrial competitiveness, this loss is particularly worrisome, especially as it pertains to operational and professional managers at the middle and upper-middle levels.

SCOPE AND NATURE OF DEMANAGERIALIZATION

Demanagerialization is having serious emotional, physical, and financial repercussions among the affected managers and staff professionals. Of even greater importance is the serious impact this process is likely to have on the future economy and social fabric of the United States. Between 1980 and 1987, nearly 15,000 companies were merged or acquired at a total cost of over $1 trillion,

Table 18.1

Quantitative Assessment of Demanagerialization

A. MERGERS & ACQUISITIONS   (Source: W. T. Grimm & Co.)

Co. Size

Year	$1B +	$500M-$1B	$100M-$500M	Other	Total
1982	8	14	116	2,208	2,346
1983	12	34	120	2,377	2,543
1984 (E)	18	40	101	2,515	2,674
1985	36	45	353	2,567	3,001
1986	26	50	270	3,010	3,356
	100	183	960	12,677	13,920

B. NUMBER OF MANAGERS EMPLOYED IN STAFF & NON-OPERATIONAL POSITIONS

YEAR	$1B +	$500M-$1B	$100M-$500M	Others	Total
1982	8,000	2,800	5,800	22,080	38,680
1983	12,000	6,800	6,000	23,770	48,570
1984	18,000	8,000	5,050	25,150	56,200
1985	36,000	9,000	17,650	25,670	88,320
1986	26,000	10,000	13,500	25,670	88,320
1987 (Est.)	-	-	-	30,100	79,600
					88,630
	100,000	36,600	48,000	126,770	400,000

*   ASSUMPTION: The following number of staff positions (overheads) are assumed in each category:

$1B +	1000
$500M	200
$100M	50
Others	10

a.   Contribution from lay-offs from the financial services industry ranges between 50,000 to 100,000.

affecting between 350,000 to 400,000 mid-level professional managers. The restructuring, which until 1987 had been confined primarily to the U.S. manufacturing sector, has subsequently spread to the U.S. financial services industry, particularly following the free fall of the U.S. stock market on Monday, October 19, 1987. Since then a number of financial services companies have either been merged or acquired, and the remaining companies are downsizing their operations. The process of restructuring and downsizing in the financial services industry has raised the ranks of unemployed or laid-off managers to between 400,000 and 500,000 (see Table 18.1). Of these, 50 percent have already lost their jobs and are prematurely retired. Another 20 to 25 percent will be out of their jobs permanently by the end of this decade. According to one estimate, "Fortune 500 companies alone have eliminated almost 2.8 million jobs since 1980, a million of them managerial."[8] These displaced workers are facing difficulty in locating comparable positions in the industry. The executive recruiting agencies are being flooded with unsolicited resumes. According to a recent *Wall Street Journal* study, one executive recruiting firm, Thorndike Deland Associates, is getting 50 percent more resumes than six months ago. At another firm, Russell Reynolds Associates, the current inflow approximates 10,000 resumes for 1,500 jobs. As most of these resumes are unsolicited, they are likely to be put into shredders. At Heidrick & Struggles, the heightened inflow of unsolicited resumes is from the troubled financial services industry.[9]

The immediate impact of the current demanagerialization is dysfunctional. It is defeating the very purpose for which it is justified. Instead of gaining increased productivity and cost economies, U.S. industry continues to suffer from sustained inefficiency. The demanagerialization has created a highly unstable work environment. The surviving employees find themselves overburdened and operating in an environment of fear, uncertainty, and stress. Undoubtedly, such an atmosphere is not conducive to employee morale, performance, and productivity.

The stressful atmosphere is causing a growing incidence of personal and behavioral problems among the current employees. In addition to lost productivity, U.S. industry is suffering from a mounting burden of health care costs related to employees' personal problems. It is hard to estimate the exact costs involved in lost productivity and health care treatment. According to Willis B. Goldbeck, head of the Washington Group on Health, U.S. industry is spending roughly 20 to 30 percent of its total health care budget in dealing with the employees' personal problems.[10] Many companies are organizing and supporting stress management programs. The cost to society in dealing with the behavioral problems of the affected employees and their families is also significant.

The current trend toward demanagerialization has two distinct characteristics:

1. It is discriminatory in its impact. In general, employees (managers) in staff functions of fifty years of age and older, and who meet the company's criteria, are being offered early retirement. With industry trends unfavorable to "50-plus" employees, these managers are joining the ranks of normal retirees (sixty-five and over) who are part of "maturing/graying" America. Other managers, below fifty years of age, are being given reasonable severance packages along with counseling services enabling them to find suitable alternative job opportunities. Many of these employees have to settle in positions of less responsibility and reduced pay.
2. Demanagerialization is causing elimination of jobs and functions in many corporations performed by the mid-level managers. These are overheads and part of cost economies. In the past, U.S. industry had also resorted to restructuring, consolidation, and downsizing. These, however, had resulted only in temporary lay-offs in an industrializing environment. But this time around, the current trend is different. Under growing pressure of competition from foreign countries, the shrinkage and downsizing are likely to be longer lasting.

WHAT CAN MANAGEMENT DO?

What management can and should do depends upon our answer to one key question: Is U.S industry in a secular declining trend, or can it recover its lost competitive and technological edge in world markets? We believe there is nothing fundamentally wrong with U.S. industry per se. They key problem is how it is being managed. As a trustee of U.S. productive assets, the present management has failed in its obligations to manage these assets for the benefit of the existing and future generations. The damage that has been done is substantial, but not total, and can be repaired, provided that management changes its attitude toward its own obligation as the industrial trustee.

In its obsession with short-term profits, U.S. industry has consistently ignored both people and machines. It now finds itself with a relatively inefficient labor force and obsolete plants and equipment. U.S. industry can partially regain its lost competitive edge in the world markets by treating both its machines and personnel as valuable assets. It is this very attitude that has given Japan, our greatest competitor, a leading edge in the world market.

Japan had realized early that no nation can gain and maintain a competitive advantage indefinitely simply by moving up on the experience (or cost) curve in the globalized economy. The competitive advantage would belong to those countries that combine cost advantage through exploitation of technologies with scope advantage through creating product differentiation. This strategy is evident in Japan's R&D investment, a large portion of which is spent on developing and improving process technologies. A relatively small portion of R&D investment is allocated to product development.

This is in direct contrast with U.S. industry's practice where a large portion of R&D budget is allocated to product innovation and only a small portion to process innovation and improvement. Hence, Japan has developed an integrated production system which is capable of producing high quality products at competitive prices to be sold in the world market. "The Japanese have achieved their manufacturing excellence by doing simple things very well, and slowly improving them all the time."[11] Japanese factories have achieved efficiency and growth through continuous improvements in manufacturing processes and heavy investments in R&D. This is not unique to Japan. Even in the United States, where management has the will and foresight to invest in plant updating and cares about product quality and consumer satisfaction, the results have been excellent. Like Japan, U.S. industry needs to develop integrated manufacturing processes that would enable it to build greater added value into its products, thereby increasing product variety while maintaining product quality.[12] Unfortunately, during the current process of restructuring of U.S. industry, cash reserves are being used primarily to pay off the existing shareholders, to service the debts involved in takeovers or leveraged buyouts, and in buying financial assets.

Japan's competitive strength is not based simply on its continuing ability to improve product and process technologies, but equally on its effective management of human resources. Our intent is not to prescribe an outright adoption of Japanese labor practices by U.S. industry, but to emphasize the Japanese attitude toward human resources. In Japan, labor mobility is almost nonexistent. Employees are guaranteed security and career opportunities within a corporation. All employees share in the overall performance of the business and are motivated to perform well. Japanese companies treat their employees as a scarce resource and a valuable asset, instead of considering them as merely an overhead cost that must be minimized. This attitude has enabled Japanese industry to have a loyal, dedicated, efficient, and cooperative labor force.

As opposed to Japan, U.S. industry treats labor as one of the factors of production which can be substituted with capital. The staff is treated as overhead to be sacrificed at the altar of efficiency and cost-cutting. It is surprising to see that U.S. industry, in spite of cost-cutting efforts, has not succeeded in improving its competitiveness, while Japan, with its lifetime employment practices, has enhanced its competitive position in the world market. American business needs to change its attitude toward human resources and induce the work force to be cooperative and efficient. In other words, U.S. industry should stop the deindustrialization and demanagerialization processes intended to regain a short-term competitive position. Instead, it should invest in capital and human resources to build a sound foundation for its future growth.

Within an economy, a shift in sectoral emphasis for growth is a natural developmental phenomenon. But there is no specific evidence of an outright displacement of one sector by another in a sequential process of economic development. During the first industrial revolution, the United States experienced a major shift of labor from agriculture to the manufacturing industry, but not

a shift out of agricultural production (something parallel to the curtailing or offshoring of U.S. manufacturing production). . . . The United States did not shift out of agricultural production, as we are now often advised to shift out of manufacturing. American agricultural production did not go offshore or shrivel up. Instead, it increased by colossal amounts; whether measured in tons or dollars or whatever. Agricultural output rose, but farm labor inputs decreased; they were replaced by capital, education and new technologies. To extend an analogy, we automated agriculture; we did not offshore it or shift out. The difference between the two approaches—keeping production by automating versus shifting out—makes all the difference in the world to the wealth of nations and to the composition of employment.[13]

Moreover, it should not be overlooked that the productive agricultural sector supported a well-developed industrial sector, partly based on its output and partly servicing its requirements. By analogy, one can argue that a weak or disappearing manufacturing industrial sector will make it difficult for the United States to have an efficient and self-sustaining service sector. Hence, if the United States loses mastery and control of manufacturing, the high-paying service jobs that are directly linked to manufacturing will, in a few short rounds of product and process innovation, seem to whither away (only to sprout up offshore, where they went). In the final analysis this is the core of the manufacturing matters argument, the proverbial bottom line. It is the high-value-added service roles tied directly to manufacturing (whether they are located in service or manufacturing categories) that we must hold and develop if we are to remain a (viable and) powerful economy. It is not manufacturing jobs per se. In brief, in order for the shift of employment to service to be developmental and not become a shift to poverty, we must maintain mastery and control of manufacturing production.[14]

Obviously, with greater emphasis on productivity within the manufacturing sector, there will be some "de-skilling" at certain operational levels, but ultimately there will be greater need for highly skilled and knowledgeable white-collar workers servicing industry.[15]

CONCLUSION

U.S. industry finds itself in a "Catch–22" position. It needs both cost-competitiveness and increased productivity to regain its markets at home and abroad. The economies achieved to date through demanagerialization and other measures have failed in providing U.S. industry with the necessary competitive edge in the marketplace. Demanagerialization has also created an environment of uncertainty which is unhealthy for efficient production, both in quantity and quality.

U.S. industry has lost one major battle in its global competitiveness by failing to modernize and improve efficiency of production. Its current efforts at downsizing are, however, likely to be quite counterproductive. It is like preparing for tomorrow's battles with yesterday's weapons.

The future, however, does not lie with improving existing production technology. Instead, future progress lies in harnessing new technologies, in other words, biogenetics, ceramics, superconducting, and information processing. The nature of emerging technology is revolutionary, not evolutionary. It carries with it increased risk and uncertainty. The success in developing and harnessing these technologies will lie not so much in raising large amounts of new capital, but in hiring, motivating, and retaining a larger number of talented and creative people in various skills who can work together in an environment of trust and enthusiasm. It would do us no good to imitate the Japanese in what they have already accomplished. Even if we succeed, it would be the wrong thing to do at the wrong time, and for the wrong reasons.[16]

Our emphasis must be on the future. Like physical capital, we must learn to invest in human capital for the long haul. American corporations would need more, not fewer, professionals and managers. These professionals will also be in high demand and unlikely to work in organizations that are rigid, bureaucratic, and short-term-oriented.[17] Therefore, to keep them involved and motivated, top management will have to learn to share real decision-making power with them. This will call for the development of new types of organization structures and

212 S. Prakash Sethi & Bharat B. Bhalla

decision-making processes to manage these "high discretion" employees.[18] American business is facing both a challenge and an opportunity. We earnestly hope that our top managers will see the opportunity and accept the challenge. They are certainly capable of doing both. What is lacking is not ability, but the vision and the will. Will they accept it? Only time will tell.

NOTES

1. Robert Bell in his forthcoming book, *Surviving the Ten Ordeals of the Takeover*, cites some interesting examples and studies supporting the fact that mergers and acquisitions are not profitable and do not contribute to efficiency.

2. Lester Thurow, "Revitalizing American Industry: Managing in a Competitive World Economy," *California Management Review* 27, no. 1 (Fall 1984): 9–41.

3. S. Prakash Sethi, Nobuaki Namiki, and Carl Swanson, *The False Promise of the Japanese Miracle* (Cambridge, Mass.: Ballinger Publishing Co., 1984), 284.

4. "XEROX says 800 Marketing Jobs to be Dropped," *The Wall Street Journal*, May 11, 1988, p. 6.

5. "Chrysler to Stop Building K-Cars in U.S. Plants," *The Wall Street Journal*, April 25, 1988, p. 10.

6. "GM is Ahead of Timetable for White-Collar Layoffs," *The Wall Street Journal*, November 4, 1987, p. 6.

7. "Honeywell-Bull to Cut By 10% U.S. Job Force," *The Wall Street Journal*, November 13, 1987, p. 2.

8. Amanda Bennett, "Is Your Job Making You Sick?," *The Wall Street Journal*, April 22, 1988, section 3, p. 11R.

9. "Unsolicited Resumes Flood into Executive Search Firms," *The Wall Street Journal*, May 10, 1988, p. 1.

10. Rhoda L. Rundle, "The Company As Shrink," *The Wall Street Journal*, April 22, 1988, section 3, p. 5R.

11. Robert H. Hays, "Why Japanese Factories Work," *Harvard Business Review* 59, no. 4 (July-August 1981): 57.

12. Sethi, Namiki, and Swanson, *The False Promise of the Japanese Miracle*, 285.

13. Stephen S. Cohen and John Zysman, "Why Manufacturing Matters: The Myth of the Post-Industrial Economy," *California Management Review* 29, no. 3 (Spring 1987): 9–10.

14. Ibid., 16.

15. Paul S. Adler, "New Technologies, New Skills," *California Management Review* 29, no. 11 (Fall 1986): 9–28. Adler's entire thesis provides a logical reasoning for advancing skills and more competent professionals in the postindustrial society.

16. Sethi, Namiki, and Swanson, *The False Promise of the Japanese Miracle*, viii.

17. Ibid., 276–99.

18. Ibid.

Insider Trading: The Secret Seduction

JOANNE B. CIULLA

Ben Franklin once remarked, "Three may keep a secret if two of them are dead."[1] If this were true, just think of how many dead people it would take to keep a secret on Wall Street. Consider, for example, the multiservice nature of the modern brokerage or banking firm. Underwriting, merger and acquisition advisory services, investment management, research, arbitrage, proprietary trading, program trading, broker and retail sales, and service on boards of directors all potentially provide broker dealers with inside information on the firm's clients. And, while the Glass-Steagall Act prohibits banking institutions from corporate underwriting activities, banks are, nonetheless, involved in a variety of securities industry functions, such as financial consulting, municipal bond underwriting, and corporate finance. Inside information from these activities can easily come in conflict with a bank's commercial lending and trust department activities. A list of institutions supplied with inside information could go on from insurance companies to law firms to newspapers. In this environment, the practice of trading on inside or secret information is not as surprising as its absence.

The current dialogue on insider trading generally focuses on the adequacy of current regulations and self-policing policies (such as "Chinese Walls"), and the ethics of individuals. Among these concerns, the moral flaws of people like Ivan Boesky and Dennis Levine capture the public's imagination most dramatically. Playing to the public, the media have put business ethics in the limelight and given the subject its fifteen minutes of fame. The publicity link between insider trading and business ethics courses has led some people to believe that our classes are nothing but discussions of the demonic Boesky and the greedy Levine. Those who blame business schools for producing amoral or immoral MBAs are often the same ones who oppose more government regulation of the securities industry—in other words, the system's ok, it's the people who are rotten.

As one who believes that research in business ethics should be more than just a rehash of the latest scandal, I begin by looking at the role of secrecy in business and the social impact of insider trading. I then argue that if one views secrecy as an attitude toward knowledge, then there are ways in which business schools might better prepare students to deal with the temptations of Wall Street.

SECRETS AND THE PRIVACY OF PROPERTY

Adam Smith recognized the utility of concealing information about prices, if only for a short period of time. In *The Wealth of Nations*, he tells us that when the market price of a commodity goes up substantially above the natural price, it is wise for those who supply the market with that commodity to conceal price change. According to Smith, if this change in price became known, rivals would enter the market, satiate demand, and knock the price down to its natural level. He says, "Secrets of this kind, however, it must be acknowledged, can seldom be long kept; and the extraordinary profit can last very little longer than they are kept."[2] While, on the other hand, Smith notes that secrets in manufacturers last longer than secrets in trade and can give a businessperson the competitive edge. Richard Posner, one of the many Smith clones around today, similarly argues that "some measure of privacy is necessary to enable people, by concealing their ideas from other people, to appropriate the social benefits of their discoveries and inventions."[3]

Early on, Smith noticed that it is not just private use, but private knowledge that made property valuable. He saw that success in business can rest on the ability to keep some information secret, even while competing in a public market system. Ironically, the owner's prerogative to keep information private mitigates against the ability of the market to function according to Smith's rational ideal— making trade a bit more like gambling, because information is either uncertain or incomplete.

The privacy of private property troubled Karl Marx. In his early writings, he named private property as the root of alienation.[4] Ownership of property gave a person the right to exclude others from it and do with it what he or she pleased. Factories could be moved, wages cut, people fired, work processes altered—all without mention to those affected. One ramification of alienation was that workers did not have control over their lives and well-being. The privacy of ownership and business decisions denied workers important knowledge of the future. This is especially true today. When a company faces a hostile takeover, employees suffer enormous stress because they are not given up-to-date information on the future of their jobs.

Writing at the turn of the century, German sociologist Georg Simmel argued that money, not property, allowed all exchanges to become secret and silent transactions. But, the concealability of money is, according to Simmel, "the symptom, or the extreme form of its relationship to private ownership."[5] In his book *The Philosophy of Money*, Simmel says, "Money's formlessness and abstractness makes it possible to invest in the most varied and most remote values and thereby to remove it from the gaze of neighbors. Its anonymity and colorlessness does not reveal the source from which it came to the present owner.''[6] Simmel goes on to say that money hides many secrets as long as it is not transformed into property.

Investigators who work on Wall Street are well aware of the invisible properties of money. For example, Wall Street private investigator Jules B. Kroll has noted that Martin Siegel and Ivan Boesky were involved in cash transactions of which there was no record or system in the corporate structure to detect. As a result of this, he believes that when you are suspicious of employees, you need to look at their life-styles, not their bank books.[7] Money itself is abstract and secretive; it only becomes public when it's transformed into goods and services.

To combat the dangers inherent in money, such as concealment, misleading estimates, and illegitimate use, Simmel points to laws that require public disclosure of the financial policies of the government and corporations. However, Simmel does not believe that the requirement for public disclosure really addresses the dangers of money. Rather, what the legal requirement for public disclosure actually does, according to him, is further differentiate public knowledge from private knowledge.

Smith, Marx, and Simmel present some interesting insights into the uses and problems of secrecy in business. Smith appreciates the usefulness of secrets as part of a business' competitive strategy, but also realizes that the lifetime of a secret in a market setting is short-lived. Although I doubt that Marx would say it this way, in his early writings I see the worry that the secrecy allowed by private property under the capitalist system can and does lead to social irresponsibility. Simmel tells us openness (required by law) is one way to combat the danger of secrecy in business. However, he says that in its effect, mandated disclosure actually creates even more secrets, by making a sharp distinction between the public and the private realms of knowledge.

These insights raise some provocative questions. For example, ''Would more regulation concerning disclosure on Wall Street have the adverse affect of increasing stakes and making insider trading an even greater temptation?'' If this question seems too farfetched we might ask, ''Given the short life of a secret, such as one concerning a takeover, would regulations eliminate secrets or simply shorten their lives?''

Sissela Bok's distinction between privacy and private property sheds some light on these two questions. She defines ''secrecy'' as intentional concealment and ''privacy'' as ''the condition of being protected from unwanted access by others—either physical access, personal information, or attention.''[8] So, according to Bok, a privately owned company is not a secretly owned one, and the privacy of this kind of private property is the right to limit access. The question that we have to ask today is, ''What kind of privacy does a corporation have?''

Bok says secrecy and privacy do overlap in cases where secrecy must be used to guard against unwanted access.[9] Hence, secrets can guard access to the private lives of individuals and corporations that are threatened by raiders. Secrets, then, tend to proliferate and become even more valuable in a dangerous environment. Corporations today live under the threat of a hostile takeover. Do their secrets protect them from unwanted access? Since corporations are not privately owned, do they have a right to protect themselves from unwanted access with a cloak of secrecy? Or are they up for grabs by anyone who can pay the price of admission? These questions are outside of the scope of this chapter, but are not unrelated to the ethical issues related to insider trading.

SECRETS AND CHINESE WALLS

If regulating secrecy from the outside is paradoxical, then consider how secrets are managed internally. In a *National Law Journal* article, Edward D. Herlihy argues that the internal self-policing systems that brokerage firms have used for the past fifty years, called "Chinese Walls," are effective. Herlihy defines a Chinese Wall as "a set of internal written policies designed to control and prevent the dissemination of non-public information acquired by one department to other separate departments in the organization."[10]

In 1980 the SEC adopted Rule 14e–3, which prohibits insider trading while in possession of material information; however, Paragraph b of the rule provides for a safe-harbor exclusion of "the disclose or abstain from trading" proscription for multiservice firms who adopt a Chinese Wall and can show that individuals making investments have had no knowledge of inside information. Rule 17j–1, also adopted in 1980, requires every registered investment company and each investment advisor of, or principal underwriter for, such a company to adopt a written code of ethics.

Segregating people and information into departments has some obvious limitations, as do codes of ethics. Because of their bureaucratic nature, modern organizations all run the risk of, as Hannah Arendt once said, "looking like they're ruled by nobody," and this greatly obscures individual responsibility. Unless you literally lock your employees up every night and put Big Brother in the bathrooms, businesses are left depending on the morals of their employees.

Hence, in our world of fancy management systems, expensive consultants, behavioral psychologists and economists, pious CEOs, and complex rules and regulations, we still do not have complete control. In the end we are left hanging by the fragile threads of trust. These threads are crucial for the maintenance of social order in organizations and society. Since professionals are supposed to represent the height of trustworthiness with respect to technically competent performance and fiduciary obligation and responsibility, it was not unreasonable for the public eye to critically scrutinize the training ground for MBAs.

ETHICS AS AN ATTITUDE TOWARD KNOWLEDGE

Many different motifs have been used to explain insider trading. Some of the more common ones are: poor moral upbringing, ethical relativism or lack of shared moral values, amoral business schools, greed, lust for power, the Reagan era, deregulation, rapid growth in the securities industries, inadequate supervision, cracks in the Chinese Wall, and, just to round things out, secular humanism. In some ways, the publicity and concern over insider trading, although distant from most people's lives, has been a catalyst for moral, social, and legal soul searching.

The question that has intrigued me is, "Is there anything about the way that business schools train MBAs that makes them more prone to do something like trade on inside information?" Several press reports about Dennis Levine have said that for him money had become "a way of keeping score." Game theory and game analogies are often used in business schools to formulate strategies. But problems arise when people come to think of themselves as players. Viewing business as a game allows people to distance themselves from their actions and the effect of their actions on others. Game-playing engenders a delight in manipulation and technical expertise that is disjointed from responsibilities that one has to others and the organization. In particular, the game attitude fosters the development of technical excellence in isolation from any notion of moral excellence.

By compartmentalizing learning in business schools, teachers often fail to integrate how the "hard" areas like finance relate to the "soft" areas of management. For example, if, after two years at a top business school, the only way that a student can tell if a business is mismanaged is if its stock is undervalued, then I think that we've failed. What's at stake here is not just a matter of teaching values—its a failure to give students an integrated understanding of business.

Some of our students who go on to work in the financial industry take with them a rationalist view of knowledge. They believe that quantitative methods and information (deductive knowledge) are superior to information collected through observation (inductive knowledge). Systems and models allow for deductive reasoning and yield information that has the sound ring of certainty and truth. I call this view "knowledge in a box." The problem with knowledge in a box is that it's not always clear whether what is true in the box is true in the world. So, for example, hostile takeovers might be shown to be good for the economy in one box, even if they don't appear to be good for the messy society in which the box sits.

If you look at insider trading from the perspective of finance, it may be hard to show that it does any harm; hence, so the argument goes, it may not be unethical. It is also difficult to demonstrate how insider trading violates current laws and regulations. But ethical thinking (and philosophical thinking in general) forces one to look at a far broader picture. For example, one might reasonably ask a transcendental question like "What are the ethical understandings that make business possible?" Here the harm is somewhat clearer. Business transactions cannot take place without trust. By betraying this trust, the inside trader causes social chaos. He or she is like a terrorist who sends the message that institutions do not have control. This shakes public confidence, not only in financial institutions, but in the ideals of fairness that underlie the market system.

Hence, an ethical attitude toward business requires that you clearly understand how your actions affect other people, your employer, the economic system, and society in general. Trading on inside information is a private action based on one area of expertise. There doesn't seem to be any harm or victim. It's an anonymous crime, if you haven't been trained to integrate what you know so as to understand the ramifications. Acts that "don't hurt anyone" are much easier to perform and rationalize than those that do.

One striking difference between graduate education in business and education in the liberal arts is the uncritical way in which information is presented and absorbed by students. With classes, cases to prepare, resumes to write, and the quest for the perfect job, students rarely take the time to reflect on or question what they've learned. The arrogance of some MBAs is often derived from the mistaken belief that they possess certain knowledge about how to get things done in the world. This special knowledge sets them apart from organizations and sometimes leads them to believe that they can outsmart everyone else. These unfortunate few have come to view knowledge only as a tool, not a guide.

CONCLUSION

As we have seen, secrets are seductive forms of knowledge that serve to hide, protect, and corrupt through unfair advantage. The law and Chinese Walls separate knowledge insofar as it is possible. These laws and policies need to be reassessed and refreshed; however, due to the privacy of secrets, not even more or tougher rules can completely control betrayal by insiders. Businesses will always have their secrets, and Wall Street will continue to offer new unethical schemes. Many will be tempted. However, one weapon against temptation is the ability to look it critically in the eye and have a clear picture of the impact of one's actions on others. Knowledge is an important part of conscience—it doesn't guarantee that a person will resist temptation, it just makes it tougher for a rational person to give in. When it comes to the building and development of character, moral struggle is almost as important as moral victory.

We don't really need to teach students that insider trading is wrong—they know that—it's yesterday's news. We won't be able to transform demons into saints. Courses in ethics and in social responsibility can be helpful, but students need to take away more than a bag full of case discussions. We need to give them the skills to think critically and philosophically about their work, their lives, and what they have learned.

NOTES

1. Benjamin Franklin, *Poor Richard: The Almanacks for the Years 1733–1758*, ed. Van Wyck Brooks (New York: Heritage Press, 1964), July 1735, p. 30.

2. Adam Smith, *The Wealth of Nations* in *The Essential Adam Smith*, ed. Robert L. Heilbroner (New York: W. W. Norton & Company Ltd., 1986), 191.

3. Sissela Bok, *Secrets* (New York: Pantheon Books, 1982), 148.

4. Karl Marx, "1844 Manuscripts," in *Karl Marx: Selected Writings*, ed. David McLellan (Oxford: Oxford University Press, 1977), 77.

5. Georg Simmel, *The Philosophy of Money*, trans. Tom Bottomore and David Frisby (Boston: Routledge & Kegan Paul, 1978), 385.

6. Ibid., 386.

7. "A Private Eye's View: Why Wall Street is Rife with Crime," *The New York Times*, February 15, 1987, p. D2.

8. Bok, *Secrets*, 10–11.

9. Ibid., 13.

10. Edward D. Herlihy, " 'Chinese Walls' and Insider Trading: How Well Does Self-Policing Work?," *National Law Journal* (May 18, 1987): 39.

— 20

Insider Trading: What We Know and What We Don't Know

MICHAEL S. ROZEFF

INTRODUCTION

The title of this chapter is far too ambitious. When I gave Robert Frederick this title, I had in mind the finance literature, which on the subject of insider trading is not very large. However, I soon discovered that a substantial legal literature existed. There is no settled view or consensus on the issue of insider trading among lawyers and economists. After decades of law cases, people still seem to be confused about this issue and are groping for ways of understanding it. Even among Supreme Court justices, opinions on insider trading vary widely. Justice Blackmun sees it as inherently unfair. Other justices have seen it as a problem only if it involved traditional concepts of fraud or deceit. Still others have pointed to the idea that insider trading is wrong when it involves the misappropriation or theft of information. Among economists, positive and negative views are on record, depending on one's ideas of the possible benefits and costs of insider trading. The SEC seems to be the body most willing to promote restrictions against insider trading, to widen its definition from corporate insiders to anyone who possesses material nonpublic information, and generally to promote an egalitarian concept of information dispersal. My impression is that the main body of lawyers and economists views the SEC's position as extreme and unrealistic.

Based on this lack of consensus, I infer that we don't know enough about insider trading. I believe that if we had a secure base of knowledge about this subject, the divergent views would have been driven to a closer degree of consensus. This is not the only possible inference from the lack of consensus. Another is that people's feelings toward insider trading are strong, perhaps

I thank Marc Reinganum for helpful comments.

I thank Marc Reinganum for helpful comments.

because they feel that important interests are at stake. Hence there is little movement toward agreement. I also draw the inference that the subject may simply be a very difficult one to analyze, that no overwhelming case can be made either for insider trading being pernicious or being beneficial.

A full consideration of the legal, ethical, and economic doctrines relating to insider trading could easily occupy a book. I will therefore talk about six areas of particular interest to me that I hope will also be of interest to you. These include the following questions: How significant is insider trading? What are the profits earned by insider trading? Why is insider trading a matter of such concern for the Securities and Exchange Commission and others? How is insider trading related to the takeover of a company? What are the major ethical arguments against insider trading? Who is hurt by insider trading?

HOW SIGNIFICANT IS INSIDER TRADING?

Recent insider trading cases involving Ivan Boesky and others have generated lots of publicity. Are these cases the tip of an iceberg? Are there many more such cases going undetected? Or is this case more comparable to an airplane crash, a bad thing but atypical?

A previous SEC Chairman, John Shad, has stated that insider trading is "a very serious problem, but it is the exception, not the rule." The SEC spends 10 percent of its enforcement budget on insider trading. The evidence in the finance literature suggests that insider trading is not significant. In 1976 Joseph Finnerty analyzed all the insider trades reported to the SEC for the years 1969 to 1972. There were 31,089 trades, or about 7,800 per year. Nejat Seyhun recently analyzed the insider transactions in 790 large New York Stock Exchange (NYSE) firms for the seven years ending in 1981. There were 59,000 trades, or about 8,400 per year. Although these are the reported trades, not all necessarily involve insider information, since corporate officials and large owners may make many adjustments in their portfolios for personal reasons. On the other hand, there are ways to take advantage of insider information without trading directly in the affected security. At any rate, Seyhun's 59,000 trades averages eleven per company per year, or about one per month. But how big were these trades? They aggregated $11.1 billion, or about $20,000 per trade. Consider that a stock like Champion International trades 250,000 shares in a *day* at a price near $40 a share, or a value of $10 million. It appears that the amount of insider trading by corporation insiders is trivial relative to the total value of trading.

The significance of insider trading can also be measured by the number of enforcement actions against it. Michael Dooley in 1980 stated that the SEC had brought only thirty-seven cases against insider trading in the years 1966 to 1980, most involving market professionals and not corporate insiders. Most of these cases were settled and with minor penalties. Dooley noted that private actions were trivial. Kenneth Scott, surveying SEC actions since its inception, found 106 trading episodes involving allegations of nondisclosure trading by defendants. I cannot vouch for these numbers, but those who have looked into this aspect of insider trading are telling us that there are very few actions against it. Might we say that "where there is no smoke, there is no fire?" The trend in SEC actions is apparently up. Commissioner Cox has reported fifty-four civil actions and six administrative proceedings in 1986.

What other countries do about insider trading also reflects on its significance. Barry Rider and Leigh French reported in 1979 that insider trading is considered proper in Japan and that enforcement actions are almost nonexistent. Parenthetically, Japan's stock exchange now is larger than the NYSE in terms of market value, and there is no lack of investor confidence in it. Hong Kong had a law but repealed it. Italy has no law. France has few suits. England had no regulation until 1978. Dennis Carlton and Daniel Fischel summarize by saying that insider trading in other countries has been either unregulated or subject to only minor regulation. I interpret this evidence as follows. Many societies and many investors would have had to be extremely shortsighted and unobservant to have allowed insider trading to persist if it were really so criminal an offense as to cause serious and observable harm to innocent parties. Perhaps if it could or does harm people, they take care of it in their own ways without needing massive public action.

To summarize: the amount of insider trading is in fact trivial. The laws against it, even in the United States, are not very stiff. Enforcement actions against it are few here and even fewer overseas. The penalties against it have not been severe. These facts tend to make one conclude that insider trading is a nonproblem, certainly not in the same league as other social issues and concerns such as drunken driving and drug-related crimes against people and property. Perhaps private individuals have created institutions and ethics that largely resolve any potential problems.

WHAT ARE THE PROFITS EARNED BY INSIDER TRADING?

We do not know the answer to this question because we do not know the full extent of insider trading. We do know something about the profits earned by those who must report their trades to the SEC. In his recent study, Seyhun said that insiders' abnormal profits did not appear to be very large. The returns that insiders earn from their purchases that are over and above the normal market returns are estimated by Seyhun as 7.5 percent per annum for their purchases and 4.25 percent for their sales. However, these profit rates are overstated. Since insiders tend to purchase more shares in small companies and sell shares in large companies, and since small companies on average earn a normal return that is higher than the return of a large company, the insiders' profit rates must be adjusted downward for this size effect. When this is done, the buys and sells average about 3 to 3.5 percent per annum in profitability.

How much is this in dollars? Recall that the sum total of all the insider trading in 790 large companies over a seven-year period was just over $11 billion. So 3.5 percent of this in profits is $385 million by all corporation insiders in all these firms over 1975 to 1981. This figure is not large by comparison with other wealth gains by various groups in society. Two that I just happened to have read about while drafting this chapter are (1) losses from bank frauds estimated to be over $12 billion since 1980, and (2) protection of the U.S. steel industry, which works out to cost buyers of cars, appliances, and construction materials $6.8 billion per year. Nevertheless, the profits to insiders are really not known with any degree of certainty. First of all, insiders can earn profits by not trading. If they learn about good news, they can refrain from selling. Second, they can possibly earn profits by trading information with others. Even if corporation insiders do not earn very large profits, valuable information may fall into the hands of others who do. Boesky supposedly made $50 million. However, it would be unwise to think of this as being typical. Most cases have involved relatively small amounts such as the $30,000 made by a printer named Chiarella whose case wound up in the Supreme Court. Boesky was a high-stakes operator who sometimes lost heavily. He lost $70 million when T. Boone Pickens withdrew his bid for Phillips Petroleum and $24 million when Gulf Oil withdrew a bid for Cities Service. He took high risks of being caught, and in the end he was caught. In fact, it really took a rather short time before his dealings were uncovered. Commissioner Cox of the SEC has reported that the SEC recovered $30 million of insider trading profits in 1986 from all its efforts.

To sum up: We do not know the profits of insider trading. The available evidence suggests that they are not excessive by comparison with other amounts of wealth we are used to hearing about.

WHY IS INSIDER TRADING A MATTER OF SUCH CONCERN TO THE SEC AND OTHERS?

SEC rhetoric suggests a high degree of concern about insider trading. The agency wants investors to have equal access to information. Congress, on the other hand, has never been very concerned about insider trading. Apart from the very mild provisions in the initial 1934 legislation, it paid very little additional attention to this area until quite recently. The whole matter was turned over to the SEC or was left in the hands of state enforcement agencies. The public has never been very concerned with insider trading. Most investors are troubled very little by the knowledge that there are people trading in the markets who may know more then they. I believe most investors accept the existence of inside information as a fact of life.

With this background of congressional and public apathy, we have an agency that has zealously sought to expand the definition of insider trading and has taken a number of cases to the Supreme Court, only to see them defeated because the laws passed by Congress and even the case law simply did not seem to support what the agency was trying to propose. So I believe that we have a real phenomenon to understand here, namely, the zeal of the SEC when it comes to promoting a concept of equal access to information for all investors.

The SEC regulates the securities industry. Hence, a logical hypothesis is that, as in other instances, the regulators are being captured by the industry or at least certain influential segments of the industry. However, identifying which segments are likely to benefit from control over insider trading is not easy, and economists have so far devoted little thought to it. The scenario that has seemed most logical to me is that if *corporation* insiders are forbidden from trading on inside information, then those next in line to learn about it, namely investment bankers and others similarly situated close to the firm, would stand to gain the most by obtaining the information. Marc Reinganum has suggested that perhaps specialists on the New York Stock Exchange stand to gain if they can reduce trades with parties who possess information that they do not. Notice that in its current deliberations to draft a bill defining inside information, Congress is reviewing a proposed draft put forward by the New York Stock Exchange.

Recently there seems to be a heightened level of concern about insider trading. I believe that some of this is the expression of moral outrage. For example, U.S. Attorney Anton Valukas has been quoted as saying that the rash of bank frauds and the insider trading scandals are both "sad symptoms of Boesky-era ethics." Valukas has said, "There is an attitude today of being far more concerned about getting rich than about the manner of getting rich. It's pervasive." He is quite correct that the ends of getting rich do not justify the bad means that he has observed people using. I do not know whether he is correct that the ethics of 1987 vary significantly from the ethics of 1887 or 1387 or 7.

Some of the concern about insider trading is also, I hypothesize, the expression of self-interest by those who would like to use this issue to promote other items on their agenda. There are clearly important established business and political interests that wish to slow down and, if possible, prevent the reorganization of corporate assets through takeovers. The resistance to takeover shows up in attempts to thwart the democratic exercise of voting rights by shareholders and even the right to buy or sell stock freely. It shows up in statutes that make it mandatory to disclose stock ownership positions, which seem to me to violate the most elementary right to privacy. It shows up in attempts to prevent people from buying shares in the open market or voting them. It shows up in court decisions that block tender offers and in injunctions that block people from acquiring common stock or in attempting to acquire control of companies without a court order. In short, certain vested interests are attacking shareholder rights vigorously, which is another way of saying that they are attacking your right and others' rights to do what you want with your money.

HOW IS INSIDER TRADING RELATED TO THE TAKEOVER OF A COMPANY?

I think that I am safe in saying that there is a strong tendency to condemn takeovers and smear these deals, to make them seem bad when they in fact may in many respects be very good. Michael C. Jensen and others have provided substantial evidence that the typical takeover creates wealth, at least for the acquired firm's stockholders. By contrast, the antitakeover forces are long on claims and rhetoric and short on evidence.

One of the real problems faced by the buyer is to accumulate shares without revealing the information about what he is willing to pay or what he thinks the assets might be worth if they were under the management of a new team of managers. By no stretch of the imagination can this kind of information be considered inside information in the classic sense since it comes from outside the company. It is better to view it as *confidential* information. Any bidder wants to keep bids secret until the appropriate time, but this is very difficult to do within our system because to cover various legal bases, others must be brought into the picture: lawyers, investment bankers, printers, proxy specialists. In fact, the investment bankers may be the entrepreneurs who see the possibility of creating value through rearranging corporate assets and placing them under new management. In such cases they should earn rewards for their efforts. Furthermore, because there are restrictions on buying stocks in the open market to achieve control, there are large incentives to achieve the goal of takeover through cooperation among a number of parties that are willing to risk money and hold blocks of stock separately and to aggregate them at the appropriate time. Hence, arbitrageurs who take the risks of outright ownership have become prominent.

The organization and control of information is clearly a very complex issue in this entire process. And it is evident that the business of takeover can become intertwined with the issue of insider trading when the real issue is confidential information. We observe institutions in place that are designed so that various agents maintain confidences. Lawyers have stringent ethics codes on maintaining confidentiality. Printers have codes worked out to maintain secrecy. Investment bankers and brokers have audit and compliance departments. All of these are evidence that individuals have learned how to control vital information.

The bottom line is twofold. The takeover business is likely to be smeared with the same brush as matters involving insider trading. Right now the SEC's investigation of insider trading is being used as a wedge to conduct a broad inquiry into corporate takeover practices.

WHAT ARE THE MAJOR ETHICAL ARGUMENTS AGAINST INSIDER TRADING?

Many people regard insider trading as unfair and harmful. I have extracted several ethical arguments from the literature that I will summarize and of which I will give some analysis. The crudest argument is that inequality is unfair. Insider trading involves the information advantage of one person over another. *Ergo*, insider trading is unfair. This belief amounts to a feeling that it is unfair for some people to have something (often of value) that others do not have. In other words, the underlying belief might simply be that equality of resources, wealth, information, or things of value is a desirable ethical ideal. Furthermore, the believers in this argument then propose that public action is necessary to remedy the inequality.

It seems to me that any philosopher worth his stone could easily dispose of these arguments on any number of grounds. Not being a philosopher, I will not attempt to do so vigorously. I will just point out a few things that seem obvious to me. First, not all inequality is unfair. Nor is inequality always bad. Inequality sometimes occurs spontaneously, sometimes as a matter of human choice. There are daredevils and milquetoasts. There are sometimes good reasons for inequalities. I elect to be uneducated and inferior to many people in my knowledge of rock music. I believe I am doing a good thing by creating this inequality because I spend my time on things I can do better. Before attempting to get rid of an inequality or considering it to be bad, we must consider the alternatives to it and the ramifications of attempting to remove the inequality. Life is not made up of a simple series of binary choices. Finally, in attempting to remove an inequality, any economist would advise us to consider the benefits, to consider the costs, and to consider the alternative ways to bring it about. These are very general statements that are meant to counter the general proposition that inequality is unfair, from which it follows that insider trading is unfair. We have to acknowledge that we often create inequality intentionally. We want rewards to some people to be greater than to others, so we want inequality. We want some people to have more power, status, and position and some to have less.

I conclude that insider trading is not necessarily bad just because it involves inequality. I am not arguing that it is necessarily good. But I do think that the burden of proof falls upon those who want equality of disclosure. I say this because they want to interfere in essentially voluntary contractual arrangements between entrepreneurs, managers, and stockholders that have evolved over long periods of time and that could have been arranged otherwise if they were unacceptable to those involved. I say this because disclosure may run contrary to principles of privacy.

But the inequality argument is only the crudest argument against insider trading. A second argument would run as follows. Unearned profits are unfair. Insider trading that occurs when someone knows something that others do not results in unearned profits. Hence, insider trading is unfair. This argument does not say that inequality is bad when it is earned, but it is bad when it is not earned. Those who use this argument to condemn all insider trading are of the belief that as a matter of *fact*, the information that insiders use is not theirs. This leads to a closely related third argument, namely, that insider trading is wrong because it involves theft or misappropriation of information that belongs to someone else. Chiarella was a printer who broke his employer's code and figured out which stocks were going to get tender offers. He then bought stock and benefited from this information. One Supreme Court justice observed that he was practically betting on a sure thing. This seemed neither fair nor honest, and most of us would consider it to be wrong. Similarly, one might argue that Dennis Levine stole information that belonged to those who had consulted the company that he worked for. Some people have argued that a manager's use of information is wrong because it belongs to the company or to the stockholders.

Information is clearly valuable. The central issue in these second and third arguments is not an ethical issue. It is the issue of property rights in the information, that is, who owns it and should benefit from it. Not being an expert in law and property, I can at best make a few general comments that seem to be appropriate. Consider the general principle that if you create something, you own it and can do what you want with it. If you paint a picture, write a book, invent a cereal, or design a curriculum, it is possible for you to establish property rights in these things. This approach is consistent with a free society and is also consistent with creating an environment in which there are strong incentives to create. Hence, allowing property rights in information would seem in many cases to be entirely appropriate. But this general approach does not do justice to the rich variety of possible specific instances that arise. If you are inside IBM and you learn that a big customer has just placed a big order, should you benefit from this information? This is not an easy question to answer. Different answers might be appropriate for different situations. Even this situation is not a simple one. There is intense competition to find out any information that is valuable. If a job holder were well situated to find out valuable information and benefit from it, applicants would compete for the job and in the process drive down the salary necessary to attract people into the job. In effect, the stockholders would allow the employee to use the information as a form of pay and pay them a lower wage. It is also conceivable that stockholders might elect to police information and have rules and procedures (codes of ethics) forbidding its use by employees. As a philosophical matter, we cannot solve what is essentially a question that individuals must solve through actual experience of the costs and benefits of alternative ways of establishing property rights in information. What people choose will depend on what sorts of information are really valuable, who has access to them, how much competition there is to learn of them, policing costs, and other considerations. Armchair theorizing simply cannot solve the question of how to establish property rights in information. The courts may have to establish law on a case-by-case basis as with the law of trade secrets.

Another version of argument used to support fairness, by which is meant equality of information, is the golden rule concept (see Levmore). "Whatever you wish that men would do to you, do so to them." Presumably if the insiders were outsiders, they too would want to receive the valuable information known to the insiders. Hence, some say the law should enforce the golden rule concept and make insiders do unto others as they would have others do unto them if they were in the inferior position. There are many ways to analyze this fairness argument, I am sure. Again, I must defer to the philosophers and ethicists who have probably thought about the golden rule for centuries. Let me say this. If I were an outsider, and in fact I have never been a corporate insider, should I wish the insiders to give me something that doesn't belong to me? In other words, can personal envy be a good basis for applying the golden rule? Unless shareholders as a group are wishing that the insiders would give to them something that may not be theirs, it seems that applying the golden rule to this question will be fruitless.

WHO IS HURT BY INSIDER TRADING?

If insider trading hurts certain people, it has not always been very clear just who they are. The term "insider trading" probably gets in our way of understanding what is really going on. What happens is that new and valuable information is sometimes created, and this happens in a variety of ways. How is it created? Who owns it? What measures do they take to retain rights to it? When is it stolen? How should rights to information be allocated? How should these rights be protected? How do those who either create or find information first elect to profit from it? How do they elect to control its disposition? A score of questions arises that we know little about. Hence it becomes very difficult to judge when someone is stealing or when someone is being hurt.

When someone executes a trade based on an informational advantage, are the traders on the other side of the trade harmed? Cases have sometimes awarded damages on this basis, but there is a strong argument that these traders have not been harmed. When they enter the market, they do so without coercion and with the knowledge that others may know more than they. Their actions are not caused by the other traders' actions, they are independently arrived at. Hence Dennis Karjala is of the opinion that it is wrong to award compensation to supposed victims on the other side of particular insider trades. He is of the opinion that if insider trading is wrong, it is wrong on grounds that require deterrence and punishment but not compensation to supposed victims.

The literature on how people behave in experimental markets that involve real dollar rewards promises to elucidate the real effects of insider information on markets and perhaps give a more firm basis upon which to understand the market's institutions. A 1982 paper by Charles Plott and Shyam Sunder is most interesting in this respect. A series of carefully controlled experiments were conducted in which some anonymous individuals had inside information and others did not. Prices in these experimental markets approached the correct prices known only to the experimenters. The uninformed investors quickly learned to base their transactions on prices themselves, prices that incorporated the insider information. This means that the investors who were uninformed were *not* fooled into selling because prices rose higher than they thought were warranted based on their personal information. Rather they learned that this meant the market had information they did not have. Even more interesting, the profits of the insiders were virtually indistinguishable from the profits of the noninsiders. This occurred because the market price was fully revealing all the information known to the insiders. *How* this was accomplished was not clear from this series of experiments, but they suggest that it is conveyed through critical bids and offers that occur. This in turn means that the insider has great difficulty not conveying his information through his own actions. Certainly, the market operated in a rational way and no problems were encountered because of the presence of private information. The same results were found subsequently by Robert Forsythe in a replication that involved computerized bidding only and not open outcry.

A plausible case can be made that insider trading by corporate insiders harms the stockholders of the company that the insiders work for. In legal terms, this argument sees the corporation official as a fiduciary who has a duty or responsibility to the shareholders. The fiduciary concept, however, begs important questions. If information is developed, does it belong to the shareholders or to its developers or both? Shareholders could easily forbid insider trading or develop mechanisms to handle insider information, but we observe little if any attempt to control insider trading voluntarily by stockholders and managers. From this Carlton and Fischel infer that there is no insider trading problem, and no harm being done to shareholders that is worth their effort to remedy.

A clear case for who may be harmed by insider trading is made by Frank Easterbrook. He uses the business property approach to information. If there is a rightful owner to information and if secrecy is needed to preserve the information's value, then another person may not lawfully exploit the information, as this amounts to theft. There are qualifications such as that the owner may allow others to profit from the information, or the owner may make errors in its control and be subject to the sanctions of the competitive market. It is reasonably clear how this approach works out in the case of a printer's helper who steals information about tender offers. The information belongs to those making the tender offer, and the printer's helper has no right to it. How this principle would be applied in other instances such as the Texas Gulf Sulphur case would be very interesting to see. On October 7, 1987 the U.S. Supreme Court heard the Winans case. Winans, who wrote a column for the *Wall Street Journal*, was charged with violating securities law. He collected information about companies (not inside information) and wrote columns. He tipped the contents of columns that he wrote to several others, who made profits from the tips, and then he shared a small fraction of the profits. It seems that an important issue of fact is who owned the information that Winans put into his columns. The prosecution argued that Winans breached a duty to his employer by divulging confidential information. Did Winans divulge confidential information? If he did, was it a crime? What kind of contract did Winans have with the *Wall Street Journal*? Did they not sanction him by firing him and publicizing what he did? A much clearer case of the theft idea is a suit by a bidding firm against its investment banker for not having kept bidding information confidential.

CONCLUSION

The subject of insider trading is filled with an unusual number of paradoxes. The Boesky case, the Levine case, the Winans case make us think that the practice is widespread and very profitable. And yet the available evidence for corporation officials suggests that it is neither. The SEC is known for its zeal in promoting a fair market, one in which investors have equal access to information, and yet their enforcement actions have historically been few in number. Parenthetically, the SEC certainly does not make disclosure documents easy to come by. Insider trading is thought to be an evil that causes harm, and yet ethics and the law have difficulty coming up with clear definitions of what the evil is or even what insider trading is. Many countries with thriving capital markets pay little or no attention to insider trading. Recent cases termed insider information cases frequently do not involve inside information, although valuable confidential information has been involved.

All of this suggests that we know far less about insider trading than we think we do. This is because we have not given enough thought to many central questions concerning the creation of valuable information and the mechanisms that individuals have created to protect the rights of those who create it.

BIBLIOGRAPHY

Anderson, Alison G. "Fraud, Fiduciaries, and Insider Trading." *Hofstra Law Review* 10 (1982): 341–77.

Boland, John C. *Wall Street Insiders*. New York: William Morrow and Company, Inc., 1985.

Brudney, Victor. "Insiders, Outsiders, and Informational Advantages under the Federal Securities Laws." *Harvard Law Review* 93 (1979): 322–76.

Carlton, Dennis W., and Daniel R. Fischel. "The Regulation of Insider Trading." *Stanford Law Review* 35 (1983): 857–95.

Cook, Bradford. "Chairman Cook on the Evolving Role of the Professional Analyst." *Financial Analysts Journal* (May/June 1973): 18–22, 76.

Demsetz, Harold. "Perfect Competition, Regulation, and the Stock Market." In *Economic Policy and the Regulation of Corporate Securities*, ed. H. Manne. (Washington, D.C.: American Enterprise Institute, 1969).

Dooley, Michael P. "Enforcement of Insider Trading Restrictions." *Virginia Law Review* 66 (1980): 1–83.

Easterbrook, Frank H. "Insider Trading, Secret Agents, Evidentiary Privileges, and the Production of Information." *The Supreme Court Review*, (1981): 309–65.

Finnerty, Joseph E. "Insiders and Market Efficiency." *Journal of Finance* 31, (1976): 1141–48.

Forsythe, Robert, and Russell Lundholm. "Asset Price Behaviour in Experimental Markets." Unpublished manuscript. University of Iowa, College of Business Administration, 1987.

Gillis, John G. "The Tippee in Transition." *Financial Analysts Journal* (January-February 1971): 6–14. (Also see the following issues of the *Financial Analysts Journal* for other articles by Mr. Gillis on insider trading: May 1972; November 1972; March 1973; July 1973; May 1974; March 1975; November 1976; March 1977; November 1977; May 1978; November 1978; March 1980; November 1980; May 1981; July 1981; November 1981; September 1983; January 1984; March 1985; and January 1986.)

Givoly, D., and D. Palmon. "Insider Trading and the Exploitation of Inside Information: Some Empirical Evidence." *Journal of Business* 58 (1985): 69–87.

Haft, Robert J. "The Effect of Insider Trading Rules on the Internal Efficiency of the Large Corporation." *Michigan Law Review* 80 (1982): 1051–71.

Hawkins, David F. *Corporate Financial Disclosure.* (New York: Garland Publishing, 1986).

Heller, Harry. "Chiarella, SEC Rule 14e–3 and Dirks: 'Fairness' versus Economic Theory." *The Business Lawyer* 37 (1982): 517–58.

Hetherington, J. A. C. "Insider Trading and the Logic of the Law." *Wisconsin Law Review* (1967): 720–37.

Inside Information Committee of the Financial Analysts Federation. "New Guidelines on Inside Information." *Financial Analysts Journal* (January/February 1974): 20–25.

Jaffe, J. F. "The Effect of Regulation Changes on Insider Trading." *Bell Journal of Economics and Management Science* 5 (1974): 93–121.

Jensen, Michael C., and Richard S. Ruback. "The Market for Corporate Control." *Journal of Financial Economics* 11 (1983): 5–50.

Karjala, Dennis S. "Statutory regulation of Insider Trading in Impersonal Markets." *Duke Law Journal* (September 1982): 627–49.

Kripke, Homer. "Inside Information, Market Information and Efficient Markets." *Financial Analysts Journal* (March/April 1980): 20–24.

———. "Manne's Insider Trading Thesis and Other Failures of Conservative Economics." *Cato Journal* 4 (Winter 1985): 945–57.

Levmore, Saul. "Securities and Secrets: Insider Trading and the Law of Contracts." *Virginia Law Review* 68 (1982): 117–60.

Loomis, Philip. "Loomis on Inside Information." *Financial Analysts Journal* (May/June 1972): 20–25, 82–88.

Lorie, J. H., and V. Niederhoffer. "Predictive and Statistical Properties of Insider Trading." *Journal of Law and Economics* 11 (1968): 35–53.

Manne, Henry. *Insider Trading and the Stock Market.* (New York: Free Press, 1966).

———. "In Defense of Insider Trading." *Harvard Business Review* 44 (November–December 1966): 113–22.

———. "Insider Trading and the Law Professors." *Vanderbilt Law Review* 23 (1970): 547–630.

———. "Economic Aspects of Required Disclosure under Federal Securities Laws." In *Wall Street in Transition.* (New York: New York University Press, 1974).

———. "Insider Trading and Property Rights in New Information." *Cato Journal* 4 (Winter 1985): 933–43.

Mendelson, Morris. "The Economics of Insider Trading Reconsidered." *University of Pennsylvania Law Review* 117 (1969): 470–92.

Plott, Charles R., and Shyam Sunder. "Efficiency of Experimental Security Markets with Insider Information: An Application of Rational-Expectations Models." *Journal of Political Economy* 90 (1982): 663–98.

Rider, Barry, and Leigh Ffrench. *The Regulation of Insider Trading.* (Dobbs Ferry, N.Y.: Oceana Publications, 1980).

Ross, Stephen A. "Disclosure Regulation in Financial Markets: Implications of Modern Finance Theory and Signaling Theory." In *Issues in Financial Regulation*, ed. Franklin R. Edwards (New York: McGraw-Hill, 1979).

Rozeff, Michael S., and Mir A. Zaman. "Market Efficiency and Insider Trading: New Evidence." *Journal of Business*, forthcoming, 1988.

Scott, Kenneth E. "Insider Trading: Rule 10b–5, Disclosure and Corporate Privacy." *Journal of Legal Studies* 9 (1980): 801–22.

Schotland, Roy A. "Unsafe at Any Price: A Reply to Manne." *Virginia Law Review* 53 (1967): 1425–78.

Seyhun, H. Nejat. "Insider's Profits, Costs of Trading, and Market Efficiency." *Journal of Financial Economics* 16 (1986): 189–212.

Stevens, Mark. *The Insiders* (New York: G. P. Putnam's Sons, 1987).

Wang, William K. S. "Trading on Material Nonpublic Information on Impersonal Stock Markets: Who is Harmed, and Who Can Sue Whom under SEC Rule 106-b?" *Southern California Law Review* 54, (1981): 1217–321.

Winans, R. Foster. *Trading Secrets*. (New York: St. Martin's Press, 1986).

IV

CORPORATE RESTRUCTURING: ALTERNATIVE APPROACHES AND VIEWPOINTS

21

The Ideology of Corporate Restructuring

WILLARD F. ENTEMAN

INTRODUCTION

The recent increases in mergers and acquisitions, spinoffs, buybacks, recapitalization, leveraged buyouts, greenmail, golden parachutes, poison pills, and divestitures are not merely acts of corporate restructuring. They are symptoms of a continuing ideological restructuring of our political, economic, and social world. This conference on business ethics, which has so appropriately taken the matter of corporate restructuring as its major theme, needs to consider not only specific applications of ethical principles to specific moral problems, but also the ideological framework within which ethical principles are developed and applied.

THE TWO ASPECTS OF BUSINESS ETHICS

Business ethics may be seen as having two different aspects. In the first, questions about the nature of the society within which businesses operate are raised and debated. This is the ideological aspect of business ethics. The other aspect of business ethics has to do with what we might refer to as applied ethics, and it deals with ethical questions as they arise within an ideological context. The ideological context articulates the fundamental values of the society. Within the context of those values, the applied ethics aspect of business confronts the difficult questions of how to apply the broadly stated values.

This chapter devotes its primary attention to the first aspect of business ethics, and it examines an ideological change that is taking place in our society. Toward the end of the chapter, it will be shown that as the ideological framework changes, justifiable conclusions about application of ethical principles must change also.

In 1969, Peter Drucker argued that our society was moving through a period of discontinuity in which the principles which had been appropriate for an earlier time were losing their relevance to the modern setting.[1] I do not accept all of Drucker's points about the nature of the change, but I do accept the view that we have been moving through a period of discontinuity and that the cultural coherence which once prevailed no longer has a hold on the general society. In 1975, George Lodge published a book with the intriguing title *The New American Ideology*.[2] While I do not agree with some of the dimensions of the new ideology that he outlines in his book, and I do not agree that it is a peculiarly American phenomenon, nevertheless, I think that Lodge is largely correct in arguing that a substantially new ideology has been emerging in the American culture, as well as in numerous other societies. We are moving beyond the breakdown of discontinuity, and a new ideology is emerging, even though an apologist has not yet come forward.

THE PREVAILING DICHOTOMY: CAPITALISM VERSUS MARXISM

The ideological aspect of business ethics is usually underemphasized except by capitalistic ideologues or by people who are primarily concerned with what they consider to be practical issues. Both groups accept the view that ideology boils down to a dichotomy between capitalism on the one hand and Marxism (or socialism or communism) on the other hand.[3]

The capitalistic ideologues have examined many of the changes in the business sector and have concluded that the American economy (and economies of other countries in the free world) has been drifting away from capitalism as each new development has come along: for example, labor unions, affirmative action, regulatory agencies, environmentalism, consumerism, deepening government involvement in the economy, and so on. They conclude that since these developments are neither contemplated by nor consistent with capitalism, the drift must be toward Marxism.

The practicalists have accepted the same dichotomy, but they come to a different conclusion. They have recognized that business continues in aggressive and healthy ways, that private property is still a major feature of American society, that there is a largely competitive enterprise market economy, and that free world economies *are* radically different from the economies of Russia, China, and the Warsaw Pact countries. They conclude that the American economy is not a Marxist economy, and that there is no practical reason to believe that it is. Given their assumptions with regard to the dichotomy, they conclude that since the American economy is not a Marxist one, it must continue to be a capitalistic one. Finally, they view the ideological debate as having no practical significance.

There is partial truth in the conclusions that each side has held. The capitalistic ideologues are correct that the American economy is moving away from being a capitalistic one. They are also correct in thinking that ideological issues are important. However, they are wrong in thinking that the American economy is drifting toward Marxism or socialism. The practicalists are correct in thinking that the American economy is not drifting in any significant way toward Marxism or socialism, but they are wrong in thinking that the economy is still informed by the values of capitalism and, in addition, they are wrong in thinking that ideology is unimportant.

Recognition of an emergent ideology allows us to understand that the drift has been away from capitalism and toward a new ideology. Our capacity to understand the new ideology enables us to analyze the ethics of corporate restructuring in new and more productive light. As I shall show later, the ethical understanding of corporate restructuring changes substantially as one explains it through the lens of capitalism rather than through the lens of the new ideology.

NEW IDEOLOGY: MANAGERIALISM

For the sake of brevity and with no claim to originality or pride of authorship, I refer to the new ideology as "managerialism." The name is suggested to me as a result of examining transitions in business history, especially as they have been analyzed by Professors Gras and Chandler. As is well known, Gras identifies numerous stages of capitalism such as Industrial Capitalism, Finance Capitalism, National Capitalism, and others.[4] Chandler adds another stage to that list and identifies it persuasively with the terminology of "Managerial Capitalism."[5] This terminology has also been adopted independently by economists such as Robbin Marris.[6] I do not dispute the identification of the stages as outlined. I believe, however, that the economy and the society at large have been transformed into a new ideological state which is best understood by abandoning the pretense that the new ideology is capitalistic. In the previous stages of capitalism as the historians and economists have understood them, capitalism was supposed to be the constant while it was modified by a series of adjectives used to help understand the stages. Speaking linguistically, we might say now that the adjective "managerialism" has become a noun and that at most "capitalism" has become an adjective.[7] We need to come to grips with the substantive change and understand the new ideology which has developed gradually, without a clear break from the past and without a spokesperson or apologist.[8] As we understand this new ideology, we shall be able to conduct a relevant ethical analysis of specific issues in the society such as many of those associated with corporate restructuring.

At this point, I shall present a brief description of managerialism. The dichotomy to which we referred earlier gives us a good starting point for that description. Characteristically, ideologies have been divided between two approaches. The first we might label atomistic, and the second organic. In the first approach, the supposition is that the society is nothing but the accumulation of its atomistic individualistic parts. In the atomistic view, social choice is supposed to be a deterministic result of individual choices. We can see numerous examples of this kind of thinking in our society, but perhaps the clearest is in our voting procedures. As individuals, we go to the polls and vote our individual preferences. There is a summing of those preferences, and a social choice is arrived at as the consequence of the summing. The presumption is that the society itself is nothing more than the summation of its individual parts.

In the organic approach, it is argued that individuals constitute a part of the society, but that with regard to the society, the whole is greater than the sum of its parts (to use Durkheim's famous, though elusory, expression). The distinction between the atomistic and the organic approach works reasonably well, which is probably why it is so widely held. Of course, it is also reflected in capitalism and socialism. The former is atomistic; the latter is organic.

I suggest that a third possibility has been emerging. Using the language of atomism and organism, I would describe that ideology as polyorganic. The term "polyorganic" is used to suggest that, for the purposes of arriving at social decisions, the society may be seen as composed of numerous organizational units which are themselves more or less organic. Corporations are, of course, examples of the organizational units, but they are by no means the only examples. The polyorganic approach recognizes the insight of the organic approach in that it recognizes that in regard to some of the units, the whole may be greater than the sum of its parts. However, the polyorganic approach argues that national social decisions are in fact nothing more than the mechanical consequence of the interactions of the units within the society. The polyorganic view is atomistic in the sense that it presumes that social decisions are made as a result of interactions among atomic units. At the same time, it does accept the insight associated with the organic view in that it recognizes that the units may be more or less organic.

The polyorganic perspective may be refined one step further, and if we understand that refinement, we can see why the word "managerialism" was selected. Actually, it is not really the interaction of the numerous more or less organic social units which leads to broad social decisions. It is, rather, the transactions among the managers of the social units which results in the broader social decisions. Thus, as the managers bargain and negotiate with each other, they set the social choices. Desires of individuals are not primarily effective except as they are expressed within an organizational context, and success is largely dependent upon the abilities of the managers of the social units.

It is popular in civics classes and on other occasions to tell people that if they do not like a law, a regulation, or a social direction, they should write to their congressional representative (or the president) and express their personal view. That suggestion conforms nicely with democratic and atomistic views of society. However, if one were to advise people on the best way to insure that their views are heard and given credence, one would tell them to find an organization which agrees with them (or, perhaps, start an organization of like-minded people) and use the organizational power gained by the management of the organization to achieve success in the negotiating process. Thus, the emphasis of this polyorganic perspective is on the managements of the various social units, and, consequently, I select the term "managerialism" to identify the ideology.

As we consider corporate decision making within the framework of managerialism, the approach which seems to make most sense is the stakeholder approach. In the stakeholder approach, it is recognized that many groups claim to have a stake in the corporation. The management of the corporation has to balance the competing interests of those who can create effective pressure in order to make good on their claim for a stake in the corporation. It is important to recognize that it is not an undifferentiated mass of people whose stake in the corporation is the source of analysis. It is the management of the unit representing those people which presses the corporate management into making concessions. Thus, what occurs is an interaction of the managements. Having a brief glimpse of the possibility of this new ideology, then, we can turn to an examination of how values have changed in accordance with the changed ideology.

CORPORATE RESTRUCTURING IN CAPITALISTIC IDEOLOGY

Under capitalism, the corporate restructuring involved in takeovers, leveraged buyouts, greenmail, and so forth, would not take place in large measure because it could not take place. Under capitalism, ownership and management are identified with each other de facto, if not de jure, and the separations would not occur which would make sense of the corporate restructuring activities. In addition, under capitalism, the owners and managers would be too busy meeting competition for their goods and services to be distracted by nonproductive activities such as manipulation of the company's stock. Consider, for example, the debt restructuring we have witnessed in the past few months in many corporations. In many cases, that restructuring has not been done in order to improve the company; it has been done in order to make the balance sheet unattractive so that the corporation would be less vulnerable to a potential hostile takeover. Under capitalism, the management that allowed itself to be distracted with such activities would soon find its company bankrupt because others would have taken advantage of the distraction. As in the wild, the animal that is distracted from its survival tasks will soon become extinct and, thus, will not be prepared to perpetuate progeny that is easily distracted. Thus, in capitalism, the corporate restructuring activity we have been witnessing would present prima facie evidence of a serious sickness in the economy.

In fact, in capitalism, economic restructuring takes place in the way everything else takes place: by the survival of the successful and the bankruptcy of the unsuccessful and unprofitable. The mechanism of survival and bankruptcy allows the public good to be served in a capitalistic economy. Anything that successfully interferes with that mechanism is considered to be a violation of the natural laws of economics. It frustrates the achievement of the public good and is, as a consequence, morally wrong. Thus, looking through the lens of capitalism, we would have to say that what has been happening in our economy recently is a sign of sickness in the economy and that it is wrong, because automatically it frustrates the achievement of the public good.

CORPORATE RESTRUCTURING IN MANAGERIALIST IDEOLOGY

If we look at the situation from a managerialist perspective, a quite different analysis may be provided. What has been happening does not represent a sickness in managerialism. It represents a further natural development of it. Under managerialism, the corporation is managed in the face of pressures from the representatives of the stakeholder units. Historically, stakeholder representatives such as unions had already made their presence felt. Increasingly, others have implicitly understood the nature of the ideological change, and they have joined together in groups to press their case. It is understandable that the stockholders would not recognize the implications of the new ideology. Under capitalism, they were the company. Under managerialism, they become one of the stakeholders. Until recently, they have been a disorganized group which is unable to press a united case. They have accepted what is known as the Wall Street Rule: if you don't like the way the company is run, sell your stock, but don't vote against the management of the company. Since other stakeholder groups were getting an increasing role in the life of the company, it should not be surprising that the stockholders would find a way in which they could have influence on the process. Thus, there has been a natural development by virtue of the coalescence and emergence of the power of the stockholders.

As capitalism has been breaking down, stockholders have become weaker and weaker entities in the corporate structure. Management of the company has taken advantage of the weakened position of the stockholders, and it has made concessions to other stakeholders (and to itself: the notion that people act out of self-interest has not been abandoned). In the meantime, the structural conditions of the stockholders has changed. The institutional investors have an even more distant and objective interest in the security than an individual investor might. In many instances, the institutional investors are prepared to abide by the Wall Street Rule. In other instances, they see an opportunity to pick up a few points with a forced restructuring of the company. In still others, the very size of their holdings may trap them in the investment, and they find the best solution is to support restructuring. For them, corporate raiders represent an opportunity either to sell out of a security entirely or to force the management to pay more attention to running the company efficiently and to forcing the demands of other stakeholders to be moderated.

In the context of transactional managerial behavior, if a set of interests is not expressed, it will not receive much attention in the transaction process. What we are witnessing, then, is the emergence of the stockholders as organized and effective stakeholders. Some stockholders believe that management has not been paying enough attention to their interests, and the stockholders are responding in ways which make them similar to the other stakeholders. Each selects the most efficient mode of influence it can, and each tries to force management to respond to its needs and desires.

Probably as a result of the mythology of capitalism, the stockholders were late in recognizing the disadvantages to which they were being put by the management of the companies in which they had invested their monies. The Carl Ichans and T. Boone Pickens are for stockholders what the early labor organizers were for labor. They simply represent the financial interests of the stockholders, and they pose a substantial threat to the management which has become smugly self-satisfied in a structure that Richard Damon has called a corpocracy. Those seeking to restructure the corporations are unelected representatives of the stockholders forcing management to pay more attention to making the decisions which will benefit the stockholders. Management had not been making those decisions because they were not under pressure to do so.

In what may be viewed as the final irony in the death of capitalism, even bankruptcy has lost its sting. Bankruptcy is no longer the death of the corporation or an index of the failure of management. Bankruptcy is being transformed into a strategic weapon. It may be used to frustrate prospective medical claims (Manville), to outmaneuver unions (Wilson Foods, Continental Airlines), to evade the consequencies of product injury (A. H. Robbins), or even to evade the impact of a court judgment (Texaco). Through it all, management continues with its position and its perquisites. Other stakeholders have been answered. As observers of these changes, we need only wait for the inevitable: filing by management for protection under Chapter 11 in order to ''protect'' the corporation from its stockholders.

Thus, whereas within a capitalistic ideology, the restructuring should be seen at best as an indication of a sickness, within a managerialist context, it is seen that restructuring is a reasonable outcome for people whose interests have been underrepresented and consequently given diminished attention previously. It can be safely said now that probably no chief executive officer of a major corporation is entirely complacent about his or her job or his or her place in the corporation. Very large and apparently successful corporations have been the subject of successful restructurings in response to threats from investors.

Having found justification for this kind of corporate restructuring, I do not conclude that every case of it is morally appropriate. That kind of analysis is left to an applied business ethics context and needs to be looked at in the light of the particulars which are represented. Just because a generalized activity is permissible, it does not follow that all instances of that activity are permissible.

NOTES

1. Peter Drucker, *The Age of Discontinuity: Guidelines to Our Changing Society* (New York: Harper & Row, 1969).

2. George C. Lodge, *The New American Ideology* (New York: Alfred A. Knopf, Inc., 1975).

3. While I recognize the very significant ideological differences among socialism, communism, and Marxism, for the purposes of this chapter, I shall treat the terms interchangeably.

4. N. S. B. Gras, *Business and Capitalism: An Introduction to Business History* (New York: F. S. Crofts and Co., 1939).

5. Alfred D. Chandler, Jr., *The Visible Hand: The Managerial Revolution in America* (Cambridge, Mass.: Belknap Press, 1977).

6. Robbin Marris, *The Economic Theory of "Managerial Capitalism"* (New York: The Free Press of Glencoe, 1964).

7. It is reasonable to think that we might make sense of expressions like "capitalistic managerialism" and "socialistic managerialism." What is common is the managerialism, and we can observe that in spite of the supposed gulf between capitalism and socialism, what some actual societies share in common is managerialism.

8. I do not pretend to be an apologist for managerialism. In many regards, I am uncomfortable with managerialism, for I find it to be a potentially dangerous ideology. My approach is clinical. Like the physician who discovers that the patient has a new condition, I believe the first step in treatment is to have an accurate diagnosis.

___ 22 ___

Let's Restructure Labour, Too

VINCENT DI NORCIA

> They want the cash, and run. . . . The luxury of a long-term outlook was no
> longer possible.
>
> Scott Buzby, President, Goodyear Canada

The takeover trend gives a primacy to investor interests in a fast return on their
buck over sound management and employee rights, as the Goodyear case suggests.[1] Finance-driven corporate restructuring reinforces investor primacy in the
firm. This disregards directly affected interests and property rights, especially
those of employees. In takeovers financiers, shareholders and a few top management usually win; employees lose.

Financial restructuring coupled with investor primacy, I will argue, perpetuates
the discredited adversarial model of labor/management relations which divides—
and weakens—the North American firm. Such "paper entrepreneurialism" is
not the best way to respond to the current economic challenge.[2] It merely moves
us back sixty years on the Wall Street rollercoaster. It returns us to socially
irresponsible profit-maximizing capitalism, for which ethics is a negative externality. Finally, it inhibits the potential of North American business to respond
to the current global economic challenge. It makes it almost impossible to develop
a community of interest among a business' stakeholders, in contrast to the
Europeans and Japanese.[3] Accordingly, we must reexamine our old assumptions,
not reinforce them; for instance, we need to recognize labour's property rights
in acquisitions. To show this I will summarise four cases, next examine the
property right that takeovers entail, and then suggest how firms might implement
that ethic.

DEFINING THE PROBLEM: FOUR CASES

The Goodyear Case[4]

In late 1986 and early 1987 Goodyear Tire had to close a number of plants and lay off 6,700 office and plant workers, one quarter of them (1,675) in its Canadian subsidiary. This was necessary in order to finance its $2.6 billion (U.S.) stock buyback defense against a hostile takeover attempt by the Anglo-French financier, Sir James Goldsmith. The parent firm in Akron, Ohio, sought supportive antitakeover legislation from the state legislature. Buzby was addressing an Ontario Legislature committee hearing on layoffs and closures. Bob Rae, the Ontario New Democratic party leader, denounced the takeover fight as "a sign of an economic system which has lost any sense of its moral priorities." This is part of the truth, but efficiency is at issue as well as equity. It is time that labor and management *each* addressed *both* concerns.[5] Accordingly, in each case I will note the impact of the takeover on (1) the bidder, (2) the target firm, (3) labor, (4) the domestic economy, and (5) the international context. The main issues are as follows:

1. The bidder, James Goldsmith of London, prospered. "It makes me sick," said David Birrell, the Canadian union local president, "that this guy is walking away with almost $100 million and leaving the company in disarray."
2. A firm in a hard-pressed industry had to spend $2.6 billion (U.S.) solely to resist a hostile acquisition bid. As a result plants were closed and product lines (e.g., radials) cut back. Strategic diversification into oil gas, aerospace, and wheels was aborted.
3. 6,700 Goodyear employees lost their jobs.
4. No net benefit for the Canadian or U.S. economies ensued in consequence; the contrary seems rather to be the case.
5. A Canadian subsidiary had to pay penalties for its American parent's battle. (Canadian layoffs appear to have been disproportionate to those in the United States.)

The Dominion Stores Case

Argus Corp., a major Canadian holding company headed by financier Conrad Black, bought this Ontario-based supermarket chain in 1979. Argus is noted for its financialist, investor perspective and paper entrepreneurialism. But Dominion lost money. So in 1984 Black restructured it as "Mr Grocer" franchises to avoid labour costs, and ultimately sold it. The main issues here are that:

1. Argus sold ninety-three stores to A&P for $134 million (Can.) and the rest to Loblaws, a competitor, for $40 million. Argus ultimately realized $342 million, helping Black to buy the London *Daily Telegraph*. His shareholders did well, getting a $7.50 per share dividend. Black and his brother, note, have the controlling interest in Argus.
2. Black had managed the stores poorly: "They neglected the customers," a major A&P shareholder observed.

3. For three years employees were kept uninformed of Black's plans! "They wouldn't tell us anything. Nobody knew their fate. It was a nightmarish time," said Bob Bell, a head grocery clerk, now with A&P. Around 2,000 employees lost their jobs; hundreds of others were rehired at lower wages. Black attempted to avoid paying severance benefits to employees, but the union successfully challenged his action and got $7 million back. Black also withdrew $62 million from the employees' pension fund, but the Ontario government forced him to return $30 million.
5. The market sector is less competitive.
6. A formerly healthy Canadian food chain is now in American hands.

The Olympia & York (O&Y)/Gulf Canada Case

A by-product of the 1984 Chevron-Gulf U.S. merger was the complex 1985 deal in which Olympia and York, a Canadian development firm, bought Gulf Canada. O&Y is owned by the Reichmann brothers, who are noted for their personal integrity and acumen as developers (they built New York's World Trade Center). Then O&Y restructured Gulf, selling its western downstream assets to state-owned Petro-Canada and the eastern to Ultramar of Britain. The main issues here are that:

1. O&Y prospered, retaining Gulf's lucrative upstream exploration assets. Through their complex restructuring moves Gulf was made to pay for its own takeover. O&Y also got a $600 million tax break (since terminated). But the Reichmanns erred in assuming that oil prices would soon rise.
2. Gulf's research arm was eliminated; its refinery and retail stations were sold off. Due to excess capacity a Montreal refinery was closed; but the capacity assessment depended on which market you were talking about: Quebec only or neighboring states.
3. O&Y laid off thirty-two Gulf R&D staff and 750 workers in the Beaufort Sea. PetroCanada laid off 2,000 office and blue-collar workers, for which it had already budgeted $30 million. It also closed many service stations. PetroCan employee severance benefits were much less generous than Gulf's. Ultramar closed Gulf's Montreal refinery and laid off 450 workers. PetroCan cleaned out former Gulf management; but, as Diane Francis queried, why should the acquirer of a successful firm "kick out the very people that made the company attractive enough" to buy?
4. The retail gas market in Ontario became much less competitive. In the United States the FTC ordered Chevron to sell several thousand service stations; for if four firms have 75 percent of a market (now the Ontario case), it tends to act. Unfortunately, Canadian antitrust law is weaker than American.
5. Canadianization of the energy sector, a generally agreed national policy, was strengthened, but $4 billion left Canada to pay for the deal. And Canada lost a good multinational corporate citizen, with a solid exploration and charitable donations record. Nonetheless, a formerly American firm with important upstream exploration and development capacity was patriated.

In sum, a mixed result. Should Canadianization of energy mean stripping a sound operation, enriching wealthy developers, decreasing competition in the downstream refinery and retail end, and bringing on huge job losses, including managers and researchers? One has one's doubts.

The O&Y/Hiram Walker Case

In order to finance the Gulf Canada acquisition, O&Y acquired Hiram Walker, a holding company including gas, oil, and distillery divisions, in early 1986. The Reichmanns miscalculated twice: (1) in ignoring the five-year decline in the hard liquor market, and (2) in arousing Walker board, management, and labour opposition. The issues here are that:

1. One bad deal had led to another. Walker people, having watched the O&Y dismemberment of Gulf, saw little hope of retaining their independence under the Reichmanns, who for the first time became unwanted suitors. Instead of helping to finance their Gulf acquisition they were faced with opposition, and ultimately a $9 billion suit, from Allied-Lyons PLC, a U.K. firm. The battle cost O&Y $35 million.
2. Allied-Lyons won and obtained the Walker distillery, partly because of union resistance to O&Y's takeover bid.
3. The alert Canadian Autoworkers local in Windsor (460 members) saw that the result of a likely O&Y/Seagram deal, on which O&Y had tabled a letter before the Ontario Securities Commission, would be the "rationalization" of duplicated plants and worker layoffs. The union worked with Walker management and board to prevent an O&Y takeover and supported the Allied-Lyons white knight, despite a personal no-layoff promise from Paul Reichmann.
4. O&Y is a conglomerate. An O&Y-Walker/Seagram merger would moreover have meant unacceptable concentration (40 percent of the U.S. hard liquor market). In contrast to O&Y, Allied-Lyons is in food and drink; but their offer would not entail decreased competition.
5. Although a foreign firm, Allied-Lyons promised to maintain Walker's employment levels, list Walker as a separate Canadian distilling company, sell shares in Canada, give local management autonomy, and keep the corporate head office in Canada.

In sum, despite a loss in domestic ownership, jobs have been saved, and competitiveness in the liquor market has not decreased. Furthermore Allied-Lyons' decentralized style gives Walker significant autonomy.

To summarize, first, the cases show that investor primacy reigns and that it occludes any recognition of employees' property rights in their job. The financialist perspective leads acquirers to neglect pension, health benefits, and severance costs.[6] Only top management parachute out in style. Merger anxiety and job loss hurt most management and line employees. Hence "labour" is meant broadly here. The real issue is the ethical and economic soundness of the deals, not the probity of the financiers (which the Wall Street insider scandals have raised).

Takeovers commonly have international ramifications. Many mergers fail because they are poorly managed. The difficulty of meshing different cultures is usually underestimated. Indeed O&Y's mistakes caused Diane Francis to ask, "Doesn't anybody know how to run a takeover?" A moot point.

Now to examine the central underlying issue: property.

THE MISSING ELEMENT: A PROPERTY ETHIC

Ownership transfers bring the ultimate property right into play. Transferring the ownership of a firm (TOF) in addition directly affects the interests of all internal stakeholders: investors, owners, management, and employees. A property ethic, C. B. Macpherson holds, begins with the principle that there is a basic human right of access to productive labour, through which persons appropriate property in things and/or an income as a means of living.[7] Since in our economy labour means employment in a firm, the firm is the major arena in which the property ethic is worked out.

As I see it the property ethic involves rights and utilities and is articulated in four elements: ownership, control, interests, and rights-holders:

O = The power to transfer to others the ownership of possessions, here the firm; TOFs directly exercise O.

C = The power to control continuously (or manage) the possession.

I = The interests to be maximized by O and C (any economic good, not just money).

H = The rights-holder structure. It defines those who hold O, C, enjoy I, and those who don't.

"I" represents the economic interests affected by the TOF, or "utility," "O" and "C" denote the rights and powers whose exercise allocates benefits/costs and limits utility maximization. For instance, the conventional focus on ownership, reinforced by investor primacy, implies that basic employee rights in TOFs are deemed secondary to investors'. Employees are almost chattels. At this point rights must constrain utilities. Here "H" takes the classic form of the *private* property right, which Macpherson describes as other-excluding (in contrast to the inclusive *common* property right). "Private" refers to *how* one defines who holds the property right: by excluding others (private) or including others (common). In all four cases, investors and owners alone exercise "O," the transfer power, and exclude management and employees. Investor primacy in TOFs then reflects the old private ownership right and the profit-maximizing interest structure of the firm. "H" usually means that shareholder rights are recognized in TOFs, but labor's property right in their job is not.

In the four cases moreover we encountered financiers, not ordinary shareholders. In each, corporate ownership is complex. Although one parent firm is state-owned, PetroCan, its rights-holder structure (H) is still private; for it, too, excludes employees. With Argus and Dominion we have divisions of a holding company; the others involve subsidiaries owned by parent firms, domestic and foreign. We must therefore address the subsidiary (or division)/parent relation. Ownership transfer (O) is an all-at-once affair, but control (C) denotes the ongoing matter of management. Both concern the firm as a whole; but their perspectives may clash, as in the Gulf and Dominion cases. This is especially true in hostile TOFs like the Walker case; or when the merger is poorly managed, as in all four cases. The Goodyear case is noteworthy in that opposition to Goldsmith unified labor and the firm; and both paid a price for their resistance.

In most acquisitions ownership (O) is sought by investors to maximize their gains (I) from the TOF. Obversely, management faces loss of control and income (C&I). Investor primacy means their (and top management's) financial interests (I) are maximized in a TOF and those of employees minimized, if not endangered. This reinforces the old outdated divisive, adversarial model of business. It is the underlying ethical issue in all the cases. In a TOF the claims of owners and investors are deemed less than those of labour respecting: their comparative financial stake, time invested, wealth, and mobility. The takeover wave, in sum, demonstrates the hypermobility of international capital in contrast to the relative rigidity of labour.[8]

Unions too have focussed collective bargaining on financial concerns (I). They commonly ignore "O" and "H" until a crisis occurs. They have addressed "C," or management rights, only in narrow areas like work conditions and safety. Like small investors, they focus on "I," the interest structure of the firm, but not on "C" and "O," its control and ownership structure. Consequently, both unions and management restrict worker property rights purely to "I." The time has come to correct that view.

The utilitarian interest structure of the property right suggests a common rationale for depriving people of their property rights, namely, efficiency. Most TOFs assume that if corporate efficiencies are sufficiently increased by a TOF, layoffs are legitimate, for the good of the firm as a whole overrides that of its parts. But closures and employee layoffs are often required purely to finance a TOF (e.g., Dominion, PetroCan). They benefit only the other rights-holders (e.g., investors and owners). As Diane Francis remarked, "One conglomerate's 'economies of scale' justification for mergers are another man's pink slip." The economic rationale for layoffs is circular. Ethically such TOFs are unjustified, and probably economically, too.

Of course some TOFs may be legitimate, for instance, where management or labor has little choice (Goodyear), or where management is incompetent and can *only* be changed by new ownership (e.g., Argus, U.S. Steel, Diamond Shamrock). Some TOFs might even help labour (Allied-Lyons). Layoffs here might be termed necessary evils; but even then harms should be minimized and rights respected. Many TOFs introduce international concerns like competitiveness as a rationale for layoffs, such as in the Goodyear, Chevron/Gulf, and Allied-Lyons cases. Also, home nation ownership, (e.g., of energy resources) is deemed preferable to foreign in Canada and most other nations. A national economic efficiency rationale not only legitimizes layoffs, but state intervention, regulation, and ownership, too (e.g., respectively, Canada's old National Energy Policy, Foreign Investment Review Agency, and PetroCanada). But such policy levers must be measured against other concerns, as we saw in the Gulf case.

Finally, one should not define economic benefits in narrow stock market terms. This evades a nest of hard economic questions about more productive uses of capital: enhancing productivity, marketing, modernization, and so on. The financial efficiency rationale, then, is increasingly under fire.[9] Equity, moreover, must be addressed, as well as efficiency. Utility maximizing must be limited by the property rights of all stakeholders—not just investors and top management, but employees, too. Such considerations imply a fundamental restructuring of the corporation's property right system.

MEETING THE CHALLENGE: REAL RESTRUCTURING

Takeovers and layoffs are commonly legitimized by the need to meet the new international economic challenge. Now, the old private property system of investor primacy, which TOFS reinforce, is an anachronism. Management primacy is not much better. Both are dodo birds: they only fly backwards. Nor would employee primacy help much. Real restructuring should move us beyond such narrow exclusivities. But current restructuring is a financial exercise, not unlike subdividing real estate. Financial restructuring merely reinforces the old clashes among labor, management, owners, and investors. It is the problem, not the solution. Indeed the current crisis renders many old assumptions inoperative, like the old private corporate ownership right.[10] Hence, this essay focuses on what North American business often neglects: the people or labour element in the equation, and how to restructure it. TOFs, moreover, entail a property ethic which requires that we recognize labour's rights (of both workers and management). The current economic challenge demands that we integrate all factors of production—people, capital, and technology—into a more equitable and efficient system. Real restructuring would balance employee, management, and shareholder rights and interests. This would help create a mutually supportive economic community committed to riding the wave of the economic future instead of becoming flotsam on the ebbtide of the past. Just as a more participatory control or management style is becoming accepted because it can mean better results, so, too, we need a much more inclusive ownership system.[11]

"In a period of intense technological change and restructuring," observes Ivor Richards, an advocate of the EEC's Vredeling Directive (requiring greater employee consultation), "you actually make it easier for the workforce to accept that change and restructuring if you tell them more rather than if you tell them less . . . , particularly if decisions are being taken that affect their very livelihood. (And especially) if what you want is . . . a workforce . . . prepared to cooperate more with management." The AFL-CIO has also called for a mechanism to protect the interests of workers and communities in mergers and takeovers.[12] Japanese and European experience here is instructive.

Employees must be informed, consulted, and even given a say in major corporate strategic decisions like TOFs, which directly affect their property right in their job. Indeed, the four elements of the property ethic suggest the dimensions of corporate restructuring.

Improving the Interest Structure (I)

Positively, by profit sharing, QWL (Quality of Working Life), and so forth; negatively, by making TOF- induced layoffs more costly. This can be done by high severance pay, job placement, and retraining requirements. Constraints should be imposed on hostile TOFs, like early announcement of bids, minimum stock-holding periods, delays, leverage limits, and tax disincentives.

Improving Controls: Information and Consultation (C)

Many firms are experimenting with increased, ongoing information disclosure by management to employee representatives about matters involving substantive impact on employee interests, such as prenotification of closures and layoffs. The property ethic demands such disclosure.[13] Management might also consult employees' views, not just inform them. Both can be achieved through joint labour/management committees, moving from subsidiaries into the parent firms, as Vredeling suggests. Some firms have already developed open information policies (e.g., a chemical, electronics, and supermarket chain). Openness is often traded for concessions in bargaining, and it is a common response to the competitive challenge (which, however, leads other firms to shy away from it). However, concerns about leakage and the old proprietary tradition inhibit openness, especially in acquisitions.

Moving Toward Co-Ownership (O and H)

We must also consider still more thorough corporate restructuring. Various means might be used, from employee stock ownership plans (ESOPs), to electing employee representatives to the board. But unions and management have each attacked "codetermination." To me that suggests it really challenges current assumptions. And employees in a subsidiary, as the cases show, have a claim on the parent firm for greater openness and representation, especially concerning TOFs.

Note that I am not calling for a blind imitation of Europe, which itself is varied. Rather, we have to adapt the traditions of Canadian and American labour and business, with their greater emphasis on collective bargaining, professional management, and shareholder rights in the United States of America, and on state action and social democracy in Canada. European and North American experience with participation and openness shows that it can reinforce a community of interest among owners, management, and employees, unlike investor primacy. It can help firms to resist high finance and takeover artists, as the cases show.

Finally, only when equity is integrated with efficiency will real restructuring result. Not before. And real restructuring can prepare North American business to respond to the global challenge facing us. To refuse it is to repeat the mistakes of the past, and hasten a tragic future.

NOTES

1. *Toronto Globe and Mail*, February 20, 1987. On investor primacy see J. C. Coffee, Jr., "Shareholders vs. Managers: The Strain in the Corporate Web," a paper from the November 1986 Conference on Takeovers at the Columbia University Center for Law and Economic Studies (for receipt of which I am indebted to Susan Rose-Ackerman).

2. See Diane Francis, *Controlling Interest: Who Owns Canada?* (Toronto: MacMillan, 1986), chap. 3; and R. Reich, *The Next American Frontier* (New York: New York Times Press, 1983).

3. See J. Crispo, *Industrial Democracy in Western Europe* (Toronto: McGraw-Hill-Reyerson, 1978); A. Athos, and R. Pascale, *The Art of Japanese Management* (New York: Avon, 1981); and W. Ouchi, *Theory Z* (New York: Avon, 1982).

4. Sources for the cases are reports in the *Toronto Star, Toronto Globe and Mail* and Francis' book and columns. I am indebted to her, Jim Waters (formerly Associate Dean of the York University Faculty of Management, now Dean, College of Management, Boston College), and the Canadian Broadcasting Corporation for help in developing this material.

5. See L. Thurow, *The Zero-Sum Society* (Harmondsworth, U.K.: Penguin, 1983), 181f; B. Harrison, "The International Movement for Prenotification of Plant Closures," *Industrial Relations* 23, no. 3 (Fall 1984): 404f. For this and many other references I am indebted to the University of Toronto's Centre for Industrial Relations.

6. See, for example, E. M. Kanter and T. K. Seggerman, "Managing Mergers," *Management Review* (October 1986): 16–17; D. Robino and K. DeMeuse, "Corporate Mergers and Acquisitions: Their Impact on HRM," *Personnel Administrator* 30, no. 11 (November 1985): 33–44; and D. W. Merrell, "Playing Hardball on a Mergers and Acquisitions Team," *Personnel* (October 1985): 22–27.

7. See C. B. Macpherson, ed., *Property* (Toronto: University of Toronto Press, 1978), especially the first and last essays; also G. C. Lodge, "The New Property," in *Ethical Issues in Business*, eds. T. Donaldson and P. Werhane (Englewood Cliffs, N.J.: Prentice-Hall, 1983).

8. See Harrison, "The International Movement," 404f; V. di Norcia, "Mergers, Takeovers and a Property Ethic," *Journal of Business Ethics* 7, nos. 1 and 2 (January-February, 1988): 109–16; also see J. D. Richman, "Merger Decision-Making: An Ethical Analysis and Recommendation," *California Management Review* 27, no. 1 (Fall 1984): 177–84.

9. See the forthcoming Columbia studies by D. J. Ravenscraft and F. M. Scherer, "Life after Takeover;" and E. S. Herman and L. Lowenstein, "The Efficiency Effects of Hostile Takeovers," *The Brookings Review* (Winter/Spring 1986). I have also consulted the *New York Times, Business Week*, and *Harvard Business Review* issues since 1985.

10. See D. Cohen and K. Shannon, *The Next Canadian Economy* (Toronto: Eden, 1985).

11. See D. V. Nightingale, *Workplace Democracy* (Toronto: University of Toronto Press, 1982); H. Mintzberg, "Who Should Control the Corporation?" *California Management Review* 27, no. 1 (Fall 1984): 90–115; J. O'Toole, *Vanguard Management* (New York, 1985); and S. Bowles, D. Gordon, and T. Weisskopf, *Beyond the Wasteland: A Democratic Alternative to Economic Decline* (New York: Doubleday, 1983).

12. "Special Report: Vredeling," *Personnel Administrator* 28, no. 9 (1983): 556–57. Also see R. Blanpain, F. Blanquet, F. Herman, and A. Mouty, *The Vredeling Proposal: Information and Consultation of Employees of Multinational Enterprises* (Deventer: Kluwer, 1983); Foreword AFL-CIO Statement to a Subcommittee of the U.S. House of Representatives Committee on Energy and Commerce made by Wayne E. Glenn, President, United Paperworkers Union.

13. See the 1984 Conference Board Study (#167) by D. Lewin, *Opening the Books: Corporate Information-Sharing with Employees*; Harrison, "The International Movement;" and Crispo, *Industrial Democracy*, chs. 7, 9–12.

23

On Regulating Corporate Takeovers: Small May Not Be Beautiful, But Bigger Is Not Necessarily Better

JOHN R. DANLEY

The issue is not simply whether to regulate corporate takeovers. After all, a regulatory framework is already in existence. The issue is whether that framework should be modified, and if so, how? In what follows I will defend the position that we should at the very least amend the regulatory process to prevent corporate combinations involving very large firms (i.e., more than $350 million in assets) unless two conditions are satisfied. First, the acquiring firm or merging firms must demonstrate that the proposed combination will yield significant efficiencies. Second, the relevant governmental agency or Congress must judge that those efficiencies are sufficiently compelling to warrant the risk which attends increasing economic size of large corporations.

This proposal was inspired by (critics would say that it has been misled by) recommendations formulated during the closing years of the Carter administration by the Justice Department and the Federal Trade Commission (FTC). At hearings in 1978 before the Senate Antitrust and Monopoly Subcommittee, representatives from the Justice Department and the FTC testified that the kinds of megamergers which had become increasingly common could not be prevented under current law.[1] This means that even under an administration intent on enforcing current regulations there would be little change in the trend. Indeed, since 1980, mergers and takeovers of colossal scale have continued unabated.

The proposals from Justice and FTC would likely have prevented a few of the largest takeovers. The Justice Department proposal would have reversed the burden of proof in antitrust cases and have required that the acquiring firm demonstrate that the new combination would enhance competition. The FTC proposal would have required divestiture of the acquiring firm equal in size to the target firm. These proposals were reflected in the bill introduced by Senators Howard Metzenbaum and Edward Kennedy, The Small and Independent Business Protection Act of 1979,[2] but the bill aroused the fierce resistance of the Business Roundtable,[3] which apparently orchestrated opposition by the Chamber of Commerce, the American Petroleum Institute, and the National Association of Manufacturers. Now, on the other side of the "Reagan Revolution," it is worth reconsidering this kind of regulation. The proposal here remains programmatic, but I am more interested in expressing the concerns that give rise to the proposal than confronting difficult problems of implementation.

Although building upon earlier proposals, this one differs in important respects. For instance, unlike the FTC cap and spin-off proposal—which would place a cap on bigness and force firms to spin off parts of the corporation equal in assets to the firm being acquired—this one does not prevent megamergers. Bigness is not per se illegitimate. The major defenders of corporate bigness have relied upon arguments for efficiencies of scale or, more vaguely, upon synergistic effects. This proposal would not block unreasonable combinations out of hand if they show prospect for efficiencies.

The proposal also differs in a couple of important respects from the Justice Department proposal. That proposal would have shifted the burden of proof in antitrust cases, requiring that the new acquiring firm demonstrate that the new combination would enhance competition. Shifting the burden of proof is a good idea, but our concern should not be focused narrowly upon competition. Competition is desirable on economic grounds because it is widely believed to foster efficiency. Competition is also valued for political reasons. Aside from Jeffersonian concerns for rather wide dispersal of economic power to insure political balance, there are more modest pluralist concerns that the balance of power between more limited numbers of groups not be disturbed. Thus, the proposal here focuses on both the economic and political concerns rather than merely upon competition. From this perspective, bigness is suspect. Gigantic combinations not only raise the possibility of economic abuse, but of political abuse. Hence, the proposal requires that a political judgment be made on behalf of the public interest that the consolidation be worth the risks. Perhaps something like a political impact statement should be considered by FTC, Justice, or Congress.

As a philosopher defending a policy recommendation, I am more than a little uncomfortable. There is an enormous corpus of law, economic theory, political theory, and a complicated history all bearing directly and immediately upon this issue. Philosophers tend to have a professional aversion to knowing too much about the world. Nonetheless, as philosopher and citizen I can listen to opposing arguments for and against policy recommendations and attempt to evaluate them, developing a reasoned position. In this connection, allow me to make an observation. Philosophers are trained to identify and evaluate those parts of policy arguments which appeal to values and principles. What is notable in the debate over the regulation of corporate takeovers is the extent to which opponents do not disagree over moral or political values or principles. As Lionel Trilling once quipped, it is not that liberalism is the dominant political tradition in America, it is the only tradition. Conservatives here are nineteenth-century liberals. Today's liberals have modified that classical liberal framework slightly. At root the most serious disagreement appears to revolve not around values and principles but economic disputes. Hence, in this chapter, the philosophical is largely absent. The defense of the proposal rests upon appeals to economic research and conclusions from that research. My position is that there is a substantial body of evidence to suggest that there is reasonable doubt that corporate takeovers involving very large firms offer economic efficiencies. Given the widely accepted value of efficiency, and the widely shared concern over concentrations of economic power yielding undue political influence, the proposed policy should be adopted.

Allow me one final preliminary remark before entering into a discussion for which philosophers are in one sense poorly prepared. To a layperson, or even a philosopher, simple questions about why we are involved in this new wave of corporate takeovers or what the economic impact on the economy will be, would seem to be rather straightforward. These, however, are the kinds of questions over which there are serious, profound, and perhaps fundamental disagreements. One is tempted to characterize these disputes as interminable. Disagreements over policy disputes which appear at first blush to rest on "factual" and descriptive disputes, are upon close inspection usually fueled by disagreements over methodologies, disagreements over concepts, disagreements over what counts as evidence, or disagreements over the relative importance of different pieces of evidence. In short, there is a sense in which these factual disputes rest upon meta-economic if not philosophical disputes. Ironically, then, these purely economic disputes often merge with philosophical ones. This is not the place to enter into that kind of discussion, but the relevant point is that policy disputes in this area, as in so many others, are not primarily the result of opponents appealing to different moral values or principles, not at all the result of appeals to fuzzy or vague moral concepts and ideas. If anything, opponents appeal to different economic theories and principles, employing economic concepts and ideas often no less fuzzy or value than those in ethical theory or moral discourse. With this face-saving gesture, let a philosopher sketch an argument in defense of curtailing large corporate takeovers.

Generally speaking, the arena for corporate takeovers is circumscribed by three different bodies of law. First, there is federal antitrust law. Second, there is the federal law regulating tender offers, setting time periods and disclosure requirements. Of most consequence here is the Williams Act of 1968 and the Hart-Scott-Rodino Antitrust Improvement Act of 1976. Third, there is that body of law from the state in which the target company is located.

The statutory foundation for antitrust in this nation, The Sherman Act,[4] the Clayton Act,[5] and the Federal Trade Commission Act,[6] were largely responses to the first of four merger waves.[7] Although legislators favoring those acts were explicitly concerned with abuses of political power which might flow from corporate bigness, the law did not reflect this, focusing primarily upon monopoly power, tendencies to reduce competition, unfair practices, and other behavior which were deemed undesirable in a competitive framework. The legislation also focused on one firm purchasing the stock of another firm, but did not forbid the alternative strategy of buying a firm by purchasing all the assets, a popular technique employed during the second merger wave of the 1920s. This so-called assets loophole was not closed until the Celler-Kefauver Act of 1950,[8] an act that also tightened antitrust policy in other ways. Paralleling the statutory changes, the Supreme Court began attempting to interpret cases consistent with legislative intent of the earlier acts—such as the fear of economic concentration yielding political problems—and reflected an academic and political consensus which evolved in the 1950s and 1960s. It became very difficult to avoid the restrictions against horizontal mergers, and vertical integration was prohibited if it might substantially lessen competition. Nearly all large mergers between competing firms or between large firms and suppliers or customers were eliminated.

Nonetheless, during the 1960s a third major merger wave gathered momentum. Antitrust policy had little effect on the acquisition of unrelated firms, and consequently, huge conglomerate mergers began to reshape the structure of the economy. In addition to the economic factors that precipitated this wave, American managers had begun to have confidence that a corporation involved in radically different industries could be managed. Numbers became important, not knowledge of production techniques or industrial specifics. Today, as the fourth wave crashes through the American economy, takeovers by firms in diverse industries are common. Corporate takeovers are no longer primarily the business of corporate mavericks, but have now become an orthodox strategy for growth.[9]

By the time the fourth merger wave gained momentum, however, the academic consensus on antitrust policy which had emerged in the 1950s and 1960s had dissolved.[10] Although economists who could be identified with the Chicago school, such as George Stigler, had earlier been strong supporters of antitrust, by 1974 a considerable number of economists began arguing that the free market itself could cure the competitive problems and that the regulatory procedures actually injured consumers. This academic schism reflected the growing political division over antitrust. Antitrust policy began to abandon the attention given to the kinds of political concerns that had originally motivated antitrust, and bureaucratic professionals began to employ refined statistical instruments focusing on product markets and tending to limit antitrust to the problem of explicit economic injury. During the Reagan years, the four largest pending antitrust suits were resolved. Reagan's then Attorney General William French Smith aptly sums up not only administration attitude but the status of antitrust policy when he quipped that "bigness does not necessarily mean badness." Current policy has little to say about conglomerate mergers and takeovers unless there is a problem relating to monopoly power in a specific product market.

If antitrust poses no obstacle to the current surge of takeovers, neither does that body of law that regulates tender offers. The most important components of this law are the Williams Act of 1968[11] and the Antitrust Improvement Act of 1976.[12] Each of these acts regulate only in the sense of setting minimal disclosure requirements and establishing time frames for offering periods. In fact, neither act was drafted with the intent of discouraging mergers. The Antitrust Improvement Act of 1976 complicates the situation. This requires notification of target and federal antitrust agencies of the pending acquisition or merger, and the filing of relevant antitrust information. Although the explicit legislative intent of the Antitrust Improvement Act was to clarify antitrust matters before a merger was consumated, and the explicit intent of the Williams Act was to protect the interests of the stockholders and the integrity of the securities markets, both provide better opportunities for managerial resistance than previously existed. Management of a target is now given valuable time to locate a white knight or to implement a resistance strategy to maintain independence. Although these acts provide management the opportunity for the resistance, they themselves pose no serious deterrent to takeovers.

State law has generally encouraged managerial resistance tactics by default. As states moved from tightly restrictive special incorporation charters to general incorporation charters in the nineteenth century, New York, New Jersey, and Delaware became involved in competition to offer the most flexible charters possible. These became rather standard. Such flexibility means flexibility for managers. The managerial revolution became legitimized in part through the charters, while stockholder control was continually eroded. State laws allow corporations the latitude within which they now routinely adopt antitakeover amendments that stagger elections of board members, for instance, offer golden parachutes to managers and, less frequently, tin parachutes to employees, buy up outstanding shares of stock, or offer special prices to stockholders. These tactics are all permissible under state law and under the "business necessity rule," which allows managers great discretionary authority in determining what is necessary. Quite recently states have taken an even more active role in preventing hostile takeovers of hometown favorites. In 1986 Indiana passed a law, similar to those in Ohio, Pennsylvania, and other states, which denies voting rights to those making tender offers or any investors who increase their holdings beyond a certain level.[13] The law allows only "disinterested" shares to be voted. Hence, bidders are not allowed to vote on corporate developments, which means it is difficult to gain control. In April of 1987 the Supreme Court ruled (6–3) that the law did not violate the Williams Act, nor was it a violation of the commerce clause of the constitution. If a number of states adopt this kind of law, hostile takeovers could be significantly deterred. Such laws dramatically alter the takeover battlefield by shifting the advantage to the defense and existing management of a target. The Justice Department and SEC argued against the constitutionality of the law. But as Justice Antonin Scalia puts it for the majority, the legal issue was whether the law was constitutional, not whether or not it was an economic folly. The court is not in the business of judging what is in the best interests of the people of Indiana. Whether such modifications of the regulatory framework are economic folly, however, is a critical issue. An answer to that question shapes our attitudes about how the framework should be altered.

The debate over altering the regulatory framework is national in scope. Obviously, those who feel that corporate takeovers are a good thing oppose tightening the framework in any of the three arenas. That the Supreme Court did not strike down state laws which provided greater advantage to the defense was viewed as a setback for the Reagan administration. A number of critics, including Commerce Secretary Malcolm Baldrige, Attorney General Edwin Meese, and (on the left) Lester Thurow, have proposed rolling back the existing antitrust framework, in the name of increasing efficiency and competition. Those who believe that corporate takeovers are bad support tightening the regulatory framework.

Recent attempts to defend corporate takeovers have done little more than embellish the position developed by Henry Manne in the early 1960s.[14] According to Manne, corporate takeovers play an important role in the market. A well-managed firm is assumed to be one with highly valued stocks. Corporate takeovers are the result of acquiring firms seeking bargains. That is, poorly managed firms have undervalued stocks that invite takeovers. After the takeover, poor management can be replaced with efficient managers, the stockholders will benefit because of the change in management, and the entire economy will be better off as the result of the increased efficiency. The threat of takeover also functions to deter other managers in the economy from deviating from the straight and narrow path of profit maximization. In a sense, this scenario is offered as a response to the problem posed by Adolf Augustus Berle and Gardiner Coit Means. If, in the modern corporation, management is entrenched and stockholders have lost the ability to directly discipline management, as they suggest, the market for corporate control may constitute an alternative market with incentives to ensure that managers act in the interest of the stockholders.

This model provides a simple means by which to legitimize corporate takeovers. Unfortunately, the elegant austerity of this picture is not only beguiling but misleading. Empirically there are serious problems that must be addressed. A number of these can be mentioned. For one thing, the model assumes that the market correctly values the stocks of a corporation. This is a highly controversial claim. Unless one means by value "market price," then one must specify value (such as "future flow of earnings," etc.) and demonstrate an empirical connection. The case is still out on this claim. Moreover, even if one grants this speculative claim, the model assumes that the only reasonable explanation of undervalued stocks is bad management. There are a host of other reasons. For one thing, there is an incentive for corporations not to return dividends as high as possible, since the tax rates on dividends are high. Corporations may reinvest earnings for stockholders, as it were, without returning the earnings to the stockholders, which would be taxed, rather than having stockholders reinvest again, losing a commission on the sale in the process. From the economic point of view, returning higher earnings to stockholders may also result in less investment, given that much of the returned earning might be consumed. This is not a defense of corporations keeping dividends low—it is merely an attempt to explain that the situation is much more complicated than the Manne model assumes. It is occasionally the case that stocks are undervalued because the market does not yet understand the opportunities of the new technology or new product being developed. Exciting entrepeneurial corporations then get bought up by stodgy large corporations who market the product and reap a large benefit. As some have put it in the high tech electronics field, "You know the pioneers; they're the ones with the arrows in their backs."

Further, proponents of takeovers point to studies which indicate that takeovers create new wealth.[15] But, these studies focus narrowly upon the market value of the stock of the acquiring firms and target firms from a period either shortly before the announced offer or from the date of the announcement to some later date near the time of the completed takeover. These studies indicate that stockholder wealth of target firms does increase in successful takeovers when management has resisted. What these studies also demonstrate is that the market value of the shares of the acquiring firms are relatively unchanged. This is a peculiar result which goes without comment by proponents of the "creates wealth" defense. If takeovers are motivated by principles of profit maximization and efficiency, then why is it that the acquiring firm's stocks do not reflect the increased efficiency which will result? Is this not evidence that takeover decisions are judged by stockholders of acquiring firms as irrelevant (if one wishes to assume that the market perfectly values shares)?

Or, again, the model assumes that acquiring firms can manage better. One of the problems with this assumption is that it ignores the obvious problems associated not only with bigness but with managing a firm in diverse industries. More than 40 percent of all the mergers of the 1960s and 1970s have ended in divorces.[16] That is not strong testimony to the viability of these mergers. The model ignores a fundamental notion of economics, the diminishing marginal returns of increased scale. At some point, which should be determined empirically rather than in an a priori fashion, bigger means worse. Why should we assume that megamergers are good or bad without attending to the evidence at hand? This is an important point to which I shall return.

Finally, the model assumes the takeover market is efficiently distributing resources. In 1986 $190 billion dollars were spent on mergers and acquisitions.[17] Much of that involves the megamergers. This is more than two times what was spent on research and development. Or, this is capital which could have been spent upon new plants and equipment. It would be easier to accept that these are efficient and desirable allocations except that tax laws distort investment decisions. As then Assistant Director of the FTC's Bureau of Competition, Albert Foer testified to the House Ways and Means Committee, summarizing the tentative conclusions of the staff investigation,

The structure of tax laws tends to encourage large diversified firms to acquire profitable (or potentially profitable) smaller, newer, single line firms, among others, by effectively subsidizing the acquisition.[18]

262   John R. Danley

Table 23.1
Percentage of Total Nonfinancial Assets Owned by the 400 Largest Nonfinancial Firms

Group	1958	1963	1967	1972	1975
Largest 50	24.4%	24.4%	24.5%	23.4%	23.3%
Largest 100	32.1	32.7	32.0	30.7	30.6
Largest 200	41.4	40.5	41.2	39.9	39.5
Largest 400	49.5	48.9	50.0	48.8	48.6

Source: Hearings before the Senate Judiciary Committee on S.600, 96th Congress, 1st sess., March/April 1979, Serial No. 96-26, Part I, statement of Alfred F. Dougherty, Jr., p. 146.

These considerations suggest that something more than a doctrinaire policy that treats takeovers as simply good or bad. Laws like those in Indiana suffer the flaw of protecting all firms in a blanket proscription, denying contenders voting rights in a struggle for control. Others, relying upon Manne-like models, assume that they are always good. What is needed is a nuanced proposal. That is what is being proposed here.

This proposal would allow increasing size if efficient. However, there is strong evidence, marshalled by the Federal Trade Commission in hearings before the Subcommittee on Antitrust, Monopoly and Business Rights in the spring of 1979, to suggest that large firms are among the more inefficient.[19] Consider, for example, Table 23.1.

Contrary to the popular perception, the economic concentration declined slightly from 1958 to 1975. This was in spite of the conglomerate merger wave of the 1960s and the beginning of the merger wave of the 1970s. At the same time, large firms continue to grow dramatically in size. Consider Table 23.2.

Moreover, there is evidence to suggest that in the aggregate the largest firms have grown at a much slower rate than smaller firms. Further, much of the growth in sales and assets of the largest firms is the result of corporate acquisition. To put it somewhat differently, the largest corporations have attempted to keep pace with the growth of smaller corporations by buying up other corporations. A 1969 study by the FTC determined that between 1960 and 1969 the relative concentration of the largest 200 nonfinancial firms would likely have *decreased* without growth through merger.[20] In the important manufacturing sector the story is more dramatic. From 1947 to 1968 the assets held by the top 200 largest

Table 23.2

Number of Industrial Firms with Assets of Over $1 Billion (constant 1977 dollars)

Year	$10 Billion	$5 Billion	$2 Billion	$1 Billion
1955	2	8	23	65
1965	5	16	46	101
1977	12	26	93	193

Source: Hearings before the Senate Judiciary Committee on S.600, statement of Alfred F. Dougherty, Jr., p. 148.

manufacturing corporations grew from 42.4 percent to 60.9 percent, or by 18.5 percent.[21] Acquisitions accounted for 15.6 percentage points. This trend seems to continue. Kenneth Davidson points out in his book on megamergers that, according to *Fortune*, in 1978 the sales and assets of its first set of 500 companies increased more quickly than those of its second 500 because of acquisition targets drawn from the top 500.[22] Between 1970 and 1977, firms in the top 500 acquired eighty-six firms from the Fortune 1000. That is, huge firms have recorded growth in sales and assets only by acquiring other huge firms. This suggests that if one is genuinely interested in economic growth, large firms should be deterred from buying up small firms.[23] Moreover, insofar as efficiency involves innovation, there is good reason to believe that innovation occurs in smaller firms, not large ones. Large firms may do a good job in developing new techniques to refine existing processes and procedures, but not in developing more innovative means.

CONCLUSION

The proposal is grounded in the traditional concern for economic efficiency coupled with the equally traditional concern to protect the political system from potential abuses which might arise from concentrations of economic power. A system of checks and balances within the institution of government itself does not provide adequate safeguards against tyranny. While the relative concentration of the largest firms may not be increasing, the larger firms are increasing in size, usually by acquisition. Bigness is not necessarily bad, yet it is not necessarily good either. Combinations should be allowed only if they promise significant efficiencies. But, on this proposal, efficiency is not sufficient. A political judgment must be made that the increased efficiencies are worth the increased risks attendant with the increasing concentration of wealth and economic power.

NOTES

1. See U.S. Congress, Senate, *Hearings before the Senate Judiciary Committee*, 95th Congress, 2nd session, July 27, 1978.

2. U.S. Congress, Senate, *Hearings before the Senate Judiciary Committee on S.600*, 96th Congress, 1st Session, March/April 1979, Serial No. 96-26, Part I, "Mergers and Economic Concentration."

3. See the testimony by the attorney for the Business Roundtable, Ira Millerstein, in *Hearings on S.600*. See also Millerstein and Salem M. Katsh, *The Limits of Corporate Power* (New York: Macmillan, 1981), where an argument is developed that the limits of corporate power are considerable.

4. On mergers, merger policy, and on associated organizational changes see Samuel Richardson Reid, *Mergers, Managers and the Economy* (New York: McGraw-Hill, 1968); *Business Concentration and Price Policy* (Princeton, N.J.: Princeton University Press, 1955), especially Jesse W. Markham, "Survey of the Evidence and Findings on Mergers"; Peter Steiner, *Mergers: Motives, Effect, Policies* (Ann Arbor: University of Michigan Press, 1975); Alfred Chandler, "The Coming of Oligopoly and its Meaning for Antitrust," in *National Competition Policy: Historian's Perspectives on Antitrust and Government Business Relationships in U.S.* (Washington, D.C.: FTC Publications, August, 1981).

5. 15 U.S.C.§ 1 et seq. (1890).

6. 15 U.S.C.§ 12 et seq. (1914).

7. 15 U.S.C.§ 42 et seq. (1914).

8. 84 Stat. 1,125 (1950).

9. One of the most helpful books on the general topic of takeovers is *Mega-Mergers: Corporate America Billion Dollar Takeovers* (Cambridge, Mass.: Ballinger Publishing Co., 1985), by Kenneth Davidson. Chapter 8 contains an excellent discussion of strategic investment theories which lead credibility to the necessity for corporate acquisitions.

10. See Davidson, *Mega-Mergers*, chapter 5, for a description and some details of the consensus.

11. 15 U.S.C. §§78m Stat. 454 (1968).

12. 90 Stat. 1383 (1976).

13. "High Court Backs State on Curbing Corporate Takeovers," *New York Times*, April 27, 1987, p. 1.

14. Robin Marris, *The Economic Theory of "Managerial" Capitalism* (Cambridge, Mass.: The Free Press of Glencoe, 1964).

15. The most rigorous example can be found in Michael C. Jensen and Richard S. Ruback, "The Market For Corporate Control," *Journal of Financial Economics* 11 (1983): 5–50. This entire volume is devoted to empirical studies on issues relevant to corporate takeovers.

16. From "Giantism Doesn't Equal Competitiveness," *New York Times*, April 27, 1987, op-ed.

17. Ibid.

18. Subcommittee on Select Revenue Measures, Ways and Means Committee, U.S. House of Representatives, *Hearings on H.R. 6295*, June 4, 1982, statement of Albert Foer. Quoted from Davidson, *Mega-Mergers*, 297. Davidson's section on "The Perpetual Merger Machine: A Tax Digression" is a good introduction. The tax code has significantly modified some points.

19. Most of this material comes from the statement of Alfred F. Dougherty, Jr., Director of the Bureau of Competition, FTC, before the Senate Committee on the Judiciary, March 8, 1979, *Hearings on S.600.*

20. Ibid., 152.

21. Ibid., 151, quoting from the FTC Economic Report on Conglomerate Mergers (1969), 189–93.

22. Davidson, *Mega-Mergers*, 286; *Fortune*, June 19, 1978, p. 171.

23. Morton Kamien and Nancy Schwartz, "Market Structure and Innovation: A Survey," *Journal of Economic Literature* 13 (1975): 1.

24

If Colleges and Universities Could Be Restructured

LARUE TONE HOSMER

The most surprising aspect of the debate over corporate restructuring, from the viewpoint of an ethicist, is that it occurs as a debate, not as a condemnation. What do we find so distasteful about the restructuring process? Is it the greenmail payments? The golden parachutes? The excessive legal and advisory fees? Is it the insider trading and other unimaginative forms of cheating that the participants seem so surprised to find associated with the exchange of huge sums of money? Is it the white knight and "in play" terms that the participants use to indicate that this is an amazing game, with high stakes but genteel rules, in which no one is going to be hurt very badly? For me, it is the buying and selling of organizations, which seems to come perilously close to the buying and selling of another commodity that was outlawed following 1863.

Business organizations can be viewed as collections of assets, or groups of people, just as management can be viewed as the optimization of economic variables, or the direction of human beings. It seems obvious that those who believe in the legitimacy of forced takeovers and delayered staffs have adopted the former view. We hear from them about "enhancing stockholder value," "improving corporate efficiency," "purging inept management," "using neglected assets," and "pruning unproductive divisions." All the positive verbs apply to money; all the negative ones to people. My concern is that I—and I assume most members of the acquired organizations—don't want to be delayered, purged, or pruned.

How do we convince these people that there are issues that go beyond the improvement of quarterly earnings? How do we convince them that there are stakeholders as well as stockholders to be considered in any decision about the future of an organization, and that the stakeholders include employees at all levels, suppliers, distributors, customers, and members of the general public?

In short, how do we convince them that managerial ethics is a legitimate field of study, as worthy as marketing or finance or production to be included in the business curriculum and to be considered in a business decision? It is not going to be easy. There is an overwhelming belief in the efficiency and the legitimacy of the corporate takeover as a means of economic and even social change among both practitioners and academics. The overwhelming or dominating nature of this belief is indicated by the following quotation by Ralph Saul, former Chairman of CIGNA Corporation:

It is hard to imagine the power—or the tyranny—of the argument that takeover activity enhances shareholder wealth and the returns on corporate assets. Few question it. Its proponents attribute attempts to limit or restrict takeover activity to managements that want to protect their jobs or to members of the business establishment who want to preserve the status quo.[1]

The power of the argument, and the self-confidence of the arguers, comes from two related beliefs that are often advanced in favor of corporate acquisitions, leveraged buyouts and hostile takeovers. These beliefs are illustrated below.

The belief that the restructuring is beneficial

Lackluster operations and questionable strategies by the senior management lead, it is alleged, to chronic undervaluation of the stock of a firm in an efficient factor market. Undervaluation provides an opportunity for "entrepreneurs"—they never seem to call themselves "raiders," but instead use a term with more positive value connotations—to purchase control, replace management, and improve performance. The improved performance, it is felt though seldom explicitly stated, spreads the benefits of greater employment, higher wages, decreased imports, and so forth, throughout society. This belief in the beneficial nature of the changes can be illustrated with a temperate and thoughtful quotation from Professor Michael Jensen:

the common transactions that have characterized this market for corporate control—leveraged buyouts, mergers and acquisitions, restructuring transactions and hostile takeovers—have been motivated, not exclusively but to a large extent, by a necessity to bring about the exit of resources from industries that can no longer effectively make use of their capital.

I don't have much doubt that the benefits from these activities are vastly in excess of the costs that are being imposed.[2]

The belief that the restructuring is legal

Stockholders, it is alleged, own the company and consequently can do with it as they wish in order to obtain a higher return on their investment. Let me

support this view with two quotations from T. Boone Pickens, Jr., one of which
is not quite so temperate nor thoughtful:

Why should shareholders' interests take precedence over relationships with employees,
customers, and other corporate constituencies? Because shareholders own the company.
In any public corporation they bear the ultimate financial risk for management's
actions.[3] . . .
   The shareholders own the company. If you operate under a free market, the shareholders
decide. That's all there is to it.[4]

   How do we convince these people that there is another view? We could mention
the layoffs and firings and early retirements to Jensen, but I somehow have the
feeling that his response would be a mention of the labor markets for both
executives and workers and the probability of prompt reemployment at rates that
would match the supply to the demand. We could mention the transfer of the
"ultimate financial risk" from the shareholders to the employees of most acquired
firms to Pickens, but I somehow have the feeling that he would not be receptive.
Let me quote one more brief comment from Pickens to show that reasoned
discussion may not work:

In reality, the short-term theory (i.e., the theory that short-term increases in earnings per
share are not the same thing as long-term improvements in corporate worth) is pure
hokum. Any observer who believes in even a modicum of market efficiency should be
able to see through the smoke.[5]

   I believe that we have to adopt other arguments, beyond the typical teleological
and deontological theories of the ethicist, to convey to the proponents of corporate
restructuring a recognition of the potential harms to individuals, organizations,
and our society. I have two suggestions here, one that is unfortunately very
impractical—though enjoyable to contemplate—and one that is unfortunately
inevitable.
   First, let us look at the impractical but pleasant means of conveying the
concepts of ethical benefits and duties to management scholars who advocate
corporate restructuring. Admittedly this method will not work with T. Boone
Pickens, but perhaps nothing that is merely logical will be effective in that
quarter. I was at lunch with a colleague one day, and the conversation turned
to the operational restructuring of General Motors. At the time, that huge company had not been the victim of a takeover attempt, but its profits had declined
markedly and complaints had been heard from the financial community. The
chairman responded with an unusual letter addressed to the stockholders, promising a reduction of the work force and a redeployment of the assets. Eleven car
assembly and component manufacturing plants were to be sold. Some 25,000
mid-level managers were to be laid off in 1987, and 15,000 more in 1988. Even
the corporate staff was to be affected, though only for an apparently token
decrease of $200 million in an anticipated total savings of $10.0 billion annually.

The closing sentence made a cheerful reference to an immediate increase in benefits for all of the stockholders: "these cost savings are designed to enhance stockholder value and promote achievement of an after-tax return on stockholder equity of at least 15% by 1990."[6]

Nowhere in the letter was there any indication that the futures of the 40,000 mid-level managers or the uncounted but numerous hourly employees at the eleven closed plants had been considered in the decision. The colleague, whose field is economic finance, said that a work force reduction of that size was indeed "unfortunate," but that both wages and salaries in the automotive industry had been high for years, that the recipients must have known that the premium represented an adjustment for risk, and that the risk had now been realized. I was struck, as so many before me have been struck, by the ease with which tenured faculty members discuss the unemployment of others.

I did not respond at that time—most of us never do—but later I thought that the same argument could easily be applied to business school faculty. Certainly our salaries tend to be higher than those of faculty in the arts and the humanities, and our opportunities for consulting are considerably greater. Given an efficient market that reflects all current information about a given situation—and I see no reason to assume that the market for business school faculty is no more nor less efficient that the market for automobile industry managers—there obviously is a recognition that we bear some form of increased risk. What could be the source of that risk? Perhaps it is a future restructuring of our colleges and universities, and the sale to the public of equity in our schools of business administration.

The public ownership of schools of business administration may be an idea whose time has come. It may not be as farfetched a proposal as it might at first glance appear. Schools of business tend to be separated both geographically and academically at most universities. They generally are on the edge of the campus— the "other side of the river" in the most famous instance—so that ownership of the land and buildings could be transferred with few complications. They usually are not interdependent with the other disciplines—despite the obvious interrelationships—so that the intellectual ties could be broken with equal ease. And many of our colleges and universities need more money. What could be more natural—given the current trends which some in this room may decry but which seem to win the approval of so many others—than to raise the needed funds by selling these underused assets?

There is no question but that these assets are underused. The return on capital at our nation's business schools is not computed as part of our national income statistics, but it doubtless has not kept pace with the increase in student demand. Any casual observer can see that economies of scale have not been realized, and that advances in technology have not been used. It is immediately apparent that staffs have expanded, that new levels of management have crept in, and that administrators have focused on long-range planning—how many times have you heard the goal of being "in the top ten" or even "top twenty-five" expressed by a dean?— rather than short-term returns.

Business school profits brought down to the bottom line, the return on capital, which apparently is such a critical measure of performance, could easily be increased with some slight investment in automation (i.e., computer-assisted instruction), some slight easing of restrictive work practices (i.e., heavier teaching loads) and some slight emphasis upon current rather than future output (i.e., students rather than research). Our colleges and universities would be transferring scarce resources to higher-valued uses, benefiting themselves and benefiting society. Who could possibly object?

A public sale of the equity in our nation's business schools might prima facie seem unfair to the faculty who doubtless felt that they were joining a private, religious, or state institution at the time that they accepted their appointments. Yet, the situation is not dissimilar to the process of "taking a firm private," by which senior executives and investment bankers combine to change a public corporation to a private partnership, without regard to the employees, and I have been assured by the numerous persons whose opinions I respect that there is nothing either illegal or immoral about that. Instead, they say, it is easier for a small group of investors to take the necessary though unpopular actions that will increase the return on capital and the value of the firm, and that is all that I am proposing here. Academic administrators have been unable or unwilling to take those actions—perhaps due to some misplaced collegial association with the faculty—and consequently it is essential to change the administration. Public ownership will accomplish that goal.

Public ownership of business schools, and the concomitant need to increase profits and advance shareholder value, will also open up all sorts of interesting alternatives for strategic planners who wish to intensify the return on capital through various synergistic combinations. Mergers, acquisitions, and forced takeovers suddenly become possible in this important sector of our economy. Let us consider some of the possibilities.

The Harvard Business School would be a prime candidate for takeover. One might think that the well-known Eastern business school would be approached first by a corporate-level consulting firm such as Bain, McKinsey, or Boston Consulting Group, that wished to integrate backward into the supply of MBAs. Another possibility for acquisition would be a four-year college such as Amherst, Williams, or Wellesley, that wanted to integrate forward, and get closer to the market. I would think, however, that those consulting firms and undergraduate colleges would be outbid by a new entrant: a second-level school—I will give no illustrative examples here—that wanted a greater endowment. Companies in the petroleum industry were told numerous times that searching for new oil reserves was a waste of resources, when existing reserves could be acquired more cheaply in the financial markets. Once again, we can turn to Jensen for support:

[There were] well-known accusations that Wall Street wasn't efficient because you could buy oil on Wall Street for three to four dollars a barrel when it was costing seventeen dollars a barrel to get it out of the ground. The truth was exactly the opposite. Those financial markets were providing some very important signals—and not only signals but incentives—for the players to respond in the right way. Wall Street was valuing those reserves correctly.[7]

It is exactly the same situation in business education as in petroleum exploration. Why search for endowment among alumni when you can buy it more easily on Wall Street? Granted that the country may run out of business school endowments, if no one is out looking for new sources, but I accept the fact that the market is efficient and correctly values the proper cost of locating those sources.

The business schools at Chicago, Wharton, Rochester, and Carnegie-Mellon might be acquired by large investment banking firms that wanted their break-up value more than their financial expertise. The marketing management and organizational behavior areas at those schools doubtless have been undervalued for years, due to the errors made by the senior administrators in focusing on much too narrow a portion of their full product line. It would be possible to sell off the accounting and finance departments as being redundant, and keep the undervalued assets for appreciation. Sir James Goldsmith has done exactly this in his series of raids upon paper companies, keeping the timberland while disposing of the manufacturing facilities, and his action has been applauded as efficient, constructive, and essential to the restoration of our national competitiveness.

It is interesting to speculate on the possible attractions of the other major business schools. UCLA and Berkeley might be acquired by real estate firms willing to speculate on their land values. Notre Dame and USC would have an obvious attraction to the New York Giants, who would want to establish a "presence" on campus. Michigan, Northwestern, Purdue, and Illinois might be purchased by New York University in a concerted effort to improve their already impressive economies of scale. The business schools at New Mexico, Colorado, and Utah have an obvious opportunity to diversify, and combine winter sports activities with discounted cash flows. Who would purchase Stanford? My apologies to anyone from Palo Alto, but Club Med comes to mind. Who would acquire Bentley? Let us assume that they have the intelligence to remain above this financial wrangling, and never issue stock, for otherwise I am afraid that these National Conferences on Business Ethics would fall victim to the first corporate cost-cutter that appeared. I value these conferences, but doubtless their return on capital is abysmally low.

Early investors in business schools will do very well. After all, this has been a growth industry since 1980, not unlike luxury automobiles and quality ice creams, and think how an investment in BMW and Haagen Das would have fared over the years. Mutual funds will accumulate stocks of business schools, buying and selling on rumors of increasing or decreasing enrollments. Market letters will develop, listing student backgrounds, research projects, and some index of article acceptances by the major journals. Pension funds, estate trusts, and insurance companies will join in this "institutionalization" of the market, and between 60 to 70 percent of the total of business school shares will be managed by the professionals who are evaluated by a quarterly increase in value. Do not be alarmed by this short-term orientation, however; exactly the same phenomenon has occurred in the manufacturing sector of our economy, and we have been assured by Jensen and Pickens that there have been no harmful effects.

What will happen to the faculty? I am surprised that you would ask, though ethicists do have an unfortunate interest in the duties and benefits owed to others. The change in orientation from research toward teaching, the trend in requirements for greater class sizes and heavier teaching loads, and the demands from the financial community for improved performance ratios, will bring a dramatic decrease in faculty numbers, perhaps in the order of 50 to 70 percent. Cover articles will appear in *Business Week* lauding the new "lean and mean" approach to business education; raiders will be quoted in the *Wall Street Journal* explaining that they have "downsized the faculty," "pruned the professors," and "purged the Ph.D.'s."

Tenure contracts, of course, will be negated by the change in ownership of the schools. Doubtless some disgruntled faculty will sue, as have some disgruntled managers who mistakenly believed that there was an implicit duty owed by the stockholders to long-service employees just as there was an explicit duty owed by the employees to the stockholders. Large law firms, however, will quickly develop expertise in tenure abrogation, and individual faculty members will discover how difficult it is to defend an employment contract against an entrenched institution. Some of the more generous institutions now owning the nation's business schools will provide personal counseling, outplacement services, and severance pay based upon length of service; others will continue medical insurance and staff benefits for sixty days. The benefits of early retirement will be widely mentioned; the costs will be nowhere discussed. With any luck, however, none of these business school raiders or their supporting MBA analysts will discover that TIAA/CREF has become "overfunded" due to the early retirements—before the benefits come due—and therefore no one will attempt a "reversion" of our academic pension funds.

Why am I so happy, faced with this forecast? I am not vindictive, and am shocked that you would even consider that as a possibility. Business ethicists, however, are human, and so some of us may take some slight degree of pleasure in the turnabout nature of this situation, but that will not be excessive. We will not chortle in the presence of our colleagues. If for no other reason, I have no doubt that we who teach business ethics will be the first to be "delayered," far ahead of those colleagues. We are considered to be an unwarranted intrusion now; we will be thought to be an unnecessary expense under the new regime.

Yet, I forecast that all of the business ethicists who are "outplaced" will find immediate employment, at much higher rates of pay. We will become expert witnesses, engaged by our prior colleagues from finance, accounting, operations research, business economics, and the other disciplines that have stressed the optimization of short-term profits. They will say to us, "Yes, I recognize that this restructuring—this process of buying and selling and changing an organization to which I was devoting my life—is beneficial in the sense of an immediate increase in quarterly earnings and shareholder value, and I admit that it is legal in the sense that I cannot defend an implied employment contract, but I need you as a witness in court to say that it is not right."

It is not right! This is the essential quality of so many of the mergers and acquisitions and takeovers, of the greenmail and golden parachutes and "putting companies in plan." Whether one approaches the human costs of restructuring from the basic principles of utilitarianism or universalism, or from the primary values of distributive justice or personal liberty, it is impossible to defend the massive benefits to one small group and the substantial harms to all others.

It is necessary to recognize, however, that the distribution of benefits and harms is outside the paradigm of economic thought. Given that the scenario that I have proposed is not going to occur—our schools of business administration are not going to be purchased, sold, combined, and changed by T. Boone Pickens or anyone else—how do we in reality convey our ethical values about distribution to persons who support the present restructuring process? I think they will be conveyed inevitably through two means:

1. Organizational disruption. Business organizations are more than the tangible buildings, equipment, and people; they also consist of intangible structures, systems, cultures, goals, norms, beliefs, and values. These intangible resources, which enable people to work together productively, may be of greater worth than all of the physical and financial assets combined. When a company is restructured—when assets are sold and people move or are discharged—the intangible resources are torn apart. It may be very difficult to put them back together.
2. Individual disloyalty. Business obligations are more than the efforts and profits owed by employees to the stockholders; they also include the concepts of dignity and worth, of truthfulness and adherence to contracts, that are owed by the stockholders to the employees. Obligations truly are reciprocal. We owe something to people only because they in turn owe something to us. When obligations are broken on one side, there is an immediate erosion of loyalty and duty on the other. It may be very difficult to reconstitute those personal feelings of responsibility to the organization.

Empirical research on organizational performance takes time. There is the time required to gather and analyze the data, but even more there is the time needed for causal events to affect performance variables in measurable ways. I have no doubt but that the organizational disruption and personal disloyalty associated with corporate restructuring will eventually be shown to result in markedly reduced performance measures, lower profits, and smaller shareholder values. This is another instance when to be proven right will not be personally satisfying.

NOTES

1. Ralph Saul, "Hostile Takeovers: What Should Be Done?" *Harvard Business Review* (September/October 1985): 19.

2. Michael Jensen, quoted in "Corporate Takeovers: Are the Raiders Right?" Robert Howard, ed., *HBS Bulletin* (February 1987): 47.

3. T. Boone Pickens, "Professions of a Short-Termer," *Harvard Business Review* (May/June 1986): 78.

4. Ibid.

5. Ibid., 76.

6. Roger B. Smith, letter to the shareholders of General Motors (not published, but distributed by the General Motors Corporation), February 10, 1987, p. 4.

7. Michael Jensen, quoted in Robert Howard, "Corporate Takeovers," 51.

STUDIES IN CORPORATE RESTRUCTURING: CASES AND ANALYSES

Ethical Dilemmas of Bankruptcy Reorganization—The Manville Case

W. T. STEPHENS

Manville, the asbestos tragedy, and the plan of reorganization for Manville are prime subjects for a discussion on ethics. The Manville case is a classic and will probably be referred to for years to come in any serious review of business ethics. There are lessons to be learned from asbestos which are in fact changing business practices. I would like to discuss my view of some of the ethical issues that arise out of Manville's bankruptcy. Before I do, however, it's important that you understand my perspective, which is not without some bias.

Two and a half years ago, I had the job of my dreams running a forest products company in Louisiana. In 1985 I was asked to move to Denver and dive into one of the biggest messes in corporate America. In the last two and one half years, this is what I've learned. The use of Chapter 11 to deal with Manville's problem was the right decision and the ethical decision. Behind the veil of a negative reputation that had descended on Manville are 19,000 excellent people who can and will make our plan of reorganization work. The plan of reorganization that has been confirmed and that is now working its way through the appeal process is the only economic, legal, moral, practical, and ethical solution to Manville's asbestos compensation problem. We in industry must completely change the way we approach product safety and product liability. No one has the right to sell a product that can harm someone and not warn them of the risk. Stated very simply, the days of let the buyer beware are over. Today it's let the seller beware. We do have a problem with ethics in American business today. The solution to that problem lies in the hands of the leadership of corporate America and teachers like those at Bentley College and others who attend its annual conference.

Let me start by talking about Manville and the Chapter 11 filing. To do that let me tell you a little bit about asbestos:

- It is a natural material.
- It has been used since before Christ.
- It has useful properties.
- Over 4 million tons of asbestos have been mined.
- Unfortunately, asbestos could also kill.

In as early as 1902 the British Inspector of Factories classified asbestos as a dust injurious to people. In 1906 both British and French doctors published findings on lung disease in asbestos workers. In June 1918 insurance company records showed notations of increased mortality in asbestos workers. From this point forward there were a series of medical reports, government reports, and insurance studies that all indicated there was a hazard associated with asbestos dust.

The asbestos industry responded to these studies in several ways. It worked to reduce dust levels in the plants. It assumed that the visible dust was the problem, but in reality it was the tiny fibers you could not see that were the real problem. It sponsored studies on the hazards of asbestos. It failed to recognize that asbestos disease had a latency period of up to forty years between exposure and manifestation. It continued to produce asbestos products in new applications. By today's standards it did not tell its employees and its customers enough about the dangers of asbestos exposure.

The experience with asbestos was not limited to industry; the Navy played a key role also. One of the growing uses of asbestos was in naval construction both in the United States and abroad. During World War II, millions of shipyard workers were exposed to high levels of asbestos dust in the holds of ships as we rushed to build ships for the war effort. Fire abroad ship is the nightmare of all sailors, and asbestos was used extensively to make the ships safer. Of course, the irony is that in cutting and fitting the asbestos insulation, thousands of shipyard workers had time bombs planted in their lungs. Navy records show that the government was aware that there was a problem in these shipyards, but because of concerns over worker morale the Navy decided not to tell the shipyard workers about the danger they faced. Today, half of all claims against Manville stem from that mistake by the U.S. Navy.

Even though it was known that asbestos fiber had the potential to injure, three sad mistakes were made. First, it was generally assumed that only heavy dust levels caused a health problem. Second, it was assumed that the health risk was limited to asbestosis. Third, the long latency period of asbestos disease masked the real gravity of the problem.

Based on the landmark work of Dr. Irving Selikoff that began in 1962 and was published in 1964, the true extent of the risk of disease from asbestos exposure became apparent. Dr. Selikoff found that not only was the threshold of dangerous exposure much lower than previously thought, but that there was a direct link between asbestos and lung cancer.

In 1964 Manville labeled its asbestos with a warning, but it was too late for thousands of people already exposed. It was not until 1971 that the Environmental Protection Agency (EPA) and Occupational Safety and Health Administration (OSHA) began to control the use of asbestos. In 1973 the Navy banned the use of asbestos in ships. In 1974, 448 asbestos workers in Texas filed suit in court against asbestos manufacturing companies and the U.S. government. The race to the courthouse was on.

From the mid 1970s until 1982, Manville settled over 4,100 cases against it, either by arbitration agreement or by court trial. Of those cases that went to trial, it was winning about half. By August 1982, new cases were being filed at the rate of 500 per month. The backlog of cases had grown to 17,000. As the number of cases grew, Manville's insurance carriers stopped paying claims, and litigation between Manville and its twenty-eight carriers began in the now-famous California proceedings. In 1981 juries began to return punitive damage judgments against Manville, and the cost per claim went up dramatically. Also in 1981, the company had an outside firm do an estimate of the number of claims it might expect as a part of the lawsuit it filed against its insurers. The results of that study indicated that conservatively, 50,000 claims could be expected.

At this point the company was faced with the dilemma that has caused so much misunderstanding. Here was the dilemma: under SEC and accounting rules, if you can reasonably estimate a liability, it must be recorded as such. In recording the liability for 50,000 claims at an average cost of $40,000 or $2 billion, the net worth of the company would have been wiped out. With a negative net worth, all the company's public and bank debt would be in default. It would have been either due and payable or must be secured under the loan agreements and indentures outstanding. The company would be cut off from the capital markets. Without access to capital, Manville would be unable to operate its businesses or to pay the ballooning asbestos claims.

The board of directors appointed a special committee made up of primarily outside directors to study the situation and make recommendations to the board. The board had a difficult job. Only in the last two years have I appreciated the real difficulty of that decision process. Of course we also know that the board of Manville voted to take the company into bankruptcy in August 1982. It's interesting to note some of the reasons that swayed the directors to make that historic decision.

The decision would put everyone on a level playing field—present claimant, bank creditor, future claimant. Filing Chapter 11 would declare a time out to resolve the company's insurance litigation. The use of Chapter 11 would allow Manville to find a way to deliver compensation more efficiently, with more net dollars going to the claimant and less to the legal system. It would allow Manville to protect the jobs and security of the majority of the 25,000 employees then working for the company. It also is interesting to note that the decision to go Chapter 11 was made over the strong objections of the president of the company as well as the chairman, who both felt that the problem might be solved without this step.

We are now over five years past the decision, and an account is due. One of the underlying assumptions of the filing was that the process would take a year, or at most, two. That was one of the first lessons we learned. Things move painfully slow in bankruptcy court. We also found out that bankruptcy is expensive. To date Manville has paid out over $100 million in legal and professional fees, and, sadly, not one claimant has been paid. We learned that in bankruptcy, it is a process not of litigation, but of negotiation. We also found out we had more people to negotiate with than we thought. It turned out to be an eight-party negotiation fighting over what surely are the most complex legal, economic, social, and emotional problems yet faced by an American company. If you think getting two parties to agree can be difficult, try this list:

Present claimants

Future claimants

Commercial and trade creditors

Codefendants

Property claims

Government

Insurance companies

I joined the negotiations in 1985 when, after three years, the parties still were deadlocked. It was at that point that most of the parties and the court agreed on some basic points: There would be more claims than there were assets to be divided. The plaintiff's bar would never agree to give up the right to go to trial nor to reduce its legal fees. The equity of the company had to be used to generate value to pay debts and claims. The claims of the property damage groups must be subordinated to the health claims. As the bankruptcy judge said in court, flesh and blood must come before bricks and mortar. The support of the banks and other lenders was essential to reaching a consensus. With the rapidly increasing number of claims filed against other companies, the original estimate of 50,000 claims would be far too low. Any plan must provide for an unknown number of future claims over an unknown period of time.

In August 1985 Manville and the court-appointed representative for future victims reached agreement on a plan. These basic concepts were expanded over the next six months as different groups were negotiated into that basic plan. At the end of the process, Manville's common shareholders were essentially wiped out, and Manville was to be owned by the trust set up for the asbestos claimants and by its other creditors.

The plan that was finally confirmed by the bankruptcy court in 1986 called for the creation of two trusts. A trust set up to pay asbestos health claims would be funded with:

- $700 million in insurance proceeds
- $150 million in case
- $1.6 billion in bonds payable over twenty-five years
- Up to 80 percent of the stock of Manville
- 20 percent of the company's profits for as long as they are needed to pay claims.

A separate trust was set up to pay property damage claims and was funded with $125 million in cash and rights to any residuals of the health trust at its termination. The company's commercial creditors will be paid off over four years. The preferred shareholders will start receiving a dividend after seven years. The common shareholders were left with as little as 2 percent of the stock of the reorganized company.

This plan is the result of thousands of hours of debate. Some of the best legal minds of our country worked on putting together this plan. All parties overwhelmingly voted in favor of the plan, except for the common shareholders. What this plan simply means is, that, in order to pay its claims, Manville must become a strong viable company that has the cash flow to pay its debts. It means that when Manville makes a profit, asbestos victims share in it. It means that when we increase the value of Manville stock, the trust can pay more claims. That's the mission of Manville today. Its new management team is committed to making the plan work.

I can assure you that the new Manville has learned from the past. Our earnings releases show that it is working and that we can meet the obligations of the plan. We have set a goal: that the new Manville will be the model of ethical corporate behavior. We have demonstrated what we can and will do this. I'm proud of our record.

Manville's Search for the Ring of Gyges

ARTHUR SHARPLIN[1]

In Plato's *The Republic* is found the story of a Lydian named Gyges, who discovered a ring which made the wearer invisible when turned a certain way. Using his new-found power, the story goes, Gyges seduced the queen, and together with her killed the king, seizing the throne for himself. In the surrounding dialogue, Socrates' fellow traveler Glaucon argues that such license as conferred by the ring of Gyges would cause just and unjust to behave alike. "We shall catch the just man taking the same road as the unjust," says Glaucon, "He will be moved by self-interest, the end which is natural to every creature to pursue as good."[2]

To his credit, Glaucon presents this cynical doctrine not as his own but as one common in intellectual circles—or perhaps he just anticipates Socrates' excellent refutation, which is soon to follow. In any case, Glaucon continues, "No one, it is commonly believed, would have such iron strength of mind as to stand fast in doing right or keep his hands off other men's goods, when he could go to the market-place and fearlessly help himself to anything he wanted, enter houses and sleep with any woman he chose, set prisoners free and kill men at his pleasure, and in a word go about among men with the powers of a god. . . . Granted full license to do as he liked, people would think him a miserable fool if they found him refusing to wrong his neighbours or to touch their belongings, though in public they would keep up a pretence of praising his conduct, for fear of being wronged themselves."[3]

IS CHAPTER 11 A RING OF GYGES?

Harvard ethics professor Kenneth Goodpaster once asked, perhaps rhetorically, if Chapter 11 of the U.S. Bankruptcy Code might be a ring of Gyges of sorts for executives.[4] Apparently Goodpaster was referring to the possibility that the protection of the bankruptcy court and the awesome power of the "debtor in possession" in the typical Chapter 11 proceeding would shield managers from accountability for past or anticipated corporate misdeeds and missteps. A number of Chapter 11 cases could well have provoked such a question. Continental Airlines, for example, was able to break its union contracts with impunity under the protection of a bankruptcy court. Through its filing, Texaco evaded payment of a massive civil judgment to Pennzoil, at least for a time. A. H. Robins Corporation filed its Chapter 11 petition to escape pursuit by thousands of Dalkon Shield claimants. In all these cases, senior corporate managers kept their jobs and, in general, improved their wages and benefits.

Goodpaster was particularly familiar with a somewhat contrary case, Braniff International.[5] At Braniff, the top managers who led the company into Chapter 11 had no part in the company's decline, having been brought in only eight months before what turned out to be the filing date (May 13, 1982). They say they chose bankruptcy reorganization not as an objective strategy, but only as a last resort. Then, they apparently concerned themselves with protecting stake-holders other than themselves, and left the company—without extraordinary benefits—when the reorganization was complete.[6]

MANVILLE'S NEED FOR A RING OF GYGES

But, when Goodpaster asked the question, he was surely thinking of Manville Corporation, a more ignoble company than any of those mentioned above. That firm's Chief Executive Officer, W. Thomas Stephens, was scheduled to appear opposite the present author, a Fellow of the Bentley College Center for Business Ethics, at the Seventh National Conference on Business Ethics in a session entitled "Ethical Dilemmas of Chapter 11: The Manville Case."[7] Goodpaster was to moderate that session.

Nowhere has the escape from accountability which might have provoked Goodpaster's question been more needful for managers than at Stephens' company. Manville sought bankruptcy court protection on August 26, 1982. At that time, there were 20,000 asbestos-health claims against the company, and new suits were being filed at the rate of three an hour every business day.[8] The average cost per case, the company said, was "sharply higher" than in prior years, averaging $40,000 per claim.[9] To make matters worse, a growing number of judgments during 1981 and 1982 had assessed punitive damages, as much as $1 million per claimant, and many named current and former Manville executives as defendants.[10]

In 1972 Manville and five other defendants had lost the landmark Clarence Borel A-H lawsuit, in which the appeals court wrote, "The evidence . . . tended to establish that none of the defendants ever tested its product to determine its effect on industrial insulation workers . . . . The unpalatable facts are that in the twenties and thirties the hazards of working with asbestos was recognized."[11]

In an April 1976 deposition, Dr. Kenneth Smith, former Manville Medical Director, had told of his knowledge of asbestos dangers during the 1940s, of his circa 1950 finding that the lungs of 704 of the 708 Manville asbestos workers he studied showed asbestos damage, and of his unsuccessful efforts to get caution labels put on Manville asbestos products.[12] Then, in April 1977, a mass of correspondence variously called the Sumner Simpson Papers and the Raybestos-Manhattan Correspondence came into public view. Included were many letters and memoranda among Manville officials and other asbestos industry executives. Concerning the documents, a South Carolina judge soon wrote, "The Raybestos-Manhattan Correspondence very arguably shows a pattern of denial of disease and attempts at suppression of information which is highly probative [and] reflects a conscious effort by the industry in the 1930s to downplay, or arguably suppress, the dissemination of information to employees and the public."[13]

The managers and directors at Manville were particularly vulnerable to charges of conspiring to hide past sins of the company, if not for committing them. The top five executives had each been with Manville twenty-nine to thirty-three years, and each had been a senior official since at least the early 1970s.[14] The outside directors, too, though imminent in their respective fields, could hardly claim noninvolvement.[15] Of the eleven 1982 directors (including two of the managers just mentioned), only two had less than ten years' tenure. The average tenure of the others was seventeen years. Six had joined the board in the 1960s, and two others, the inside directors, had worked for Manville since about 1950.[16]

Five months after the Smith deposition, the nine outside directors of Manville had demanded the resignation of psychologist Richard Goodwin, an outsider who had been installed as President in 1970 and who had been aggressively diversifying the company. *Fortune* reported that the three directors who transmitted the demand allegedly refused to explain their action. Corporate counsel John McKinney, whose tenure with Manville dated back to 1951, was the new choice for President.[17] The directors and officers were guaranteed indemnification by Manville, a contract they firmed up in 1981.[18] But the company's financial fortunes had turned sharply downward after 1978—so the indemnity might not mean much. And Manville's insurers provided little solace; they had stopped paying for most of the asbestos claims by 1981, and could not pay punitive damages anyway.[19]

After 1978, the company had begun what seems an irreversible downward slide financially, despite strategic moves undertaken by McKinney. Revenues (expressed in constant 1986 dollars—CPI adjustment) had fallen from $2.74 billion in 1978 to a $2.18 billion annual rate for the first half of 1982 (1982 revenues turned out to be $2.04 billion, a 26 percent drop). And earnings available to common stock (also in 1986 dollars) had simply evaporated, going from $198 million to an $85 million annual-rate *loss* (the 1982 loss turned out to be $125 million).[20] Manville's auditor, Coopers and Lybrand, had qualified its opinion on the company's 1980 and 1981 annual reports,[21] and its insurance companies were refusing to pay most of the asbestos-health litigation costs.[22]

Of course, Standard and Poor's and Moody's had downgraded Manville's debt.[23] And the small amounts actually paid for "asbestos health costs"—$13 million in 1981 and $16 million in 1982—could hardly be blamed for the financial collapse.[24]

Loss of easy asbestos profits was clearly a major factor. Until at least 1978, asbestos had been the company's mainstay. Sales of the raw fiber alone produced 41 percent of operating profit as late as 1976, though accounting for only 12 percent of revenues that year.[25] And many of the company's other products were asbestos-based.[26] U.S. asbestos consumption fell after 1976, by 36 percent in 1980 alone.[27] By 1982 Manville's asbestos fiber revenues were half the 1976 level.[28] And each dollar of fiber sales produced markedly less operating profit, 18 cents versus 33 cents in 1976.[29]

THE RING WORKS

The Chapter 11 filing solved—or at least deferred—all these problems. Legal actions against the company outside the bankruptcy court were placed on hold for at least five years, and virtually no earlier judgments were paid. A reorganization plan, which provided for a trust (the A-H Trust)— charged, among other obligations, with compensating asbestos victims—was filed by Manville management in 1986, but was held up pending the outcome of three appeals of the judge's confirmation order.[30] By that time, there were an estimated 41,500 new A-H claims waiting to be filed against Manville and, of course, many of the 1982 claimants had died.[31] In July 1987, the A-H trustees estimated that payments from the trust could begin during the spring of 1988,[32] although not even the official notices of all the appeals mentioned above had yet been filed.[33]

In the meantime, the company experienced a cash windfall, as receivables flowed in and $736 million in liabilities were frozen, most to be paid only after "conclusion of the Chapter 11 proceedings."[34] Manville's cash and marketable securities balance varied from a little over $200 million in December 1982 to over $440 million December 31, 1986—compared to $27 million on June 30, 1982, shortly before the filing.[35] The 1982 slate of directors and top executives, mostly unchanged after the 1960s, increased their pay and improved their benefits.[36] They were also able to exercise extraordinary discretion in influencing political developments and in spreading the largess preserved by Chapter 11 among a host of consultants and attorneys.[37] And the most senior managers were able to retire in economic security, shielded by the bankruptcy court and indemnified by Manville, and prospectively by the A-H Trust, against asbestos-related liabilities.[38] The executives left behind were also reassured of large termination payments upon choosing or being asked to leave[39] and of probable bonuses in the meantime.[40]

The power of the prefiling directors and senior managers promised to remain firm for at least four years after plan consummation, if and when that was to occur. Two new directors were appointed at the insistence of a group of preferred shareholders in 1984,[41] but there was no other new outside director on the 1986 board.[42] J. T. Hulce, a lawyer who had joined Manville as Assistant Corporate Counsel in 1972 was appointed President in 1984, but resigned in 1986, allegedly under pressure from asbestos plaintiff attorneys.[43] His replacement, W. Thomas Stephens, who later also became Chief Executive Officer, was not identified with Manville's distant past,[44] but was required to work with no employment or termination contract, serving "from Board meeting to Board meeting at the discretion of the Board."[45] No annual or special meetings of common shareholders, at which new directors might have been elected, were permitted after the bankruptcy filing.[46] Further, the Manville reorganization plan provided that at least half of all common shares, those held by the A-H Trust, would be voted for management's nominees to the board of directors for four years after the consummation date.[47] While the initial post-consummation board of directors was to include seven new outside members, six of the prefiling directors were to remain on the board, as was W. Thomas Stephens.[48]

And while management was able to claim to be out of the asbestos business after 1983, the company reaped continuing cash flows from "mining, milling and distributing asbestos fiber."[49] On July 1, 1983, Manville had completed the sale of its remaining asbestos operations to a Canadian group headed by former Manville executives. Aside from about $47 million apparently borrowed on the assets and remitted to Manville, the $117 million (Canadian) to $150 million (Canadian) selling price was payable "out of 85.5 percent of available future cash flows from asbestos fiber operations."[50]

NOTES

1. The continuing encouragement of the Bentley College Center for Business Ethics, of which the author is a Fellow, is gratefully acknowledged.

2. Francis MacDonald Cornford, trans., *The Republic of Plato* (New York: Oxford University Press, 1966), 44.

3. Ibid., 45.

4. Conversation with author.

5. David E. Whiteside (under the supervision of Kenneth E. Goodpaster), "Braniff International: The Ethics of Bankruptcy (A)" (Case no. 385-001), "Braniff International: The Ethics of Bankruptcy (B)" (Case no. 385-001), and accompanying teaching note (5-384-182), in Harvard Business School's "Cases and Notes on Business Ethics," 1984.

6. An "organizational stakeholder" is an individual or group whose interests are affected by organizational activities. See Arthur Sharplin, *Strategic Management* (New York: McGraw-Hill Book Company, 1985), p. 28.

7. Conducted annually at Bentley College in Waltham, Massachusetts, under the auspices of the Center for Business Ethics. The 1987 conference was scheduled for October 15–16, 1987.

8. G. Earl Parker, "The Manville Decision," paper presented at the symposium "Bankruptcy Proceedings—The Effect on Product Liability," conducted by Andrews Publications, Inc., at Miami, Florida, March 1983, p. 3.

Arthur Sharplin

9. Manville Corporation, "Manville Files for Reorganization," media release, August 26, 1982, p. 2.

10. Ronald L. Motley (leading asbestos plaintiff attorney), conversation with author, October 9, 1987. Also see Manville Corporation, *Quarterly Report on U.S. Securities and Exchange Commission Form 10-Q*, for quarter ended June 30, 1982, II-8 (discussion of Louisiana cases).

11. *Clarence Borel vs. Fibreboard Paper Products Corporation, et al.*, Fifth Circuit U.S. Court of Appeals, 1973, *Federal Reporter*, Vol. 493 F. 2d, pp. 1076–109.

12. Dr. Kenneth W. Smith, Discovery deposition (file no. 164-122), *Louisville Trust Company, Administrator of the estate of William Virgil Sampson, vs. Johns-Manville Corporation*, Jefferson (County, Kentucky) Circuit Court, Common Pleas Branch, April 21, 1987.

13. Amended Order (Survival and Wrongful Death Actions), *Bennie M. Barnett, Administrator, for Gordon Luther Barnett, deceased, vs. Owens-Corning Fiberglass Corp., et al.*, Court of Common Pleas, Greenville County, South Carolina, August 23, 1978, pp. 10 and 5.

14. Manville Corporation, *1982 Proxy Statement*, March 25, 1982, p. 12, and *Moody's Industrial Manual*, 1971, 1424; 1972, 3222; 1973, 2907–8; and 1974, 2040.

15. Manville Corporation, *1982 Proxy Statement*, March 25, 1982, pp. 4–7. The outside directors included the Dean of the School of Architecture at Princeton, the Dean of the Graduate School of Business Administration at New York University (who had previously been Chairman/CEO of American Can Company), the Chairman/CEO of Ideal Basic Industries, Inc. (who had earlier been elected three times as Governor of Colorado), the Chairman/President/CEO of Phelps Dodge Corporation, and the top managers of three other companies.

16. Manville Corporation, *1982 Proxy Statement*, March 25, 1982, pp. 4–7.

17. See Herbert E. Meyer, "Shootout at the Johns-Manville Corral," *Fortune*, October 1976, pp. 146–54.

18. Manville Corporation, *1981 Proxy Statement*, September 11, 1981, Exhibit 2, pp. 5–7.

19. Manville Corporation, *Report on U.S. Securities and Exchange Commission Form 10-Q*, for quarter ended June 30, 1982, pp. II-11–II-14.

20. Manville Corporation, *1982 Annual Report and Form 10-K*, 7; and *Quarterly Report on U.S. Securities and Exchange Commission Form 10- Q*, for quarter ended June 30, 1982, pp. I–2. Also, Johns-Manville Corporation, *1978 Annual Report*, p. 36. U.S. Consumer Price Index figures were obtained from Ibbotson Associates, *Stocks, Bonds, Bills, and Inflation: 1987 Yearbook* (Chicago: Ibbotson Associates, Inc., 1987), 30. It is interesting that "Asbestos-Health Costs," which were only $13 million in 1981 and $16 million in 1982, were not the cause of Manville's financial decline.

21. Manville Corporation, *1980 Annual Report*, 21, and *1981 Annual Report*, p. 15.

22. Manville Corporation, *Report on U.S. Securities and Exchange Commission Form 10-Q*, for quarter ended June 30, 1982, pp. II-11–II-14.

23. See, for example, "Manville Ratings Cut by Standard and Poor's," *Wall Street Journal*, June 11, 1982, p. 36.

24. Manville Corporation, *1982 Annual Report and Form 10-K*, p. 7.

25. Manville Corporation, *1977 Annual Report*, p. 1.

26. See, for example, Johns-Manville Corporation, *1977 Annual Report*, pp. 8, 10, and 13, which list many such items, including "Asbestos Felts, Papers & Textiles,"

"Asbestos-Cement Shingles," "Asbestos-Cement Water & Sewer Pipe," and "Asbestos Paper and Millboard."

27. Raymond A. Joseph, "Problems Have Long Plagued Asbestos Firms," *The Wall Street Journal*, August 30, 1982, p. 15 (U.S. Interior Department figures in thousands of metric tons for 1976–1981 are given as 659, 610, 619, 561, 359, and 350, respectively).

28. Manville Corporation, *1982 Annual Report and Form 10-K*, p. 18 (also see p. 30, where it is reported "Approximately 60% of the Company's asbestos fiber is sold in international markets, principally Western Europe."), and Johns-Manville Corporation, *1977 Annual Report*, p. 1.

29. Ibid.

30. See, for example, "Appeals Consolidated in 2nd Circut [sic], Possible Hearing in October," *Stockholders & Creditors News Service Re. Johns-Manville Corp., et al.*, September 21, 1987, p. 6,953.

31. "Plan Protects Manville, Shortchanges Victims," *Asbestos Watch* 4, no. 1 (Fall 1986): 1. Also see "JM Trust to Accept Claims in January, Negotiate Even Before Consummation," *Stockholders & Creditors News Service Re. Johns-Manville Corp., et al.*, July 6, 1987, p. 6,681, which states, "It is now estimated that 70,000 asbestos cases have been filed throughout the country."

32. "JM Trust to Accept Claims in January," p. 6,680.

33. See, for example, Aaron H. Simon, Vern Countryman, and Doros & Blessey, P.C., "Notice of Appeal to U.S. Court of Appeals for Second Circuit," August 13, 1987, in *Stockholders & Creditors News Service Re. Johns-Manville, et al.*, August 24, 1987, p. 6,816. Assuming the Second Circuit affirms the confirmation order, further appeals to the U.S. Supreme Court seem certain.

34. Manville Corporation, *1982 Annual Report and Form 10-K*, December 31, 1982, pp. 6 and 11.

35. Manville Corporation, *1982 Annual Report and Form 10-K*, 6; *1986 Annual Report and Form 10-K*, 39; and *Quarterly Report on U. S. Securities and Exchange Commission Form 10-Q*, for the quarter ended June 30, 1982, p. I–3.

36. See Manville Corporation, *1982 Proxy Statement*, 10; *1985 Annual Report and Form 10-K*, p. 79; and *1986 Annual Report and Form 10-K*, p. 63. McKinney's cash compensation went from $408,750 in early 1982 to $638,005 in 1985, his last full year of employment. Senior Vice Presicent Chester Sulewski's increased by 88 percent from 1982 to 1986. The cash compensation of W. Thomas Stephens, who took over from McKinney in September 1986, was 39 percent higher that year than in 1985, the first year he appeared in the company's Compensation Table. The cash compensation of the nine outside directors and twenty-three officers of Manville was shown as $3,882,995 in the March 25, *1982 Proxy Statement*, p. 10, while the *1986 Annual Report and Form 10-K*, p. 63, reports cash compensation of $5,456,403 for the twenty-five "executive officers" during 1986.

37. By the end of 1986, Manville had dispensed $64 million in Chapter 11 costs (*1986 Annual Report and Form 10-K*, p. 40, and *1983 Annual Report and Form 10-K*, p. 6). For example, Davis, Polk and Wardwell, a New York Law firm that had represented Manville since 1928, was cocounsel for the Chapter 11 proceedings and charged over $200,000 a month early in the proceedings. (*Stockholders and Creditors News Service Re. Johns-Manville, et al.*, March 14, 1983, p. 794). First Boston Corporation was authorized $100,000 a month in late 1984 to serve as financial advisor to certain creditor groups (*Stockholders and Creditors News Service Re. Johns-Manville, et al.*, December

10, 1984, p. 3,184). Leon Silverman, the "Legal Representative for Future Claimants" appointed by the bankruptcy court, retained his own law firm as counsel to himself. He and his firm submitted bills for $2.3 million for August 1, 1984, through December 31, 1986, although they had only been paid $1.5 million of that by August 1987 (*Stockholders and Creditors News Service Re. Johns-Manville, et al.*, September 7, 1987, p. 6,945). Dr. Frederick W. Kilbourne, Mercer-Future Cost Analysts, was paid $73,550 for work as Manville's "actuarial experts" during November 1983 through April 1984 (*Stockholders and Creditors News Service Re. Johns-Manville, et al.*, August 24, 1987, p. 6,819). The Executive Director of the Association of Trial Lawyers of America, Marianna S. Smith, was hired as Chief Executive Officer of the A-H Trust. The pattern continued in 1987. For the first six months of 1987, twenty-two law firms submitted bills in the Manville Chapter 11 proceeding for $5,733,983 (*Stockholders and Creditors News Service Re. Johns-Manville, et al.*, September 7, 1987, p. 6,905). The "provisional" trust budget for January-August 1987 provided $4.6 million to administer the trust, including $194,000 for executive searches, $840,000 to pay Smith and three assistants, and $257,000 for the six trustees, who were scheduled to meet seven times (*Stockholders and Creditors News Service Re. Johns-Manville, et al.*, August 10, 1987, pp. 6,779 and 6,800).

38. See Arthur Sharplin, "Liquidation versus 'The Plan,' " *The Asbestos Litigation Reporter*, November 21, 1986. Also see Johns-Manville Corporation, et al., "Application for an Order Approving Severance Pay Agreements," *Stockholders & Creditors News Service Re. Johns-Manville Corp., et al.*, September 8, 1986, pp. 5,569–72; and "Judge Approves Severance Pay for G. Earl Parker," *Stockholders & Creditors News Service Re. Johns-Manville Corp., et al.*, pp. 6988–89. CEO John McKinney's severance agreement, effective September 1, 1986, provided for cash payments totaling $1.3 million, two extra years of fringe benefits, and two extra years of longevity for retirement purposes. Two other executives were given severance agreements at the same time providing for payments totaling $1,030,000 and certain other benefits. By December 1986, four of the five most highly paid executives shown in the *1982 Proxy Statement*, p. 10, had left the company (*1986 Annual Report and Form 10-K*, p. 62). G. Earl Parker, Manville's legal chief under McKinney, retired as Executive Vice President and Director in March 1987. His severance agreement, approved by the bankruptcy court in September 1987, provided payments of $430,000 a year through 1989, a total of $1.2 million, counting from March 1987. But the board of directors remained mostly unchanged, with only one of the nine 1982 outside directors having departed (*1982 Proxy Statement*, pp. 4–7, and *1986 Annual Report and Form 10-K*, pp. 56–61). The importance of the protection against lawsuits naming the officers and directors in their personal capacities is illustrated by the fact that the estate of Vandiver Brown, Manville Vice President and Secretary during the 1930s, was still being attacked by asbestos victims. See "Stay Sought for Lawsuits Against Estate of Vandiver Brown," *Stockholders & Creditors News Service Re. Johns-Manville Corp., et al.*, November 5, 1984, p. 3,082.

39. *Stockholders and Creditors News Service Re. Johns-Manville Corp., et al.*, April 7, 1986, pp. 5,004–6. At a special board meeting in New York held on October 11, 1985, J. A. McKinney discussed "Confidential Minute Number 13," which was said to address severance pay of up to two times annual salary for officers and other "key managerial personnel" upon any termination of employment. It was agreed that the special pay would even apply to persons terminated after any assignment of a trustee in the bankruptcy case.

40. "New Bonus Plan for Executives Approved by Court," *Stockholders and Creditors*

News Service Re. Johns-Manville Corp., et al., August 10, 1987, pp. 6,778 and 6,779. In mid-July 1987 Manville obtained court approval for a new executive bonus plan for that year, increasing the possible bonuses for certain managers from 57.5 percent of annual salaries to 97.1 percent. The allowable bonuses for achieving less than 80 percent of goals were reduced.

41. "Manville Adds 3 to Board to Increase Shareholder Input," *Wall Street Journal*, August 3, 1984, p. 4. The third director, Randall Smith, was a limited partner in Bear Stearns & Co., appointed after Bear Stearns accumulated a large holding of Manville common stock (see Dean Rotbart and Jonathan Dahl, "Manville's Common Stockholders May Have Potent Ally as Bear Stearns Bolsters Holdings," *Wall Street Journal*, July 25, 1984, p. 51). Smith resigned his directorship in late 1985.

42. Manville Corporation, *1986 Annual Report and Form 10-K*, pp. 56–59.

43. Cynthia F. Mitchell, "Manville President Quits After Dispute with Asbestos Plaintiff over Top Posts," *Wall Street Journal*, April 30, 1986, p. 34.

44. Stephens had been an employee of Olinkraft Corporation, a major wood products company which Manville acquired in 1978 (see Manville Corporation, *1986 Annual Report and Form 10-K*, p. 59).

45. W. T. Stephens, personal correspondence with author, April 10, 1987.

46. See, for example, Manville Corporation, *1986 Annual Report and Form 10-K*, p. 33.

47. Manville Corporation, *First Amended Disclosure Statement, Second Amended and Restated Plan of Reorganization, and Related Documents*, August 22, 1986, p. 41.

48. Manville Corporation, *1986 Annual Report and Form 10-K*, pp. 56–61.

49. Manville Corporation, *1983 Annual Report and Form 10-K*, p. 15.

50. Ibid.

27

Organizational Downsizing in "MADD" Times: Balancing Humanity and Efficiency

LAURENCE J. STYBEL

These are "MADD" days for American industry—Mergers, Acquisitions, Divestitures, and Downsizing. (In keeping with the spirit of the times, I do not claim that I originated the word. I heard it from Manny Kay, a psychologist in Marblehead.)

According to the October 8, 1987, issue of the *Wall Street Journal*, announced mergers and acquisitions increased by 5 percent during the last year, to a total of 3,355 in one year. Total dollar value jumped 28 percent to $182 billion. I would think divestitures and corporate downsizing would have increased by 5 percent at least.

A MADD decision normally will hurt some employees. Hardest hit will be staff-level and middle managers who believed that they were part of the management team, the ones who always thought, "If you take care of the company, the company takes care of you."

A MADD decision ultimately places senior management in the role of having to strike a balance between being people-oriented and being profit-oriented. It is a particularly painful experience because it puts people in a situation where their professional responsibility may conflict with their genuine concern for people. How do managers strike that balance between compassion and efficiency?

DOWNSIZING OPTIONS IN "MADD" DECISIONS

How do companies decide the rationale for who will be let go? Companies have a variety of options: LIFO, FIFO, Surgical Strike, Performance-Based, or Mixed Bag.

This chapter previously appeared in *Industry* (January 1988).

LIFO (Last in/First out)

This is a seniority-based system. Unions love this approach, since it offers most protection to their members. Managers like it because it is totally impersonal. Dismissed employees like it because it is totally impersonal.

Problems with LIFO are that it does not really address the issue of downsizing very effectively, in that it still leaves the bulk of entrenched middle management intact. In addition, use of LIFO puts greater pressure on the younger members of the employee population, making it more difficult to attract and retain young people in the future.

LIFO really eliminates some payroll costs without regard to the strategic contribution of the people being eliminated. Middle-management/staff-level fat is often retained while muscle—janitors, receptionists, entry level accountants—is eliminated.

For this reason, LIFO is often followed up by downward mobility of those who remain behind in the organization. The federal government calls this bumping down. The morale of those who remain in such organizations is sometimes as bad as the morale of those who were forced to leave.

FIFO (First in/First out)

An example would be Polaroid's attempt to reduce its work force population through a program of offering attractive financial incentives for early retirement, commonly known as "open windows," since *all* employees of a given age/seniority level must be eligible to avoid a wrongful termination suit on the grounds of age discrimination. Once you get selective about who you push out, you leave yourself open to discrimination suits.

The key advantage of FIFO is that it does effectively get rid of middle-management bulge. Yes, you do loose some valuable talent as Polaroid did. But you can get back some of that knowledge by offering consulting contracts to key employees, as Xerox in Europe did. Another advantage of FIFO is that it is impersonal. The Japanese use a complex version of FIFO in their layoff decisions.

Surgical Strike

This approach involves the elimination of a function or an organization for a strategic reason. Examples would be General Dynamics' decision to close the Quincy Shipyard Division; Johnson & Johnson's decision to exit from certain high-technology medical instrumentation businesses, thus closing down Ortho Diagnostics Systems and Magnetic Corporation of America. Boston University's decision to close its School of Nursing is another example.

This decision is also impersonal and based on strategic business needs. But it requires a sound strategy and the guts to implement that strategy.

Performance-Based

Here, the decision of who is going to be let go is highly personal and is orientated at individuals. Examples would be law firms who constantly introduce fresh blood of first-year associates and promote a few into the partnership but let the rest go. University tenure decisions are performance-based. A well-known commercial bank in Boston recently downsized using performance as the criterion.

From an organization perspective, this rationale makes sense . . . keep the wheat and throw the chaff away. It clearly signals that the culture of the company is going to be performance-oriented.

Of course, there are some ethical problems with this approach. One is that performance standards at the professional level are often highly subjective, and performance-based decisions may indeed be based on personality factors that are not job related.

Second, once the outside world knows an organization is using a performance-based criterion, the company in effect stigmatizes its ex-employees. Many potential employers take the attitude, "We don't want to take other people's rejects."

Sometimes organizations go to great lengths to cover up that they employ performance-based methods, partly for humanitarian reasons. It also doesn't help the organization to let it be known that they have hired incompetent or ineffective people. No one gets fired from law firms; they all leave voluntarily for better opportunities.

On the other hand, most industries operate within small incestuous communities. It may be impossible for the organization to disguise a performance-based termination. For example, when a university associate professor leaves after six years with the same institution, there is little need to ask what happened.

Mixed Bag

This approach represents a combination of all these methods. Two variations of Mixed Bag are "Performance-Based Disguised as Surgical Strike" and "LIFO Disguised as Performance-Based."

Performance-Based Disguised as Surgical Strike. This approach is very common in U.S. industry at the management levels. A specific person is targeted for elimination on the basis of performance. The rationale given to the employee and to the outside world is that it is a surgical strike, elimination of the position.

The advantage of this tactic is that it avoids bitter fights and arguments between bosses and subordinates; it helps subordinates find new employment by masking an intensely personal decision as impersonal. Company X lets go the Director of Engineering, saying it has combined engineering and manufacturing under the Director of Operations. They plan to hire a new Director of Engineering once the ex-director gets a job.

The major problem with this approach is that it does not allow ex-employees to learn from the experience. They too readily want to believe the cover story. Thus, employees may be doomed to repeat the same mistakes over and over.

LIFO Disguised as Performance-Based. A well-known high-technology company followed intensely by the investment community is experiencing a drop in sales and market share. It wishes to disguise how bad things are for fear of hurting sales even more.

The company decides to downsize its employee population slowly to avoid the appearance of downsizing. Instead, what the public will perceive is an aggressive separation of chaff from the wheat—a tough performance-oriented system for eliminating ineffective employees.

What publicly appears to be a tough organization going through a blood-letting of ineffective employees is in reality a reduction in force, often of younger and less trusted subordinates. The pain for affected individuals can be quite severe; they are lied to at an individual level and stigmatized as failures, when the reality is quite different. If the company were growing, they would still be employed. It hurts those who leave, and it hurts the managers who must implement the plan.

CONCLUSIONS

My purpose is not to say that one strategic option is better than others. Much depends upon the larger corporate framework of its strategy and how the company wants to differentiate itself in the marketplace for talent.

Johnson & Johnson, for example, wants to be perceived in the human resource marketplace as a company that really cares for its people. Even among the people fired by Johnson & Johnson, that perception will hold fast. Other companies couldn't care less how they are perceived in the marketplace, feeling that a warm body is a warm body or that good old cash compensation will win over any objectives relating to touchy/feely issues.

As we help managers thrash with themselves about what course to take, managers' attitudes toward downsizing fall along a dimension whose two ends are expressed in the following way:

- I need to strike the right balance between the competing and irreconcilable conflicts between ex-employees who want good severance packages, shareholders who want good profits, and managers who want to minimize their discomfort in the whole business of getting rid of people.

- Assuming we can afford it, the things we do to help terminated employees are the things that will be right for our shareholders in the long run:

  —The people who leave will speak of us as a class organization and this will help us recruit in the future.

—We will keep our managers from feeling they are in ethical binds when firing people, because we are trying to make termination as rehabilitative as possible.

Our involvement with the General Dynamics (GD) Corporation Quincy Shipyard Division is an example of this second value in action. As a result of the decision to shut down the division, over 6,000 employees would be out of work. More than out of work—out of an industry where they, their fathers, and their grandfathers had been employed.

GD took the attitude that they owed it to their employees to find alternative work for them. A serious attempt was made to place employees with other divisions of General Dynamics, including some arm-twisting at times. For those not placed within GD, an outplacement center was created. This center included:

- Space for State Department of Employment Security to provide information regarding state services.
- An active outreach program to local businesses to place people. GD became an employment agency.
- Outplacement assistance to provide employees with tools necessary to perform an effective job search.

The unique partnership between the Commonwealth of Massachusetts and General Dynamics was recognized by the U.S. Department of Commerce and the National Alliance of Business.

Obviously, as a representative of an outplacement firm, I have a vested interest in pushing management toward the latter end of the moral continuum. But I *know* it is possible to create win/win outcomes for companies and for employees in the aftermath of a MADD decision. And that knowledge is one of the major gratifications of my job as an outplacement consultant.

28

Dynamics versus CTS—A Case Study of the Ethical Questions in Hostile Takeovers

FRED J. NAFFZIGER

JEFF KUROWSKI

In September 1980 Dynamics Corporation of America (DCA) began one of the longest and most bitter takeover battles in American business when a six-and-a-half-year fight for the control of the CTS Corporation was initiated with the announcement that DCA held 5 percent of CTS common stock. Eventually the contest between these two publicly traded, albeit somewhat obscure, corporations would encompass a proxy fight, adoption of three forms of poison pills, a search for a white knight to buy 100 percent of the target, the payment of greenmail to ward off yet another potential raider, the attempted use of a state antitakeover statute as a shield, litigation in a multiplicity of forums—one portion of which would result in a major U.S. Supreme Court decision—and finally, a negotiated settlement between the two hostile adversaries.

This struggle for corporate control provides an example for studying the techniques of mounting hostile takeovers and the strategies for fending them off, in other than an abstract manner. We are not interested in the broad perspective, that is, what is best for the overall American economy or how the takeover rules inhibit or enhance the competitive position of U.S. companies in a global market. We wish to examine what actions the parties took, why they used them, and what their effect was ultimately.

We have chosen DCA versus CTS for a variety of reasons. The target is a locally headquartered corporation. One coauthor extensively covered the struggle in his capacity as a business reporter. The latter also was able to interview the ousted CEO of the target for a retrospective discussion of the matter. (The other CEO declined an interview request.) In addition, we believe that some individuals do not fully realize how sophisticated, complex, and interrelated is the corporate world. Illustrating the manner by which the federal securities and state corporation laws interact to create a dramatic effect upon what may be viewed as a local company may assist in disspelling such misconceptions.

DESCRIPTIONS OF THE ANTAGONISTS

Although both companies have their stock traded on the NYSE, they are relatively small, obscure manufacturing companies. CTS, headquartered in Elkhart, Indiana, manufactures a broad line of custom electronic components. It was founded in 1896 as the Chicago Telephone Supply Company. It quickly outgrew its facilities in Chicago and moved to Elkhart, Indiana, in 1902, because local governmental officials provided free land and tax breaks.

CTS made hand-crank telephones until 1940 and began supplying parts to radio manufacturers during the 1920s. For most of its history, CTS operated only one manufacturing plant, in Elkhart. Variable resistors and associated on-off switches used on televisions and radios were CTS's most important product from the 1950s through the 1970s.

In 1976, components sold to consumer electronics manufacturers accounted for 40 percent of CTS's sales. However, because of the transfer of consumer electronics manufacturing to Japan and Southeast Asia, that market accounted for only 3 percent of CTS's sales revenue by 1985.

Its 1986 sales totaled $245.5 million. It has twenty plants, both in the United States and Asia, with a work force of 6,500. In the 1970s it began minimizing investments in products for mature or declining markets in order to concentrate in products for growing markets.

This policy led to two costly acquisitions. In September 1981 it paid $13.3 million in cash for Printex, a manufacturer of printed circuit boards. Mounting losses in the operation led to a January 1987 CTS board announcement that it would phase out the Printex operations and take an $18 million pretax charge against its fourth quarter 1986 earnings. In June 1983 CTS used cash and stock to purchase Micro Peripherals, Inc., a manufacturer of floppy disk drives for home computers. In September 1984 CTS announced its decision to close down the Micro operations and take a $37 million pretax writedown. Actually, after its initial purchase, CTS stock increased to over $57 per share after trading as low as $33.50 during the second quarter of 1983.

Between these two acquisitions it became known that the Belzberg family of Canada owned 5.7 percent of CTS. They were relatively quickly dispatched by a greenmail payment, by our calculations carrying a premium of about $884,800. The CTS chief executive during most of this long saga, Robert D. Hostetler, does not believe that the payment to the Belzbergs put CTS "into play." In fact, he believes that it reduced arbitrage interest in CTS. The payment did generate a derivative suit settled for $50,000, and a by-law was subsequently adopted prohibiting future greenmail payments.

Beginning in the 1970s, CTS management had followed a strategy of minimizing investments in products intended for mature or declining markets, and investing in products serving growing markets. Hostetler attempted to accelerate the implementation of that strategy.

CTS is about the fifth largest employer of Elkhart, with 800 to 850 production workers and about 150 people in its corporate headquarters staff. Its largest manufacturing plant is in Berne, Indiana, about 120 miles southeast of Elkhart. CTS's Elkhart manufacturing plant is approximately the same size, in terms of employment, as its plants in Singapore and Taiwan.

Hostetler said he did not make an extra effort to preserve manufacturing jobs in Elkhart because it is CTS's homebase. "The Elkhart people would accuse me of being overly aggressive in moving things (production lines) out of Elkhart (to Mexico or Southeast Asia where labor costs are much lower)," he said.

DCA is a manufacturing concern about one-half the size of CTS. In 1986 sales were $139.2 million. Three business segments—environmental systems, electrical appliances and electrical devices, and fabricated metal products—generate those sales dollars.

The environmental systems division has manufacturing plants in Cincinnati and Bridgeport, Connecticut. The electronic appliances and devices division has plants in Burbank, California, Carlisle, Pennsylvania, and New Hartford, Connecticut. DCA's fabricated metal products plant is in Scranton, Pennsylvania. In 1986, DCA sold its farm machinery manufacturing plant in Minnesota to a privately held company in that state. DCA received an equity position in Farmland, Inc., as a result of the exchange.

CTS and DCA may be direct competitors in their quartz crystal product lines. If that turns out to be the case, then DCA stated in its proxy material dated March 27, 1986, that it would sell its quartz crystal manufacturing business.

DCA filed a Chapter 11 bankruptcy petition in 1972 and emerged in 1974. The bankruptcy was related to litigation with a money-center bank. It is chartered in New York (CTS is an Indiana corporation), and its chief executive during this struggle was Andrew Lozyniak. In 1980 it disclosed that it owned 5 percent of CTS stock. It subsequently bought and sold varying amounts and currently owns 27.5 percent of the 5.6 million outstanding shares of CTS common stock.

Lozyniak had DCA made the investment in CTS because he believed that "it could be a significant and supportive investor of CTS and make a positive contribution to its continued growth." It did not turn out well, and the two companies soon turned to fighting each other in a variety of arenas. DCA tried to oust the CTS management, viewing CTS's subsequent poor financial performance as justification. Hostetler of CTS feared that DCA would attempt to maximize short-term gains and, as a minority holder but one large enough to control the company, would have obtained control without paying holders the premium that accompanies a change in control.

CHRONOLOGY OF EVENTS

In September 1980, DCA filed an SEC Schedule 13D disclosing that it owned 5 percent, or about 220,000 shares, of the 4.5 million shares of CTS stock then outstanding. The SEC Act of 1934 requires an investor to file a Schedule 13D within ten business days of buying 5 percent or more of a company's stock. The purpose of a 13D filing is to provide other investors with timely information upon which they could base decisions on whether to buy, sell, or hold the company's stock.

It is believed that an investor owing 5 percent or more of a company's stock can have a significant impact on the market value of the company's stock. Usually, the market price of a company's stock will rise when a 13D is filed by an outsider, because market professionals believe that puts the company's management and board of directors under pressure to raise the value of the company's stock. The price of CTS stock ranged from $16.75 to $25.50 a share during the third quarter of 1980.

Clinton W. Hartman was the Chairman and CEO of CTS when DCA made its initial purchase. Hartman retired as Chairman and CEO after the annual shareholders meeting on April 20, 1981. Hostetler became the CTS President, Chief Administrative Officer, and Treasurer at the time.

On October 16, 1980, the first of several lawsuits was filed. CTS claimed in U.S. District Court in the Northern District of Indiana that DCA embarked upon a "creeping takeover" of CTS. An example of a creeping takeover, or creeping tender, would be an investor buying 4.9 percent of the company's stock, and then arranging financing to buy another large block of the company's stock. That way, the unfriendly investor could own much more than 5 percent of the target company's stock when it has to disclose its purchases in a Schedule 13D filing.

CTS also used the creeping tender claim in an effort to get the Indiana Securities Commissioner to block DCA from buying any more CTS stock. The Commissioner dismissed CTS's claim on November 21, 1980, and his decision was affirmed by the Indiana Court of Appeals on December 1, 1981.

On October 31, 1980, DCA sued CTS, the Indiana Secretary of State, and the state Securities Comissioner, seeking to have the Indiana business takeover offers act declared unconstitutional. CTS filed a counterclaim seeking to recover $415,675 plus interest and attorneys' fees. CTS claimed DCA made materially false and misleading statements on its Schedule 13D. (DCA and CTS settled this lawsuit on June 11, 1985. DCA paid CTS $215,000 and each side released the other from liability.) Meanwhile, DCA increased its stake from 8 percent to 16.5 percent of CTS during 1981, according to the CTS 1981 annual report, dated March 2, 1982.

On June 4, 1981, DCA also sued CTS in an attempt to get CTS to reveal confidential information about its R&D expenditures. In October 1983, the Elkhart Circuit Court ruled CTS did not have to reveal the information to DCA. The Indiana Court of Appeals affirmed that judgment on July 9, 1985.

During September 1981, CTS made the first of two costly acquisitions that eventually led to Hostetler's ouster. It paid $13.3 million in cash to buy all of the stock of Printex Corporation, a printed circuit boards manufacturer based in Mountain View, California. Printex had net earnings of $1.4 million for its 1980 fiscal year, and it earned $1.1 million in 1984. However, it lost $5.3 million in 1985 and $6.3 million in 1986. Concern over the mounting losses at Printex was one of the reasons why DCA launched its tender offer and proxy contest in March 1986.

Finally, in January 1987, the CTS board announced it would phase out its Printex operations and take an $18 million pretax charge against its fourth quarter 1986 earnings.

Between January 1, 1983, and March 7, 1983, DCA increased its stake to 23.2 percent of CTS. During 1981, the market price of CTS stock ranged from $22 to $31.25 a share. During the first quarter of 1982, CTS stock ranged from $23 to $28.625 a share.

The Belzberg family of Canada, notorious corporate raiders, was paid greenmail by CTS during May 1982, Hostetler admitted. CTS, according to a press release dated May 10, 1982, paid $7,963,200, or $31.50 a share, for the 252,800 shares, or 5.7 percent of CTS that the Belzbergs owned. CTS also paid $162,500 for the call options, exercisable at $25 a share, for 25,000 shares, from the Belzbergs. (The 1984 CTS annual report stated the Belzbergs were paid $8.3 million for their stock and options.) During the second quarter of 1982, CTS stock traded from $21,875 to $28 a share. (Hostetler said the market price was $26 to $28 when the Belzbergs were paid a premium to sell their shares.) Hostetler said the greenmail premium paid to the Belzbergs was "$600,000 to $800,000."

The CTS Board was worried about a bidding war between DCA and the Belzbergs that would result in CTS losing its independence under unattractive terms. They decided to pay greenmail because "the Belzbergs did not put up much of a fight and they made a reasonable [settlement] offer," Hostetler said.

The Belzbergs may have owned 4.9 percent of CTS for years, forgot about it, and then decided to sell out, Hostetler speculated. As stated previously, he does not believe that paying greenmail to the Belzbergs put CTS "in play," but, rather, that the board's actions reduced arbitrage interest in CTS.

"The Belzbergs' goals were of a short term nature impairing CTS's ability to maximize opportunities for the benefit of all shareholders," according to the May 10, 1982, CTS press release.

A derivative action was filed against CTS later in 1982 by Ann Brown of Edgewater, New Jersey, an owner of ten CTS shares, over the Belzberg greenmail payment. Hostetler said CTS paid $50,000 for an out-of-court settlement of Brown's suit. "For $200,000 we could have won the suit, or paid $50,000 to settle," Hostetler said.

The acquisition by CTS of Micro Peripherals, Inc. (MPI), headquartered in Chatsworth, California, with manufacturing plants in Singapore and Mexico, was the next major event in the CTS-DCA saga. CTS announced plans to buy MPI on April 27, 1983, and it closed the deal on June 17, 1983. CTS stock sold for $33.50 to $57.75 a share during the second quarter of 1983. The price shot up to over $57 a share after the MPI acquisition was announced because "we [CTS] told the market what it wanted to hear—high tech," Hostetler said.

For MPI, a manufacturer of floppy disk drives for home computers, CTS paid $1,884,000 in cash and issued 1,302,136 shares of CTS common stock that were held in treasury. CTS had about 4.2 million shares outstanding at the time, of which DCA owned 977,400 shares. The MPI acquisition diluted DCA's holding from 23.2 percent to 17 percent of CTS.

Lozyniak first objected to the MPI acquisition during May 1983. "CTS ignored our advice and completed the transaction," he wrote in a letter to CTS shareholders on March 27, 1986. Its dissatisfaction plus the run-up in the price of CTS stock apparently led to DCA selling 500,000 shares of CTS stock for $50.25 a share on July 23, 1983, CTS reported in a press release on that date.

Lozyniak's fears were justified. During 1983, MPI posted a $7.7 million operating loss, and that swelled to $13.7 million in 1984. On September 24, 1984, CTS announced plans to close MPI, for which CTS took a $37 million pretax writedown.

"We bought MPI at the worst possible time, shortly before a recession in the home computer market," Hostetler said.

Lozyniak was not as kind. "The MPI misadventure involved far more than a business judgment which happened to turn out badly, but rather a reckless disregard of sound business practices," he wrote to CTS shareholders.

Except for the litigation that was settled during 1985, the CTS-DCA situation was at a standstill until March 10, 1986, when DCA announced its $43 a share cash tender offer for 1 million shares of CTS. DCA stipulated it would buy only the tendered shares for which it would also have voting rights. The additional 1 million shares would increase DCA's stake to 27.5 percent of CTS, which DCA wanted to vote to oust the incumbent CTS board during the CTS annual shareholders meeting on April 25, 1986. CTS hired Smith Barney, Harris Upham & Co., Inc., on March 11 as its financial advisor.

On March 7, 1986, the last full day of trading before DCA announced its tender offer and proxy contest, CTS stock closed at $35.625 a share. On March 13, 1986, the first full day of trading before it was possible to tender to DCA, CTS stock sold for $40.125 a share. (Actually, CTS traded between $30.25 and $36 during most of the first quarter of 1986. The price rose to near $36 shortly before DCA announced its tender offer because there were rumors that the CTS board would repurchase some of the corporation's stock, according to Henry Kensing, Vice President and General Counsel for DCA, who serves as DCA's spokesman.)

Hostetler replied in a letter to shareholders on March 13, 1986, by urging them to reject DCA's "limited tender offer" because it was "essentially a vote-buying scheme to obtain control of CTS for the benefit of DCA without paying all stockholders the premium normally associated with a change of control." He was worried about a coercive two-tiered tender offer with an assumed lower back end. Hostetler said that the board would study DCA's offer and report to the shareholders prior to March 27. He urged shareholders to wait at least until then before tendering their shares. His letter of March 24 noted that the DCA offer would not expire until midnight on April 10.

The eight-member CTS board, five of whom were outside directors, declared on March 24, 1986, "the partial tender offer is unfair (as determined by its financial advisor, Smith Barney, Harris Upham & Co., Inc.) and urges shareholders to reject the offer. If DCA is successful in the offer, CTS may be controlled by a dominant minority shareholder whose interest may conflict with those of other shareholders."

The DCA tender offer expired at midnight April 10, 1986, so CTS had only seventeen days to erect a defense. It set out on a two-pronged strategy. It requested a hearing before the Indiana Securities Commissioner, which was scheduled for April 10, seeking an injunction to prevent DCA from buying tendered shares and for protection under Indiana's control share acquisitions provision. Because DCA was attempting to increase its stake in CTS to more than 20 percent, the new law, passed by the Indiana legislature only a few weeks earlier, applied. Under the new law, DCA would not have been allowed to vote its newly acquired 1 million shares unless a majority of disinterested shareholders, all of those except DCA and CTS management, voted to grant voting rights to DCA's newly acquired 1 million shares.

The other feature of CTS's defense was the adoption by its board of the first of three poison pill shareholders' rights plans. Smith Barney presented the plan on March 22. The first CTS poison pill was a "flip-in/flip-over" plan which would have been triggered if DCA or any other unfriendly shareholder acquired more than 15 percent of CTS. The plan would dissuade a hostile acquirer from buying more than 15 percent of CTS, because it would allow other CTS shareholders to exchange their "rights." One right was attached to each share, for a unit consisting of one CTS share and a senior subordinated debenture. The right allowed shareholders to buy each share-debt unit for one-fourth its market price at the time. The debt-equity proportion would be adjusted so that no more than $80 million in new debt would be issued. In addition to diluting the hostile acquirer's investment in CTS, the rights plan also would have allowed CTS shareholders to buy the acquirer's common stock for half price.

The pace of activity accelerated during mid-April. On April 10, Susan Getzendanner, a U.S. District Court judge for the Northern District of Illinois, ruled Indiana's control share acquisition provision could not be used against DCA because it "creates an impermissable indirect burden on interstate commerce." On April 15, the Indiana Securities Commissioner ruled DCA's tender offer could continue, and on April 17, Getzendanner enjoined CTS from using its first poison pill plan against DCA. CTS then appealed to the 7th Circuit Court of Appeals. Meanwhile, DCA extended its tender offer deadline from April 10 to April 14, then April 17 and finally April 24.

After the conclusion of NYSE trading on April 23, 1986, the 7th Circuit affirmed Judge Getzendanner's decisions (April 9 and 16) enjoining CTS from using the flip-in/flip-over poison pill and affirming her decision that Indiana's control share acquisition provision was an unconstitutional burden on interstate commerce.

DCA then agreed to buy 1 million of the 2,093,826 CTS shares that were tendered to it as of 5 P.M., April 24. Because its offer was oversubscribed, DCA purchased on a pro rata basis as required by the Williams Act. If one tendered 100 shares, DCA purchased forty-eight for $43 each and returned the other fifty-two shares.

On April 24, the price of CTS stock jumped $6.75 a share, closing at $44.50 in NYSE trading. Some CTS shares sold for $44.75 that day. In retrospect, "smart" shareholders would have sold all their stock in the open market.

The CTS board and senior management scrambled to erect new defenses on April 24. The board adopted a second, significantly different poison pill that would have been triggered by any shareholder acquiring 28 percent or more of CTS, and more radically, it announced a white knight strategy. "While the board believes that the long-term interest of CTS shareholders would be best served if CTS remains independent, the board recognizes that, as a practical matter, this is no longer consistent with the goal of maximizing value for all shareholders given DCA's stock ownership and apparent intentions."

The second poison pill, when triggered, would have allowed CTS shareholders to exchange each of their shares for a one-year note worth $50 in principal that would pay 10 percent interest per annum. This was intended to discourage a hostile acquirer from buying a large stake in a company that was overloaded with debt. Looking back, this was a desperate act, because it required the CTS board auctioneers to prove that $50 a share, or $280 million, was a reasonable price to pay to control CTS.

The CTS board would redeem, by paying five cents a share, the poison pill if a white knight was willing to pay at least $50 a share for all 5.6 million outstanding CTS shares. DCA, owning 1 million more votes and believing the other CTS shareholders would be angry about what it believed were the CTS board and management's entrenchment efforts, wanted the annual shareholders' meeting to take place on schedule on April 25, 1986. The CTS board wanted the meeting postponed until May 16, 1986, and the 7th Circuit Court of Appeals allowed the postponement, despite DCA's objections. CTS announced that a special committee made up of its five outside directors would be in charge of attempts to sell the company, and CTS hired Merrill Lynch Capital Markets to assist the special committee and Smith Barney.

Although she enjoined the first poison pill, Judge Getzendanner denied, on May 5, DCA's request for an injunction to prevent CTS from usng the second poison pill. Judge Getzendanner stated that would involve "too much second-guessing" of management decisions.

However, Judge Getzendanner ordered CTS to correct the "materially misleading" statements and "several material misrepresentations and omissions" in CTS's press release on April 24 and letter to shareholders on April 29, so that they could be better informed when deciding which slate of directors to elect.

Concerning the $50 a share asking price that was tied to the white knight strategy, Judge Getzendanner wrote, "$50 a share in the near term is highly unlikely and in a year's time is an outside high value based substantially on untested optimistic management projections of CTS's 1987 sales and earnings. According to Smith Barney, if the company is in fact sold within the next 50 days, the most likely price is $40 a share."

She also ordered the CTS board to admit to the shareholders that the spring of 1986 "is not the right time to sell and that its plan to sell is based on the Board's fear that DCA would win the proxy contest unless the white knight strategy was adopted and on the Board's general distrust of DCA."

Judge Getzendanner also agreed with DCA's belief that CTS shareholders needed to be aware that CTS might be prevented by restrictive covenants with its current lenders from issuing all $200 million of the new debt as stated in the second poison pill plan.

If CTS could not issue all of the debt once the pill is triggered, then Judge Getzendanner wrote that some "shareholders will remain shareholders and they will be shareholders of a company that may have incurred substantial debt." So the value of their equity investment would be greatly reduced, as CTS claimed would be the result if DCA pulled off a two-tier takeover.

Because they could not get the second poison pill invalidated, and out of concern that shareholders would vote for the incumbent CTS board because of the $50 a share asking price white knight plan, DCA responded on May 7 by saying it would also sell CTS, if the DCA slate was elected to the CTS board.

Apparently, this was DCA's attempt to win more proxy contest votes. "It is unlikely that a price in excess of $50 a share can be obtained," Lozyniak wrote. "Our proxy solicitation efforts with some of CTS's more substantial shareholders have convinced us that the decision by the CTS board to sell, which in our judgment is ill-timed, cannot be reversed without substantial damage to CTS shareholders."

According to the Circuit Court of Appeals Judge Richard Pozner, DCA, at a time during the proxy contest, said it could sell CTS for $45 a share. Lozyniak added that DCA would not sell its 27.5 percent of CTS for at least six months and that DCA had more incentive to find a buyer willing to pay the highest price than "the outside directors of CTS who own virtually no CTS stock."

On May 8, CTS disclosed that its financial advisors had been contacted by "over 30 companies" interested in buying CTS, some of whom entered into confidentiality agreements. The $50 asking price white knight strategy was successful because the incumbent CTS board was reelected with 53 percent of the shareholder votes cast on May 16. (CTS bylaws required only a simple majority.) That means the incumbent CTS board received 73 percent of the votes that were not controlled by DCA. CTS's slate got about 2,989,200 votes; 50 percent of 5,649,900 is 2,824,700.

The setback in the shareholder vote prompted DCA to go to the 7th Circuit Court of Appeals again, to seek an injunction against the second poison pill.

However, because the next CTS annual meeting was a year away, the 7th Circuit did not advance the DCA-CTS case on its calendar as it did with the first poison pill case. On June 20, George Sommer replaced Hostetler as chairman. Hostetler continued as CEO and a director. On July 29, CTS disclosed a $2.7 million loss in second quarter due to slack electronic components demand, the cost of new product startups, and $2.8 million expense due to fighting the tender offer, the proxy contest, litigation, and sale process. To reduce operating costs CTS closed plants in Bentonville, Arkansas, and Ashville, North Carolina.

The Court of Appeals refused to enjoin the second poison pill, in a ruling issued November 3, 1986. However, Judge Pozner, the author of the opinion, was very critical of the methods CTS and its financial advisors used in setting the $50 a share asking price and the 28 percent trigger. Judge Pozner remanded the case back to Judge Getzendanner because he did not believe the Court of Appeals had enough information to enjoin the pill. However, he wrote that there were indications the poison pill defense primarily was intended so "the current management and directors would keep their jobs."

DCA used Judge Pozner's criticisms as a reason for demanding, on November 11, that the CTS board either redeem the poison pill or put the question of adopting a poison pill defense up to the shareholder vote. That apparently prompted the CTS board, on November 21, to redeem the second poison pill and to immediately adopt a third pill, which was identical to the second, except the asking price was lowered from $50 to $35 a share. The lower price "more closely reflects the price at which the board presently believes CTS may be sold," wrote Ted Ross, the outside director who headed the CTS special committee in charge of finding a white knight. As with the second poison pill, the third shareholder rights plan was to expire on April 23, 1987.

Lozyniak responded by going to the 7th Circuit Court of Appeals seeking the appointment of a receiver to manage CTS, a court-ordered special shareholders' meeting, and an injunction against the third pill. He wrote that the lower asking price showed "CTS has recklessly and irrationally abandoned the goal of shareholder wealth maximization and is now completely out of control. . . . DCA will hold the directors of CTS personally responsible for damages for huge losses incurred by shareholders by reason of their unlawful efforts to entrench themselves at CTS."

The lower asking price finally produced a prospective white knight, the AVX Corporation, another electronics manufacturer headquartered in Great Neck, New York, which offered $35 worth of securities for each of the 5.6 million outstanding shares of CTS. "We'd certainly not do anything that is not friendly or pleasant," AVX Chairman and CEO Marshall Butler said about the proposed CTS-AVX merger.[1]

AVX disclosed its $35 a share offer on December 16, 1986, and on December 17, the CTS board announced it would accept other bids, including bids from

DCA. One can say DCA called their bluff by submitting two bids on December 19 to exchange DCA securities worth $37.50 for each CTS share.

For each CTS share, AVX offered one AVX share plus a senior convertible debenture paying an interest rate that would raise the value of the unit to $35. One of DCA's offers was identical, except the interest rate on the DCA debt, plus the share of DCA stock, would total $37.50. The other offer would have provided one DCA cumulative preferred share, paying a $1 annual dividend, for each CTS share. The DCA preferred would have been convertible into two shares of DCA common stock after five years.

AVX did not match DCA's offers. Possibly it could not, as Standard & Poor's and Moody's both placed AVX's senior subordinated debentures on their credit watch lists for possible downgrading if the CTS-AVX merger was completed.

AVX let its offer expire on December 23, 1986, while DCA extended its offers several times during December and January so it could perform a "due diligence" investigation of CTS, after signing a confidentiality accord.

However, on January 23, 1987, DCA withdrew its offers because its financial advisors, Kidder, Peabody & Co., concluded that $37.50 a share was too high a price to pay for CTS. Kidder, Peabody concluded it would be unfair to DCA shareholders to pay $37.50 a share for CTS, said Henry Kensing, the spokesman for Lozyniak.

The news did not get any better. On January 26, 1987, CTS announced it would phase out Printex and take an $18 million pretax loss against its fourth quarter 1986 earnings. When it revealed its 1986 financial results in late February, CTS posted a $26.6 million loss from continuing operations during 1986. That was reduced to a net loss for the year of $13.1 million because of CTS's $7.2 million profit from the sales of another subsidiary in January 1986, and a $6.3 million tax benefit for a net operating loss carry forward.

Contributing to CTS's $26.6 million operating loss was $7.6 million in expenses related to the lawsuits and proxy fight against DCA and the efforts to sell CTS. Questions began to be raised about whether CTS could survive.

Finally, the CTS and DCA board reached an agreement, ratified on March 3 and disclosed March 4, 1987, calling for Lozyniak and two other DCA directors to join the CTS board. The three DCA representatives replaced three CTS board incumbents, including Hostetler, who also lost his jobs as the President and CEO and CTS. (The agreement called for Hostetler to receive a $450,000 severance payment.)

The financial market reacted negatively because the agreement took away any chance shareholders had of being paid a takeover premium in the immediate future. The price of CTS stock fell $2.125, to $27.50 a share, the fifty-two week low at the time, on March 4.

Both sides agreed to drop all pending litigation and to place two questions before CTS shareholders during the annual meeting scheduled for May 22, 1987: whether CTS should reimburse DCA $2,178,00 for expenses incurred in the takeover fight; and whether to grant an option allowing DCA to purchase up to

35 percent of the outstanding CTS shares, at $29.625 a share, within a year after the 1987 meeting.

During the period from May 22, 1987, to May 22, 1988, an 80 percent vote by the new seven-member CTS board would be needed to amend the CTS bylaws, adopt poison pills, and change the size of the CTS board or the date of the annual meeting, according to the agreement. The third poison pill was allowed to expire on schedule on April 23, 1987, and DCA agreed not to increase its holding to more then 35 percent prior to May 22, 1988.

Under the agreement, if 80 percent of the CTS board could agree on a slate of director candidates by March 1, 1988, then both sides could solicit proxies, and the annual meeting would be postponed sixty days. Ultimately, the parties agreed on a slate and this clause did not become effective.

Ironically, after CTS and DCA reached the settlement, the U.S. Supreme Court, on April 21, 1987, surprised most observers by declaring the Indiana Control Share Acquisitions provision to be constitutional. In a 6 to 3 vote, the Court ruled that the Indiana law did not violate the Williams Act by preventing tender offers.[2]

The March 3 agreement stated that both parties would be bound by the Supreme Court ruling on whether DCA would have voting rights for 1,020,000 of its shares. (That included the 1 million bought as a result of the tender offer and 20,000 shares that DCA bought on January 28, 1986, which the Indiana law considers a part of the same purchase, because it was made within ninety days of the tender offer purchase.)

The agreement also amended the CTS bylaws to "opt out" of the Indiana Control Share Acquisitions provision. That means the law would not apply to any shares bought by DCA after March 4, 1987.

The landmark Supreme Court decision set the stage for the first vote on the question of whether a large shareholder should be granted voting rights for the shares of an assumed target corporation that exceeds a specified threshold. That vote occurred during the CTS annual shareholders meeting on May 22, 1987, and the result was surprising.

The new CTS board amended the proxy materials and recommended that disinterested shareholders grant the voting rights to DCA's 1,020,000 shares, along with the recommendations to pay the reimbursement to DCA and grant the stock option to DCA. We assumed CTS shareholders would either grant DCA the voting rights, pay the reimbursement and provide the stock option, or they would reject all three. Because the CTS board recommended that the shareholders approve the voting rights, the reimbursement and the option, we thought all three proposals would pass. The only split decision we anticipated would have been the approval of the voting rights but denial of the reimbursement and the option. However, the shareholders refused to provide the voting rights, but agreed to pay the reimbursement and provide the stock option.

On the voting rights question, the owners of 1.6 million shares voted to grant voting rights to DCA's 1,020,000 shares. That was not enough, because the

Indiana law required a majority of the "eligible shares" to be voted in favor of providing the voting rights to DCA.

Because DCA and CTS insiders could not vote their shares on the voting rights question, there were 4,088,930 eligible shares, and DCA needed a favorable vote from the owners of at least 2,044,465 shares.

The owners of about 1 million shares voted against providing the voting rights to DCA, the owners of another 150,000 shares voted to abstain, and 1.5 million shares were not voted at all. According to the Value Line Investment Survey, institutional investors owned slightly less than 2.5 million CTS shares during the first quarter of 1987, the mostly timely information available.[3] We assumed institutional investors would be short-term profit maximizers who would vote, as a matter of principle, to grant voting rights to DCA's 1,020,000 shares.

DCA did receive 1.6 million favorable votes on the voting rights question, so maybe most of those votes came from institutional shareholders opposed to antitakeover legislation what could reduce the amount of quick profit opportunities from hostile takeover battles.

If all institutionally held shares were voted (and that is a big assumption, because 1.5 million shares were not voted at all), then DCA would have needed affirmative votes from 80 percent of the institutional holders. Instead, it received favorable votes from, at most, 64 percent of the institutionally held shares. Possibly this shows that there are significant numbers of institutional shareholders who are long-term investors, who look to a company's fundamentals when deciding whether to hold or sell.

This proposition is substantiated by comparing the amounts of CTS shares held by institutions during 1986 and the first quarter of 1987. During the first quarter of 1986, institutions owned a little more than 2.8 million CTS shares, and that fell 2.1 to 2.2 million shares during the final three-quarters of 1986. The number of CTS shares held by institutions then climbed to almost 2.5 million during the first quarter of 1987.[4]

We can assume arbitrageurs bought significant amounts of CTS stock during March and April 1986 when DCA's tender offer was open and then sold their stock because no white knight appeared and the courts upheld the second poison pill. As a result, there were few if any arbitrageurs owning CTS stock prior to the CTS shareholders vote on the CCA voting rights question during the spring of 1987. Despite losing the right to vote 1,020,000 of its shares, DCA won the reimbursement and option votes because it needed fewer affirmative votes.

There had to be more shares voted in favor of paying DCA the reimbursement than shares voted against. To be granted the stock option, DCA only needed affirmative votes from a majority of the votes cast during the meeting.

DCA received 2.1 and 2.2 million affirmative votes on the reimbursement and stock option questions. Both Kensing and Jeannine Davis, CTS's Corporate Counsel, assume DCA voted its 534,000 eligible shares and CTS insiders voted their 236,000 shares in favor of paying the reimbursement and granting the option to DCA. Most of the 1.6 million shares voted in favor of voting rights for DCA, plus the 770,00 shares controlled by DCA and CTS insiders apparently provided the 2.1 and 2.2 million share vote totals in favor of paying the reimbursement and stock options. DCA prevailed on the reimbursement question because it received 65 percent of the eligible shares and 70 percent of the eligible votes on the option question.

OTHER DEVELOPMENTS

The CTS board voted on June 29 to cut the second quarter dividend from 25 cents to 12.5 cents a share. The market's reaction was neutral to slightly bullish. The dividend cut had a neglible affect on the price of CTS stock. The stock price fell $1 a share immediately following the announcement, but the stock price remained within the $25 to $30 a share trading range that CTS occupied for much of the second quarter of 1987. Quite possibly, the dividend reduction was viewed positively by the market because it would allow CTS to reinvest a larger amount of income to bring new products to market.

For the second quarter of 1987, CTS reported pretax operating income of $2.1 million, $3.6 million for the first half of the year (sixty-four cents per share).

Although the prospect of being paid a takeover premium had dropped to nil, institutional investors were beginning to load up on CTS stock because they were coming to view it as a growth company that could be bought relatively cheaply. The amount of CTS shares held by institutions increased from slightly less than 2.1 million during the fourth quarter of 1986 to slightly less than 2.5 million in the first quarter of 1987.

Value Line forecast that CTS would earn $1.35 a share during 1987, $1.75 a share during 1988, and $3.50 a share annually from 1990 to 1992. Value Line also forecast an average price-earnings ratio of 13 for CTS during the 1990–1992 period, which would place its stock price at about $45.50 a share.[5]

As a reason for the improved outlook, Kensing took a slap at Hostetler when he said CTS's performance had improved because, "The new board and management has returned the operation to basics rather than a grand strategy of being the OEMs' favorite supplier."

During the due diligence process in January 1987, Kensing said Lozyniak and George Sommer, who was appointed to replace Hostetler, developed "a mutual respect." Davis agreed that a healthy, cooperative atmosphere developed between CTS and DCA executives.

There were days in late August when the price of CTS was slightly above the $29.625 a share price at which DCA could exercise its option to buy more CTS shares. CTS would issue about 650,000 new shares for purchase by DCA at $29.625 each if DCA exercises its option. Kensing declined to say at what market price DCA might exercise its option to buy the additional 650,000 shares, which would increase DCA's holding from 27.5 to 35 percent. Kensing said he did not know if such a target price had been computed and that he would not reveal it if he did. The price of CTS backed off to between $28 and $29 a share during mid-September, and was between $27 and $28 in late September. It was assumed by brokers who follow CTS that its price fell due to a general stock market correction. All this proves that CTS shareholders who held onto their CTS stock from January 1986 until September 1987 did not benefit from any capital appreciation despite the record setting bull market. Shareholders who did not sell when the company was in play during March and April 1986 had the value of their investment reduced by CTS's defensive measures, particularly the second poison pill with the unrealistically high $50 a share reservation price. Had the agreement between DCA and CTS, which included dropping all pending and potential legal claims, not been reached, then we believe the previous CTS board could have been found liable for a breach of fiduciary duty for approving the second poison pill.

STATE REGULATION OF CORPORATE MATTERS—A UNIFORM CORE

Although the federal government plays an important regulatory role in corporate matters, primarily through securities legislation, the basic governance of corporations occurs at the state level. The fact that corporation law is state law has not resulted in a crazy quilt pattern of fifty different rules. To a large degree, uniformity exists in the corporate law field. Practicality requires such a result if corporations are to flourish in sophisticated markets which neither respect the geographical boundaries of the states nor even national borders. The entrepreneur is free to incorporate within the venue of his or her choice, and this also tends to encourage uniformity. If a particular state offered a system of corporate governance superior to that of other states, one would expect not only new incorporations to disproportionately originate there, but also existing corporations to transfer their state of incorporation to that location. With tangible benefits, such as tax revenue, and intangibles, such as state pride and reputation, being at stake, it is natural that states do not allow themselves to be placed in such circumstances. If one state adopts a regulatory scheme unusually attractive to the business world, the remaining states gradually amend their statutes to conform.

This copying of statutes, frequently word for word, strengthens uniformity two ways. First, of course, is the fact that a regulatory philosophy spreads from one state to another. There is a second subtle, albeit strong, influence toward uniformity. The initial state to adopt the legislation is where one expects the first litigation over its application and interpretation to occur. If the state is home base legally of a multiplicity of corporations, one also expects litigation under the state's business corporation law to occur with greater frequency. The result is a judicially created body of law developing within the jurisprudence of the model state. Thus, when the courts in the second state must interpret its law, the greatest body of interpretative decisions is by the highest court of the model state. Although those decisions are only of a persuasive value, and not precedently binding, they tend to be followed, thereby increasing a tendency toward uniformity.

Finally, there is a constitutional basis that places outer limits upon the diversity permitted the individual states. Governments are recognized as having the inherent power of legislating for the promotion of the health, welfare, safety, and morals of their citizenry. This so-called police power enables the states to regulate corporate affairs. Nonetheless, this power is not unbridled. The United States Constitution bestows upon persons a right to due process, equal protection of the laws, privileges of citizenship, free speech and assembly rights, and so forth, as well as granting to the federal government the power to regulate interstate commerce. These constitutional provisions place parameters upon the states exercise of their police powers. The states retain a substantial degree of flexibility in making public-policy judgments when enacting legislation. However, the Constitution does tie together the sovereign states into one nation by creating a uniform system of boundaries beyond which the states may not regulate. This constitutional bar against certain forms of regulations, which applies uniformly to all states, tends to create, if not one uniform system, similar legislative responses to common problems. Thus, there exists a strong degree of homogeneity within the business corporation statutes of the fifty states.

THE LEGAL OBLIGATIONS OF DIRECTORS

The board of directors possesses the exclusive legal authority to manage the corporation. The shareholders own it, and the officers may operate it on a day-to-day basis, but it is to be managed by the directors.[6] In the words of the Delaware law: "The business and affairs of every corporation . . . shall be managed by or under the direction of a board of directors."[7] This authority is balanced by an obligation to exercise it in a prudent manner. The directors must exercise business judgment in making corporate decisions or, put another way, they owe a duty of care to the corporation.

The problems inherent in conflict of interest situations have long been recognized in both the religious ("No man can serve two masters," Matthew 6:24) and secular ("A house divided against itself cannot stand," A. Lincoln, 1865) domains. The corporate law imposes upon corporate directors a fiduciary obligation. The fiduciary concept is not confined to corporate law, or within corporate law, to only directors. It is a concept of widespread broad applicability that exists in relationships where one is acting for and on behalf of another. Both parties stand in a fiduciary relationship to each other and owe each other the utmost loyalty and good faith. One violates this duty if, without the knowledge and consent of the other, one acts in any manner that is inimical to the interests of the other. Directors are to act in the best interests of their corporation. Their self-interest and the interests of third parties are to be disgarded when making corporate decisions.[8]

Adolf Augustus Berle and Gardiner Coit Means in their famous book, *The Modern Corporation and Private Property* (1932) point out how the control of large corporations has been separated from ownership of those corporations. Professional managers operate the entity for its diverse owner-stockholders. The directors owe a duty of loyalty and due care to their corporation. They do not owe it to other directors.[9] We are not speaking of the type of disloyalty involved in embezzlement, although such faithlessness is both criminally illegal and in violation of a director's fiduciary duty. We are considering the nature of the due care to be exercised when directors of a target company make corporate decisions which affect both the raider and other shareholders. Directors exercise such due care by making decisions based upon informed business judgment. This duty mandates that the board's action recognize that it acts on behalf of another— the corporation.

Complicating the matter is determining exactly who the corporation is. The corporation is the legal entity created and recognized by the state of incorporation. That definition does not provide practical guidance to a director pondering what course is in the best interest of a corporation when he or she does not perceive a legal fiction, but instead beholds a mosaic consisting of employees, retirees, customers, suppliers, a community at large, and the stockholders. Not only may the interests of these various groups vary, but the groups themselves are not homogeneous. The interests of a worker eligible for early retirement differ from those of a more recently hired employee. The institutional investor has a different perspective from that of a small stockholder. The CTS directors hold only 4.17 percent of the stock, as opposed to DCA, the largest holder, who has 27.5 percent. Recognizing the quandary that directors face, let us turn to how they frequently act when confronted by the threat of a hostile takeover.

REJECTION OF OFFER FOR INADEQUACY OF PRICE

A common response of the target company's management to a hostile bid is to label it financially inadequate. This characterization is communicated to the shareholders as a major reason why they should rebuff the offerer's unsolicited bid, despite the fact that it is greatly in excess of the stock's market price before the announced offer. The fact that the market had previously valued the securities at a lower price raises some doubt as to management's assertion that the offer does not reflect the true value of the stock.

Occasionally, management seems to be sincere in opposing not a takeover per se, but a takeover at that price. If the bidder increases the bid, the stockholders are enriched by management's tactic. Sometimes, particularly if the entrance of a white knight touches off a bidding war, the shareholders of the target are compensated munificently beyond the initial offer (for example, the T. Boone Pickens versus Chevron struggle for Gulf Oil).

Management often appears to oppose a takeover at any price and uses the inadequacy argument as a mere artifice. Let us examine a few select, but by no means isolated, egregious illustrations. In 1981 Chevron (then named Standard Oil of California or Socal) offered $78.50 for each share of Amax, Inc., stock, approximately double its current market price. Amax spurned the offer, and Chevron did not mount a hostile takeover. In May 1982, Amax announced a quarterly loss and cut its dividends, and its stock traded around $26.50.

In December 1977 the stock of Marshall Field traded at approximately $22 per share. Carter Hawley Hale proposed a friendly offer of $36.00. It was rejected, and in February 1978 an offer of $42 in a cash-stock combination was made. Marshall Field's acquisition of certain Texas department stores placed antitrust obstacles in front of the merger. Field stock, which had climbed as high as $34 during the struggle, collapsed to $19. If a Marshall Field stockholder held his or her stock until March 1982, he or she would have received a communication from management recommending a merger offer of $25.50 from Batus, Inc. Subsequently, to ward off a possible hostile takeover by another group, Batus raised its offer to $30, and the merger was consumated.

Diamond Shamrock has been involved in several episodes of this nature. In 1985 it tentatively agreed to sell out to Occidental Petroleum for $28 of Occidental stock per share. Later, it decided not to complete the transaction, and by the year's end its stock price had sagged to $14. In 1986 T. Boone Pickens offered limited partnership units of approximately $16 for each share. Management rejected the proposal and bought back some of its own stock, but at year's end the stock still traded in the $14 range. In 1987 Pickens offered $15 a share for 20 percent of Diamond's stock, and once again management opposed it. Notice how, in a general bull market, the successive offers decline in amount, but meet the same fate from management—rejection. When Diamond's Chief Executive Officer, William Bricker, announced in February 1987 that he was stepping down, he commented to the press, "I am proud of the value we have delivered to shareholders."[10] This was the comment of the person who had been the CEO of the organization for about a decade.

DCA was not merely a passive investor. Although it had no representation on the CTS board, it was not at all reticent about commenting publicly upon the policies and strategies of CTS management. Eventually DCA came to attempt to gain an official voice in CTS affairs.

In March 1986 DCA announced a tender offer of $43 per share for 1 million shares of CTS stock. The stock, which had been trading at about $36, was eventually bid up to $42. CTS instituted its first poison pill at this point. When the federal district court enjoined its implementation, DCA bought the shares. The offer was oversubscribed by attracting 2,093,826 shares.

DCA had also begun a proxy fight over management of CTS by proposing its own slate of directors. Since the tender offer had boosted its stockholdings to a 27.5 percent level, and since management personally controlled such a small block of stock, DCA seemed to be in a good position. Institutional investors held the bulk of the stock, and with a disappointing record of financial performance over the past several years by current management, they might be persuaded to vote their proxies for DCA. At this point CTS management announced stunning news. The board had decided to maximize the value of all stockholders by seeking the sale of the company at $50 a share of all the outstanding shares to a white knight. The stock jumped $6.75 to $44.50 a share on the NYSE in reaction to the news. In the meantime, another poison pill had been adopted to prevent DCA from going above a stock position of 28 percent.

DCA attacked the poison pill and the proxy statement announcing the open invitation to a white knight. The poison pill challenge failed. However, the district court ruled that the press release and proxy material contained material misrepresentations and omissions and ruled that CTS could not vote any proxies received after their distribution until the accurate information was submitted to the holders. As to the white knight strategy, the judge ruled it had been adopted by the board out of distrust of DCA and a fear that DCA would win the proxy contest without it, and that the directors did not believe it was the right time to sell. Additionally, the court said the holders must be informed that they should not conclude that any bidder will in fact offer $50 per share and that the CTS financial advisor had indicated that most likely price was only $40.

Whether it was the new poison pill, the belief that current management could best negotiate a sale of the corporation, satisfaction with CTS's prior management performance, or some combination of all of these, CTS was a victor in the proxy contest, with 53 percent of the stock supporting the incumbent board of directors. Chairman Hostetler of CTS said after the results of the proxy contest were announced that he could not predict a sale date, but they would attempt to arrange the sale ''as expeditiously as possible.''

Approximately one year later, management was still seeking a white knight. However, unlike 1986 when the price was $50 a share, management was now in effect shopping the company around for $35 a share. In the 1986 tax year, CTS had lost $13.3 million, or $1.83 per share of common stock.

While it is true that the market price of a stock does reflect the price of only one share, and while a controlling block of stock will bring a premium (which reflects the value of the control element), stockholders of a target company should retain a healthy degree of skepticism when evaluating management's claim that the raider's offering price does not reflect the fundamental value of the stock.

There can always be legitimate differences of opinion when one is attempting to compute the correct valuation of a business. Yet, one must question the objectivity of management that opposes an offer that exceeds by a substantial premium (in this case about 21 percent) the previous market value of a stock that is traded on a recognized stock exchange. Does the board members' incumbency actually provide that much greater insight into the true value of their corporation's securities than that possessed by industry analysts, current stockholders, those who have chosen not to buy the stock, those who have decided to sell the stock—in other words, the market as a whole? Or rather, does their incumbency, with all of its inherent perks, distort their judgment when evaluating a proposal of another, particularly that of a raider? Is acceptance of a raider's offer an admission to the stockholders, and possibly more importantly to themselves, that under their tutelage the full value of the company has not been realized?

In legal terms, the CTS announcement that it was seeking a white knight to buy all the stock of $50 per share was materially misleading, and it contained material misstatements and omissions. Yet, was it not more than that? Was it also unethical? Management did all in its power to prevent the stockholders from availing themselves of a tender offer at $43 a share, substantially in excess of its market price per share at that time. When this effort failed and the tender offer was oversubscribed, management squeaked out a victory in the proxy fight. The latter was tainted to a degree by the implication that a white knight would pay $50, when in fact there were no discussions with a potential white knight and the financial advisor of the board's own choosing stated that $40 was a more likely price. In the letter to the stockholders that honestly appraised them of the facts, which was sent at the direction of the court, the CTS directors expressed their concern that the long-term value of CTS would not be realized if the DCA nominees were elected. Hindsight shows that those same directors have accomplished little in enhancing the value of CTS shares. In a sense, the prophecy they sketched for CTS under the direction of DCA has become a self-fulfilling prophecy achieved under their own direction.

POISON PILLS—A PANACEA OR A CURSE?

The "poison pill" is an extremely popular, albeit controversial, antitakeover device. Defenders of the device often refer to it as "shareholder rights provisions." Basically, shareholders are granted the right to purchase securities of the raider at a steep discount if the raider acquires more than a certain percentage of the target's stock. If management wishes to pursue a friendly acquisition, it can redeem the rights for a token payment to its stockholders. While not halting friendly mergers, such instruments are effective barriers against hostile acquisitions. If the raider triggers the pill, it effectively commits financial suicide by diluting the holdings of its stockholders, making them angry as they observe unrelated persons acquiring shares at a discounted price unavailable to them, and increasing the overall cost of the acquisition by a substantial dollar amount by burdening the company with debt.

Opinions on poison pills run the gamut. Those at one end of the spectrum who view hostile takeovers as negative, believe them to be a legitimate defense. At the opposite end are those believing that shareholders should determine their own destiny, and they regard the pills as merely another method for management to entrench itself in office, regardless of what is best for the corporation. The legal attitude falls somewhere between the two extremes. Exactly where along the spectrum a poison pill crosses over the boundary from legal to illegal remains a subject of legal dispute. Again this is illustrated by CTS—one of its poison pills was struck down by the court, while a second was reviewed by the very same court and not struck down.

The conflict of interest inherent in poison pills is quite clear in the CTS matter. Based not only upon DCA's public criticism of various management decisions by CTS but also on its proxy fight to elect its own set of directors, it is clear that a defeat in the struggle with DCA would result in some replacement of high level CTS personnel. (Three of the CTS directors were company employees.) Thus, adoption of the poison pill makes a hostile takeover less unlikely and simultaneously decreases the chances that CTS management will lose their jobs.

The Delaware courts take this conflict-of-interest factor into account when judging the validity of defensive measures adopted by a board to thwart hostile takeovers. Why are we discussing the attitude of the Delaware courts when CTS is an Indiana corporation? The Indiana Supreme Court has not ruled in this area.

Delaware permits directors to adopt, without shareholder approval, defensive measures against hostile takeovers. Included in the category of approved defenses is the poison pill.[11] Ordinarily, when challenging board action, a shareholder has the burden of proving that the directors have not exercised proper business judgment. The Delaware Supreme Court has shifted the burden in litigation over defensive measures because of the inherent conflict of interest on the part of the board. When such measures are challenged, the directors have the initial burden of proving that they acted in good faith, exercised informed judgment, and in the honest belief that the action was in the corporation's best interests.[12]

Because of the conflict inherent in the action of directors in adopting poison pills, maybe a legal change should be legislated. To those that would argue that they possess some validity, we would respond by saying that they could be retained as a defensive device while still removing the conflict of interest by requiring that they be approved by the shareholders. The threat of a takeover is a spur in the directors' flanks to provide a superb level of performance. If poison pills too easily remove the possibility of a takeover, directors do not face as direct a challenge when their management performance has been poor. A better solution may be to eliminate poison pills completely as a legally permissible device. A more suitable replacement may be the ''fair price'' amendment to the corporation's charter. This mechanism prevents a raider from buying a controlling interest, running the acquisition as his self-interest dictates, and either ignoring or forcing out at a lower price, by means of a merger, the remaining shareholders. The conflict of interest is absent, while the goal of protecting the shareholders is advanced. An SEC study of 245 poison pill programs found that the companies' stock prices fell an average of 1.7 percent relative to the market during the two days after the pill's announcement.

The first CTS pill was enjoined by the court as a device to block DCA, regardless of the consequences to the welfare of the CTS shareholders. The initial CTS pill would have given holders the right to buy a package of securities for 25 percent of its market price whenever a stockholder would obtain 15 percent or more of CTS stock. The effect would have been to dilute DCA's position from 27.5 percent to 20.7 percent of the stock and burden CTS with $80 million of debt. The court knocked it out, saying it effectively precluded a hostile takeover, thereby making the stockholders a hostage of current management. The court viewed it as a device to block DCA regardless of the consequences to the welfare of CTS stockholders. The second was not enjoined by the court. It was characterized as not being designed to block a DCA takeover, but to maximize the price if a takeover was to occur. A legal ruling was never made on the third pill.

Looking back, it is clear that the $50-a-share reservation price set by the second poison pill was much too high and the CTS board's promise to sell the company for a minimum of $50 a share deceived CTS shareholders prior to the 1986 annual meeting. CTS's investment advisors did not fulfill their obligations to CTS shareholders by not making a reasonable effort to determine whether $50 a share was a reasonable price for CTS. Instead, CTS's investment advisors merely took management's overly optimistic 1987 earnings projection of $3.23 a share and multiplied it times 15.5, the average price-earnings ratio for electronic components manufacturers during the spring of 1986, to come up with the $50 a share value.[13] Neither Smith Barney nor Merrill Lynch Capital Markets tried to confirm independently the $3.23 a share earnings projection.

Of course, past performance does not necessarily indicate what the future performance will be, and forecasts made in good faith could end up wide from the mark. However, there are a variety of other financial valuation models, such as discounted cash flow, that analysts can select, depending on the industry in which the company operates.

The data processing industry, now CTS's primary customer, has proven itself to be cyclical. Value Line forecasts CTS's earnings per share will not reach $3.50 until the 1990–1992 period. We believe that proves that CTS's management's claim that its earnings per share would be $3.23 in 1987 was self-serving, and Smith Barney did not act as an independent financial advisor in accepting that projection without independent confirmation.[14]

The CTS board adopted the three poison pill plans to prevent DCA from establishing a blocking position. That raises the question: At what percentage of stock ownership can a large, unfriendly shareholder with a short-term profit maximization goal establish a blocking position to prevent management from implementing strategies that could maximize shareholder wealth over the long term, but which may not maximize shareholder wealth over the short term?

The first CTS poison pill assumed a shareholder owning 15 percent could establish a blocking position. The Indiana Control Share Acquisition Provision assumes a blocking position could be established by an investor owning 20 percent. The second and third CTS poison pills assumed a blocking position could be established by a holder of 28 percent, but not 27.5 percent. Judge Pozner does not believe a shareholder can establish a blocking position until it owns more than 50 percent of a company.[15] There is no conclusive empirical evidence that a minority shareholder *can* establish a blocking position.

However, to prevent shareholders from setting up blocking positions, and to prevent two-tier tender offers with a low back end, we would suggest a requirement that when a shareholder buys a certain percentage of a corporation's outstanding voting stock, the investor must then buy all remaining shares at the price at which he or she purchased the shares to reach the threshold. To prevent this measure from entrenching incompetent managements, we believe the threshold should be at 50 percent, or slightly below 50 percent, so that there could continue to be a market for corporate control.

THE ROLE OF LAWYERS AND INVESTMENT BANKERS IN TAKEOVER FIGHTS

Lawyers and investment advisors are not objective independent experts who serve in the role of providing unbiased opinions to the stockholders above whose heads the takeover battle swirls. Most stockholders probably realize that fact about the legal teams. To the distress of some in the profession, many have traditionally categorized lawyers as mere hired guns. Stockholders, knowing that management has hired the lawyers, probably regards the resulting legal advice as being tailored to fit the wishes of management—wishes that they realize may or may not conflict with their own self-interest as stockholders. If this is in fact the case, they will judge the legal opinions accordingly.

We are not so certain that the same holds true for the investment bankers. Their opinions may be viewed as unbiased, reached as a result of an objective quantitative analysis of specific financial data. As we will observe when we turn to the role of the investment advisors engaged by CTS, we believe that what holds true for the legal advisors, also holds true for the financial ones—he who pays the piper, calls the tune. Before reaching that point, we wish to first discuss why lawyers and investment bankers are necessary.

The critical need for attorneys is obvious. Takeovers, whether through mergers or tender offers, require a minimum of legal work. Frequently, it extends beyond a minimum as litigation may envelope the parties engaged in a hostile struggle. CTS and DCA have battled each other in administrative forums, the state courts, and all levels of the federal court system.

Why the need for investment bankers? Are not the members of the board intelligent individuals with diverse backgrounds who are cognizant of corporate matters and thus capable of reaching an informed judgment as to whether a takeover is or is not in the best interest of the company and, if so, what is a fair price? Yet, they often are. However, investment bankers form a shield against stockholder derivative suits.

In a 1985 case, the Delaware Supreme Court held that directors have been grossly negligent when they sold their corporation at a premium to the market without having valued it. While saying that an outside evaluation study is not required as a matter of law, the case clearly identifies outside valuation studies as being a safe harbor in which boards can most likely successfully ride out the legal storms whipped up by derivative suits. Because directors in takeovers are almost certain to anger someone, no matter what position they adopt, safe harbors are in high demand.

In 1980 Jerome Van Gorkom, the Chairman and Chief Executive Officer of Trans Union Company, a publicly traded company, approached Jay Pritzker, a takeover specialist, about acquiring Trans Union. He did it on his own, and he proposed the price per share. Pritzker subsequently offered to buy the company at $55 per share, the price named by Van Gorkom. A special meeting of the Trans Union board was convened, and the members learned for the first time of the proposal. After a meeting of approximately two hours, the board approved the proposal. As of this point, the board had never evaluated the company in an effort to value the entire enterprise nor had it ever previously considered selling the company or consenting to a merger. A stockholders' derivative suit was brought against the directors, charging them with a breach of business judgment in approving the merger. Their unsuccessful defense was to point to the premium paid for the stock above its market price and to point to the extensive business background and years of experience of the board members who approved the sale.

The Delaware Supreme Court in a 3-to-2 decision held that the board was grossly negligent in approving the transaction under the circumstances.[16] It lacked adequate valuation information for making an informed business judgment as to the fairness of the offered price. The court added, "We do not imply that an outside valuation study is essential to support an informed business judgment; nor do we state that fairness opinions by independent investment bankers are required as a matter of law."[17]

The failure of the Trans Union board to exercise proper business judgment ultimately resulted in an out-of-court settlement in the amount of $23 million. Insurance covered $10 million, Pritzker interests paid almost $11 million, and the Trans Union directors paid the remaining amount.[18]

On the same day in March 1986 that DCA announced its tender offer and declared that it would propose a director slate, CTS management announced its opposition to DCA's actions "without having studied their business and financial implications or even having consulted CTS's outside directors."[19] The following day CTS hired Smith Barney, Harris Upham & Co. as its financial advisor. The Smith Barney compensation package included the payment of a bonus if the DCA offer were defeatd. Apparently the legal advisors of CTS were aware of the Trans Union case and believed that CTS should avail itself of the safe harbor of outside financial advice, and leave to later litigation the question of the objectivity of such advice when the advisors' fee is increased if the raider is fended off.

After the DCA tender offer was successful, CTS introduced the second poison pill. It again used the services of Smith Barney, but this time a committee of outside directors actually retained it. Again the compensation package would be more favorable to Smith Barney if the wishes of CTS's board were satisfied.

Apparently it would receive an incentive fee if CTS were sold to a buyer agreeable to the board rather than acquired by a hostile raider.[20]

What did all of this cost the contestants? DCA's costs in 1986 were approximately \$4.2 million. Despite this expensive effort, it posted earnings of \$1.1 million. CTS, on the other hand, incurred expenses of \$7.6 million in fighting the takeover and lost \$13.3 million for the year. The companies provided no breakdown as to what portion of the costs were legal, investment banking, or other. Both companies would have incurred expenses in connection with the proxy solicitation effort. However, they would not have approached the magnitude of the legal and investment banking portion of the total costs. The expenses continued to mount during the first quarter of 1987 and totaled \$454,000 for CTS.

What have these costs actually purchased? A legal stalemate. The respective boards obviously believe the corporate funds to have been well spent. Stockholders and outside observers will have to decide for themselves whether the safe harbor these monies purchased for the directors also enhanced the value of the two corporations.

STATE ANTITAKEOVER STATUTES

Thus far, our discussion has focused upon the contenders in a takeover struggle—the raider, shareholders of the target corporation, and the target's management. There are others whose fate is inexorably tied to the outcome of the contest, even though they are confined to the role of observer. We are speaking, of course, of the communities where the antagonists' plants are located, the employees, the customers, and various suppliers. The states have attempted to protect their interests, and not so incidentally that of the target company, by enacting state antitakeover statutes.

The decade of the 1970s saw many states enact statutes delaying tender offers until a state official held a hearing and concluded that the offer was "fair." In 1982 the Supreme Court ruled that the Illinois statute unconstitutionally interfered with interstate commerce.[21]

With the new wave of takeovers in the early 1980s, the states began considering a new generation of such laws. In its Illinois decision, the Court indicated that states possessed the authority to legislate in this area if they carefully avoided trespassing on the domain of the federal government.

Indiana enacted a Control Share Acquisition statute in March 1986. It requires shareholder approval for a purchaser of "control" shares to vote his shares. Control shares are defined as 20 percent of the stock, or those shares that would increase one's holdings to a level of 33 or 50 percent. Only "disinterested" shareholders are entitled to vote. Shares held by the control stockholder, officers, or inside directors are not disinterested. The purchaser of the control shares can insist that a stockholders' meeting be held within fifty days for a vote on the matter.

This statute was declared unconstitutional by the lower federal courts, thereby allowing DCA to increase its holding from 9.7 to 27.5 percent of CTS.[22] In a major legal surprise, the Supreme Court upheld the law's constitutionality on April 21, 1987, by a 6-to-3 vote.

Other states moved quickly to enact similar statutes to protect their local companies who were targets of raiders, by tilting the playing field against raiders. Whether such protectionist state legislation will advance the interest and economies of a state or merely temporarily protect inefficient producers that are ultimately doomed, remains to be determined. Even though they were parties to the litigation, the case will not, at this point, affect the struggle. It has been temporarily settled.

THE SETTLEMENT

On March 4, 1987, the respective boards of DCA and CTS announced an agreement permitting three DCA directors to join the CTS board immediately. Three CTS directors, including Hostetler, resigned; Hostetler also resigned from the company. All pending litigation was dropped. The third poison pill was allowed to expire, and from May 22, 1987, until May 22, 1988, an 80 percent vote by the new CTS board was required to amend the bylaws, alter the size of the board, alter the date of the annual meeting, or adopt a poison pill. If 80 percent of the board could not agree on a directors' slate by May 1988, then both factions were free to solicit proxies. (Subsequently, this 80 percent super majority agreement was allowed to lapse in May of 1988.)

CTS probably agreed to the settlement because it faced the real chance of being defeated at the 1987 shareholders' meeting. Why did DCA agree, if it was on the verge of taking complete control? It had invested $43 million in CTS and had actually been offered three seats on the board ten months earlier. Hostetler speculates that Lozyniak discovered in the interim time that CTS was a more complicated company to run than he originally believed. Possibly DCA shareholders were becoming disenchanted with Lozyniak's pursuit of CTS. DCA's net income for 1986 of $5.3 million was reduced to $1.1 million by the auditor's recognition of DCA's share of CTS's operating losses.

Both Hostetler and Lozyniak say that they intended to maximize the value of all CTS stockholders. However, the opposite turned out to be true. An unprofitable CTS had to bear the large expenses of the takeover battle, the attention of its management was diverted from routine operations to fighting DCA, and it incurred negative publicity from the struggle.

Hostetler said he wanted to prevent Lozyniak from buying CTS "on the cheap" by establishing a blocking position which would force other shareholders to accept a lower wealth position or to sell out at a depressed price. Lozyniak offered a higher price ($43 a share) than CTS shareholders could get on the market except for a few days in late April 1986. True, he only bought about half of the shares tendered, but CTS shareholders had other opportunities to sell, after the tender offer, at prices which, if averaged with the stock sold at $43 a share, would have provided most shareholders with a profit. For example, CTS sold for as much as $37 a share during the third quarter of 1986.

Even unsophisticated shareholders realize there is a risk involved in investing in the stock market. Do they really need Hostetler to protect them from an alleged two-tier takeover by Lozyniak? Shouldn't Lozyniak's decision to invest $43 million of DCA's money in CTS during the spring of 1986 show he is interested in the future of CTS?

History proved Hostetler wrong about Lozyniak's intentions, because if DCA wanted to gain control of CTS on the cheap, it would have used a "market sweep." DCA could have canceled its tender offer and then waited for the market price to plummet before buying large numbers of CTS shares from block houses and arbitrageurs seeking to unload their CTS shares.

The fact that DCA did not engage in a market sweep bolsters its claim that it was an investor interested in the long-term future of CTS, not an opportunist looking for quick profits from market manipulations.

Hostetler said he did not set up barriers against DCA to protect manufacturing or administrative jobs in Elkhart, CTS's home base. Thus, he cannot claim that he was trying to prevent the erosion of Elkhart's economic base that could have resulted from restructurings of CTS under DCA management.

Poison pills may be adopted by competent managements, but they could end up being renewed to entrench future incompetent managements. In the 1986 DCA annual report, Lozyniak wrote that he first invested in CTS because of its "older but very successful management team" and that his dispute was with CTS's "post-1981 management."

Maybe we should be skeptical about the claims of both chief operating officers. Each probably honestly believes that he was working for the best interests of CTS, whereas the other's policies would be detrimental to the company and beneficial to his own self-interest. Yet, their own position may have colored their view and prevented an objective evaluation. The old adage "where one stands, depends upon where one sits" contains a good bit of truth. Possibly their egos could have subconsciously come into play in shaping their actions. "Ego" is a difficult concept for an efficient market to evaluate.

CONSEQUENCES OF THE SUPREME COURT DECISION

Perhaps the disinterested shareholders are merely financial intermediaries, rather than legal owners, who decide by their vote between two contesting management teams for the de jure control, and de facto ownership, of the target. Congressman John Dingell introduced legislation that in one section adopts such a viewpoint. His proposal would give any holder who owns the larger of $500,000 of stock or a 3 percent stake of the company "free and equal access" to the company's proxy machinery. This would put a raider on equal footing with the management in any proxy contest. Ideally, the shareholders would now, with full facts at their fingertips, decide which of the two competing groups, incumbent management or the raider, will be given control of the corporation.

If this viewpoint is an accurate one, the Supreme Court decision upholding the Indiana Share Control Acquisition law does not harm shareholders. Undoubtedly, it will stretch out the time necessary for a hostile acquisition and, at a minimum, thereby drive up the cost. However, if the holders view the raider as providing them more value for their stock than current management, either by offering a premium above the market or a promise of increased value by better management, one would expect them to vote rationally and permit the raider to vote the stock that he has acquired. They can vote to deny the voting rights if necessary to protect competent management or block a self-serving raider.

Judge Powell wrote that the Indiana law does not violate the Williams Act because it does not prevent tender offers and it maintains a level playing field for management and bidders. He said bidders could make conditional tender offers to the shareholders of corporations that are chartered in states with a similar provision in their business corporation laws. If the shareholders vote not to provide voting rights to the share acquired by the bidder, then the bidder can choose not to buy the tendered shares.

Many raiders need to buy shares with voting rights, so that they can take control of the company and use its cash flow to pay off the loans they obtained to buy the tendered shares. Many raiders will be unable to get all the financing they need to mount tender offers if they cannot be certain the shares they buy will have voting rights.

This could lead to fewer breakups of conglomerates by raiders. That is why Indiana-type antitakeover laws have political support. The sale of plants following the takeover of a company by an investor looking for break-up value creates anxiety among the workers, customers, and suppliers of the affected plants.

However, this may be bad economics. The breakup of conglomerates could lead to more profitable and efficient smaller companies because all energies are devoted to the core business.

The DCA experience shows that the theory may not work in practice as long as large numbers of shareholders do not vote at all. Remember, 1.5 million eligible CTS shares were not voted at all on the question of allowing DCA to vote its 1,020,000 shares. We do not know whether this shortcoming can be eliminated by more diligent proxy solicitations or whether this is a fatal flaw that disproves the theory.

Unfriendly suitors can adopt alternative strategies when pursuing targets chartered under the law of a state that contains an Indiana-type control share acquisition section. For example, the Dart Group may engage in a proxy fight to oust the Dayton Hudson board of directors before following through on its plan to buy a controlling amount of Dayton Hudson stock.

State antitakeover laws would become irrelevant if congress follows SEC Chairman David Ruder's suggestion that the SEC be given authority to preempt state laws viewed as interfering with the national market for securities. Legislation proposed by Congressmen Dingle that includes a one share/one vote could also preempt Indiana's statute, that is, if you agree with the suggestion that the CTS shareholders' vote on May 22 created two classes of CTS common stock: the 1,020,000 nonvoting shares owned by DCA and the remaining voting shares.

CONCLUSIONS

The investors who held on to their CTS shares after January 1986 had the value of their investment diminished. They were ill served by Hostetler's decisions to buy MPI and Printex. They were also ill served by Hostetler and the CTS board's defensive measures against DCA. The poison pills and the Indiana antitakeover law kept CTS shareholders from benefiting from the record-setting bull market in 1987.

One can assume the negative publicity from the long takeover fight still has a depressing effect on the market price of CTS stock. All indications are that CTS is a healthier company now than it was in January 1986. Yet, why is CTS selling for $27 to $28 a share now, when it sold for over $30 a share in January 1986?

Hostetler contends that Lozyniak is noted for a "milking management style." That involves using healthy businesses in mature industries as sources of cash to acquire other companies, instead of reinvesting in product development. He believes the lack of reinvestment in the Waring blender kitchen appliance, a product of DCA's Waring Products Division, is the best example of Lozyniak's milking style.

Hostetler said he fought Lozyniak's efforts for years because he believed that Lozyniak's management style was inappropriate for a company in electronics, a dynamic growth industry. It is apparent that the personal dislike between Hostetler and Lozyniak lengthened the battle and added to its costs. Unfortunately, the outside directors and independent legal and financial advisors, who have a duty to prevent personal opinions from affecting business decisions, did not live up to their obligations.

Hostetler eventually lost his job, as did CTS employees in Arkansas and North Carolina, due to plant closings to reduce expenses. Of course, with a $450,000 severance payment, Hostetler is more financially secure than the other CTS employees who were let go.

We can only speculate about Lozyniak's intentions toward CTS, although it appears he is a pragmatist. Certainly, with over $60 million of DCA's money invested in CTS, Lozyniak is not in a position to rock the CTS boat, at least as long as the apparent turnaround continues. Kensing, Lozyniak's very candid spokesman, does not want to speculate about whether DCA will try to gain control of the CTS board during the next CTS shareholders' meeting. If Lozyniak wanted to make a quick buck, he could have sold DCA's CTS shares long ago and invested in other companies that were in play. If he wanted to buy control of CTS on the cheap, then he could have tried a market sweep to buy 1 million or more shares for less than $43 a share.

We believe that the actions of Hostetler and Lozyniak debunk many of the arguments used to support defensive measures such as poison pills and state antitakeover laws. It appears that the CTS shareholders were financially harmed by the defensive measures that kept a CEO who needed to be replaced in office for another year. It appears that the CTS outside directors acted objectively with the shareholders' interests primarily in mind only after being threatened by DCA with personal liability suits. We believe this shows that boards of directors sometimes do not live up to their obligations to shareholders when exercising their business judgment on whether to adopt a poison pill rights plan. This is an argument in favor of federal legislation requiring shareholder votes on the question of adopting poison pills.

The Indiana antitakeover statute also creates two classes of common stock, one with voting rights and one without, if a large investor loses the disinterested shareholders' vote. The Indiana law was promoted as a way to attract corporate headquarters to the state. So far, no corporations have moved their headquarters to Indiana because of the antitakeover statute, because the corporation would also have to have a significant amount of assets in Indiana to qualify for protection under the law.

The control share acquisitions section may have protected the managements of some Indiana corporations from raiders. But the success several target corporations have had in getting their home state legislatures to pass similiar laws shows the Indiana act is irrelevant as an economic development tool.

Hostetler suggested that he looked to make CTS investments in businesses and communities that presented the greatest long-term profit opportunities. He was not out to preserve a level of investment in Elkhart for sentimental reasons. Because it only protects, at least temporarily, the jobs of senior corporate executives and is not a useful economic development tool, we believe the Indiana act interferes with the efficient functioning of the national market for securities. That is why we believe it should be preempted by federal one share/one vote legislation.

NOTES

1. "CTS Buyout," *The Elkhart Truth*, December 16, 1986.
2. CTS Corporation versus Dynamics Corporation of America, *Law Week* 55, (1986) p. 4,478.
3. Ibid.
4. Ibid.
5. Ibid.
6. While acknowledging that the legal scheme may vary dramatically from the real world, where management may be the actual powers and the directors more akin to rubber stamps, it is not within the purview of this chapter to address this issue.
7. 8 Del. C. 141 (a).

8. With some narrow exceptions, shareholders are permitted to vote on corporate matters according to their self-interest.

9. A director who aided the raider, when the other board members were assisting a white knight, may have been disloyal to the board, but did not incur liability, as his decision was based on business judgment. *Treadway v. Care*, 638 F2d 357 (1980).

10. "The Downfall of a CEO," *Business Week*, February 16, 1987, p. 76.

11. *Revlon v. MacAndres & Forbes*, 506 A2d 173 (1986).

12. *Moran v. Household Int'l.*, 500 A2d 1,346 (1985); *Unocal v. Mesa Petroleum*, 493 A2d 946 (1985).

13. *Dynamics v. CTS*, 805 F2d 705, 712 (7th Circuit, 1986).

14. Value Line Investment Survey, August 7, 1987, p. 1,040.

15. *Dynamics v. CTS*, 805 F2d 705, 712 (7th Circuit, 1986).

16. *Smith v. Van Gorkam*, 488 A2d 858 (1985).

17. Ibid., p. 876.

18. "Ruling In, Jury Still Out on Trans Union," *Chicago Tribune*, February 8, 1987, section 7, p. 9.

19. *Dynamics v. CTS*, 794 F2d 250, 257 (7th Circuit, 1986).

20. *Dynamics v. CTS*, 805 F2d 705, 710 (7th Circuit, 1986).

21. *Edgar v. Mite*, 102 S. Ct. 2,629 (1982).

22. *Dynamics v. CTS*, 794 F2d 250 (1986).

Restructuring the Airline Industry: Economics, Ethics, and Public Policy

DUANE WINDSOR

We have recently experienced a still-continuing wave of sectoral and organizational transformations involving a wide diversity of controversial business practices. These transformations include Chapter 11 reorganization bankruptcies (Continental Airline's "method" for breaking its labor contracts); privatizations (in April 1987, the United Airlines pilots' union announced its desire to buy that company for $4.5 billion); hostile takeovers (the Texas Air acquisitions of Continental, Eastern, and Frontier as viewed from a labor perspective); friendly but forced mergers (the People Express acquisition); divestitures (People tried to sell Frontier after acquiring it); employment reductions (substantial at Continental); activity relocations (Texas Air closed its Dallas hub); compensation renegotiations (which failed at Eastern, but partially succeeded in 1982 in the auto industry); and so on.[1] Corporate raiding is under close scrutiny.[2] Texaco and Pennzoil are engaged in an $11 billion litigation over the nature of contract law and third-party intervention. A great many corporate stakeholders are obviously and adversely affected by these transformations and practices. In 1986, some 3,300 firms were involved in takeovers valued at $175 billion in assets; investment banks earned commissions of $4 billion on these activities.[3]

In evaluating these changes, it is necessary to differentiate among the embedded economic, ethical, and public policy dimensions. The moral viewpoint of the economic dimension is essentially *utilitarian*: what are the social welfare impacts of sectoral and organizational transformations, given that such changes are largely driven by policy decisions (such as deregulation and free trade) or foreign competition? U.S. national security cannot be readily extricated from oil prices and the economic performance of Japan and Western Europe. Losses on certain stakeholders will clearly be imposed by these conditions. The moral viewpoint of the policy-making process is shaped heavily by such stakeholder impacts, given openness to constituency pressure. Here a *contractarian* perspective is widespread: what are the rights and political influence of the various stakeholders? The ethical dimension faces a difficult task in determining the moral obligations (or *social responsibility*) of businesses and managers under potentially conflicting utilitarian and contractarian requirements.[4]

TOWARD AN ETHICS OF ORGANIZATIONAL TRANSFORMATION

A fundamental methodological issue in any ethical investigation of business practices is to disentangle economically justifiable transformations (foreign competition, higher costs, managerial inefficiency, scale economies, market deregulation, and so on) from financial manipulations for personal gain—whether by managers with golden parachutes, corporate raiders, specialized investors, insider traders, or labor unions. It can be very difficult to distinguish political struggles over issues of financial distributions among stakeholders from genuine policy disagreements over allocative efficiency, market competitiveness, and business cycle control. There is a natural tendency to attribute moral quality to one's own position in a political struggle and to assert that preservation and expansion of one's present or desired rights is in the public interest.[5] Adopting the posture that stakeholders' present rights (to employment, income, living standards, asset values, or anything else) can never be lost is tantamount to eliminating individual risks by public policy. While certainly desirable, this process will work reasonably well only where continuous economic growth allows an ever-larger pie for distribution so that everyone gains simultaneously. Britain is now having to face the social costs of delayed economic transformation. In many respects, both our ethical and corporate governance theories are inadequate to cope with stakeholder conflicts in a static or declining economy where losses through change will necessarily be imposed on someone.[6] Furthermore, social consensus concerning profound economic restructuring and optimal public policies for such conditions is highly unlikely.

The fundamental ethical test for organizational and sectoral transformation is whether there is a redeeming social purpose or effect (utilitarian cost-benefit test) that outweighs existing contractual rights. That decision will be contestable and contested. Often the same practices (whether golden parachutes or Chapter 11 bankruptcy reorganizations) can be either faintly praised or loudly damned, depending on viewpoint.[7] A case in point is the issue of an oil import tariff, which, while clothed in national security language, is also about reversing the economic disaster in Alaska, Louisiana, Oklahoma, and Texas in particular. There are opposed sectoral and regional interests, as well as ideological beliefs at stake. Consumers would pay higher energy costs now, and may or may not have to do so for imported oil in the future. Organizational transformations are typically justified by managers and directors on the basis of maximizing shareholder wealth in changing conditions. If so, we face the perhaps unsolvable issue of interest conflict among stakeholders (investors, consumers, employees, managers, and others) that is at the heart of the corporate governance and social responsibility debate.[8]

John Shad, Chairman of the U.S. Securities and Exchange Commission (SEC), recently pledged to generate some $30 million for the Harvard Business School to study "ethics, leadership and competitiveness" (an interesting combination of purposes), evidently inspired by recent revelations of insider-trading scandals on Wall Street.[9] Yet, Michael Jensen, who holds a joint appointment with that school, argues that (1) insider trading improves market efficiency (and ultimately social welfare), and (2) the SEC should be abolished, as it impedes market competitiveness.

There is apparently a profound disagreement between the SEC legal and economic staffs over proper interpretation of insider trading, an activity that has probably increased with merger mania.[10] The SEC legal staff wants to eliminate all pre-merger-announcement stock price fluctuations as prima facie evidence of insider trading; the economics staff wonders how genuine market anticipation can be differentiated from improper tipstering. Raid targets are rarely without publicly known problems readily found in their financial statements. We can readily distinguish the intentions of raiders such as Ivan Boesky (an accused inside trader), Carl Icahn (now running TWA), and T. Boone Pickens from the causes impelling mergers. The former are concerned with financial manipulations for personal gain, regardless of their public postures about the need for organization transformations.

The crucial issues are still whether the transformations themselves are economically justified (are raiders serving a social purpose regardless of personal motivation?); and whether the resulting stakeholder and social "damages" are offset by social benefits. Economic causality and financial manipulation are typically embedded in the same transformation—together with diverse stakeholder impacts.

Evaluating the ethical dimensions of contemporary business practices is drastically complicated and intensified by the recent (and continuing) wave of both sectoral and organizational transformations in the U.S. economy. What is ultimately a profound economic restructuring in a now globalized world economy[11] has been driven by (1) violent macroeconomic and regional fluctuations (inflation, employment, income) attributable to the volatility of energy prices and profound political disagreements over federal budget policy, (2) rising international trade competition involving substantial variations in national industrial policies, and (3) long-term secular alterations in national, sectoral, and regional economic activities. In the case of the airline and telecommunications industries, we may add the effects of market deregulation adopted by public policy. With obvious scope for both community and stakeholder damage, virtually all transformations will be criticized and suspect. The legitimacy of "business judgment" will be under constant scrutiny, for both misjudgment and deliberate manipulations to obtain personal and corporate gains from changing circumstances will be widespread.

Implicit in this exposition is the existence of an underlying levels-of-analysis dilemma. By levels of analysis, I mean proper attribution of cause and effect to the international and national economy, cyclical and secular condition of the region or sector, circumstances of the particular industry and firm, stakeholder impacts, and motivations of individual actors. Only within the context of this analysis can we evaluate the intentionality of actors. I do not mean to imply that ethics depends on the situation. We may readily judge many actions and motives to be improper. Corporate raiders do not seek a public interest; the question is whether they serve it. William Agee received a $4 million golden parachute from Bendix when his attempt to take over Martin Marietta failed and Allied took over Bendix as a white knight.[12] A social purpose is hard to find in the Agee affair.

Given this framework, we may shape a series of related questions for examination by which to sharpen ethical investigation of contemporary business practices.

1. Is organizational transformation ultimately being driven by identifiable competitive stresses affecting the industry or region? Where such stresses are minimal, we may more readily suspect that financial manipulation outweighs economic justification for change.
2. If competitive stresses exist, where do they arise: in international competition, unsustainable high costs (such as debt or labor contracts, defined-benefit pension liabilities, government regulations), public policy (market deregulation in the airline and telecommunications industries)? Circumstances beyond the control of management, raiders, or investors may become mitigating factors.
3. What social purpose is finally served by the organizational transformation: economic efficiency, free trade, national security? I believe that a strong case can be made that under present conditions transformations must be scrutinized for social impact, although impacts are clearly not simply a matter of whether stakeholders are harmed. Given competitive stresses, someone is very likely going to be damaged. In the airline industry, labor compensation has been affected, and there has been considerable personnel turnover. But the rationale for the 1977 deregulation act was consumer welfare (and the alleged air safety and maintenance issue is clearly unresolved).
4. What are the contractual rights of the various stakeholders impacted directly or indirectly; and what are the social externalities of the organizational transformation? The proposed federal 1980 Corporate Democracy Act would have prevented or slowed plant relocations by requiring a Department of Labor investigation, two years' notice, and compensation to affected employees and communities.
5. To what extent do managers, raiders, and specialized investors simply benefit from economic changes driven by outside forces without providing any social value in exchange? Such gains might be halted without preventing the transformations themselves.

RESTRUCTURING OF THE AIRLINE INDUSTRY

A fundamental transformation of the airline industry has been driven largely by the 1978 air passenger deregulation act (a 1977 air freight deregulation act was also enacted). The basic outlines of that transformation should be stipulated here. A large number of firms have gone out of business through bankruptcy or merger. The most notable failure is the bankruptcy of Braniff, originally a Dallas-based regional carrier that attempted a program of national expansion. (Republic, formerly North Central, also had trouble expanding from regional to national activity; but Piedmont did not.) Delta has arranged a friendly merger with Western. Texas Air has emerged as the largest firm in the U.S. industry. Its acquisition of Continental, Eastern, and Frontier may be classified as hostile takeovers, because in such instances labor was opposed to Francisco Lorenzo's leadership. In the Eastern merger, its chairman, Frank Borman, got a $900,000 cash severance agreement, $150,000 annually as a consultant through June 1991, and fringe benefits coverage. Eastern also entered into golden parachutes with twenty-one other officers totaling (including Borman) $7.3 million.[13] Both Eastern and People Express were on the verge of bankruptcy at the time of merger with Texas Air; and Continental had been a high-cost, unprofitable carrier.

There are three main issues involved in restructuring of the airline industry: long-run impact on (1) consumer demand, industry supply, quality of service, and prices; (2) air safety and maintenance; and (3) labor employment and compensation. The purpose of deregulation was to increase consumer access to air travel at lower costs. Initially, that goal was achieved. Scheduled passenger flights have essentially doubled in the last decade. Since 1938 the industry had been a regulated oligopoly that protected monopoly power on the alleged grounds of air safety and access of many communities to air service regardless of cost. Price structure was discriminatory and reduced overall demand.[14] In July 1986, market share in the airline industry (measured as percentage of capacity) was: United 17.5 percent, American 15.1 percent, Eastern 12 percent, Delta 11.4 percent, TWA 6.4 percent, and Continental 5.9 percent.[15] TWA was taken over by an outsider raider, Carl Icahn, just ahead of Texas Air. Texas Air had unsuccessfully attempted to purchase TWA at a time when Icahn already owned 33 percent of the latter's stock.[16] After proposed mergers, Texas Air Corporation would hold 24.3 percent (590 jets compared to United's 361), adding 0.8 percent for New York Air and 5.6 percent for People Express (including 1.6 percent for Frontier, previously purchased by People Express) to Continental and Eastern. Delta rose to 19.6 percent by acquiring Western.

The first issue is whether Texas Air's emergence as the dominant carrier will reestablish monopoly power. There is reason to anticipate that demand will remain higher and prices lower than before regulation, because the market is "contestable" if not "competitive."[17] Texas Air has pursued a low price/low cost strategy. In contestable oligopolies, firms use low prices to deter new entrants. If so, the consumer is clearly better off. More obviously, the establishment of oligopolistic dominance by Texas Air resulting in higher prices and poorer service would undoubtedly result in renewed regulation by the federal government at some point.

Much of the debate has been over air safety and maintenance. This issue was much of the original rationale for regulation in 1938. However, we should note two items. This issue has been raised in part by losing stakeholders: air controllers (whose union was decertified) and labor. Second, air safety is a government responsibility assigned to the Federal Aviation Agency (FAA). If air safety needs improvement, the obvious course of action is to use a federal surcharge of the necessary amount allocated directly to the air safety and maintenance system rather than to allow excess profits to airline companies, which may or may not go to quality assurance. The Reagan administration has in fact allegedly been very slow in spending accumulated funds in the federal air trust fund.

The final issue concerns labor employment and compensation. About 40 percent of operating expenses are attributable to labor, based heavily on contracts originally structured in the pre-1978 regulated environment of high prices. The next largest operating cost components are for maintenance and fuel, which are difficult to alter. "An internal study by Arlington, Va.-based Avmark Corp. stated what many in the industry have said for years: To survive, Eastern must either get long-term economic relief from its labor unions or enter bankruptcy and impose that relief, just as now-thriving Continental Airlines did."[18] In September 1983, Continental filed for bankruptcy protection and received judicial approval to cancel its union contacts. The resulting pilot and flight attendant strike continud into 1985. Eastern was similarly facing strike deadlines and loan defaults in February 1986 when the Texas Air takeover was approved; tentative cost-cutting agreements were reached with two of three major unions, but the International Association of Machinists refused. Eastern had asked all employees to take 20 percent pay cuts and accept relaxed work rules.

Given this information, let us apply the suggested levels-of-analysis framework for evaluating organizational transformations in an industry under fundamental change. Foreign competition is deliberately excluded through selection of this case. A public policy decision to deregulate a domestic market was involved. Before 1977 the industry was a heavily regulated and largely static structure in which the same five firms had been dominant since regulation in 1938. Francisco Lorenzo clearly did not intend to serve any explicit public purpose. His regional air carrier, Texas International (TI), was being driven out of business by Southwestern Airlines; its employees, investors, and consumers, as well as himself, would have been adversely affected. The basic picture is revealed in Table 29.1. From 1977 to 1979, TI had steady financial growth. Then in 1980, net income dropped by more than 90 percent, due to competition from Southwest Airlines. The acquisition of Continental, itself a failing firm, was a desperate gamble. "In a risky legal maneuver never before made by a major American firm, Continental unilaterally scrapped its union contracts . . . as it filed its bankruptcy petition."[19] In September 1983, Continental filed bankruptcy and furloughed

Table 29.1
Five-Year Financial Summary ($ in 000's except per share data)

	1981	1980	1979	1978	1977
	Texas Air Corp. (Consolidated)		Texas International (TI)		
Operating Revenues	$ 719,400	$291,496	$234,161	$180,192	$144,787
Net Income	(47,185)	3,990	41,395	13,151	8,238
Earnings Per Share	(8.11)	0.55	5.88	2.17	1.52
Total Assets	1,301,316	385,749	319,201	194,855	108,796
Long-Term Debt	833,409	217,790	175,295	113,213	61,610
Net Worth	44,853	89,224	81,218	40,784	11,749

Source: Texas Air Corporation, 1981 Annual Report.

some 8,000 of 12,000 workers. By September 1985, employment had risen from 4,100 to 12,800 (with undoubtedly tremendous replacement); average captain's pay had risen from $43,000 to $68,000.[20] Continental is beginning to pay off its enormous debt. No doubt Lorenzo has gained by these maneuvers; and various stakeholders have suffered losses. Yet other stakeholders have arguably gained.

It is not enough to judge Lorenzo's motives and intentions, or even his wealth gains. On the contrary, a complex evaluation of social and stakeholder impacts is necessary. Many will argue correctly that consumers are suffering from complex pricing structures, air safety hazards, long delays, deceptive practices, lost luggage, and other woes. And undoubtedly they are suffering (the author has been through these experiences). Other stakeholders, especially labor, have also been adversely affected. Determining optimal public policy, however, requires weighing these losses against the manifest increase in flight availability and consumer demand combined with lower average price structure than existed before 1978. On balance, there may be substantial justification for improved safety and service regulation (the FAA is already moving to reduce flight delays and correct maintenance practices), but there exists little justification for price-quantity regulation of the type practiced before 1978 as methods for tackling these problems. Some stakeholders have gained while others have lost. Much of the recent research on the airline industry continues to sustain the deregulation argument that overall consumer welfare has been improved.

A FORMAL FRAMEWORK

This section formalizes the levels-of-analysis framework introduced above and applied to the airline industry. Figure 29.1 explicates the framework; Figure 29.2 evaluates organizational transformations at a microeconomic level of markets and stakeholders. The methodological issue in the levels-of-analysis framework introduced here is how (1) to differentiate individual motives from economic forces, and (2) to determine whether personal gain serves any legitimate social purpose. Figure 29.1 outlines the complexity of public policy trade-offs involved in both sectoral and organizational transformation. Markets (in which I include sectoral and regional economic effects) are the mechanisms by which macroeconomic effects are transmitted to stakeholders. The airline case study deliberately excludes international competition as a factor. The issue is a purely domestic policy decision about stakeholder impacts and air safety. But much of the organizational and sectoral transformations with which we must be concerned are driven by macroeconomic changes substantially affected by globalization and intensification of competition. There has been a worsening foreign trade deficit in an economy with moderately high unemployment concentrated in particular sectors and regions. The various organizational stakeholders are affectd by both the macroeconomic (effcts on economic aggregates) and microeconomic (effects on specific industry markets) impacts operating through the sectoral and regional structure of the economy. Public policy goals are a mix of real growth, free

Figure 29.1
Levels of Analysis Framework for Evaluating the Public Policy Trade-offs Involved in Economic Transformations

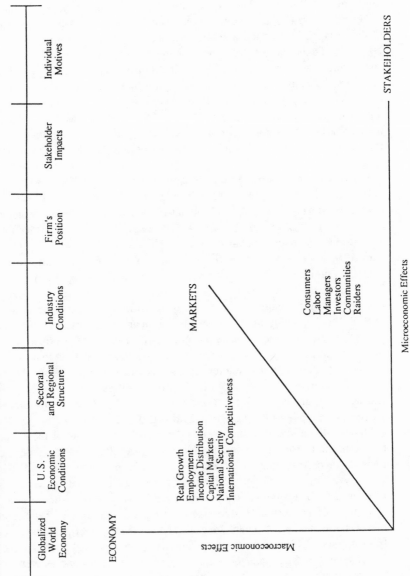

trade, income distribution, technical progress, national security, and international competitiveness issues.

Macroeconomic effects appear to be the most important. For example, many hostile takeovers are funded with junk bonds (defined as high interest rates due to speculative B rating). The widespread objection is that these bonds may prove to be worthless, shaking capital markets already viewed as precarious because of the large federal deficit and debt partially dependent on foreign (especially Japanese) purchases. At least some of the pressure on corporate management and raiders alike, however, is driven by the short-term perspective of institutional investors. Pension funds control about a third of all public equity.[21] New bonds issued in connection with target firms were less than 1 percent of new debt in nonfinancial companies during the period 1980–1983, while financial credit for the largest takeovers during 1984 was less than 1.5 percent of domestic debt.[22] By contrast, Japanese firms rely on bank debt and can take a more long-term approach.

Figure 29.2 takes a more microeconomic approach and focuses on the interaction of markets and stakeholders. The latter are categorized into external and internal wealth seekers. William Fruhan suggests that profits are allocated among consumers, marketing costs, external shareholders, and internal stakeholders.[23] Microeconomic theory contains a well-developed standard for evaluating market performance. Neoclassical welfare economics argues for consumer sovereignty through atomistic competition. Given any degree of monopoly power beyond atomistic competition, the principle of consumer sovereignty is violated, and excess consumer wealth is transferred to the firm of industry. Economic justification for this violation might be found in marketing costs such as improved product quality through technical progress. Advertising and product differentiation may simply be methods of market segmentation and thus manipulation of consumer preferences. The interesting issue is whether excess profits beyond the costs of product improvement go to the firm's external shareholders (its equity and debt capital investors) or to internal stakeholders (such as managers, employees, or suppliers) through organizational slack.[24]

Organizational transformations may be classified in terms of their types and their effects on shareholder wealth. The issue is whether transformations create, transfer, or destroy economic value; and for whom. Following Mark Hirschey we may differentiate among friendly mergers, fakeout defenses, and hostile takeovers.[25] The economic justification for a friendly merger should lie in some form of scale economy. Hostile takeovers must be justified by replacement of inefficient management. There are costs to what Hirschey terms fakeout defenses (poison pills, shark repellent, greenmail, white knights, and golden parachutes) by which entrenched management attempts to fend off raiders; as well as to the devices such as junk bonds that raiders themselves employ. Ross Perot received a $748 million payment to step down as a director of GM after a public dispute over strategy with Chairman Roger Smith. The financial economics literature tends to endorse the view that takeover mechanisms improve the market for

Figure 29.2
A Microeconomic Framework for Evaluating Organizational Transformations

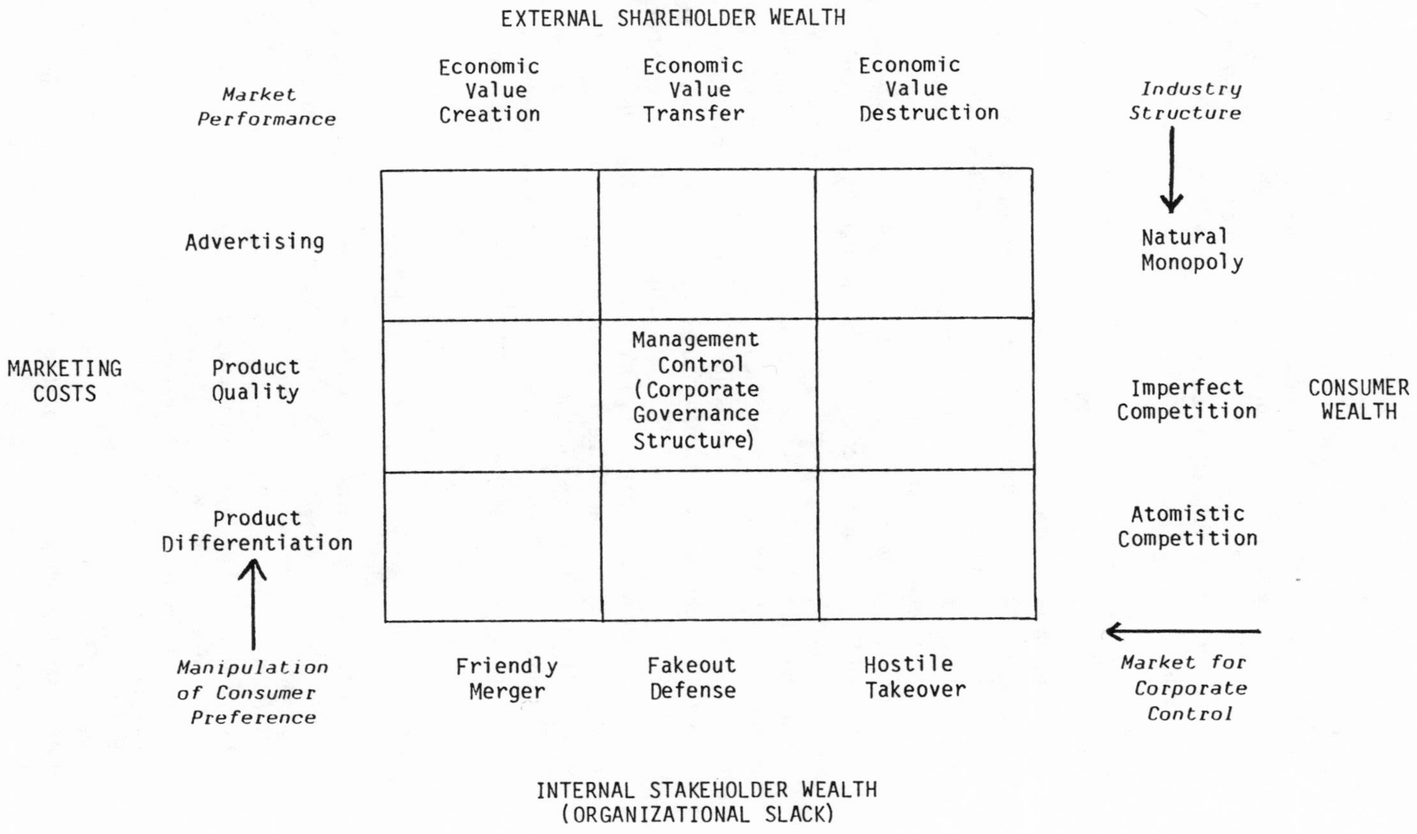

EXTERNAL SHAREHOLDER WEALTH

	Economic Value Creation	Economic Value Transfer	Economic Value Destruction
	Friendly Merger	Management Control (Corporate Governance Structure)	Hostile Takeover
		Fakeout Defense	

INTERNAL STAKEHOLDER WEALTH
(ORGANIZATIONAL SLACK)

Industry Structure →

Natural Monopoly

Imperfect Competition

Atomistic Competition

↓ *Market for Corporate Control*

CONSUMER WEALTH

Market Performance

Advertising

Product Quality

Product Differentiation ←

Manipulation of Consumer Preference

MARKETING COSTS

corporate control.[26] Hostile takeovers are only a small fraction of changes in corporate control, while "considerable evidence shows that takeover contests are beneficial for stockholders of target companies."[27] Hirschey concludes that "the perceived benefit to target firm management, and cost to target firm stockholders, resulting from a successful hostile takeover defense is more apparent than real."[28] However, Murray Weidenbaum comments that, "The cold, hard reality is that there is little organized data to affirm or discredit the efficiency hypothesis."[29]

CONCLUSION

Much of the debate over recent organizational transformations is occurring at a microeconomic level of analysis: What is happening to particular firms and their various stakeholders? Naturally, this is the general perspective of the political process, which is necessarily constituency-oriented.[30] Nevertheless, the critical test of organizational transformation is the macroeconomic effects of all the changes taken together in aggregate. Here a basic social judgment must be made about the value of competitiveness or contestability in both domestic and foreign markets. Raids and takeovers, hostile or friendly, take place in a volatile environment. The revolution in the airline industry, traceable to a public policy decision to undertake deregulation for the benefit of consumers, is a highly revealing case illustration. Since it is likely that various stakeholders will in fact suffer and that the actions of all participants (losers or gainers) are activated by financial self-interest, what must be judged is the social purpose served or damaged by economic restructuring. As I have argued elsewhere, the true essence of the problem is not that businesses fail to pursue social responsibility (they may or may not have proper incentives to do), but that social responsibility admits of no clear definition absent political struggle among stakeholders. Our legal and economic conceptions of corporate behavior do not match this political reality.[31]

NOTES

1. "1982 Auto Negotiations," Harvard Case Services 9-484-010 (revised 1984).

2. See Michael C. Jensen, ed., "Symposium on the Market for Corporate Control: The Scientific Evidence," *Journal of Financial Economics* 11, nos. 1–4 (April 1983): 1–475; and U.S. Council of Economic Advisers, *Economic Report of the President* (Washington, D.C.: U.S. Government Printing Office, 1985), 187–216.

3. ABC News Telecast, March 2, 1987.

4. These distinctions among goals (utilitarian), rights (contractarian), and obligations ("pluralistic") based ethical systems are made in Kenneth Goodpaster, "Some Avenues for Ethical Analysis in General Management," in *Policies and Persons: A Casebook in Business Ethics*, ed. John B. Matthews et al. (New York: McGraw-Hill, 1985), 492–99. I have redesignated obligations as "social responsibility," a more widely understood term.

5. See Morton H. Halperin, "Why Bureaucrats Play Games," *National Security Policy-Making: Analyses, Cases, and Proposals* (Lexington, Mass.: Lexington Books, 1975), 3–16.

6. Robert H. Hayes and William J. Abernathy, "Managing Our Way to Economic Decline," *Harvard Business Review* 58, no. 4 (July–August 1980): 67–77.

7. Peter F. Drucker, "To End the Raiding Roulette Game," *Across the Board* 23, no. 4 (April 1986): 30–39, views hostile takeovers as bad for the economy and not justified in terms of allocative efficiency, despite being arguably good for shareholders in the short run. But even Drucker observes that hostile takeovers are merely symptomatic of underlying structural problems with defined-benefit pension funds and corporate governance. Michael C. Jensen, "The Takeover Controversy: Shareholders versus Managers," *Cato Policy Report* 8, no. 6 (May/June 1986): 6–15, stresses the benefits for shareholders and the economy if the corporate-control market functions as a check on inefficient and entrenched managements.

8. R. Edward Freeman, *Strategic Management: A Stakeholder Approach* (Boston: Pitman, 1984).

9. *Business Week*, April 13, 1987, p. 40.

10. *Wall Street Journal*, March 19, 1987.

11. Theodore Levitt, "The Globalization of Markets," *Harvard Business Review* 61, no. 3 (May-June 1983): 92–102.

12. Philip L. Cochran and Steven L. Wartick, "Golden Parachutes: A Closer Look," *California Management Review* 26, no. 4 (Summer 1984): 111–25.

13. *Wall Street Journal*, September 16, 1986.

14. Duane Windsor and George Greanias, "Deregulation of the Airline Industry" (1981), case available from author; and Paul W. Mac Avoy and John W. Snow, eds., *Regulation of Passenger Fares and Competition among the Airlines* (Washington, D.C.: University of America, 1977).

15. *Wall Street Journal*, September 16, 1986.

16. "Carl Icahn: Raider or Manager?", *Business Week*, October 27, 1986, pp. 98–102 and 104.

17. William J. Baumol et al., *Contestable Markets and the Theory of Industry Structure* (New York: Harcourt Brace Jovanovich, 1982).

18. *Houston Chronicle*, February 24, 1986.

19. *Houston Chronicle*, September 8, 1985.

20. Ibid.

21. ABC News Telecast, March 2, 1987.

22. Murray Weidenbaum, "Responding to Corporate Takeovers: Raiders, Management, and Boards of Directors," Contemporary Issues Series 21, (St. Louis: Center for the Study of American Business, Washington University, October 1986), p. 7.

23. William Fruhan, *Financial Strategy* (Homewood, Ill.: Irwin, 1979).

24. The term "organizational slack" implies that costs are higher than economically optimal due to side payments to internal stakeholders. Richard E. Cyert and James G. March, *A Behavioral Theory of the Firm* (Englewood Cliffs, N.J.: Prentice-Hall, 1963).

25. Mark Hirschey, "Mergers, Buyouts and Fakeouts," *American Economic Review: Papers and Proceedings* 76, no. 2 (May 1986): 317–22.

26. Eugene F. Fama, "Efficient Capital Markets: A Review of Theory and Empirical Work," *Journal of Finance* 25, no. 2 (May 1970): 597–610; Michael C. Jensen and Richard S. Ruback, "The Market for Corporate Control: The Scientific Evidence,"

Journal of Financial Economics 11, nos. 1–4 (April 1983): 5–50; Henry G. Manne, "Mergers and the Market for Corporate Control," *Journal of Political Economy* 73, no. 2 (April 1965): 110–20. This conclusion is based on the underlying argument that managers are self-interested and therefore imperfect agents; if so, connective devices such as hostile takeovers would presumably improve allocative efficiency. Eugene F. Fama, "Agency Problems and the Theory of the the Firm," *Journal of Political Economy* 88, no. 2 (April 1980): 288–308; Michael C. Jensen and William H. Meckling, "Theory of the Firm: Managerial Behavior, Agency Costs and Ownership Structure," *Journal of Financial Economics* 3, no. 3 (October 1986): 305–60; Oliver E. Williamson, "Managerial Discretion and Business Behavior," *American Economic Review* 53, no. 5 (December 1963): 1032–57.

27. Weidenbaum, "Responding to Corporate Takeovers," 9.

28. Hirschey, *Mergers, Buyouts and Fakeouts*, 321.

29. Weidenbaum, "Responding to Corporate Takeovers," 10.

30. Joseph L. Badaracco and David B. Yoffie, " 'Industrial Policy': It Can't Happen Here," *Harvard Business Review* 61, no. 6 (November-December 1983): 97–105.

31. Duane Windsor and George Greanias, "Improving Corporate Accountability: Concepts and Proposals," in Lee E. Preston ed., *Research in Corporate Social Performance and Policy: A Research Annual* 6 (Greenwich, Conn.: JAI Press, 1984): 1–25; George Greanias and Duane Windsor, "Corporate Governance: The Legal Framework for Institutionalizing Ethical Responsibility," in *Corporate Governance and Institutionalizing Ethics: Proceedings of the Fifth National Conference on Business Ethics*, ed. William M. Hoffman et al. (Lexington, Mass.: Lexington Books, 1985), 95–106. See also Henry G. Manne, "Our Two Corporate Systems: Law and Economics," *Virginia Law Review* 53 (March 1967): 259–85.

Index

About the Editors and Contributors

BHARAT B. BHALLA is Professor, School of Business, Fairfield University.

JOHN R. BOATRIGHT is Professor of Philosophy, John Carroll University.

JAMES L. BOWDITCH is Associate Professor of Organizational Studies, Boston College.

ROBERT F. BRUNER is Associate Professor, The Colgate Darden Graduate School of Business Administration, University of Virginia.

ANTHONY F. BUONO is Associate Professor of Management at Bentley College.

ELIZABETH CALLISON is Assistant Professor of Finance, University of Colorado at Boulder.

JOANNE B. CIULLA is Senior Fellow, The Wharton School, University of Pennsylvania.

JOHN R. DANLEY is Associate Professor, School of Humanities, Department of Philosophical Studies, Southern Illinois University at Edwardsville.

VINCENT di NORCIA is Professor of Philosophy, University of Sudbury.

THOMAS DONALDSON is Wirtenberger Professor of Ethics, Loyola University of Chicago.

THOMAS W. DUNFEE is Kolodny Professor of Social Responsibility, University of Pennsylvania.

WILLARD F. ENTEMAN is Provost, Rhode Island College.

ROBERT FREDERICK is Assistant Professor of Philosophy and the Assistant Director of the Center for Business Ethics, Bentley College.

EDWARD L. HENNESSY, JR. is Chairman and Chief Executive Officer of Allied-Signal, Inc.

W. MICHAEL HOFFMAN is Professor of Philosophy, Chair of the Philosophy Department, and Director of the Center for Business Ethics, Bentley College.

LARUE TONE HOSMER is Professor of Corporate Strategy and Managerial Ethics, Graduate School of Business, University of Michigan.

HERBERT W. JARVIS is Adjunct Professor, College of Business, Rochester Institute of Technology.

JEFF KUROWSKI is a business writer for the South Bend Tribune, Indiana.

PETER LINNEMAN is Professor of Finance, The Wharton School, University of Pennsylvania.

EDWARD J. MARKEY is a member of the U.S. House of Representatives, Seventh District of Massachusetts.

ROBERT E. MERCER is Chairman and Chief Executive Officer of Goodyear Tire and Rubber Company.

FRED J. NAFFZIGER is Professor of Business Law, Indiana University at South Bend.

LISA H. NEWTON is Director, Program in Applied Ethics, Fairfield University.

WILLIAM C. NORRIS is Chairman of the Board Emeritus of Control Data Corporation.

LYNN SHARP PAINE is Assistant Professor, School of Business Administration, Georgetown University.

ROBERT F. PEARSE is Professor of Management, College of Business, Rochester Institute of Technology.

EDWARD S. PETRY, JR. is Instructor of Philosophy at Bentley College and Clark University and the Research Associate for the Center for Business Ethics, Bentley College.

DIANA C. ROBERTSON is Lecturer, The Wharton School, University of Pennsylvania.

MICHAEL S. ROZEFF is Chester A. Phillips Professor of Finance, The University of Iowa.

DAVID T. SCHEFFMAN is Director, Bureau of Economics Federal Trade Commission.

S. PRAKASH SETHI is Associate Director, Center for Management, Bernard Baruch College, City University of New York.

ARTHUR SHARPLIN is Distinguished Professor of Management, McNeese University.

DANIEL W. SHERRICK is Associate General Counsel, International Union, United Automobile, Aerospace and Agricultural Implement Workers of America (UAW).

ANDREW SIGLER is Chairman and Chief Executive Officer of Champion International Corporation.

PAUL STEIDLMEIER is Assistant Professor, School of Management, State University of New York at Binghamton.

W. T. STEPHENS is President and Chief Executive Officer, Manville Corporation.

LAURENCE J. STYBEL is President, Stybel, Peabody and Associates, Boston.

DUANE WINDSOR is Associate Professor of Administrative Sciences, The Jesse H. Jones Graduate School of Administration, Rice University.

In the wake of major insider trading scandals on Wall Street and serious debates over the benefits of corporate mergers and takeovers, ethics in business has become a topic of paramount importance—both in the corporate world itself and in the business school community. This volume presents a discussion by a distinguished group of corporate executives and academic specialists of the ethical issues involved in mergers, acquisitions, and takeovers. The result of a major conference sponsored by the Center for Business Ethics at Bentley College, the book seeks to relate ethical and philosophical considerations to the pragmatic concerns of business operation. In their provocative exploration of the issues involved, the contributors address such subjects as employee interests, stakeholder welfare, managerial ethics, the problem of insider trading, and more.

Divided into five major sections, the volume begins with several chapters that offer an overview of ethical and moral issues in organizational transformations. The second section presents corporate, labor, and government views of the issues involved and includes chapters by Edward L. Hennessy, Jr. of Allied-Signal; Daniel W. Sherrick of the UAW; and David T. Scheffman of the Federal Trade Commission among others. In the following chapters, the contributors address ethical aspects of the strategies and tactics used to effect mergers and takeovers, paying particular attention to their impact on management and employee interests. Section Four presents some alternative approaches to corporate restructuring, while the final section includes actual case studies of the relationship between ethical issues and practical bottom-line business concerns. Must reading for corporate executives and financial experts involved in the business of mergers and takeovers, this book is also an ideal supplemental text for graduate courses in business ethics.